Y0-BUB-678

RENEWALS 458-4574

WITHDRAWN
UTSA LIBRARIES

Piety and Politics

RELIGION AND GLOBAL POLITICS SERIES
SERIES EDITOR
John L. Esposito
University Professor and Director
Center for Muslim-Christian Understanding
Georgetown University

ISLAMIC LEVIATHAN
Islam and the Making of State Power
Seyyed Vali Reza Nasr

RACHID GHANNOUCHI
A Democrat within Islamism
Azzam S. Tamimi

BALKAN IDOLS
Religion and Nationalism in Yugoslav States
Vjekoslav Perica

ISLAMIC POLITICAL IDENTITY IN TURKEY
M. Hakan Yavuz

RELIGION AND POLITICS IN POST-COMMUNIST ROMANIA
Lavinia Stan and Lucian Turcescu

PIETY AND POLITICS
Islamism in Contemporary Malaysia
Joseph Chinyong Liow

Piety and Politics

Islamism in Contemporary Malaysia

JOSEPH CHINYONG LIOW

OXFORD
UNIVERSITY PRESS
2009

OXFORD
UNIVERSITY PRESS

Oxford University Press, Inc., publishes works that further
Oxford University's objective of excellence
in research, scholarship, and education.

Oxford   New York
Auckland   Cape Town   Dar es Salaam   Hong Kong   Karachi
Kuala Lumpur   Madrid   Melbourne   Mexico City   Nairobi
New Delhi   Shanghai   Taipei   Toronto

With offices in
Argentina   Austria   Brazil   Chile   Czech Republic   France   Greece
Guatemala   Hungary   Italy   Japan   Poland   Portugal   Singapore
South Korea   Switzerland   Thailand   Turkey   Ukraine   Vietnam

Copyright © 2009 by Oxford University Press, Inc.

Published by Oxford University Press, Inc.
198 Madison Avenue, New York, New York 10016

www.oup.com

Oxford is a registered trademark of Oxford University Press.

Library of Congress Cataloging-in-Publication Data
Liow, Joseph Chinyong.
Piety and politics : Islamism in contemporary Malaysia / Joseph Chinyong Liow.
    p. cm.—(Religion and global politics series)
Includes bibliographical references.
ISBN 978-0-19-537708-8
1. Islam and politics—Malaysia.   2. Islam and state—Malaysia.
3. Islamism—Malaysia.   4. Malaysia—Politics and government.
5. United Malays National Organisation.   I. Title.
BP63.M27L56   2009
320.5'5709595—dc22   2008035278

9 8 7 6 5 4 3 2 1
Printed in the United States of America
on acid-free paper

Dedicated to Ai Vee, Euan, and Megan

We do not want to pretend and say everything is okay. We do not want to be in a state of denial. Tell the truth even if it is painful.

—Abdullah Ahmad Badawi, President of UMNO
and Prime Minister of Malaysia, 6 October 2007

UMNO are more Islamic and dangerous than PAS. Who break your temples? Who put 5 in ISA [Internal Security Act]? Who declare Malaysia Islamic state? Who snatch dead bodies? Who kill in police custody? Who create bumiputra? Who break family using shari'a law? Who break statues? Who use khalwat to spy on people? Who implement Islamic policy in schools? It is BN [Barisan Nasional]. For 50 years they brainwashed us to think that they are moderate. They are the extremists.

—Excerpt from a text message that was circulated
widely in Malaysia prior to general elections on
8 March 2008

We do not scold them. We ask them to rethink, not to be extreme but to return to the moderate path. According to some politicians, Malaysia is already an Islamic state. We have syariah. It is not complete but it is a process. We told them they should be patient. It is better now than before.

—Excerpt from the response of a member of
Malaysia's religious rehabilitation program for
members of Jemaah Islamiyah (JI) and Kumpulan
Militan Malaysia (KMM) when asked what was
the theme of their rehabilitation strategy. Cited in
"Persuading Terrorists to Disengage," *New Sunday
Times*, 5 October 2008

Preface

When queried about the possibility of creating an Islamic state in Malaysia immediately after independence, Tunku Abdul Rahman, Malaysia's first prime minister and the country's *Bapa Kemerdekaan* (Father of Independence), famously quipped that to do so he would have to "drown every non-Muslim in Malaysia." Some forty-five years later, Malaysia's fourth prime minister and the architect of Vision 2020, Mahathir Mohamad, openly declared that Malaysia was already an Islamic state. While Mahathir's comment could be partly attributed to the need to shore up his Islamic credentials as his party engaged in the politics of brinkmanship with an Islamic opposition, it was in fact the culmination of several decades of gradual Islamization of Malaysia that had been engineered, paradoxically enough, by the very party and government that Tunku led many years ago. How did this shift come about, and what does it portend for Malaysia?

Malaysia has a population of approximately 22 million people. Of these, close to 60% are Muslims, who are virtually all ethnic Malay. Since independence, the country has undergone tremendous transformation. Once primarily a rural backwater, several decades of urbanization and industralization have created the tenth largest economy in Asia, one that quickly joined the ranks of the original "Asian tigers." Modernization of the economy was a key policy objective of the Mahathir administration, the foundation of his "Vision 2020" plan to make Malaysia a developed country by the year 2020. Much of this modernization hinged on policies that encouraged an influx of foreign investments and multinational corporations into Malaysia. This foreign influx was so critical to the government's development strategies that it was prepared to make exceptions to various aspects of its affirmative-action policies, which required firms based in Malaysia to allot a specified number of jobs and a certain percentage of ownership to *bumiputra* ("sons of the soil," a term that refers primarily to ethnic Malays). Its track record of development and steady economic growth has made the Malaysian economy one of the most vibrant in the Muslim world today.

Malaysia's admirable economic growth was to a great extent made possible by an equally admirable record of social and political stability since the end of World War II. During an immediate postwar period in which Southeast Asia was widely known as a "region in revolt," Malaysia (known as Malaya until 1963) stood out as an oasis of relative calm. Still, ethnic tension was simmering beneath the surface, as Malay political parties sought to enshrine Malay racial primacy in the political constellation of postcolonial Malaysia, a problem compounded by the existence of a recalcitrant Chinese-dominated Communist insurgency. This move was intermittently challenged by non-Malay minorities, particularly opposition political movements. These included the Singapore-based People's Action Party (PAP), which fronted the Malaysian Solidarity Convention, an umbrella organization that championed a "Malaysian Malaysia"; and the Democratic Action Party (DAP), which inherited this mantra following Singapore's separation from Malaysia.

Ethnic tensions notwithstanding, the creation of a multiethnic governing coalition and sound economic and investment-friendly policies ensured that, apart from the riots of 13 May 1969, no major outbreaks of interethnic violence occurred in Malaysia. In the Southeast Asian context, the relative peace in Malaysia contrasted starkly with the Communist coup and countercoup in Indonesia, ethnic separatist violence in Burma, multiple military coups in Thailand, and the institution of authoritarian rule in the Philippines. A broader comparison of Malaysia with the Muslim world during this period makes for a similar contrast, particularly with respect to the Middle East and North Africa.

Despite an acute sense of ethnic identity that has occasionally been manipulated by political interests, relations among ethnic groups in Malaysia have largely remained stable. In Malaysia there has traditionally been close interaction among ethnic groups. Indeed, the very notion of the Peranakan Chinese—Malaysians of mixed Chinese and Malay parentage, known colloquially as the *Nyonya* or *Baba*—is indicative of the extent to which cultural groups have interacted and integrated in Malaysia. Among older generations of Malaysians, anecdotal evidence abounds of how ethnic and religious festivals were celebrated in an inclusive manner and how bonds between families and individuals often transcended ethnic, racial, and religious boundaries. Underlying this stability was the minorities' tacit acceptance of Malay-Muslim primacy and a reciprocal preservation of minority rights and freedoms on the part of the Malay-Muslim majority.

Against this broad cultural tapestry of traditional Malaysian society, and the continued centrality of Malay-Muslim identity in national affairs, recent trends of Malaysian Islamization are striking. In this regard, the obvious point of entry is the question, raised recently by a number of political leaders and repeated in public discourse, of whether Malaysia is essentially a secular or Islamic country.

Even though freedom of worship is constitutionally guaranteed in Malaysia, Islam is enshrined in the nation's constitution as the sole official religion of the country. Moreover, constitutional articles, such as the controversial Article 121 1(A), accord Islamic *shari'a* law equal status with civil law in jurisprudential matters in the private lives of Muslims. The constitution grants Islam further dominance by stating that being Muslim is one of the chief criteria for being Malay. The relationship between ethnicity and religion is so intimate that the popular term for having converted to Islam, *masuk melayu,* means having "become a Malay." Islam's role at the core of Malay identity is more salient than ever because the two other pillars of Malay identity, language and royalty, no longer carry the weight they did several decades ago. The Malay language remains important politically, but for precisely this reason the state implemented an education policy establishing the language's primacy in the national curriculum. The result of this policy is that knowledge of the Malay language is no longer the exclusive prerogative of Malays. Similarly, royalty in Malaysia today has a highly problematic relationship with the Malay ruling elite, who see constitutional monarchs as competitors for legitimacy in the eyes of the population. Royals have also further undermined their own legitimacy in the public eye as a result of a number of recent controversial episodes and scandals.

The centrality of Islam in Malaysian culture is further augmented by the prevalence of a state-orchestrated discourse of Malay dominance encapsulated in the concepts of *ketuanan melayu* (Malay primacy) and *bumiputra* rights. These concepts have given rise to Malay-Muslim demands for privileged status and access in the realms of politics and economics, effectively turning members of other ethnic groups and religions into second-class citizens.[1] In fact, while ethnicity has long been seen as the primary identity marker for Malays in Malaysia, recent research indicates that identity criteria may be shifting away from ethnicity and toward religion, with Malays seeing themselves first as Muslim rather than Malay.[2]

Finally, in the context of Malaysia's federal system of governance, it is telling that significant aspects of Islamic strictures come under the direct purview and jurisdiction of local state governments. This arrangement came about by way of colonial-era juridical norms bequeathed to the postcolonial state. Even as British colonial authorities arrogated political and economic power to themselves, they made an important (if merely symbolic) concession to local authorities, permitting sultans and rulers to remain the heads of religion in their respective states.[3] The continuation of this tradition, provided for in the constitution, has effectively meant that several aspects of religious matters are controlled within the various states by local *mufti*, religious departments, and state administrations, at least at the level of policy formulation. That is not to say, however, that the lines between federal and state jurisdictions are clearly defined. Indeed, as ensuing chapters will illustrate, the questions of who legislates on matters of religion, who implements the ensuing requirements, and who polices them have caused considerable confusion and tension within the larger Malaysian polity. Compounding the confusion are the facts that Islam is the religion of the Federation, Malays are constitutionally defined as Muslims, and, notwithstanding the constitutional guarantee of religious freedom, no Muslim can opt out of the jurisdiction of *shari'a* laws, administered by state religious authorities.

Given the historical, cultural, constitutional, and functional factors that codify Malay dominance in Malaysia, it follows that Malay-Muslim identity must determine the shapes, contours, and trajectories of Malaysian politics. Against this backdrop, political Islam has taken center stage in Malaysian politics, because the objective of "safeguarding" Malay rights invariably means preserving and defending the status of Islam. This was made abundantly clear when former Prime Minister Mahathir openly contested the description of Malaysia as "secular": "Many Muslims will of course disagree with us and try to make out that we are secular. We are not going to argue with them because we know that debating with them or opposing them will not convince them that we are right. But we believe and we are equally convinced in our beliefs that what we do is in the service and in accordance with Islam."[4]

With the structure and historical process of Malaysian politics sketched above, it should be no surprise that Islam has become firmly entrenched in the Malaysian political psyche today. In relation to non-Muslims, Islam is defended as religion and race. Within the Malay-Muslim community, Islam provides reference points for questions of authority and legitimacy. The United Malays National Organization (UMNO), the *Parti Islam Se-Malaysia* (Islamic Party of Malaysia, or PAS), and elements within the Malaysian state itself have internalized the discourse and vocabulary of the Islamic state, turning Islam into an organizing principle of Malaysian society and politics. In other words, Islam has emerged to supplement—and, in certain respects, to supplant—the paradigms of race and ethnicity that for so long provided the basis for Malaysian politics and dominated political discourse in Malaysia. This book, then, is an attempt to understand how this shift came about and how Islam—in particular its ideological and institutional expressions—informs the configurations of power, the nature of legitimacy, and the sources of authority in Malaysian politics and society today.

Acknowledgments

In the course of writing this book, I received support from many different individuals and organizations. I wish foremost to thank Barry Desker, dean of the S. Rajaratnam School of International Studies, for his encouragement and support.

The conceptualization of this book benefited greatly from many conversations and discussions with friends, colleagues, Malaysianists, and activists. I would particularly like to thank Premarani Somasundram, Lee Sue-Ann, Farish Noor, Patricia Martinez, Greg Fealy, Bridget Welsh, Greg Barton, Tom McKenna, Riaz Hassan, John Funston, Syed Ahmad Hussein, Johan Saravanamuttu, Anil Netto, Zaharom Nain, Hermen Shastri, Jacqueline Ann Surin, Yang Razali Kassim, and Don Emmerson. Several political party leaders and members were also very generous with their time and opinions, particularly Anwar Ibrahim, Hasan Shukri, Kamaruddin Jaafar, Dzulkefly Ahmad, Salahuddin Ayub, Fadli Ghani, Liew Chin Tong, Nor Jaslan, Abdul Rahman Dahlan, and Ahmad Ikmal Ismail.

The writing of this book benefited from a brief period of leave spent at the Southeast Asia Forum, Shorenstein Asia Pacific Research Center, Stanford University. I wish to thank Don Emmerson for facilitating this leave and the rich intellectual exchange that came with it, as well as Denise Matsumoto and Debbie Warren for providing administrative support. Thanks also to the participants at the APARC speaker series who attended my presentation of the ideas of the book and provided immensely helpful critiques and suggestions. Mohamed Nawab, Shahirah Mahmood, Vidia Arianti, Chan Wenling, and Mustafa Izzuddin provided valuable research assistance, as did several others who have asked to remain unnamed and who assisted in the procurement of documents not readily available. Shahirah Mahmood and Adeline Lim ably assisted in preparation of the final manuscript for submission to the publishers. Theo Calderara at Oxford University Press New York was highly supportive of this project from the very beginning, and the anonymous reviewers made important suggestions and comments for revisions. Liz Smith was immensely helpful with the preparation of the manuscript for publication.

Those who have written books will fully understand the burdens that such endeavors impose on an author's family. I wish to express my gratitude and love to my wife, Ai Vee, and my children, Euan and Megan, for tolerating my periods of absence in the course of researching and writing this book. None of this would have been possible without the sustaining grace of my Lord Jesus Christ. To him be the glory.

A final caveat is in order here. The manuscript for this book was completed before the monumental general election on 8 March 2008, when the Malaysian opposition posted its most impressive performance to date. While the consensus among analysts is that the election result can be attributed as much to failures on the part of Prime Minister Abdullah Badawi and his embattled *Barisan Nasional* coalition as to the strength of oppositionist forces, many of the undercurrents that framed the politics surrounding the election are traceable to trends identified in the following chapters. To that end, Oxford University Press has kindly accommodated an epilogue to address some of the pertinent issues flowing from the elections that are related to the themes of this book.

Contents

Abbreviations

ABIM	*Angkatan Belia Islam Malaysia* (Malaysian Islamic Youth Movement)
ACCIN	Allied Coordinating Committee of Islamic NGOs
APU	*Angkatan Perpaduan Ummah*
ASEAN	Association of Southeast Asian Nations
Badai	Anti-Interfaith Commission Body
DAP	Democratic Action Party
FELDA	Federal Land Development Authority
FIS	Islamic Salvation Front in Algeria
GAM	*Gerakan Aceh Merdeka* (Free Aceh Movement)
Gerak	Malaysian People's Movement for Justice
HINDRAF	Hindu Rights Action Force
HIZBI	*Al-Hizbul Islami*
HT	*Hizbut Tahrir*
HTM	*Hizbut Tahrir Malaysia*
IFCM	Inter-Faith Commission of Malaysia
IIUM	International Islamic University Malaysia
IKIM	*Institut Kefahaman Islam Malaysia* (Malaysian Institute of Islamic Understanding)
IKIN	Network of Intellectuals in the Malay World
IMP	Independence of Malaya Party
INGO	Islamic nongovernmental organization
IRC	Inter-Religious Council
ISA	Internal Security Act
JAIS	Selangor State Religious Department

JAKIM   *Jabatan Kemajuan Islam Malaysia* (Malaysian Islamic Development Department)

JIM   *Jemaah Islah Malaysia*

JUST   International Movement for a Just World

KARIM   *Koperasi Angkatan Revolusi Islam Malaysia* (Malaysian Islamic Revolutionary Front)

KMM   *Kumpulan Militan Malaysia*

LEPAK   Let's Enhance Positive Attitudes and Knowledge

MATA   *Majlis Agama Tertinggi Malaya* (Malayan Supreme Religious Council)

MCA   Malayan Chinese Association

MCCBCHS   Malaysian Consultative Council of Buddhism, Christianity, Hinduism, and Sikhism

MCP   Malayan Communist Party

MIC   Malayan Indian Congress

MKHIM   *Majlis Kebangsaan Halehwal Islam Malaysia*

MNP   Malay Nationalist Party

MPF   Muslim Professionals Forum

NAM   Nonaligned Movement

NASAKOM   *Nasionalisme, Agama, Komunisme* (Nationalism, Religion, and Communism)

NEP   New Economic Policy

NGO   Nongovernmental organization

NOC   National Operations Council

OIC   Organization of Islamic Conferences

PAS   *Parti Islam Se-Malaysia* (Islamic Party of Malaysia)

PBM   *Parti Buruh Malaya* (Labor Party of Malaya)

PBMUM   *Persatuan Bahasa Melayu Universiti Malaya* (University of Malaya Malay Language Society)

PEMBELA   *Pertubuhan-Pertubuhan Pembela Islam* (Defenders of Islam)

PETA   *Pembela Tanah Ayer*

PGSM   Malaysian *Shari'a* Lawyers Association

PKMM   *Partai Kebangsaan Melayu Malaya* (Malay Nationalist Party of Malaya)

PKPIM   *Persatuan Kebangsaan Pelajar-Pelajar Islam Malaysia* (National Union of Malaysian Muslim Students)

PMIA   Pan-Malayan Islamic Association

PMIP   Pan-Malayan Islamic Party

PPI   *Peguam Pembela Islam*

PRM   *Parti Rakyat Malaya* (People's Party of Malaya)

PULO   Pattani United Liberation Organization

PUM   *Persatuan Ulama Se-Malaya*

SIS   Sisters in Islam

SMS	Short Message Service
SUHAKAM	Government-Appointed Human Rights Commission
Teras	*Teras Pengupayaan Melayu*
UMNO	United Malays National Organization
WADAH	*Wadah Percedasan Umat*
YDIM	*Yayasan Dakwah Islamiah Malaysia*

Piety and Politics

Introduction

More than two decades after the Iranian Revolution of 1979, the tragic events of September 11, 2001, have thrust political Islam to the forefront of policy and academic interest yet again. The concomitant "global war on terror" targeting radicals, militants, Jihadis, and terrorists who claim legitimacy in the name of Islam for their heinous actions is taking place concurrently with a critical interrogation and examination of political systems throughout the Muslim world, which is thought in many quarters (correctly or otherwise) to spawn extremists. Events in more recent years—such as riots involving disenfranchised Muslim youths in France, the return of conservative, anti-Western elements to power in Iran, the increasing popularity of radical Muslim parties in Bangladesh, persistent separatist violence in Muslim-majority provinces in Thailand, and the triumph of Hamas in free elections in Palestine—have served only to focus greater attention on political developments in the Muslim world.

Against this seemingly tumultuous backdrop, Malaysia appears to stand out as an oasis of calm. With its stable, developing economy and relative social and political stability, the country is widely celebrated as the epitome of progressive, moderate Islam by the international media and major Western governments. No doubt with one eye cast toward foreign investments, Malaysian leaders regularly announce that religious radicalism and "deviancy" from the state-defined "norms" of Islamic practice are not tolerated in a society where ethnocultural harmony reigns within a sociopolitical configuration based on Malay-Muslim dominance. This representation of Malaysia is nested in a wider discourse, promulgated and carefully tended by former Prime Minister Mahathir Mohamad, of Malaysian ambitions to be a fully industrialized, modern, developed country by 2020.

To be sure, this message has more than a modicum of truth to it. Compared to other multiethnic, multireligious countries, Malaysia has witnessed an admirably low rate of racial and religious conflict. Save for the race riots of 13 May 1969, which in any case had little immediate association with religious issues, Malaysia has managed to avoid major outbreaks of violence. Impressive economic growth rates over the past three decades strengthen Malaysia's image as a Muslim country firmly committed to economic development and modernization. These facts have convinced many that Malaysia will play a major role in international affairs as a model of Muslim governance. Indeed, Malaysia has won accolades for its tough stance on terrorism and has been extolled in many Western capitals as a "beacon of stability" and valuable ally in the war on terror, while at the same time receiving an equally impressive "report card" from the countries of the Organization of Islamic Conferences (OIC) for its model of Islamic leadership and governance.

Beneath this surface, however, lies a striking paradox. Beyond the energetic world of Kuala Lumpur, defined by consumerism and a vibrant night life worthy of any capital in the Western world, Malaysian society on the whole has been experiencing a swing toward Islamic conservatism in ways that would undoubtedly disturb the very same Westerners who have endorsed the country as the epitome of moderate Muslim governance. More important, this swing seems to be gaining momentum, as demonstrated by the increasing popularity of *shari'a* in public discourse, state-sanctioned curtailment of civil rights and liberties in the name of Islam, the incapacity of civil courts to challenge controversial *shari'a* court decisions, increasing incidences of moral policing by Islamic religious authorities (including policing of non-Muslims in some instances), and the alarming regularity of references to the "Islamic state."[1] Tellingly, the increasing visibility of Islam in Malaysian society and politics is being driven not only by the Islamist opposition party *Parti Islam Se-Malaysia* (Islamic Party of Malaysia, or PAS), as one would anticipate, but also by the United Malays National Organization (UMNO), whose members were presumably the architects of Malaysia's brand of progressive, moderate Islam.[2] In addition, alternative actors such as nongovernmental organizations (NGOs) and civil society groups are increasingly weighing in on the discursive politicization of Islam in Malaysia today. In certain respects, this active engagement in Islamic discourse and counterdiscourse is eclipsing mainstream political parties in terms of intensity.

Of course, one could reply that this dichotomy, striking though it is, may not amount to much in the larger scheme of things, particularly when compared to other, less palatable models of Islamist governance. Nevertheless, the gradual Islamization of Malaysia and this uneasy paradox it has spawned will transform the complexion of Islam and politics in the country in substantive, fundamental ways. This book, then, is an attempt to unpack and unravel this dichotomy and examine its implications for politics in Malaysia. Put differently, this book is an attempt to understand the shape of Islamism and its institutional expressions as it has evolved.

Islamism as Political Ideology

Most discussion and analysis of political Islam begins by pointing to the fact that Islam is inherently "political." Proponents of this logic have noted that Islam is *ad-din*, a way of life that encompasses *din wa dawla*, or faith along with polity—religion and state. The essentially political character of Islam was categorically demonstrated, if not in doctrine, then certainly in the development of the faith. The Prophet Muhammad established the first religiously governed polity in Medina; soon after his death in 632 A.D., internecine conflict emerged within the Muslim community over questions of succession and legitimacy. The rule of the first four caliphs was a highly politicized epoch of Islamic history, defined by competition over power, authority, legitimacy, authenticity, and the driving seat of Islam vacated by the Prophet. Indeed, it is this fusion of religion and politics that has captured the imagination of generations of Muslim intellectuals, from the reform movements of the late nineteenth and early twentieth centuries, to the rise of Islamism in the wake of the failure of Arab nationalism in the 1970s, then to the Iranian Revolution, and right up to the current post–September 11 milieu and beyond. By definition then, to an Islamist, a Muslim cannot be indifferent to politics.

At the same time, Islam is also *tawhid*, oneness and unity in the name of Allah. Yet the theological notion of *tawhid* belies an extraordinary diversity in popular expression and practice of Islam, often determined by cultural and historical contexts. This diversity is driving an energetic intellectual debate over the universal and particularistic characteristics of Muslims—and, some would argue, of Islam as well. The uneasy conjunction of *tawhid* and diversity explains the wide variety of social-political discourses and movements that claim authenticity and legitimacy in the name of Islam.

According to conventional wisdom, Islamism is at its heart a social-political phenomenon that has a history traceable to Muslim anticolonial movements but whose modern permutation came about in reaction to the failure of Arab nationalist states to empower their Muslim populations. In contrast to the romanticized legacy of the Prophet's seventh-century construction of an Islamic society or the precepts of *ad-din* and *tawhid* that ostensibly transcend time and space, Islamism today is a decidedly modern phenomenon dictated by its contexts. Its origins as a reaction to perceived injustice in the social, political, and economic spheres made it attractive as a populist civic phenomenon, which explains its rapid expansion as a social-political ideology (or, as

Yusuf Qaradawi would have it, an "Islamic solution") in the 1970s and early 1980s among disenfranchised Muslim populations throughout the world. As authoritarian structures of power gradually loosened, Islamism also became an outgrowth of democratic processes as a counterhegemonic social movement, and it flourished as a voice of dissidence in contemporary politics.

In light of these historical and intellectual roots, for our purposes Islamism can simply be defined as the ideological politicization of Islam.[3] In this manner, Islamism is as much a study of Muslims as peoples, communities, and societies with political ideals and aspirations as it is of Islam as a religion. It should also be noted that while Islamism is essentially revivalist in nature, it is nevertheless different from other forms of Islamic revivalism represented by missionary groups and Islamic charity organizations, which understand change as a longer-term process occurring outside the realm of politics. If Islamism is the ideology, then "political Islam" is its institutional expression: the institutional mobilization of this ideology—and the religious symbols and idioms that draw from and build on it—toward political ends. It follows, then, that the hallmark of political Islam is its quintessentially political agenda; it is a political order that is articulated in religious terms, the politicization of Islam through the aligning of structures of governance and society with Islamic strictures. It is on this basis that social scientists often view and refer to political Islam and Islamism interchangeably.

There is a tendency in some quarters to conflate Islamism with fundamentalism and Islamists with fundamentalists. This tendency must be addressed. While there are undoubtedly some shared characteristics between the two groups, and while some Islamists can certainly be categorized as fundamentalists in terms of their outlook, there are also substantive distinctions between the two which need to be recognized. The major distinction between fundamentalism and Islamism is, again, the question of politics. Fundamentalism can be understood as "a particular mode of thought and logic, a distinctive style of discourse or rhetoric . . . that . . . purveys a particular worldview, a binary universe of good and evil with no nuances in between."[4] Islamic fundamentalism implies an outlook that idealizes the "golden age" of Islam and offers a return to this golden age through the restoration of primary values and rules of social and personal behavior on the basis of timeless precepts. The fundamentalist agenda, however, need not be political in nature. Research conducted by the International Crisis Group, for instance, has suggested that the strictest Salafi fundamentalists are religious activists, not political ones, who in fact eschew political allegiances.[5] This is understandable given that to many fundamentalists, involvement in politics causes rifts and divisions within the Muslim community and diverts resources and attention from the more important task of *dakwah* (proselytization).[6] Islamism, on the other hand, is a decidedly political phenomenon. Islamists believe that any return to the "golden age" can in the final analysis only be possible with the establishment of an Islamic state, although the precise form it should take and the process through which this is to take place remain matters of great debate among Muslims. Azza Karam sums up this dichotomy when she writes: "Whereas a fundamentalist may or may not become engaged in political thought, debate and activism, an Islamist, by definition, does. Political engagement is the *sine qua non* of being an Islamist."[7]

While there are obvious common denominators of Islamism among most, if not all, Islamist movements, Islamism need not be considered a unitary phenomenon, at least not in terms of the scope, extent, and process of its institutional expression, for Islamism might originate from different causes and serve different purposes in each particular instance. Thus, it is imperative that analysis of Islamism and Islamist movements also elucidate the contingency and variety within them, taking into account the complexity generated by contemporary and contextual social and political factors. This complexity and variety are clearly demonstrated by the Malaysian case, where Islamism has found several modes and avenues of expression, by the broader literature on Islamism, and more generally by the applicability of prevailing conceptual frameworks to the subject.

Malaysia and the Study of Islamism

The literature on political Islam has long been dominated by empirical studies centered on the Middle East and North Africa, despite the fact that only 14 percent of the global Muslim population lives there. This belief in the "authenticity" of Arab and Middle Eastern Islam as a model for Muslim politics ignores the vibrant historical and intellectual tradition of Islam in Southeast Asia, where a substantial number of Muslims reside, and where, as Michael Laffan has noted, indigenous Muslims "have long been primary actors rather than the passive subjects of a global discourse."[8] Indeed, on closer inspection one realizes that the conditions for Islamism are entirely different in Southeast Asia.

In the Middle East and North Africa, the growth of Islamism was largely a response to the state on two counts: the prevalence of autocratic and authoritarian regimes on the one hand, and the failure of secular pan-Arab nationalism on the other. It has also been suggested that Islamism in this region was a reaction to the denial of economic opportunities and social mobility. In Southeast Asia, on the other hand, Malaysia offers a compelling case for the emergence of Islamism under different circumstances and along different trajectories. First, rather than a reaction to the state, the mobilization of Islamic vocabulary, idioms, and symbols for political ends was very much a process orchestrated and structured by the state since the 1980s. Second, Malaysian Islamism was not the response to the bankruptcy of modernization projects that appeared to drive the phenomenon elsewhere. The economic

deprivation and uneven distribution of wealth that are thought to be so instrumental to the Islamist project of discrediting the state were relatively absent
from the economic landscape of Malaysia.[9] On the contrary, the politicization of Islam was taking place in tandem with economic growth and under
the watchful eye of the Mahathir administration; it was in fact mobilized to
justify industrialization and development policies, which in turn were premised upon the Malay-Muslim community being benefactors of a state-driven
affirmative-action program that gave them privileged political and economic
access.[10] In other words, if, according to received wisdom, the rise of Islamism
in Muslim societies stemmed from the younger generation's alienation from a
state that seemed no longer to offer them viable prospects, then Malaysia, with
its affirmative-action support of the Muslim majority through the provision
of education, exclusive scholarships, job placement, and prospects for career
advancement, should not be witnessing trends toward Islamism. Yet this is
certainly not the case.

This book is essentially an in-depth investigation into the contours of
Islamism in Malaysia, but it does not claim that the Malaysian case has been
insulated from developments elsewhere in the Muslim world. While Malaysia
may be exceptional in the sense that all narratives of Islamism are ultimately
conditioned by their own unique social, political, historical, and economic set-
tings, the country has also been exposed to external forces that have helped
shape internal dynamics and frame Muslim politics within the local milieu.
A case in point is the impact of the global Islamic resurgence, which, as this
book will endeavor to demonstrate, had a pervasive impact on the increasing
"Islamization" of politics in Malaysia since the early 1970s. Consider also the
instrumental role that early-twentieth-century Islamist political thought played
in providing ideological fodder for the Malay anticolonial movement in the prewar years; Malaysian Islamists' establishment and maintenance of ties with
transnational movements such as the *Ikhwanul Muslimin* (Muslim Brotherhood), ties that continue to this day; the existence of a Malaysian Muslim student
diaspora across the Middle East and South Asia (demonstrated by the existence
of Malay *kampung melayu* communities in Cairo and Malay *halaqah* study circles
in Mecca); and the impact of such events as the Iranian Revolution. In short,
while Islamism within contemporary Malaysia has by and large been shaped by
specific, local conditions, the transnational nature of Islamism in general needs
to be appreciated in terms of how it inevitably (and predictably) generates cross-
border influences, where global developments affect the local context.

Conceptual Points of Entry: Islamists, Politics, and the State

In the study of Islamism today, one of the most widely accepted conceptual
frameworks argues for the mitigating effects that mainstream democratic

political processes have on strident Islamist political agendas. According to the proponents of this school of thought, participation in the political process will inevitably blunt the dogmatic edges of Islamist political parties as they carve out their own spaces in the public domain, get socialized into the political game, and internalize the pragmatism required to survive as relevant political actors. Piscatori argues, for instance, that Islamists will find in a democracy that they "are unable to dominate over others, they must compromise and engage in the give-and-take of electoral politics common everywhere."[11] Others, such as Esposito and Voll, further suggest that "processes of democratization and Islamic resurgence have become complementary forces in many countries."[12]

These persuasive arguments are undoubtedly a necessary riposte to the essentialist and orientalist literature that portrays Islamism as a monolithic expression of a fundamentalism that is the antithesis of democracy. At first glance, the suggestion that Islamists have to negotiate their agendas in order to survive politically resonates to some extent with developments in Malaysia, where, as the book will demonstrate, doctrinaire positions taken by the Islamist opposition PAS, for instance, often proved to be their undoing, particularly when the party was confronted with the challenge of making itself relevant to non-Muslim constituencies.

This resonance notwithstanding, this argument explains only part of the picture in Malaysia. Indeed, upon closer investigation several conundrums emerge. The argument that participation in the political process will dilute the Islamist agenda is a structural one that assumes a mainstream political sphere that is inherently, if not explicitly, a secular space. The argument also assumes that society itself, which provides the context in which Islamist parties operate, is equally committed to secularism or is at least ill-disposed to Islamism. This may not necessarily be self-evident in contemporary Malaysia, where the vocabulary and praxis of mainstream political contestation has in fact become discernibly Islamic in character. In this manner, the (hypothetical) question of whether PAS might mitigate its Islamist agenda if it gains political power and leverage in Malaysia is complicated by the fact that the incumbent, UMNO, and the state over which it presides have already defined the terms of engagement in Islamist fashion. In other words, PAS is entering and operating on a terrain that is already "Islamist" in many ways. This should hardly be surprising, given the fragmentation of authority and the contestations over who speaks for Islam that define much of Islamism today.

Second, the overemphasis on party politics distracts from equally important and indicative subterranean trends. The focus on state power and partisan politics leaves out, for the most part, Islamic actors and organizations whose most important "political" act is to seek to sidestep the "unclean" business of politics and the influence of those who seek to wield state power to control the organization and practice of Islam. Even though the state and mainstream political parties play important roles in defining the parameters of Islamism, civil society groups (political and nonpolitical ones) and popular discourses (expressed in blogs, e-mail discussion lists, and other alternative media) have come to assume mounting importance in negotiating these parameters. Given the growing popularity of Islamic activism across the Muslim world and the broad consensus that the rise of Islamism was traceable to the Islamic resurgence of the late 1960s and early 1970s (which was essentially a bottom-up phenomenon), popular perspectives on the direction of Islam as represented by these alternative voices simply cannot be ignored.[13] In fact, it is worth noting here that in Malaysia, these shades of gray are captured in the recent emergence of a decidedly Islamic civil society that has proven strikingly strident in its use of Islamist vocabulary during its engagement in political discourse. This development is indicative of a gradual but discernible shift of Malaysian Muslim society toward the conservative end of the religious spectrum. Consequently, any study of Islamism will have to account for the role of a burgeoning and increasingly influential parallel Islamist civil society and popular discourse. This parallel society's contribution to the rise and trajectory of Islamism highlights the fact that the Islamist agenda is neither unitary nor unilinear, nor is it confined to political parties; it is in fact highly contested, both within as well as across the boundaries of mainstream politics.

This stress on contingency and agency is important for the way it illuminates how governments deal with the Islamist challenge. Mohammed Ayoob has noted that references to Islamism and the state within prevailing academic discourse produce at least three different ontological registers in which this relationship can be positioned: co-optation, competition, and suppression.[14] Co-optation of the Islamist agenda provides the state with publicity and attention, while suppression drives Islamists underground and possibly to violence. As for competition, Ayoob suggests that it could lead to the surrendering of rhetorical ground to Islamists and ultimately places the regime in a precarious position of "failing to live up to their own words." It is likely that state responses oscillate among these three strategies, and combinations of some or all of the three may well have been pursued by any given state toward its Islamist opposition over time. One will also often find that some strategies invariably flow into others; for example, competition can lead to suppression if the former strategy fails to blunt the influence of the Islamists. Underlying this typology of responses to Islamism is a single assumption: whether by virtue of ideology or politics, Islamists and the state are polar opposites. Before discussing this assumption, it is perhaps appropriate to first consider in greater detail the three strategies elucidated and how they illuminate the nature of relations between Islamism and the state in several Muslim contexts.

A cursory survey of Muslim politics might suggest that co-optation is the most popular strategy. Ruling governments across the Muslim world have at some time or other "co-opted" Islamists for the very reasons cited above, namely, "publicity and attention," not to mention more fundamental interests such as augmenting incumbent legitimacy. Attempts at such strategies were evident, for instance, in Zulfikar Ali Bhutto's model of "Islamic Socialism" in Pakistan, where his 1970 election campaign platform—"Islam is our faith. Democracy is our polity. Socialism is our economy."—allowed him to dispense of Islamist opposition in the form of the Muslim League and *Jamaat-e-Islami*. They were evident also when Hosni Mubarak co-opted the *Ikhwanul Muslimin* in Egypt during the early years of his tenure, where "by legitimizing the Brotherhood as the primary representatives of centrist Islam, Mubarak could place militants outside the mainstream. Once they were isolated, he could take forceful measures against them with little protest from Egyptians sympathetic to the centrist Islamist."[15]

Similarly, there is abundant evidence, too much to detail here, of suppression of Islamist movements across the Muslim world. One thinks immediately of Mustafa Kemal Atarturk's policy of sidelining and cracking down on Islamist opposition in Turkey, a legacy that arguably carried on to 1997 when the Turkish military launched a coup against the Welfare Party of Necmettin Erbakan; Sukarno's clampdown on the modernist Islamists from the Masyumi Party in Indonesia in the 1950s, and Suharto's marginalization of Islamist forces during the early New Order period; the heavy-handed approach of the Nasser administration toward its Islamist opposition in Egypt; and, more recently, the crackdown on the Islamic Salvation Front in Algeria in the early 1990s.

Strategies of competition rest on assumptions similar to those undergirding co-optation and suppression, namely, that the state is confronted by an Islamist "threat" from beyond its institutional borders. The state responds to the threat by competing with it, rather than by co-opting or suppressing it, even if the state is sometimes ill-equipped to do so. This conceivably occurred in Algeria in the 1980s, Turkey in the early 1990s, Indonesia in the post-Suharto era, and, more recently, Lebanon and Palestine. In all cases, incumbents competed head-on with Islamist parties in political elections on the basis of discernibly divergent political agendas. What should be noted, however, is that the normally fragile state of relations between Islamists and ruling elites in these instances, as well as the generally constricted nature of political space in many of these Muslim countries, caused these strategies of competition to lead to suppression, especially when the incumbent was unable to dispense of the Islamist challenge at the ballot box. Indeed, with the exceptions of present-day Indonesia and Palestine, this appears to be the case in all of the above examples, to say nothing of others.

While the depictions of relationships between governments and their Islamist oppositions provided by this typology are for the most part convincing and relevant, there are several issues that warrant clarification if we are to understand the contours of Islamism in Malaysia. First, the notions of co-optation and competition, as represented by the prevailing literature, tend to reify the state as a secular entity by definition. According to this logic, Islamists and the state are necessarily polar opposites: Islamism is political opposition or an extra-state actor that stands mostly at the margins of mainstream politics, while the state consolidates power and circumscribes Islamists through a combination of coercion and conciliation. The reification of the state as secular stems from the Enlightenment-tradition assumption that the state is an inherently secular institution; thus, the state will not and indeed cannot evince Islamist traits and tendencies unless it "imports" Islamism. In this conception, Islamism can only originate from outside the state, and the two are entwined in an action-reaction relationship.

Yet interactions between states and Islamists may not be so straightforward. Consider, for instance, the matter of what happens to the complexion of the state after Islamists have been co-opted. While some have made the persuasive argument, discussed earlier, that such a strategy might "tame" Islamists and socialize them to the "mainstream," others would contend that it is equally conceivable that this might instead be tantamount to letting the fox into the henhouse. More important, a distinction of this nature does not allow for the possibility that the process of Islamization of societal structures and institutions may well be engineered by the state itself without reference to Islamist forces outside it. In other words, the state may not necessarily be forced by Islamists to react or compete. In Malaysia, as this book will argue, instead of religion being subservient to the state, an Islamization process emerged from within the establishment, accounting for the gradual Islamization of the bureaucracy. Rather than having its hand forced by Islamists situated outside of its institutional and ideological fold, in Malaysia the state itself has been part of—and, to a large extent, has orchestrated—aspects of the Islamist project. Put simply, the state didn't so much co-opt Islamists as it became Islamist. Thus, the politicization of Islam cannot be described as merely the response of an otherwise secular and disinterested state to a stout challenge from oppositional Islamists. Such a rationale is insufficient to explain the shape, tenor, and trajectory of Islamism in Malaysia, where the state has clearly become its vehicle, if not its architect.

In the same vein, while some are inclined to caution (in almost teleological fashion, it appears) that competition with Islamists might ultimately doom the state to failure with dire consequences, the question remains: What if these strategies succeed, particularly if one accepts that the state can compete with the opposition on distinctly Islamist terms, thereby "out-Islamizing" the Islamists?[16] What are the consequences (or costs) of success, particularly for a pluralist society where protection of minority rights are supposedly the responsibility of the state? The Malaysian case is striking not only because state-orchestrated policies and politics appear to have succeeded in deepening Islamism in the country, but also because the Islamist opposition has consequently been forced to raise the stakes in the contest. Consider Jan Stark's prescient observation: "Politically, PAS soon found itself in a similar situation as the government when it came to the implementation of Islam: bound by constitutional and multiracial predicaments, PAS had to abide by the same standards as Mahathir whom it had often criticized for introducing Islamic symbols into politics without thoroughly changing the system."[17] This argument is a challenge to the received wisdom that suggests UMNO's Islamization strategy was essentially a reaction to PAS. According to Stark, the relationship is in fact reversed—PAS has been compelled to react to UMNO, not least because of UMNO's "successful" politicization of Islam. This observation agrees with Salbiah Ahmad's contention that "the PAS electoral victory in the state of Kelantan in 1990 marked *the beginning of a challenge* to Mahathir's Islamization agenda," and Stark's further suggestion that after 1990 "PAS had to shape an even more decisively Islamic profile to counter Mahathir's Islamic policies."[18]

Indeed, one tends to forget that while states certainly do instrumentalize Islam and mobilize its attendant metaphors and symbols to bolster their legitimacy, so too do Islamist parties, whose objectives are ultimately to seize power. In any case, it is also debatable whether the Islamist opposition in Malaysia ever posed such an existential threat to the popularity and legitimacy of the ruling government that it required a vigorous rejoinder on the part of the state.[19] In this regard, none should overlook the Mahathir administration's occasional penchant for "securitizing" all sources of threats to regime legitimacy, be they Islamist or secularist in nature, and consequently mobilizing physical and legal instruments of coercion to address them. This consideration is crucial, for it calls into question the relevance of popular assumptions, highlighted above, that are premised on the problematic notion that while opposition forces may be Islamist, the state is always assumed to be secular, and that if states do embark on Islamization programs, it is purely for the calculated and reactionary purpose of fending off pressure from Islamist political opposition.

It can be argued that while there are traces of all three of the abovementioned strategies in the Malaysian context, the primary dynamic has been one of competition, albeit a competition that is not expressed in the dichotomous manner assumed in the literature. Rather, the defining feature of the connection between Islamism and state power in Malaysia is the government's attempt to "outbid" the Islamist opposition by taking a proactive approach to Islamization and becoming more Islamist than the opposition, even as the government uses its arsenal of tools to constrict avenues of political expression for Islamist elements in the opposition and civil society.[20] While the terms of the "competition" between the state (incumbent government) and the Islamist opposition in Malaysia are dyadic, they are not antithetical but rather mutually reinforcing. This is evident in how the state fought to define, protect, and promote Islam and claim Islamic legitimacy through "piety-trumping," where the points of reference are decidedly Islamist. The apex of this process was surely Prime Minister Mahathir's declaration that Malaysia was an "Islamic state" (a declaration that was repeated by Deputy Prime Minister Najib Tun Razak) and the attempt of his successor, Abdullah Badawi, to refine this Malaysian "Islamic state" with the concept of *Islam Hadhari* (Civilizational Islam). Such declarations on the part of UMNO leaders are significant when considered alongside developments in other Muslim countries. For instance, in Egypt the concept of the Islamic state is associated with the *Ihkwanul Muslimin* and not the Mubarak regime. In Algeria, it is the Islamic Salvation Front and not the government that mobilizes around the Islamic state. While Morocco is constitutionally an Islamic state, the king has outlawed parties with a "religious, ethnic or regional base."[21]

It is precisely this mobilization of decidedly Islamist referents on the part of the UMNO-dominated government that has facilitated the entry of conservative and exclusivist trends into the state's discourse and practice of Islamism. This resonates partially with Seyyed Vali Nasr's contention that states that have chosen the path of Islamization "have done so not merely in reaction to pressure from Islamist movements but to serve their own interests. State leaders have construed Islamism as a threat, but at times also as an opportunity, and in so doing have found added incentive to pursue Islamic politics."[22] While a valuable assertion, Nasr's argument still assumes an implicit dichotomy between Islamism (the religious) and state (the secular), thereby reflecting the church-state (or mosque-state, as it were) separation bias. Returning to an earlier point, this relationship may not be as polarized, and may be more dynamic, than is often understood. Indeed, Nasr himself concedes that "Islamism defies the facile religion versus secularism conception that has been prevalent in the social sciences. As a religious idea that has internalized many aspects of modernity and seeks to operate in the modern world, Islamism shows that religion is adaptable to ideological change and will do so in a continuous dialectic with society."[23] Here he is right on the mark.

Central Arguments

Using the above discussion as its conceptual point of entry, this book argues that tectonic movements and subterranean shifts that underscore the gradual politicization of Islam and the rise of Islamism in political discourse have long been at work in Malaysia, despite popular media representations of Malaysia as being the epitome of moderate, progressive Islamic governance—a characterization that is regularly proclaimed by its leaders as well. While the opposition PAS party is widely regarded as the main Islamist player in the drama, the ruling UMNO regime has proven equally strident in its Islamist predilections, such that sometimes there is little to differentiate the regime from the Islamist opposition. At the same time, even as the majority of its religious leadership persists in conservative renditions of Islamic politics, certain quarters within the leadership of the fundamentalist and "parochial" PAS have also demonstrated democratic and perceptibly conciliatory tendencies in their attempts to negotiate the complexities of mainstream politics in pluralist Malaysia against the backdrop of UMNO hegemony and Malay-Muslim primacy.[24] On balance, however, the net effect of UMNO-PAS contestation has been the accelerated politicization of Islam. Islamic credentials have assumed greater importance for politicians, and Muslim attitudes and perspectives have in general become discernibly more conservative.

The final point in the preceding paragraph leads to another major contention asserted here. Notwithstanding their considerable political power, mainstream political players have not been the sole actors in expanding the Islamist agenda. Most studies of Muslim politics in Malaysia are confined to the UMNO-PAS "Islamization race" and locate this relationship at the center of their analysis.[25] While such an approach has obvious merits, it creates the impression, first, that UMNO and PAS lie at opposing ends of the spectrum of Islamism, with ideologies as fundamentally divergent and antagonistic as their political relationship; and second, that it is only this political contest that dictates the shape and tenor of political Islam in Malaysia. The picture is in fact far more complex.

To be sure, there is a tide of conservatism and distinctly exclusivist Islamism emanating from both UMNO and PAS, as noted earlier, even as segments in both parties also strive to demonstrate moderation. But the UMNO-PAS Islamization race is as much shaped by the dynamics of Islamism as it is a driver of it. Hence, in order to fully appreciate the kaleidoscope of Islamist politics, one must consider not merely the UMNO-PAS contest but also other actors, institutions, and movements through which broader trends of Islamism have come to be expressed, as well as historical trajectories and variations in Islamism in postcolonial Malaysia; the contributions of civil society, NGOs, and non-Muslim communities to Islamic discourses and narratives; and the relationship of Islamism with the practice of democracy and pluralism in the context of Muslim-dominated politics in Malaysia. The point to stress here is that while UMNO and PAS have been instrumental in facilitating the rise of Islamism in Malaysia today, they are by no means the only agents in this scenario. Increasingly, civil society groups and NGOs, not to mention a burgeoning public discourse, are playing an important role either engaging, expanding, or at times even constricting the parameters of the Islamist debate in Malaysia.

These developments raise a number of issues pertaining to the prospects for Islamism, pluralism, and secularism in Malaysia. First, "piety-trumping" may prove very difficult to manage, let alone reverse, as the line between instrumentalism and ideology becomes increasingly blurred and the process begins to assume a life of its own, particularly given the rise of "alternative" Islamisms embedded in the discursive sphere of civil society, outside the parameters of mainstream politics. Once escalated, this process will be difficult to de-escalate without having the legitimacy of the state and ruling party, or of opposition parties for that matter, called into question. Consider for instance, the declarations made by UMNO leaders that Malaysia already is an Islamic state. While skeptics may dismiss these declarations as mere showmanship (and there is no doubt that such statements are articulated partly for popular consumption), it is difficult to fathom how such discourse, once initiated, can be reversed or even moderated. Put differently, with the genie out of the bottle, it is difficult to conceive of future UMNO leaders rescinding such declarations or revoking Islamic laws that have been formulated by various state governments. Hence, while political elites are culpable for initiating the process, they might gradually lose their ability to control and dictate its parameters or trajectory. Telltale signs of this loss of control are already apparent, as later chapters will discuss, in the nature, tenor, and politics of popular discourses on topics such as *murtad* (apostasy), where dangerously vituperative positions are increasingly articulated not by government leaders or political opposition but by civil society groups and members of the general population with no immediate stake in the political process.

Second, because the process cannot but be conceived as an endgame, it constricts the maneuvering room for other players even as they emerge to engage with the narrative of the main Islamist protagonists. Though this book does not take the position that Islamism is inherently antithetical to democracy, developments in Malaysia have caused democratic processes to give rise to patently undemocratic outcomes. To be sure, this state of affairs may have materialized in part because the incumbent regime's Islamization program has reduced the social and political space available for alternative voices. What is more interesting, however, is the fact that the emergence of undemocratic tendencies may also stem from a curious paradox embedded in political Islam in Malaysia today: an increasingly active nonpartisan civil society debate has emerged to further narrow and polarize debate, even though by their very presence such participants represent a welcome expansion of voices and actors of consequence. There are now more Islamic civil society groups and NGOs actively engaging in the debate today, but because they mostly share the positions of the primary protagonists (UMNO and PAS), in many instances their voices have reinforced dominant Islamist narratives, if not outright setting the agenda for these narratives, rather than providing alternatives to them. At its current pace, this phenomenon might well entrench further the highly political and exclusivist Islamism that lies at the heart of the UMNO-PAS "Islamization race."

At the heart of the issue in this respect then, is the question of whether the role of Islam in configuring Malaysian society and politics proves constructive, where Islam provides a platform for reform and democratization in a way that reassures non-Muslims and neutralizes the corrosive effects of highly politicized racial discourses, or whether it polarizes by taking on increasingly insular and exclusivist forms that undermine fundamentally the erstwhile "consociational democracy" in Malaysia and in so doing further alienate and marginalize already apprehensive non-Muslim Malaysians.

Structure of the Book

To make its case, this book is divided into five chapters. Chapter 1 looks at the genesis of the Islamist agenda in Malaysia from the perspective of both PAS and UMNO. Using the history of the Islamist opposition PAS and UMNO's concomitant early responses to its rise as a lens through which to perceive the early tenor of Islamism in the Malaysian context, the chapter will demonstrate how the party underwent several metamorphoses as it evolved to locate Islamism at the heart of its social-political agenda.

The second chapter investigates at closer analytical quarters the phenomenon of Islamization in Malaysia and the creation of institutions of Islamic governance by the UMNO-led Malaysian government, in a process that can aptly be described as the "bureaucratization" of Islam. This process is important, for it effectively put in place the levers of Islamic governance in Malaysia, eventually facilitating the "Islamic state" proclamations by some of UMNO's senior leaders. The chapter also identifies and discusses in greater detail two prevailing contradictions that arose out of this move to bureaucratize Islam, the first between federal and state administrations, and the second between civil and religious law.

Chapter 3 explores attempts to "reframe" Islamism in the 1990s by both PAS and UMNO. The chapter investigates the contours of the ongoing debate between PAS and UMNO, and within PAS itself, over the nature and expression of Islam as an organizing principle for society and politics in pluralist Malaysia. The chapter also examines how Malaysia's non-Muslim community has responded to this renovation and negotiation exercise that these main Islamist parties have been engaged in.

The fourth chapter takes the discussion beyond the boundaries of mainstream party politics and systematically sets out the civil society agenda that has both engaged and countered the discourse of Islamism in Malaysia as propounded by the main Islamic political parties. In particular, the chapter provides a survey of major civil society groups in Malaysia that have engaged the Islamization debate in recent times from various angles, particularly in relation to legal issues such as Islamic family law, *hudud*, and apostasy. To capture the full range of positions, it discusses groups that span the spectrum from conservative to liberal, anti-establishment to pro-establishment, and also includes non-Muslim and fringe Muslim groups. The chapter also looks at popular discourses and representations of Islamism in Malaysia expressed in English, Malay, and Mandarin-language blogs, alternative media, and Internet chatrooms, which represent a separate source of "popular opinion" and space for debate (but one that has thus far eluded analytical attention).

Chapter 5 explores expressions of Muslim militancy and extremism as they have emerged in Malaysia. While small in numbers and increasingly enervated as an ideology, militant extremism is nevertheless an important expression of Islamism that has occasionally surfaced in Malaysia to influence thinking on trends and patterns. The chapter scrutinizes the Malaysian government's confrontation with Islamic militancy in its domestic political sphere by investigating its operational and ideological countermeasures against the backdrop of an escalating Islamist political discourse. Important as it is to map this militant fringe in the spectrum of Islamism in Malaysia, one should note that political activity in the country will hinge not on these extremists and their activities but on the tension between the various manifestations and articulations of the Islamist agenda described in the preceding chapters. Chapter 5 also discusses the Islamic factor in Malaysian foreign policy as another means by which the UMNO-led government bolsters its Islamic credentials, and it discusses how PAS has developed its own foreign policy agenda for similar purposes.

The book concludes with reflections on the idea of pietization and politics after the transition from the Mahathir administration to the Abdullah administration in the government, as well as from the reformist leadership of Fadzil Noor in PAS to the fundamentalist leadership of Abdul Hadi Awang. The intensification of contested authenticities between UMNO and PAS that these changes heralded is also discussed. In addition to a careful critical deconstruction of the Islamic discourse and praxis of the main political protagonists, the conclusion will draw further attention to the cultural context, meanings, and practices of contemporary Islam in Malaysia, particularly with regard to how these factors interact with mainstream elite politics as encapsulated in the UMNO-PAS "Islamization race." By listening to the voices of those outside the elites who have responded to the effects of UMNO's and PAS's mutually reinforcing Islamist politics, the conclusion further assesses the contributions of society (in contradistinction to the state and the political apparatus, as represented by these dominant political parties) either as an alternative vehicle for or as a buffer against Islamization.

I

Genesis of an Islamist Agenda

The emergence of Muslim political consciousness and the onset of Islamic political activism in Malaysia had several points of origin. Religious teachers, scholars, and students—particularly those who had ventured to the Middle East and North Africa in the early twentieth century, where they imbibed the reformist ideas centered on the writings and teachings of the Egyptian scholar Muhammad Abduh and his Syrian student Rashid Rida—were instrumental in bringing back to the Malay Peninsula these transformative ideas that provided the intellectual foundation for Islamic social and political movements.[1] They viewed Islamic reform as a social-political force for regenerating what was perceived to be a Malay-Muslim identity eroded by Western colonialism. George Kahin noted the impact of Islam on Malay-Muslim political activism when he observed that in the politics of the Indo-Malay world, "the Mohammedan religion was not just a common bond; it was indeed, a sort of in-group symbol as against an alien intruder and oppressor of a different religion."[2]

Through journals such as *Seruan Azhar, Al-Imam*, and *Al-Manar*, students from the Malay Peninsula and the Indonesian Archipelago regularly reproduced and commented on the works of Arab scholars glorifying the Islamic reformation and disseminated them not only to the Malay student diaspora in Cairo but also in local circles in Indonesia and Malaya.[3] However, as was often the case elsewhere in the Muslim world during the process of decolonization, Islamist elements in British Malaya were also closely associated with socialist and nationalist movements, with which they shared the primary objective of independence.

Emergence of Organized Political Movements

Notwithstanding its precedents in the Islamic reform movement, the organized Islamist movement in colonial Malaya appears to have emerged out of the cauldron of Malay socialism and nationalism spearheaded by the Malay Nationalist Party (MNP). Formed in 1945, the MNP was the successor of the prewar *Kesatuan Melayu Muda* (Young Malays Union) and was the first postwar political movement to champion the cause of independence. Among its leaders were prominent socialists such as Ishak Haji Mohammad, Moktarrudin Laso, and Musa Ahmad, who would later assume the post of chairman of the Malayan Communist Party (MCP). The MNP also had a religious wing, though its existence is often overlooked by scholars who focus on its socialist leanings.[4] A prominent member of this religious faction was Dr. Burhanuddin al-Helmy, a reformist Aligarh-trained philosopher and homeopath who would later assume the presidency of *Parti Islam Se-Malaysia* (PAS, or the Islamic Party of Malaysia). Among Burhanuddin's earliest and more enduring contributions to the emergence of Islamism in Malaysia was the Malay nationalist and religious leaders' conference (*Persidangan Ekonomi-Agama Se-Malaysia*) held in March 1947 at Gunung Semanggol in Perak, which he organized for the purpose of detailing the role of Islam in Malayan politics. Attendees included Islamist dissidents disillusioned with the reluctance of the United Malays National Organization (UMNO) to give Islam sufficient prominence in its political ideology after the party's formation in 1946.[5]

Following the Gunung Semanggol meeting, the *Lembaga Islam Se Malaya* (All-Malaya Islamic Council), later renamed *Majlis Agama Tertinggi Malaya* (MATA, or the Malayan Supreme Religious Council), was formed to agitate for the separation of religious matters from the control of state authorities and Malay rulers, the latter of whom were accused of not properly discharging their duties as defenders of the Islamic faith.[6] In particular, the Muslim leaders of MATA could not countenance Britain's proposals to establish an Islamic Religious Council headed by a British governor who was a Christian. MATA was described as "the first institutionalization of the Islamic reformist stream in Malay nationalism."[7] It is important to note, however, that despite its overtly political inclinations (which were partly inspired by the activism of their Indonesian *ulama* counterparts), MATA was not an official political party at its inception, but was rather a welfare organization.[8]

In response to Britain's Malayan Union plan of 1946, which attempted to plot the future of the Malayan state to which Britain would eventually bequeath administrative control, MATA called for a Malay Congress in March 1948 to discuss issues such as the formation of an Islamic political party and the establishment of an economic bureau and an Islamic university. It was at this Congress that *Hizbul Muslimin*, a reformist party and the first overtly

Islamist political organization in Malaya, was formed. At the heart of *Hizbul Muslimin*'s political agenda was independence for Malaya through the creation of an Islamic state and society anchored by Malay dominance. Because of the close association between its members and those of the nationalist party MNP, *Hizbul Muslimin* has been considered the "Islamic wing" of Malay nationalism.[9] Not surprisingly, the party was inspired not only by the perceived inability of the UMNO elite to secure a predominant role for Islam in the making of the nation and state, but also by the aspirations and struggles of international Islamist movements, most notably the Egypt-based *Ikhwanul Muslimin* (Muslim Brotherhood).[10] By August 1948, *Hizbul Muslimin* had established party branches in all the states on the Malay Peninsula. Its meteoric rise was facilitated both by an extensive network built around alumni of El-Ehya Asshariff School, a hotbed for radical Malay nationalists, and by leftist Malay organizations such as the MNP and *Pembela Tanah Ayer* (PETA, or Defenders of the Fatherland).

It must be stressed that *Hizbul Muslimin*'s objectives, though decidedly Islamist in orientation, were not articulated in dogmatic fashion. Funston has noted that the *Hizbul Muslimin* leadership was prepared to negotiate its Islamist objectives in the wake of objections and concerns raised by both Muslim and non-Muslim participants at the Congress. Funston also notes that, according to *Hizbul Muslimin* leaders, "while *Hizbul Muslimin* pursued the aims of both Malay nationalism and Islam, the former had precedence over the latter."[11] This tension between Islamist and ethnonationalist interests would prove to be an enduring trait of Muslim politics in postcolonial Malaysia, as would Malaysian Islamists' capacity for negotiation and compromise.

Hizbul Muslimin's functional ties with Malay radicals proved to be a double-edged sword. While the party leveraged its networks and organizational capabilities, it soon found itself under the scrutiny of British colonial authorities, who had launched their counterinsurgency campaign, commonly known as the Emergency, against the MCP in June 1948. Despite spirited protests and vehement denials of links with Communist elements, *Hizbul Muslimin* was caught in the crossfire between the colonial authorities and the leftist movements, which included their radical Malay nationalist counterparts. Guilty by association, *Hizbul Muslimin*'s relations with the left proved detrimental to their cause; the president and most of the executive committee were arrested under Emergency regulations as the colonial administration moved swiftly to curb the party's activities.[12]

While Islamist reformists and Malay radicals were extending and institutionalizing their collaboration against colonial authority, the mainstream nationalists of UMNO were also attempting to establish their own religious identity. UMNO came to power with the protection of the Malay race as its raison d'être. Given the demographic constraints at the time of independence, when a substantial proportion of the population of British Malaya was non-Muslim,

UMNO could not afford to take a dogmatic position on the matter of the role of religion in the postcolonial state for fear of alienating this substantial constituency—and, more important, antagonizing the British colonial administration, which wanted assurance that UMNO could oversee a moderate governing structure that would maintain multiracial stability. UMNO's caution was evidenced in its constitutional deliberations with the Reid Commission, tasked with drafting the constitution of an independent Malaya. The UMNO-led Alliance submitted a memorandum indicating that while the religion of Malaya would be Islam, this fact would not prejudice the secular nature of the state.[13]

In an obvious concession to more radical Islamist elements in UMNO, the final constitutional document deliberately avoided characterizing Malaya as secular. Under the administration of Tunku Abdul Rahman, numerous assertions were made to the effect that it was unrealistic to consider postcolonial Malaya an Islamic state. Be that as it may, early concern about the presence and activism of *Hizbul Muslimin* threatened to further fragment an already fragile Malay community whose loyalties were divided along ideological and class lines. UMNO awoke to the potentially critical role that Islam would play in the shaping of Malay politics and in 1946 established an *ulama* wing under the leadership of Shaikh Abdullah Pahim. An UMNO Religious Affairs Department was also established, and its Advisory Committee was chaired by Haji Ahmad Fuad Hassan, who would later become the first president of PAS.

Some have suggested that the emergence of this religious wing in UMNO had less to do with the immediate need to assert an Islamic imprint than with differences between UMNO's two senior leaders, Dato Onn bin Jaafar and Tunku Abdul Rahman, over the question of Malay primacy and concessions to the non-Malay population.[14] While the UMNO leadership were skeptical about the sultans' fitness as religious leaders, their criticisms of these traditional structures of authority were decidedly measured compared to the radicalism associated with Islamists from *Hizbul Muslimin*, MATA, and MNP. Moreover, given the party's great reluctance to support the Singapore Malay Union's call to situate the establishment of an Islamic state at the heart of UMNO's decolonization program, it was apparent that UMNO's commitment to an Islamic political agenda was at first fairly weak. At that stage the party was far more concerned with the leftist challenge. This, however, did not stop the UMNO leadership from making symbolic gestures of Islamic leadership in the immediate postindependence years, which included building some two thousand mosques and prayer houses within the first decade of independence, conducting annual Qur'an-reading competitions, and launching various state-sponsored initiatives for the conduct of the *haj* pilgrimage.[15]

Gaining support from Islamic religious leaders was a major strategy for UMNO to shore up its religious flanks. To that end, the Education Act of 1956 provided for an Islamic religious teacher for all public schools that had twelve or more Muslim students. While a number of these teachers were locally trained at university Islamic studies departments, the vast majority were state-sponsored religious students who had attended tertiary Islamic education institutions in North Africa and the Middle East. Locally, the government actively supported the creation of an Islamic religious school system and provided financial assistance for private religious institutions.

In February 1950, UMNO sponsored its own Islamic conference in Johore, which was attended by *ulama* from the party and various other state religious councils. While several issues concerning education and the general welfare of the Muslim community were discussed, by far the most significant outcome of that meeting was the decision to form *Persatuan Ulama Se-Malaya* (PUM or the Ulama Association of Malaya), a body tasked with spreading the message of Islam under the UMNO umbrella. In August of the following year, a second Ulama Conference was held in Kuala Lumpur, at which it was decided to make PUM an organization independent of UMNO. This conference was further noteworthy for the attendance of several former *Hizbul Muslimin* leaders such as Ustaz Osman Hamzah, Baharuddin Latiff, and Khaidir Khatib, who were evidently invited to bolster UMNO's Islamist credentials.[16] Several months later, in November, a third Ulama Conference was held in Butterworth, Penang, in which PUM's name was changed to *Persatuan Islam Se-tanah Malaya* (Pan Malayan Islamic Association, or PMIA). Ironically, it would be "this small, marginalized body, made up of a number of *ulama*, *imam* and conservative nationalists from both within and without UMNO" that would form the "nucleus of the Malayan Islamic party which later developed and came to be known as PAS."[17]

Widening the Schism: Malay Rights and the Islamic State

From the beginning, the PMIA was an ardent supporter of Malay rights and privileges, owing to its origins within UMNO. Still, PMIA members were not afraid to actively criticize the Malay nationalists, which they vehemently did in opposition to what they saw as UMNO's excessive concessions to non-Malay communities. PMIA rejected the granting of Malayan citizenship and voting rights to non-Malays on the basis of *jus soli* (birthright), a move that UMNO was then considering in the course of negotiations with its non-Malay Alliance counterparts. PMIA further criticized a number of clauses in the constitution for being threatening to Malay-Muslim primacy. These included the absence of an explicit ethnic requirement for major government posts, including that of the prime minister, and the constitution's alleged endorsement of economic policies that disadvantaged the Malay-Muslim community. PMIA also took UMNO to task for adopting economic policies that privileged elite and non-Malay interests, and for relying on the latter for financial support during elections. UMNO's rural projects came under heavy attack for introducing developmental schemes at a pace that rural Malay communities could not keep up.[18] UMNO responded to PMIA's criticisms with counterproposals such as one that urged the government not to approve non-Malay business-operating licenses in Malay *kampung* (villages).[19]

While concerned with the Malay cause, PMIA also saw itself as a champion of Islamism in Malaya. It criticized UMNO for not instituting Islamic administration even as it paid lip service to Islam as the religion of the state, and for not designating the Qur'an and *sunnah* (the religious actions of the Prophet) as the chief source of public law in the land. To the PMIA, the Islamic laws that UMNO had implemented to demonstrate its religious credentials, such as anti-*khalwat* legislation, were welcome but insufficient gestures toward the implementation of Islamic governance.[20] The party further denounced UMNO's support and provision of aid to churches and temples, actions which to the PMIA's mind raised questions about UMNO's commitment to Islam.

PMIA's attempt to marry Islam with Malay primacy was given expression in its 1951 constitution, which listed among its objectives the realization of a union of Islamic brotherhood; the unification of constitutional and religious administrations in Malaya; the defense of Islam's honor and of the rights and interests of the *ummah*; and cooperation with other political organizations whose principles and objectives were not opposed to Islam.[21] The centrality of religion was further emphasized in PMIA's declaration of intent to establish a society and government that abided by and upheld Islamic values as it sought to champion the independence of the country. This was to be achieved by way of the propagation of Islam through *dakwah* (proselytization); the introduction of religious values in political, economic, social, and educational realms; and the propagation of Arabic, the language of the Qur'an. To oversee these initiatives, a *Dewan Ulama* (*Ulama* Council) was formed to play an advisory role in the overall hierarchy of the organization.[22] As for the preservation of Malay primacy, this was to be guaranteed through the promotion of Malay as the sole national official language, the establishment of Malay culture as the core of a national culture without undermining Islamic teachings, and the protection of the rights and interests of the Malays in the broader context of interethnic harmony.[23] Despite its strident commitment to Islam and Malay nationalism, the PMIA leadership also demonstrated a capacity for political pragmatism where necessary. For instance, the PMIA resolved to cooperate with other organizations in the spirit of democracy and human rights as long as this cooperation did not oppose the teachings of Islam.[24] This resolution would prove portentous of the party's participation in numerous political coalitions in the years to come.

The backbone of PMIA's intellectual leadership consisted of rural populists and religious scholars, with scores of them coming from the ranks of *Hizbul Muslimin* and MNP. Many disillusioned religious leaders from UMNO also flocked to the organization and assumed positions of leadership. These included Haji Ahmad Fuad Hassan, Ahmad Badawi (father of the current prime minister), and others from UMNO's Bureau of Religious Affairs. The rank and file of the party consisted mostly of religious teachers and students from the *pondok* (traditional Malay religious boarding school) system of religious education.[25]

The PMIA's early influence was primarily confined to the west coast of the Malay Peninsula. It was not until 1953 that the party began expanding into Kelantan and Terengganu on the east coast, the current strongholds of its successor, PAS.[26] This is not surprising, given the genesis of Malay-Muslim political activism at Gunung Semanggol, Perak (a state on the west coast). A dual-membership policy that permitted PMIA members to maintain their membership in UMNO further prevented the consolidation of the movement and stymied its institutional and ideological development as allegiances wavered. Even so, it was not long before the party began to distance itself from UMNO. At the fourth Ulama Conference in Kepala Batas, Penang, the PMIA leadership issued a call for the implementation of Islamic law in Malaya, signaling the first instance of Islamists articulating their agenda with explicit reference to the formation of an Islamic state in the peninsula.[27] Indeed, PMIA's defense of Malay rights and agitation for an Islamic state would dominate its platform for the 1955 federal elections, the first popular election that it would contest. It was on the eve of nomination day for this election (31 May 1955) that PMIA reregistered as the Pan-Malayan Islamic Party (PMIP) or *Parti Islam Se-Tanah Melayu* (PAS). The name change came about because the registrar of societies ruled that in order to contest elections PMIA had to incorporate the word "party" into its name.[28] With this change in nomenclature, PAS officially came into being.

While PAS had its roots in a range of organizations and parties, including UMNO, by the early 1950s it was clear that PAS was trying to package itself as the antithesis of its former nationalist and socialist associates with regard to matters of ethnicity and religion. When UMNO president Tunku Abdul Rahman questioned the formation of PAS as an Islamic alternative to UMNO, Haji Ahmad Fuad Hassan, the first PAS president, retorted by claiming that "the party's aim was to fulfil what UMNO could not accomplish."[29] Ahmad Fuad's comment portended a complex, titanic struggle between his party and UMNO for the hearts, minds, and votes of Malaysia's Malay-Muslim population for many decades to come.

First Forays into Politics

As the PMIA had done before it, PAS projected itself as the voice that represented both Islam and Malay interests, as exemplified by its repeated references to the need for the integration of more Islamic values into governance (including the occasional refrain of the need for an Islamic state) as well as its activism on ethnocultural issues, such as its strident opposition to the National Language Bill proposed by UMNO and its demands that Malay replace English as the sole official language. PAS tried to discredit UMNO as a secular nationalist party that had in fact "sold out" Malay interests to the non-Malay community. The PAS political machinery was anchored by religious teachers who played an important role not only through their stature in the community but also through their network of *pondok* and *masjid* (mosques). The party's infrastructure was generally weaker than UMNO's, so these informal networks would prove even more critical to mobilization and ideological indoctrination. Equally important for the party's political strategies was the welfare work that PAS had engaged in during its previous incarnation as PMIA, which proved instrumental in expanding its rural base and securing popular support.[30] To further exploit these informal networks, PAS relied on *ceramah* (dialogue sessions) in *kampungs* and small towns rather than public rallies to get their message across to the masses. These *ceramah* would be led by a PAS member, usually a *tok guru* (religious teacher from the *pondok*) or *alim* (religious leader). The *ceramah* would begin with a religious lecture before launching into politics through the application of analogy. Unlike public rallies, the more intimate *ceramah* setting offered the opportunity for questions from the audience, which further allowed party leaders to clarify their positions on respective issues and build rapport with followers. By using *ceramah* sessions as its chief vehicle of propaganda and mobilization, PAS laboriously expanded its support base between 1951 and 1955.[31] The *ceramah* model has been so successful that it continues to be the cornerstone of the party's strategies of mobilization today.

PAS's popularity increased among the rural Malay base, but the party was still hampered by several problems in its formative years. As alluded to earlier, the membership of PAS at its formation included a motley crew of Islamo-nationalists from the defunct *Hizbul Muslimin*, socialists from the disbanded MNP, and disenchanted members of UMNO alongside religious scholars and peasants. The ideological incoherence that this conglomeration served up among the rank and file was further aggravated by a slack policy on membership that allowed members not only to possess dual membership with other political organizations but also to assume concurrent leadership roles in a number of them. Party discipline was thus compromised in the early years, and the party itself was hampered in its ability to cobble together a coherent political agenda that could accommodate the variety of interests it represented. Some characterized the early PAS as "an Islamic welfare organization professing no clear political goals."[32] In addition, despite its attempt to discredit UMNO, the party leadership was hard-pressed to plot an agenda to distinguish itself from UMNO and the Independence of Malaya Party (IMP), formed in 1951 by UMNO founder-president Dato Onn bin Jaafar after he lost the UMNO party leadership to Tunku Abdul Rahman. Finally, much of the party's initial incapacities have also been attributed to a lack of visionary leadership. The first president of PAS, Haji Ahmad Fuad Hassan, was seen as too closely aligned to Onn bin Jaafar of IMP, whose credibility suffered from his vacillation on issues pertaining to Malay and minority rights (which accounted for his forced resignation from the presidency of UMNO in August 1951). Meanwhile, Ahmad Fuad's successor, Dr. Haji Abbas Alias, was an English-educated medical officer deemed to be too moderate and Anglophile in outlook to command any significant gravitas. The consequences of this absence of party discipline, ideological coherence, distinctive political platform, and visionary leadership became abundantly clear in PAS's lackluster performance in its first foray into national politics, the 1955 national elections.

Hoping to capitalize on its grassroots popularity, PAS concentrated its campaign efforts for the 1955 elections on the rural Malay-Muslim heartland. As von Vorys observed, "the PMIP (PAS) shunned public debates in English; it did not even try to make inroads in urban areas."[33] Consequently, the party focused its energies on its stronghold, Perak, as well as the Malay-Muslim dominated states of Kelantan and Terengganu. From its slate of three candidates each for federal and state elections, PAS managed only to secure one parliamentary seat in Perak. The seat PAS won proved to be the only seat won by a non-Alliance party, as the Alliance swept 51 of 52 parliamentary seats. The results of the 1955 elections exposed PAS's institutional and ideological weaknesses, a fact that was not lost on the leadership of the party, which acknowledged the need to recalibrate its political strategy to increase its popularity and garner more votes. This became a major issue at the party's general assembly in 1956, which saw the election of a new party president, Burhanuddin al-Helmy, to replace the ineffectual Haji Abbas.

Burhanuddin brought with him impressive credentials. He was an anti-colonialist par excellence, who had extensive experience accrued from his roles as founder, founding member, or leader of several nationalist organizations.[34] He was also an Islamist whose understanding of nationalism was informed by Islamic reformist thinking of the likes of Muhammad Abduh and Rashid Rida.[35] Some have suggested that it was precisely Burhanuddin's Islamist credentials that proved a drawback in his early career as an anticolonialist, when he lost the presidency of PKMM to radical Malay nationalist Ishak Haji Mohammad.[36] Others however, have argued that Burhanuddin's Islamist credentials were less significant than his overall reputation as an anticolonialist. It has been noted that these Islamist credentials were called into question during the contest for the PAS presidency in 1956.[37] Regardless of the ongoing academic debates over the extent to which Burhanuddin was committed to a strict Islamist agenda, his influence derived from his ability to craft a platform and an ideology that was a potent mix of leftist socialism, nationalism, and Islamic reformism, echoing the Indonesian nationalist Sukarno's concept of

NASAKOM (*Nasionalisme, Agama, Komunisme,* or Nationalism, Religion, and Communism), which had captured the imagination of nationalists in the Indo-Malay world.[38] Burhanuddin's influence would become abundantly clear by the 1959 general elections, when under his leadership PAS made significant inroads into the northern Malay states of Kelantan, Terengganu, and Kedah, capturing the state government of the first two on a political platform that married Malay nationalism with Islamism.

Although PAS under Burhanuddin emphasized its Islamic roots and traditions in its 1959 campaign platform, Islam merely provided a rallying point for the party's chief objective of a Malay nationalism that was based on a resolute criticism of the Alliance government's changes to citizenship and language laws. If indeed "its championing of Islam was one of the several factors contributing to its success in these states," the party's loyalty to Islam was certainly not the driving force in the wider context, given that the establishment of a theocratic state did not feature prominently in a campaign fixated on the controversial questions of citizenship and language.[39] Safie Ibrahim has noted that of the five basic principles enunciated by the PAS leadership at the 1957 party conference to plot an alternative constitution for Malaya, "only one was about Islam."[40] This was a reflection of the overall political agenda of PAS under Burhanuddin, in which Islam only assumed prominence insofar as the religion was a feature of Malay identity. The defense of this identity, not the advancement of an Islamic state, took precedence.[41]

The PAS successes in 1959 also benefited from schisms within the Alliance government over matters of education and minority representation in federal elections.[42] The Malayan Chinese Association (MCA) had pressed UMNO for the recognition of Mandarin as an official language alongside English and Malay.[43] Leaders of the respective parties subsequently resolved these differences, but radicals from the MCA and the Malayan Indian Congress (MIC) continued to challenge the dictates of UMNO over matters of education, particularly in light of the Education Ordinance of 1957, which appeared to threaten the status of vernacular education.[44] New constitutional citizenship laws enacted upon independence exacerbated discontent within the Alliance. These laws superseded the restrictive citizenship requirements of the Federation Agreement of 1948, making it easier for non-Muslims to attain citizenship status.[45] In the eyes of many from the Malay community, the passing of this new legislation was "unnecessary, improper, and a betrayal of the interests of Malays," and PAS capitalized on this controversial policy to devastating effect.[46]

Even though it chose ethnic issues as its main line of attack, PAS was also aware that reference to religion often gained currency and enjoyed widespread appeal among the rural Malay community. Consequently, while its head-on assault against UMNO focused on Malay issues, PAS also worked to outflank UMNO by raising doubts about the latter's commitment to Islam. UMNO leaders were criticized for attending non-Muslim religious ceremonies and providing financial support for the construction of non-Muslim places of worship. These criticisms were packaged colloquially and published in *Siaran PAS* (PAS Broadcast), the party's mouthpiece. The PAS attacks in *Siaran PAS* sometimes took comic form, but they nevertheless regularly took UMNO leaders to task for helping non-Muslims rather than Malay-Muslims.[47]

UMNO's precarious position in 1959 was worsened by instability within party ranks and by the economic disparities generated by government policies:

> The alliance's defeat had more tangible causes: the divisive internal struggle in the Kelantan UMNO; the inability of the powerless UMNO state councillors elected in 1955 to establish any record of achievements; and, more fundamentally, a disillusionment with the Alliance, which with independence had removed power over the Kelantanese peasantry to Kuala Lumpur, and had thus become to the peasants more remote than the British and aristocratic colonial civil servants had been. Seeing the benefits of independence concentrated on the more developed and primarily non-Malay west coast, the Kelantanese resented those Malays who enjoyed power in the new order heedless of the peasantry's concerns.[48]

Relating Islam to these more fundamental motivations, Alias Mohamed noted that as a consequence, "Muslims flocked to their religion in the event of a threat, real or imaginary, faced by their community."[49] The key point to underscore here is that social and political circumstances endowed PAS with credentials to serve as "a religiously informed popular movement for the defense of (especially) peasant interests."[50] These cleavages between UMNO and PAS were defined less by religion than by class. Indeed, it was distinctively in this area of relatively slower economic development that the seeds of the campaign for Malay dominance fell on fertile ground.

PAS turned in an admirable electoral performance in 1959, but the party was not able to consolidate that success. UMNO swiftly brought the instruments of the state to bear on PAS in the early 1960s, denying PAS state governments access to developmental funds and mobilizing police powers to deny permits for PAS rallies and religious functions. Equally detrimental to the PAS cause were accusations that some among their leadership, primarily Burhanuddin and Raja Abu Hanifa, were complicit in spreading pro-Indonesia, anti-Malaysia sentiments during the period of Indonesia's diplomatic and military confrontation with Malaysia, better known in the lexicon of international politics as Confrontation or *Konfrontasi*.[51] The Malaysian government alleged that PAS was among the political parties that supported the *Gerakan Pemuda Melayu Raya* (Greater Malaysia Youth Movement), which was established by socialist revolutionaries Ahmad Boestamam and Ishak Mohammad. This movement espoused pan-Malay unity with Indonesia and opposed the UMNO-led Malaysian government.[52] PAS was dealt a crippling blow when its charismatic and respected leader, Burhanuddin, was arrested in January 1965. The party's plight was further compounded by the tragic death of its popular deputy president, Ustaz Zulkiflee Muhammad, and the rising tide among Malaysians of reactionary nationalist sentiment against Indonesian aggression. These developments forced PAS to tread cautiously so as not to give the impression that it was supporting anti-Malaysia elements working to undermine the Federation. Consequently, the party assumed a decidedly lower profile in local politics. This resulted in a significant loss of support in the Malay-Muslim heartland, and it was only in 1969, when the Alliance was faced with another crisis, that the Islamist opposition began to assert its presence again.

The Watershed of 1969

The May 1969 general election and its aftermath remains one of the most studied events in postwar Malaysian history.[53] This election was the first time that the ruling government lost its two-thirds majority in Parliament. This resulted from a massive non-Malay vote swing to the opposition. This was also the first time in Malaysian history that UMNO was denied more than half the votes of the Malay community. Not surprisingly, PAS was the main beneficiary of Malay discontent.[54]

The dominant themes in academic studies on 1969 in Malaysia have concentrated mainly on communal friction that resulted from non-Malay political assertiveness, which culminated in the race riots of 13 May. It was precisely against this background that PAS managed to regain some measure of influence at UMNO's expense. In the 1969 elections, PAS reiterated its campaign for Malay rights, into which Islam was subsumed. While routine talk of implementation of an Islamic state surfaced on the campaign trail, under the new leadership of the Malay nationalist Asri Muda, the notion of an Islamic state was once again articulated in the context of the "overriding cause": Malay supremacy.[55] What was at stake more than anything else in 1969 was the constitutional compact between the ethnic communities of Malaysia. Upon close inspection, PAS appears to have benefited again from internal problems confronting UMNO, just as it did in 1959. This time, the problems had arisen from differences within the Alliance over how to balance the demands of the non-Malays with the preservation of Malay political and economic primacy.[56]

In this tense climate, aggravated by the "Malaysian Malaysia" platform of the Democratic Action Party (DAP), battle lines were drawn along ethnic contours. This set the stage for the deepening of an internal crisis within UMNO between moderate supporters of the party's accommodationist policies and Malay "ultras" who openly questioned the government's concessions on matters of language (where familiar debates raged over which languages should be granted "official" status) and education (where emotive exchanges took place over vernacular education policies). While the UMNO leadership was caught up in internal bickering, PAS marshaled its extensive and proven *ceramah*-based grassroots network across the northern Malay states to expand its web of influence. Explaining the resurgence of PAS, Alias Mohamed surmised: "Neither religion nor poverty was the crucial factor which enabled PAS to succeed in particular areas. It was PAS' very pragmatic approach which was its real strength."[57] This view resonates with analyses of the 1969 elections which suggest that the popularity of PAS resulted less from its Islamist ideology or philosophy than from a particularistic mode of operation premised on the personal approach of its candidates at the grassroots level.[58] This analysis contradicts generalizations that Islam served as the unifying force of the party in these earlier years.

Islam did make some contributions to the success of PAS in 1969. Religion certainly featured in the PAS campaign, and this was evident in its party manifesto, which emphasized the realignment of laws with the "teachings of Islam" and the need to integrate Islam into mainstream education.[59] Even then, it was clear that the Islamic state agenda was devised primarily to draw attention to the weaknesses of the Alliance government, framed as neglect of Islamic principles of administration.[60] However, the potency of the Islamic factor really came to the fore in the context of a strident defense of Malay identity. The PAS leadership portrayed Malay identity as coming under threat from UMNO's unnecessary concessions to non-Malays, leading to the riots in 1969. By this token, the defining challenge of the PAS manifesto was above all fundamental revision of the constitution "to see that the present constitutional provision concerning citizenship is reviewed so that it will ensure the rights of the natives."[61] For PAS, Malay identity, of which Islam was but a constituent feature, took precedence.

In the early 1970s, Malaysia was still trapped in the mire of ethnic politics, and ethnic/racial polemics framed political conduct. This helps explain PAS's inability or reluctance to enunciate operational principles for its call for an Islamic state. As Hussin Mutalib notes, in the 1960s "interethnic tension among [Malaysia's] disparate ethno-religious groups, especially between Malays and Chinese, was still a salient feature of Malaysian daily life. In such a setting, Islam did not make inroads into the political system or into Malay identity politics."[62] While it was true that the usual Islamist diatribes were deployed by leaders of both parties, particularly when they criticized each other in terms of "un-Islamic" governance, Islam was essentially a component of broader concerns of ethnic identity, which "serves to demonstrate . . . that Malay [ethnic] communalism and Islam constituted two dialectical strands, which, consciously or otherwise, complement each other in a 'balance of power' situation, although in the majority of cases, the former seems to have had an edge in the Malay resolution of their socio-economic problems."[63]

The outcome of the 1969 elections heralded a period of unexpected accommodation between UMNO and PAS, which joined the ruling UMNO-led *Barisan Nasional* (National Front), the coalition that replaced the discredited Alliance in 1970. Sensing that its support among Malays had slipped significantly, UMNO moved to regain its hold on the Malay electorate and enacted a number of policies toward that end. In 1971, UMNO leveraged the advantage of incumbency by pushing constitutional changes through Parliament to remove sensitive issues such as the special position of the Malay community and the sovereignty of the Malay sultans from the arena of public discussion. This was followed by the introduction of the *Rukunnegara* (Values of the Nation) concept, which was intended to be a national ideology that transcended parochial ethnic loyalties and fostered a sense of national identity. The government also made the Malay language the sole official language of the country.

Prime Minister Tunku Abdul Rahman resigned under pressure a year after the riots, and the new administration of Tun Abdul Razak moved quickly to institute an affirmative-action program to entrench Malay dominance in the political and economic spheres. A National Operations Council was created following the proclamation of a period of emergency and the suspension of Parliament after the riots. Among its key proposals to the government was the implementation of the far-reaching New Economic Policy (NEP), which aimed to reduce and eventually eradicate poverty by raising income levels and increasing employment opportunities for all Malaysians irrespective of race, and to accelerate "the process of restructuring Malaysian society to correct economic imbalance, so as to reduce and eventually eliminate the identification of race with economic function."[64] While crafted in egalitarian and pluralistic terms, the NEP's key objective was to buttress Malay political and economic dominance.

Insofar as the defense of Malay primacy had always formed the cornerstone of the PAS political agenda, the changes initiated by the new UMNO government presented interesting implications; they brought to fruition much of what PAS had been agitating for over the previous two decades. As a consequence, differences between the two parties, which had essentially been defined by communal motivations, narrowed considerably. In fact, the split in the Malay vote in 1969 belied an "emerging congruence" between UMNO and PAS ideologies, which culminated in an alliance between the two erstwhile antagonists in 1974 as they found a point of convergence.[65] PAS leaders rationalized cooperation with UMNO as "assisting the cause of Islam";[66] others have suggested that the liaison was in fact a conduit for PAS's subsequent radicalism.[67] Indeed, a PAS leader suggested that it was only after Tun Razak had sufficiently demonstrated his commitment to place Islam squarely on the state's agenda (presumably with the announcement of *Rukunnegara*) that PAS agreed to cooperate with UMNO.[68] PAS-UMNO collaboration was also facilitated by the nature of Asri Muda's leadership of PAS, which paid substantive attention to Malay nationalism and which was considerably less dogmatic on Islamism.

Whatever the motivation, the liaison proved short-lived, and an acrimonious separation ensued.[69] Internal dissent brewed within PAS between supporters of cooperation with UMNO, most of whom were members of the PAS old guard, and a growing number of "Young Turks" who felt that such cooperation was against their principles and worked to the detriment of the party's interests.[70] By the end of the 1970s, the liaison had collapsed as a result of internal strife within PAS, with profound ramifications for the future of the party and the Islamization of politics in Malaysia. Against this backdrop of the UMNO-PAS "marriage of convenience" and its failure, processes of Islamization were set further in motion.

A New Broom Sweeps Clean: The Islamization of PAS

The repositioning of Islam from periphery to center has been identified as a consequence of the Islamization of Malay society in the 1970s, which witnessed a move to align state and social structures with Islamic teachings. As several scholars have noted, the revitalization of Islam had much to do with the global resurgence of Islamic consciousness that was then engulfing Muslim societies throughout the world.[71] Yet this process was caused not only by external events but also by fatigue within certain segments of the Malay community as a result of the heavily racialized bickering between UMNO and PAS.[72]

Equally important, the resurgence of Islamic consciousness within Malaysia coincided with the formation of the UMNO-PAS coalition, the consequence of which was "the recognition that Islamic values would be propagated without restriction. The implication of this point was the conferment of legitimacy to various Islamic groups to propagate Islam freely."[73] With the UMNO-PAS alliance anchoring the governing coalition, the seeds of an Islamic bureaucracy were sown with the inclusion of PAS leaders and members in various government organizations, such as the *Majlis Kebangsaan Halehwal Islam Malaysia* (National Council of Islamic Affairs), the *Yayasan Dakwah Islamiah Malaysia* (Islamic Missionary Foundation), and other key bureaucratic and ambassadorial posts.[74] The implications of these changes for the configuration of politics in Malaysia would prove far-reaching. Even though PAS was roundly defeated in the elections of 1978 (after leaving *Barisan* a year earlier) as a consequence of internal politicking that UMNO capitalized upon, by then there were already indications that the party was soon to undertake a renewal process that would fundamentally reorient its political trajectory.[75]

The global Islamic resurgence had a catalytic effect on the emergence of a more acute religious consciousness among Muslims in Malaysia. This revival found expression in a general increase in religiosity among the Muslim population. Indicators included the expansion of mosque congregation sizes, proliferation of religious study groups, a heightened interest in Islamic dress, and the ubiquity of Islamic greetings and *halal* food. The most telling signal of Islamization during this period was the escalation of *dakwah* activism, particularly on university campuses, where the influence of *dakwah* groups was considerable. Some of this "Islamization" eventually precipitated political action. Indeed, PAS deputy president Nasharuddin Mat Isa offered the following conjecture, which captured the political impact of *dakwah* activism: "The hope is that the *dakwah* that we [PAS] conduct will lead to political support. We make them realise what being a Muslim entails and how important it is to live in an environment conducive to practicing Muslims. And to realise that we have to struggle in order to have that environment. We must win as many Malay-Muslims to our side."[76] The political efforts of *dakwah* also extended to Malaysian students abroad. PAS and UMNO leaders made regular trips to campuses in the Middle East, Britain, and the United States at the invitation of Malaysian student associations to deliver talks on Islamization and local politics to large groups of Malaysian Muslim students.

The transnational influence on Islamist politics in Malaysia took a further turn with the Iranian Revolution in 1979. Doctrinal and theological differences—Malaysian Muslims are almost entirely Sunni in orientation, and follow the Shafi'i school of Islamic jurisprudence, while the Iranian Revolution was a Shi'a phenomenon—did not stop the Revolution from serving as a source of inspiration for PAS leaders, particularly those intent on reinvigorating the party along religious lines. Yusof Rawa alluded to the impact of the Iranian Revolution on PAS in his inaugural presidential address:

> The fundamental difference between the Islamic Revolution in Iran and other revolutions that have taken place in Muslim countries is the fact that in Iran it was the result of agitation of the Iranian people led by *ulama*. Unlike other instances across the Muslim World, the Islamic Revolution in Iran was not led by the military elite who harboured political ambitions. Because of this, the Islamic Revolution in Iran was firmly grounded on genuine freedom to implement what was necessary in accordance to the sovereignty of Allah in all aspects of life and to shake America out of its arrogance and pride.[77]

The Malaysian ambassador to Iran in the mid-1970s, a period when popular resentment against the regime of Shah Pahlavi was building up at an alarming pace, was none other than Yusof Rawa himself. Rawa's tour of duty in Iran gave PAS critical firsthand experience of the buildup to an Islamic Revolution and the makings of an Islamic government. Even if its ideological underpinnings were incongruent with Malaysia's brand of Islam, the Iranian Revolution demonstrated the possibilities and plausibility of Islamic governance in a contemporary age. In the aftermath of the Revolution, several PAS leaders accepted invitations issued by the Islamic Republic of Iran to visit the country, while others openly admired and celebrated the authenticity of the Iranian model of Islamic governance.[78] The youth wing of PAS, which stood at the forefront of party reform, sent study groups to Iran to improve relations with the Iranian leadership and study their model of government. The first visit took place in November 1981 and involved Subky Latif, Suhaimi Haji Ahmad, and Ustaz Abu Bakar Chik. PAS Youth chief Haji Mustafa Ali, Rushdi Haji Ariff, and several others made another visit to Iran in June 1982.[79] Iranian politicians were also invited to attend PAS meetings during this time. In 1982, Fakhur Razzi, an Iranian parliamentarian, was invited to speak at the PAS Youth convention, where he urged PAS to emulate Iran in the establishment of *ulama* leadership and an *ulama* council.[80]

This period of intense activity within PAS resulted in the emergence of a new generation of leaders with impeccable religious credentials. Some scholars have identified Yusof Rawa, Asri Muda's deputy and eventual successor, as the personification of this religious resurgence in PAS.[81] However, this shift to a more Islamist register cannot be attributed to one man, influential though he was. Rather, the shift was a consequence of the influx of an entire team of prominent and inspired Islamists, such as Fadzil Noor, Abdul Hadi Awang, Mustapha Ali, Subky Latif, Yahya Othman, and Nakhaie Ahmad, most of whom had openly sought party leadership positions at the 1978 PAS *Muktamar* (General Assembly). These Young Turks injected a potent combination of Islamist romanticism and activism into PAS politics; many of them were Islamist activists and compatriots of Anwar Ibrahim in their student days at the height of Islamic revivalism. Their enthusiasm quickly infected the rank and file and inspired political agitation against the old-guard PAS leadership under Asri Muda. Explaining the motivations of this new leadership, Kamarulnizam Abdullah said these men "had dedicated their life to the cause of Islam and were very displeased with the manner in which Islam had been subordinated to Malay culture and nationalism. By joining PAS, they believed that they could effectively spread their message."[82]

Driven by the global Islamic resurgence and strengthened by the vigor of this new movement, a rejuvenated PAS began to push methodically for a more purposeful Islamic political agenda.[83] The Young Turks articulated the grievances of the PAS rank and file, most notably the party's youth movement, which had become highly critical of the incumbent leadership's lack of religious zeal. The youth movement of PAS clearly stated that UMNO was not an Islamic party because it was not conducting its affairs "according to the will of God, but the will of political interests within the party."[84] By 1981, these grievances had stimulated internal party dissent at the highest levels, culminating in Yusof Rawa defeating Abu Bakar Umar (the incumbent and an ally of Asri Muda) for the post of deputy president of the party. Faced with a likely internal coup given the complexion of the new leadership beneath him, Asri Muda was forced to resign the party presidency at the 1982 PAS Muktamar, when his presidential address was jeered in a virtual vote of no-confidence. He was replaced by Yusof Rawa, the first recognized *ulama* to head the party. With Asri's resignation, PAS leadership finally passed into the hands of the Young Turk *ulama*.

Among the most significant policies implemented by the Young Turks was the creation of the *Majlis Shura Ulama* (Consultative Council of Religious Scholars), a fifteen-member body of religious scholars, led by a *Musyidul 'Am* (spiritual leader) who sits at the top of the party hierarchy. The *Majlis Shura* had the following responsibilities (as outlined in the party's constitution):

1. Elaborate, clarify, and interpret party policies and council decisions in accordance with the party constitution, and ascertain their meanings and purpose.
2. Issue directives and decrees to ensure that policies and decisions are implemented and adhered to by the rank-and-file membership or party committees in the course of the party's activities, movements, and administration.
3. Foster, defend, and regulate party discipline (through a disciplinary committee), and appoint and screen party committee members in accordance with Clause 75 of this Constitution.[85]

While a consultative council in name, the *Majlis Shura* is in effect charged with responsibility over religious matters and remains the highest decision-making body in the party by virtue of its authority to overturn decisions made by the Central Working Committee, thereby signaling a swing in the pendulum of power toward the religious leadership. This marked the institutionalization of *ulama* rule, a characteristically Shi'a tradition that had no historical Sunni precedence and that was likely a legacy of the Iranian model that so attracted the PAS Young Turks. The *Majlis Shura* was led by Haji Nik Abdul Aziz Nik Mat, a respected Islamic scholar who had been associated with Asri Muda earlier in his career but who had gradually distanced himself from that faction as the party further Islamicized. The *Majlis Shura* decentralized power from the party president, a deliberate move on the part of the Young Turks, who had been critical of the concentration and personalization of power under Asri Muda's presidency.

A further initiative of this new *ulama* leadership was to return the Islamic state objective to a position of prominence on the PAS agenda. This motivation was articulated in the following manner:

> Implementing the laws of Allah in the form of *ibadah* [worship] such as fasting, praying, paying *zakat* [tithes], performing pilgrimage and so on is relatively easy but to implement other laws of Allah such as law, economic, political and social systems and so on is not easy,

unless by establishing an "Islamic government." Based on this fact, it is a reality that power is the main condition in implementing the laws of Allah. For this reason, the struggle for governing power is a must for every Muslim. Hence, it is the governing power that is the political power. It is this political power that has been the struggle of PAS for so long.[86]

Yusof Rawa described this stage of the PAS struggle as one that would now locate the Islamic factor at the heart of the party's pursuit of political objectives.[87] This transformation of PAS was supported by student groups in Malaysian universities, who advocated the formation of an *ulama*-led Islamic Republic along the Iranian model and who rejected the "secular" UMNO government.[88]

The introduction of *ulama* rule in PAS was no mere cosmetic change: it heralded a new era in PAS politics, marked by the injection of highly contentious and assertive religious-political rhetoric into the political discourse. This was exemplified most devastatingly in the introduction of the practice of *takfir* to Malaysian politics.

Takfir and the *Amanat Haji Hadi*

Takfir is the practice of Muslims labelling fellow Muslims as infidels. In Malaysia, *takfir* was first introduced to the political scene by the *ulama* of PAS as a response to UMNO's close cooperation with its non-Muslim partners, primarily the MCA and MIC. Because the *Barisan* government comprised a significant number of non-Muslims, PAS criticized it as the illegitimate implementation of non-Muslim rule over a Muslim population, despite the fact that the coalition government was headed by UMNO. Ahmad Fauzi traces the earliest PAS public branding of UMNO as *kafir* (infidel) to November 1979, when Mustapha Abu Bakar, a leader from the Kelantan PAS, called UMNO members *kafir* during a *ceramah* in Ulu Besut, Terengganu.[89] PAS leaders deemed their UMNO counterparts unfit to undertake religious duties such as leading congregational prayers, slaughtering livestock for consumption, and solemnizing Muslim marriages.[90] Mustapha was eventually tried and convicted in the *shari'a* court for delivering a religious lecture without *tauliah* (formal letter of authority) and for issuing a *fatwa* without *tauliah*, which contravened religious law and convention.

Despite the court ruling against Mustapha, the PAS *Ulama* Council escalated tension by publishing *Islam dan Politik: Hasil Kajian Ilmiah Ulama PAS* [Islam and Politics: Results of Scholarly Research by PAS's Ulama] and declaring in it that Muslims who condoned the separation of religion from politics or who placed manmade laws above God's laws were apostates.[91] This declaration was followed by a swift deterioration of relations between Malay-Muslims of differing political persuasions and loyalties. A wealth of anecdotal evidence describes tensions within many *kampung* leading to the construction of alternative mosques or *surau* (prayer house), one used by UMNO supporters and the other by PAS supporters. Because of this tension, some marriages had to be solemnized twice, once each by an UMNO and a PAS *alim*. Cemeteries were segregated, and families were fractured along party lines.

At its height, *kafir-mengafir* (allegations and counterallegations of being an infidel) was crystallized as a national issue by the controversial speech delivered on 7 April 1981 by Haji Abdul Hadi Awang, a Medina and al-Azhar graduate who was then PAS state commissioner for Terengganu, during a *ceramah* in Banggol Peradong, Terengganu. This speech, which gained notoriety as the *Amanat Haji Hadi* (Edict of Haji Hadi), outlined three major principles that governed the PAS political struggle against UMNO. First, PAS opposed UMNO and the *Barisan Nasional* government it fronted because they had maintained the infidel colonial constitution inherited at independence. Second, given the struggle between PAS and UMNO, speeches and financial contributions of PAS members were all *jihad*, and should they die in the course of fighting UMNO members, they would die as martyrs. Third, one need not officially convert to other religions to become a *kafir*; simply condoning the separation between religion and politics was sufficient to render one an opponent of Islam and worthy of condemnation.

Amanat Haji Hadi further deepened the polarization of Malay society into PAS and UMNO camps. The situation was particularly acute in the rural Malay heartlands of Kelantan, Terengganu, and Kedah.[92] Burgeoning audiences at PAS-organized lectures prompted the government to step up security measures. Three PAS Youth leaders (Abu Bakar Chik, Bunyamin Yaakob, and Muhammad Sabu) were detained under the Internal Security Act, and rumor had it that PAS members were preparing themselves for an armed *jihad*. A ban was imposed in August 1984 on PAS gatherings in its four stronghold states.[93] A live television debate on the *kafir-mengafir* issue, scheduled for 11 November 1984, would have pitted UMNO leaders against their PAS counterparts, but the debate was canceled after the intervention of the *Yang diPertuan Agong* (king).[94] Further attempts at public discussion of this issue between PAS and UMNO representatives got nowhere.

The National Fatwa Council ruled in December 1984 that the *Amanat Haji Hadi* was contrary to the teaching of Islam. State governments never publicized the ruling, probably because of the controversial nature of the *Amanat* and of the ruling itself, given the highly politicized climate. The government's silence further fueled popular perception that the state was incapacitated by the PAS challenge to its religious legitimacy.[95] Indeed, it was likely that religious leaders and scholars within state religious institutions sympathized with the PAS leadership on matters pertaining to Islam, even if they moved cautiously on the specific issue of the *Amanat*, given the political freight associated with it.

In 1985, the government issued a white paper titled *The Threat to Muslim Unity and National Security*, which implicated PAS members in the subversive activities of extremist Islamic groups and created the impression that Communists were manipulating PAS to generate rifts that would achieve their antidemocratic aims.[96]

Hostility spawned by the political polarization in the country also led to sporadic outbreaks of violence. An incident in the village of Memali, Kedah, in November 1985 was arguably the most extreme example of the severity of repercussions caused by this escalating political contest (the Memali incident will be discussed in greater detail later). There was also a clash between UMNO and PAS supporters at the Padang Terap by-election in 1985, resulting in one death. These developments put a severe stress on Malay unity. As Alias Mohamed notes: "Since Haji Abdul Hadi Awang's appearance in the political arena, religious issues which once had more or less lurked in the background now loomed large, threatening to destroy the Malay social fabric."[97] The matter of the *Amanat* was raised again, this time by *Jabatan Kemajuan Islam Malaysia* (Malaysian Islamic Development Department), in 2001. The Council of Rulers, vested with constitutional powers to monitor and regulate religious affairs, spoke out firmly in criticism of the *Amanat Haji Hadi*.[98] Even then, state *mufti* remained reluctant to publicize the decision.

The acute religious turn in the PAS political discourse, and the considerable extent to which extremism appeared to flow from that turn, proved unnerving for Malaysia's sizable non-Muslim community. To assuage these concerns, the *ulama*-led PAS sought to dissociate the party from its tradition of ethnonationalist agitation. The party's religious elite criticized the government's pro-Malay policies for encouraging *assabiyah* (communalism or tribalism), and several leaders went so far as to condemn the NEP as "inimical to the spirit of Islam."[99]

Notwithstanding the saber-rattling and brinkmanship, the first true test of Malaysia's receptivity to the recalibrated agenda of the PAS Islamists would come with the 1986 general election—the first nationwide political contest for the party's *ulama* leadership.

The 1986 Setback

In a striking departure from earlier campaigns, in 1986 Islam began replacing Malay ethnicity as the key reference point for PAS politics. So profound was this change that PAS leaders began criticizing the NEP and condemning UMNO's "un-Islamic ethnic chauvinism" vehemently.[100] PAS leaders issued *fatwa* against the "infidels" of UMNO and called for *jihad* against them as *kafir-mengafir* brinkmanship continued between the two parties.

In 1986 the Islamic state concept took center stage in Malaysian electoral politics for the first time.[101] The establishment of an Islamic state had been a declared objective of Islamists since the 1940s, but for a long time there had been no attempt to define or clarify the terms and conditions pertaining to such a state's formation, and no election campaigns had been focused entirely on that issue.[102] Reference to the idea during election campaigning seldom moved beyond cursory allusions and remarks. Despite this reticence, PAS leaders believed that the Islamic state was a viable and necessary alternative to the Malaysian secularism they accused UMNO of propounding.[103] The pursuit of the Islamic state gained greater urgency after 1982 under the stewardship of Yusof Rawa and his deputy president, Abdul Hadi Awang, who was the party's unofficial ideologue.[104]

Given the demographic landscape of Malaysia, a necessary corollary of the reemphasis on the Islamic state was the accommodation of non-Muslims within the theocratic polity. PAS formed a Chinese Consultative Committee with that concern in mind. In addition, Abdul Hadi himself declared while campaigning that Malays were not entitled to special rights and privileges. Nevertheless, despite the party's attempt to break out of the racial boundaries of Malaysian politics, PAS found it distinctly difficult to reconcile their demands for the implementation of *shari'a* and *hudud* law with their ambitions to be an acceptable alternative to the non-Muslim population. Moreover, the party's alacrity in supporting the preservation of non-Muslim cultural practices proved a double-edged sword, as it created the perception that the PAS Islamist agenda discriminated against Malay Muslims, denying them the option of practicing pre-Islamic Malay traditions and customs that were still practiced and held in high regard in Malay society.[105]

Meanwhile, another clear indicator that Islam was making its imprint on the Malaysian political landscape was the emergence of Muslim extremism. By 1984, the Malaysian government had identified six extremist groups that it claimed were plotting to overthrow the government on the way to establishing an Islamic state, and attempts were quickly made to associate them with PAS.[106] The Memali affair of November 1985, when PAS stalwart Ibrahim Mahmood and his supporters engaged government forces in a gun battle that resulted in eighteen deaths (including Mahmood) and thirty-seven injuries, was another incident that drew attention to the radicalization of Islam. The government was quick to label Ibrahim Mahmood a criminal, but PAS eulogized him as a martyr.

In the political contest of 1986, there was a sense that the Islamic resurgence and the discernible shift in the party's ideological and policy orientation toward greater Islamic consciousness would enhance PAS's chances for the general election:

> Political observers, domestic and foreign, predicted that the BN,
> particularly UMNO, would lose numerous seats to PAS especially
> because of the resurgence of religious extremism among the Malays

and the emergence of a new PAS leadership with their own brand of religiousness and radicalism. . . . PAS had launched an extensive campaign, with the aim of regaining control of at least Kelantan and with hopes of making inroads into the other predominantly-Malay states.[107]

Given expectations like these, PAS's actual performance at the ballot box was a major setback.

After an exhaustive election campaign, the Islamists won a grand total of only one out of ninety-nine parliamentary seats contested and fifteen out of 265 state seats contested, its worst-ever performance in a national election. Paradoxically, the party's excessive emphasis on religious issues was identified as a key reason for the debacle. Many Malays, including some PAS supporters, were "upset with PAS's portrayal of the party as 'Allah's party.'"[108] Despite attempts to court non-Muslims, the staunch Islamist language employed in the PAS campaign created the impression that the party was intolerant and conservative, consequently alienating not only non-Muslims but also the average Malay-Muslim voter who was becoming increasingly conscious of Islamic identity but who was nevertheless disturbed by the overly vituperative version of Islamization that PAS seemed to be propounding.[109] Such perceptions were reinforced by the fact that many among the *ulama* leadership appeared obsessed with *kafir-mengafir* confrontation with UMNO. Conversely, PAS's attempted collaboration with the Chinese-dominated DAP was also seen as contributing to its rejection by Malays.[110] To the extent that this was true, it indicated that even in the face of Islamic resurgence, political Islam was constrained by the racial polarization endemic to Malaysian politics.

The limitations of doctrinaire Islamist politics became all too evident with PAS's dismal performance at the 1986 polls. Defeat heralded yet another transition in the party, this time in the direction of moderation, defined by an emphasis on civil justice, human rights, and democratization. But a careful examination of UMNO in the mid-1980s would reveal yet another major factor that explained the failure of the PAS Islamist agenda: by 1986, the UMNO-led government under Mahathir Mohamad had already put in place the makings of an alternative model of Islamic governance that effectively took the wind out of the PAS sails.

2

The Malaysian State and the Bureaucratization of Islam

By the early 1980s, Malaysian society was already in the throes of an Islamization process that was gaining momentum on the back of both international and domestic developments. According to prominent Malaysian activist Chandra Muzaffar, "Islamization is that process by which what are perceived as Islamic laws, values and practices are accorded greater significance in state, society and culture."[1] In the case of Malaysia, the Islamization process can be understood as a phenomenon of social change with distinct political implications. Islamization was accelerated by both UMNO and PAS in their respective quests for an Islamic ideal that would translate into legitimacy, popularity, and electoral support. Hence, in attempting to accord greater significance to Islamic laws, values, and practices, UMNO and PAS essentially entered a "race" to see which of the two parties was able to package, sell, and execute its Islamization campaign most effectively in Malaysia.

Yet even as Islamization acquired a distinct political edge, it was firmly rooted in the civil sphere and had its origins as a social movement, otherwise known in Malaysian parlance as *dakwah*. Chapter 1 introduced the concept of *dakwah* and its role in facilitating and expressing the phenomenon of Islamization in the Malaysian context. In this chapter we will delve deeper into the movement, given its instrumental role in the transformation of state and society.

The domestic roots of *dakwah* can be traced to the post–13 May 1969 recalibration of affirmative-action policies aimed at alleviating Malay concerns that their status as the dominant ethnic group was under threat. As noted previously, the race riots of May 1969 led to the formulation of several far-reaching policies, including the introduction of a New Economic Policy (NEP) that was designed to reduce wealth disparity among races. According to the logic behind the NEP, this objective was to be attained through policies aimed at cementing the "special status" of the Malays, thereby adding substance to the concept of *ketuanan melayu* (Malay primacy). One such policy entailed the allocation of large numbers of government scholarships to Malay students seeking to pursue tertiary education abroad and, specifically, heavy investment in the field of Islamic education. The impact of this policy of sending Malay-Muslim students overseas during the height of the worldwide resurgence of Islamic identity and consciousness cannot be overemphasized. Their overseas travels offered students the opportunity to acquaint themselves with Muslim student movements on university campuses in Europe, North America, and Australia, as well as the Middle East and North Africa.[2] During this period, students engaged in activities organized by well-structured and well-endowed social networks and Islamic charities that were underwriting much of the civil activism associated with the Islamic resurgence of the 1970s. PAS deputy president Nasharuddin Mat Isa shared the following experience that typified the impact of such sojourns on the political socialization of Malaysian Muslim students:

> I became a PAS member when I was a student in Jordan. PAS leaders visited us often in Jordan—either on the way to perform the *umrah* or on special visits that they organised. So I met and got to know leaders such as the late Datuk Fadzil Noor, Datuk Abdul Hadi Awang, Datuk Nik Aziz Nik Mat and a number of others. The number of students in Jordan was not very many but we organised quite a number of activities; sometimes with other Islamic movements in the Middle East. I was more exposed to other Islamic study groups while in the UK and that kept my interest in being a PAS member going.[3]

Through interactions such as these, Malaysian students imbibed the general Muslim disdain for Westernization and the social "decadence" associated with it. At the same time, they were exposed to new streams of Islamic scholarship. This allowed them access to a wider pool of knowledge about their faith, leading one observer to suggest that "the new approach to the study of Islam with its emphasis on Islam as a way of life and its recognition of Islam's political aspect was the greatest single factor that had brought about this transformation."[4] Further elaborating on the *dakwah* model of socialization, Judith Nagata observed that these youths came to a consciousness of their Islamic identity "through attendance at *dakwah* lectures and conferences, and through the study of Arabic as well as of the voluminous Islamic literature. . . . These youths are deeply preoccupied with theological issues, particularly of a fundamentalist cast, which tend to take priority in their relationship with fellow Muslims and in evaluating behaviours."[5]

These students brought strong Islamic values and perspectives back home to Malaysia upon completion of their education. Their newfound values informed how they viewed their own society, where Westernization was perceived to be rampant and Islam was practiced in ways that did not adhere to strict, purist interpretations of its creeds. This transplanted movement found institutional expression locally in the formation of numerous Islamic student associations and societies (*Persatuan Islam*) on campuses throughout the country. Some scholars have observed that when imported to Malaysian soil, the Islamic resurgence had a profound impact on traditional Malay society, where the practice of Islam was steeped in folk and syncretic traditions that had for a long time characterized the religion in Southeast Asia.[6] Aside from various *Persatuan Islam*, *dakwah* adherents also formed several nongovernmental organizations (NGOs) that surfaced on the Malaysian socioreligious landscape during this time.

Though there was some consensus among these organizations that drank from the well of *dakwah*, particularly their unity in opposition to Westernization, rampant modernization, and the rapid economic development that had dislocated Malay-Muslim society, the *dakwah* movement was not monolithic. Differences soon emerged over the very nature of *dakwah*, with some groups such as *Jemaat Tabligh* and *Al Arqam* preferring to remain apolitical, while others, like *Angkatan Belia Islam Malaysia* (ABIM, or the Malaysian Islamic Youth Movement), saw political activism as the *sine qua non* of the movement. These competing approaches to dealing with politics indicated how the nature of *dakwah* lent itself to political machinations. Describing how *dakwah* evolved, Nagata asserted:

> One characteristic the various *dakwah* elements in Malaysia have in common is the fact that they are "non-establishment" groups in that they have no traditional, legal, historical or other institutional basis for their authority, but have risen spontaneously and independently. They are easily vulnerable to representations that they are non-legitimate by government authorities, who prefer to keep to themselves all rights of political power in its broadest sense. Religious power and authority is likewise jealously guarded by those who have held it longer, that is, the *ulama* of the older rural tradition, religious councils, and sometimes even the sultans. *Dakwah* in Malaysia, therefore, reflects aspects of relationships and conflicts which have long existed under other names and banners.[7]

Islamic revivalism and the *dakwah* movement inspired major changes in the PAS leadership, structure, and ideology. It has been suggested that UMNO and the Malaysian government had "an ambivalent attitude toward the rising tide of Islam."[8] In hindsight, however, it appears that this assessment was a misrepresentation of the impact of the revivalist movement on mainstream politics in general and on UMNO and the Malaysian government in particular.

Syed Ahmad Hussein has observed, for instance, that "as early as 1972, [Prime Minister] Razak had begun to speak of the 'necessity of *dakwah*' and 'religious revolution to check declining morals.' The dominant media too published editorials on Islam."[9] The UMNO-led government's concern for greater Islamization would intensify after Mahathir Mohamad assumed the party presidency and the office of prime minister of Malaysia. He moved immediately to harness and direct these social forces spawning from Islamic revivalism. In his insightful study of "Mahathirism," Khoo Boo Teik argued convincingly how "a politician and his religion are not easily parted," and he demonstrated how Mahathir's Islamization policies were driven not solely by the expediency of politics but also by an intense desire to locate Islam at the heart of the Malaysian social-political orbit and to contribute to the resurgence of Islam as an intellectual and cultural force.[10]

The Beginnings of an Islamic Bureaucracy

Mahathir assumed office in July 1981, as the Islamic resurgence reached its peak internationally with the success of the Iranian Revolution and the increasing popularity (at least in the Muslim world) of the Afghan Mujahideen resistance against Soviet occupation. Mahathir reacted immediately to this changing environment by making a conscious decision to Islamize the government, and a number of policies were enacted to achieve these ends. This decision was communicated at the UMNO general assembly in 1982, when Mahathir announced that UMNO would be embarking on a new strategy focused on "the struggle to change the attitude of the Malays in line with the requirements of Islam in this modern age."[11] This logic took the form of a policy of *Penerapan Nilai-nilai Islam* (inculcation of Islamic values), which sought to create a Muslim work ethic to underscore the modernization of Malaysia.[12] To add intellectual weight to the policy, a widely publicized conference titled "The Concept of Development in Islam" kick-started a plethora of Islam-related programs and policy directives that would span Mahathir's 22 years in power.[13] According to Mahathir,

> Islamization is the inculcation of Islamic values in government administration. Such inculcation is not the same as implementation of Islamic laws in the country. Islamic laws are for Muslims and meant for their personal laws. But laws of the nation, although not Islamic-based, can be used as long as they do not come in conflict with Islamic principles. Islamic laws can be implemented if all the people agree to them.[14]

Mahathir moved to delineate the parameters of Islamic governance and invest heavily in the Islamization of the state machinery and bureaucracy. This calculated move to enact policies that framed and guided his Islamic agenda was calibrated to manage the domestic Islamic resurgence on his own terms.

Conventional wisdom has always maintained that Mahathir's Islamization project (implemented via the hegemonic ruling party, UMNO) took place against the backdrop of intensifying political pressure from PAS. In truth, however, the project was conceptualized and set in motion long before a PAS threat materialized concretely. Moreover, while Mahathir's initiative was indeed significant, it was not entirely novel. The previous administrations of Tun Abdul Razak and Tun Hussein Onn had already implemented policies in realms such as education that introduced the first steps in the creation of a bureaucratic apparatus that was imbued with the *dakwah* ethos. For instance, the Razak era saw the continued proliferation of mosques, the continuation of national Qur'an-reading competitions, and the increased popularity of seminars and courses on Islam sponsored by state authorities. New Islamic institutions established at the federal level through the 1970s included the Islamic Research Center, the Institute of Islamic Missionary and Training, and the Malaysian Foundation of Islamic Missionaries. In addition, the secretariat for the National Council of Islamic Affairs was elevated to a full division of the prime minister's department in 1974. Theologically trained people were recruited en masse by the civil service. As a result of these measures, an increasing number of *ulama* and *ustaz* were mobilized, trained, and employed by the UMNO-led government as Islamic court officials, schoolteachers, and state and federal department officials.[15] On the one hand, these newly employed people were heavily dependent on the state for their authority and their livelihood; on the other hand, this policy facilitated the injection of decidedly Islamic perspectives into the everyday running of the administration. This ideological pollination would prove to have significant ramifications, particularly when the process was expanded and accelerated under Mahathir.

One of the most significant initial steps in Mahathir's Islamization program was the successful enticement of Anwar Ibrahim, a popular and charismatic Islamist activist, and his followers into the UMNO fold. Anwar's pedigree as both an Islamist and a populist, and the fact that he had also been courted by PAS, made his incorporation into the ranks of UMNO nothing short of a coup, a move of strategic consequence that further strengthened and legitimized Mahathir's Islamization campaign. Another compelling reason to bring Anwar into the UMNO fold was his vast support network within ABIM and the *dakwah* movement at large, many of whom eventually became *ulama* and religious teachers. Though not all followed him into UMNO—indeed, a large number flocked to PAS—with Anwar and his compatriots in government, the stage was set for the creation of an Islamic bureaucracy.

By virtue of their positions and appointments within the state bureaucracy, the *ulama* were effectively empowered to define the parameters of Islamic discourse in Malaysia, and they lent their considerable weight and gravitas as religious scholars to the legitimacy of the UMNO government's Islamization programs.[16] A number of scholars have noted that the government had managed to harness the support of the *ulama* through formal institutions such as the respective state offices of *Mufti*, the *Majlis Ugama* (Religious Council), and the National Fatwa Council.[17] Aside from state *mufti*, the more prominent religious personalities in UMNO's federal bureaucracy include Abdul Hamid Othman (chairman of the UMNO Religious Bureau), Wan Mokhtar (former secretary of the bureau), Yusuf Noor (chairman of the Federal Land Development Authority, or FELDA), Zainal Abidin Kadir (former director of *Jabatan Kemajuan Islam Malaysia*, the Malaysian Islamic Development Department, or JAKIM), and Che Min Che Mat (also a former JAKIM director). While not of the caliber or prominence of PAS *ulama* such as Nik Aziz Nik Mat, Abdul Hadi Awang, Harun Din, Harun Taib, or the late Fadzil Noor, the mobilization of these religious commissars nevertheless bolstered the Mahathir administration's religious credentials and legitimacy, allowed him to concentrate power and stem potential resistance from the religious elite, and enabled him to engineer a decidedly Islamic turn in the governing of the country.

Mahathir's overall Islamization strategy was based on the creation of think tanks, whose purpose was to provide intellectual and ideological impetus for policy. Georg Stauth described this process as "the socialization and institutionalization" of Islam.[18] The think tanks were important because they made available to Mahathir and his government the necessary knowledge and expertise to design and implement Islamization policies that would undercut and outbid PAS by ensuring that the state was "pro-Islam" while still modernizing the country, and in particular the Malay community, without sacrificing Islamic values. A number of institutions were either created or augmented to this end. Two institutions that featured prominently were JAKIM, which was the upgraded Islamic Center (*Pusat Islam*), and *Institut Kefahaman Islam Malaysia* (IKIM, or Malaysian Institute of Islamic Understanding).

From *Pusat Islam* to JAKIM

Pusat Islam was established in 1980 by Mahathir's predecessor, Tun Hussein Onn. At its formation, it was seen as a "government-sponsored *dakwah* group intended to compete with other *dakwah* groups and to report on their activities."[19] *Pusat Islam* was placed directly under the supervision of a cabinet minister inside the prime minister's department. The agency was upgraded in 1996 to the Department of Islamic Development in Malaysia or *Jabatan Kemajuan Islam Malaysia* (JAKIM). Along with the change in its name, a *dakwah* foundation was also established under its auspices, with the mandate to coordinate all *dakwah* activities throughout the country.[20] Thus, not only did JAKIM serve to "compete" with *dakwah* groups, it also sought to harness the popularity and efficacy of the *dakwah* movement to the advantage of the state. In an indication of the increasing magnitude and influence of the *Pusat Islam* in the early years of the Mahathir tenure, its staff strength increased from 100 in 1982 to 608 in 1987.[21]

According to its Web site, "JAKIM has been responsible to ascertain policies pertaining to the advancement of Islamic affairs in Malaysia by fostering and promoting the sanctity of the *aqidah* [faith] and Islamic *shari'a*."[22] JAKIM (and before it *Pusat Islam*) has also been relied upon to enact and standardize laws and procedures and to coordinate their implementation with the respective state religious authorities in all states across Malaysia. One of the key functions of *Pusat Islam* was to mobilize state-affiliated *ulama* as civil servants whose task was to propose and discuss *shari'a*-based legal responses to a range of issues. *Pusat Islam* played a crucial role in supervising and scrutinizing the drafting of *shari'a* legislation by the respective state religious authorities and preparing these proposed laws for parliamentary deliberation and adoption. Moreover, *Pusat Islam* also played an important political function as an advisory body to government institutions on proper legal statements and responses to PAS positions on religious and social matters, including PAS's persistent agitation for the introduction of the Islamic penal code encapsulated in *hudud* (restrictions), *qisas* (laws of retaliation covering homicide and injury), and *ta'zirat* (penal stipulations).[23] In other words, UMNO's response to PAS policies and positions on religious issues, as well as those of other religious groups such as ABIM and *Al Arqam*, were dependent on the proposals made by *Pusat Islam* (and later JAKIM). JAKIM served a critical function in Mahathir's accelerated Islamization campaign, which involved "institutionalizing the state Islamic administrative apparatus as well as incorporating *ulama* into the formal state structure."[24]

JAKIM has also contributed significantly to the state's attempt to define the parameters of Islamic thinking and praxis in Malaysia by actively monitoring "deviant" teachings in Malaysia. According to its own yardsticks, JAKIM has identified and documented up to ninety-eight "deviant" strains of Islam in the country, of which twenty-five are apparently still being actively propounded and followed.[25] Among the more prominent of these are the *Al Arqam* movement, led by Ashaari Muhammad, and the Sky Kingdom cult, a religious commune previously congregated in Hulu Besut, Terengganu, led by a man called Ayah Pin. Followers of both groups have either gone through or are currently undergoing rehabilitation at JAKIM's rehabilitation centers in Jerebu and Kuala Terengganu. According to JAKIM statistics, there are 2,383 rehabilitants in its centers, 500 of whom have been classified "hardcore"—those who refuse to recant or repent despite efforts to rehabilitate them.[26] JAKIM also monitors groups (especially among intellectual and academic circles) practicing and promoting Wahhabi Islam, particularly in the northern state of Perlis, which follows the Hanbali school of jurisprudence closely. According to JAKIM's

director-general, Mustapha Abdul Rahman, this monitoring is important because "Wahhabi practices could encourage religious extremism and adversely
affect the moderation of Malaysia's mainstream Sunni Islam followers."[27]

While JAKIM's role involves monitoring deviant teachings and rehabili-
tating wayward adherents, it lacks legal authority to arrest and prosecute dis-
seminators of "deviant" Islamic doctrine. This lack of authority has led some
to question JAKIM's ability to circumscribe the activities of deviant religious
groups. To make matters worse, a whole new range of deviant groups have surfaced over the past few years, including the *Jangan Ikut Tuhan* (Don't Conform
to God) cult and the "Black Metal" antireligion cult, consisting of Malay youth
who routinely engage in abuse of the Qur'an, which they are known to burn.
Consequently, parliamentarians have appealed for JAKIM to be given some
measure of policing power so it can arrest and prosecute leaders and followers
of deviant religious cults.[28]

JAKIM also plays a pivotal role when it comes to issues of family, marriage,
and divorce legislation. For instance, the government has tasked JAKIM with
fine-tuning the Islamic Family Law (Federal Territories) Amendment Act of
2005, which has been heavily criticized for favoring Muslim men on issues of
polygamy and divorce. JAKIM has been instructed by the Malaysian Cabinet
to clarify the benefits to women in the proposed (amended) Islamic Family
Law.[29] A pertinent issue that has come to the fore in this regard is the use
of cellphone SMS (Short Message Service, i.e., text messages) for purposes of
divorcing one's spouse. This issue arose following the actions of Senator Kamaruddin Ambok, who was fined RM550 for attempting to divorce his wife via
SMS and voice mail in 2001. On this issue, JAKIM has pushed for heftier fines
to be imposed on Muslim men who try to divorce their wives through text
messages. According to Mustapha, "it is an offence for men to divorce their
wife outside the courtroom and thus this review [for stiffer fines] is to ensure Muslims do not take matters pertaining to divorce lightly."[30] On matters
of marriage, JAKIM has recommended that Muslim couples be subjected to
health screening before marriage. This recommendation came after the Johore
Religious Department made HIV screening compulsory for all Muslim couples
registered in Johore in 2001.[31]

JAKIM has also weighed in on the state's response to the proliferation of
acts of "indecency" committed by Muslims. JAKIM has publicly called for immediate action against Muslims who commit "indecent acts," even though the
question of what constitutes "indecency" is debatable (acts such as kissing in
public are deemed "indecent" by some state religious authorities). Mustapha
noted that non-Muslims found committing indecent acts with Muslims would
be handed over to the police, while their Muslim partners would be dealt with
under the *shari'a*.[32] Mustapha further argued that it was the responsibility of the
government to ensure that everyone in the country lived in harmony and subscribed to "high moral standards." JAKIM's position on such "indecent acts"

is clear: they exemplify the Western decadence that is shunned and forbidden in Islam.[33]

Finally, another issue that has caused uproar in Malaysia and challenged JAKIM to act decisively was an unsubstantiated but highly controversial claim made by Perak Mufti Harussani Zakaria that there were as many as 100,000 Muslims in the country who had become apostates (*murtad*).[34] Apostasy and the laws governing it will be discussed at several points in this book, because apostasy has become a contentious political issue that has elicited emotional responses from Muslims and non-Muslims alike. For this reason, apostasy has become a key point of contention in the discursive terrain of political Islam in Malaysia. JAKIM has been noticeably slow and reactive in its investigations of apostasy. Such was JAKIM's incapacity on this issue that PAS Youth chief Salahuddin Ayub had to provoke the organization to explain Islam's position on apostasy to non-Muslims.[35] Salahuddin also noted that the patience of Muslims was "wearing thin" on the question of apostasy.[36]

In response, JAKIM said it was exploring a system of registration that would enable converts to Islam to be documented by the government for purposes of monitoring and possible follow-up.[37] JAKIM has also made it compulsory for all converts to attend counseling sessions to improve their understanding of Islam.[38] The implication is that, in JAKIM's view, the apostasy problem pertains mostly to converts to the religion rather than to those born into it. In a related matter, a study revealed that 40 percent of Muslim patients did not comprehend the full spectrum of Islamic prayers that could be performed while they were sick or bedridden, so it has been proposed that JAKIM officials be deployed at hospitals to help Muslim patients (including converts) perform prayers.[39]

Aside from its contribution to the ongoing debate over the boundaries of Islamic doctrine, JAKIM has also been active in framing the practice of Islam in everyday Malaysian life. To that end, the department has undertaken the major responsibility of issuing *halal* ("permissible in Islam") certification for food products distributed in Malaysia. In fact, all states in Malaysia have been directed to use the *halal* logo issued by JAKIM instead of those from respective state Islamic religious departments. Thus, JAKIM's *halal* logo has become the national logo for *halal* food.[40] The JAKIM logo has since won further recognition as requisite certification by Muslim authorities in other countries in the region and hence has evolved into a distinctive Malaysian brand. JAKIM is scheduled to move into its own 18.4-hectare *halal* complex, which will include a *halal* accreditation center, by the end of the year.[41] Such an institution will further enhance Malaysia's reputation as a global *halal* accreditation and reference hub. Similarly, JAKIM will undertake a Malaysia International *Halal* Showcase project, which aims to make Malaysia a global player in the production of certified *halal* products.

This seemingly innocuous discussion of *halal* certification should not be seen as inconsequential in light of larger political concerns. JAKIM's monopoly on *halal* certification has in effect augmented the state's hegemony over the practice of Islam, such that even opposition forces have had to subscribe to their established standards. The prominence of JAKIM in this area has also given the state a high degree of visibility in Malaysian society, allowing it in this instance to define the parameters of religiocultural practice. The demand for *halal* products in ASEAN countries has reached US$46 billion, so it is likely that Malaysia's international reputation will be further enhanced with JAKIM's initiatives on this front.[42] To further emphasize its control over *halal* certification, JAKIM is currently drafting a *halal* standard for the production and use of cosmetics according to Islam, because many cosmetic products contain a mixture of animal and fruit substances.[43]

In sum, JAKIM functions along the lines of a religious affairs ministry, because its roles and responsibilities are geared to elevating and sustaining Islam as the official religion in Malaysia. While JAKIM has been criticized on a number of fronts, such as its rigorous censorship of information and Islamic literature as well as its lethargy on certain controversial matters pertaining to the practice of Islam, it remains a vital institutional pillar of UMNO's objective of defining and safeguarding the parameters of Islam while augmenting the party's and the government's Islamic credentials. These objectives were facilitated by a major publicity campaign in which JAKIM used prime-time television to conduct discussions on issues pertaining to Islamic doctrine and governance. Given the structure of religious authority in Malaysia, where states are the final arbiter on religious affairs, there are constitutional constraints on the expansion of JAKIM's influence. Nevertheless, the organization remains a major instrument in the government's policy on Islam.

A major challenge for JAKIM, though, is its need for consultation and engagement with non-Muslim groups. The need for established and clear channels of communication gains greater urgency when JAKIM policies and programs have a direct impact on Malaysia's substantial non-Muslim minority, as is increasingly the case in Malaysia today. Harcharan Singh, president of the Malaysian Consultative Council of Buddhism, Christianity, Hinduism and Sikhism, indicated as much when he called for JAKIM to consult with non-Muslims before proposing religious guidelines on public issues (such as forms of entertainment) that might affect all Malaysians, Muslim and non-Muslim alike.[44]

Institut Kefahaman Islam Malaysia (Malaysian Institute of Islamic Understanding, or IKIM)

IKIM was established in 1992 with the explicit mandate to work with other national Islamic agencies to propagate "progressive" Islamic views congruent with UMNO's version of "modern" Islam, or as some scholars term it, "Islamic Modernism."[45] This was evident in the regularity of its references, both direct and oblique, that perpetuate Mahathir's articulation of Islam. For instance, IKIM's objectives of "Vision Islam," as detailed in its publication *An Inspiration for the Future of Islam*, dovetailed with Mahathir's objectives of Islamic modernity encapsulated in his Vision 2020 proposal, which stressed the Islamic basis of development. IKIM operates its own radio station, IKIM-FM, which was officially launched on 6 July 2001. The main purpose of this media outlet is purportedly to elevate the understanding of Islam among both Muslim and non-Muslim communities by presenting radio programs that address misconceptions about the religion.[46] IKIM-FM has specially designed programs for youths, adults, and seniors, as well as programs that focus on politics, economics, and education. Illustrative of this is the popular *Suara FELDA* (Voice of the Federal Land Development Authority) program, which has been broadcast on the channel since June 2003 and which presents news and information related to FELDA schemes in the agricultural sector. The program is funded by the FELDA Foundation, which aims to encourage community service and social enterprise among both Muslims and non-Muslims in Malaysia.[47]

Additionally, Milne and Mauzy observed that IKIM's objectives were not only to "channel the challenge of the Islamic resurgence along state-defined lines" but also to "establish a dialogue with non-Muslims both inside and outside Malaysia."[48] To that end, IKIM has engaged leaders of other religions in dialogue. Its chairman, Ahmad Sarji Abdul Hamid, has also reiterated that "IKIM would intensify its activities to create a better understanding of Islam both in the country and international level."[49] In pursuit of this objective, IKIM has continued its efforts to meet with non-Islamic organizations to facilitate an understanding of Islam as the official religion of Malaysia.

One could argue that, similar to JAKIM, IKIM has been instrumental in providing intellectual capital for the Mahathir government, in this instance in relations with non-Muslims. Given that IKIM provided a vehicle for the Mahathir administration to realize, propagate, and operationalize (with a clear Islamic bent) its Vision 2020 program through both academic and popular discourse, one could also argue that IKIM has in effect allowed Mahathir to successfully pursue a kind of "intellectual assimilation" of Islamic precepts into his blueprint of modernization. IKIM helped to articulate and promote an understanding of Islam that was defined by the Mahathir administration.

IKIM is not without its detractors, though. While it has produced numerous articles (mostly published in the local Malaysian media) to explain how Islam fosters economic progress and development, IKIM often comes under criticism from more conservative Islamic quarters for not basing its "Islamic" pronouncements sufficiently on the Qur'an, *hadith*, or *shari'a*.[50] For example, an IKIM-linked feature article appeared in the *New Straits Times* on 13 February 1999 describing how research, development, and the Internet were important components of modernity, and the article was criticized for lacking references to Islamic teachings on these matters.[51] IKIM's partiality and objectivity have also come under considerable scrutiny. IKIM's contribution to Islamic discourse in Malaysia is clearly geared primarily toward explaining and endorsing the government's Islamization policies and programs.

UMNO's think-tank strategy essentially amounted to the creation of the ideological machinery through which the state managed and harnessed Islamic discourse in Malaysia, by perpetuating an "official" position on intellectual, cultural, educational, and legal matters in relation to Islam. The UMNO government also embarked on an unprecedented degree of restructuring (both in scale and in scope) for a range of Islamic institutions. We have already seen how the state bureaucracy was expanded to accommodate the return of a growing number of Malaysian students who had been dispatched abroad on government scholarships during the Mahathir administration for degrees in Islamic studies, not to mention the products of local Islamic institutions as well. In addition, the government changed how the *shari'a* courts and mosques were run, and it reorganized banking structures, foundation and charity work, *zakat* collection, and educational institutions.

Among the Mahathir administration's most significant (and controversial) efforts was the move to make religious knowledge an examinable subject in the mainstream school curriculum. This policy was premised on Mahathir's desire to "ensure that the Malay community truly adheres to Islamic teachings."[52] To facilitate this shift, the Islamic Teachers Training College was established in 1982. Mahathir also sanctioned the establishment of the Islamic Development Foundation in 1984 and the Islamic Insurance Company in 1985, the same year in which an increased emphasis on Islamic studies in the curriculums of secular institutions was initiated, although it was referred to with the more nebulous phrase "religious knowledge."

One of the Mahathir administration's chief initiatives in the realm of the Islamization of education was the development and launch of an Islamic university (later renamed International Islamic University Malaysia, or IIUM) in 1983. The opening of IIUM had both symbolic and functional value. As Milne and Mauzy observe, "IIUM aspired to be the counterpart of the renowned Egyptian al-Azhar University where many Malay nationalists had been educated."[53] It is worth noting, however, that the administrative structure and organization of IIUM was in fact modeled along the lines of American universities. Although IIUM is situated in Malaysia and is sponsored by the Malaysian government, it is also cosponsored by the Organization of Islamic Conferences (OIC).[54] Indeed, this was the first instance when the OIC sponsored a tertiary education institution in a Muslim country.

The international character of IIUM is noteworthy. The university has attracted students not only from Muslim countries but also from Europe and North America. English is the language of instruction. In addition to Islamic studies, the curriculum includes subjects such as engineering, economics, management, and political science. Interestingly, faculty and students are not required to be Muslims. While IIUM was envisaged as playing an important role in making Malaysia a center for tertiary Islamic education, the university has not been immune to the broader currents of politics that both caused and resulted from Mahathir's Islamization project. Indeed, as IIUM has grown, some have suggested that the university had transformed into a major power base for Anwar Ibrahim, through which he exerted his influence over educated Muslim youths.[55]

A final milestone of Mahathir's enterprise of creating and restructuring Islamic institutions was the establishment of an Islamic bank.[56] The creation of an Islamic bank was instrumental to the larger objective of the Islamization of the economy; it was also an important expression of Islamic values (*Nilai-nilai Islam*) articulated by Mahathir, whereby Malays will be able to "seek wealth in a moral and legal way" and to "obtain prosperity in this world and hereafter."[57] The Islamic banking project also served as a response to criticisms by PAS and elements from the Islamic civil sphere that economic development involving a secular-banking system would incur "*riba*" or profit maximization through usury, an activity shunned in Islam.[58] Thus, when the Islamic Bank was established in 1984, its marketing drive focused on a rural Muslim community that put a great deal of stock in criticisms of conventional banking practices. It should be noted that Mahathir never intended his robust Islamic banking system to be a challenge to the conventional banking system; rather, he wanted it to complement conventional banking and provide an alternative system that generally adhered to conventional secular banking practices.

The popularity of the Islamic Bank skyrocketed, not only among the Muslim community but also among non-Muslims who were drawn to its favorable terms, especially for personal, housing, and auto loans. So strong was the support for the Islamic Bank that it became the nation's third-largest bank within four years of its opening.

On balance, the Islamic Bank has proven to be such a major boost to the government's Islamic credentials that even PAS was forced to acknowledge its contribution to Malaysia's Muslim community. Still, PAS leaders were quick to point out that their party had long advocated for the creation of an Islamic bank in Malaysia, and features of Islamic banking had already been introduced and practiced in Kelantan under PAS administration. PAS also noted that while the Islamic Bank was a laudable initiative, the Malaysian government should not claim too much credit for the idea, given that Islamic banks were proliferating even in non-Muslim countries.[59]

Policing Islamization

Mahathir's approach to Islamization also exposed the authoritarian nature of his government. Malaysian observers have noted how social and political activities were closely monitored and policed during the Mahathir administration by way of instruments of surveillance and coercion.[60] Mahathir had at his disposal mechanisms of control that he could mobilize to keep the Islamic resurgence in check and to pursue his Islamic agenda by silencing "deviationist" and dissident voices. A major tool from this arsenal was the Internal Security Act (ISA), which has been described as "a draconian law whose use is justified as ostensibly the only means of maintaining political stability."[61] Against the backdrop of Mahathir's Islamization agenda, the ISA became a notorious yet convenient way for the state to neutralize the political threat posed by political opposition, civil society groups, and radical Islamist movements, all in the name of "national security." Operation Lallang in 1987, the banning of Al Arqam in 1994, and the arrests of several political figures, most notably from PAS, were some of the events that illustrated how the Mahathir administration used the ISA to weed out what Mahathir perceived as obstacles to his Islamization policies and broader political agenda, even if the actual threat posed by these forces was questionable.

Operation Lallang was carried out by the Malaysian police on 27 October 1987 to crack down on opposition leaders and social activists who were accused of engaging in activities with strong racial overtones. According to the white paper released by the government following the episode, various groups had played up "sensitive issues" and had generated "racial tension" in the country, which threatened to boil over in a volatile multiethnic climate. The operation culminated in the arrest of 106 people under the ISA, including Democratic Action Party deputy chairman Karpal Singh, Democratic Action Party secretary-general Lim Kit Siang, and PAS Youth chief Halim Arshat. The government also revoked the publishing licenses of two dailies, the Star and the Sin Chew Jit Poh, and two weeklies, the Sunday Star and Watan.

Although it was not directly related to Mahathir's Islamization policies, Operation Lallang did indicate that the administration was prepared to use draconian measures in order to curtail dissent against its policies, including those related to Islam. The incident provided the Mahathir government with a convenient excuse to tighten the executive stranglehold on politics by further restricting fundamental liberties. The government exerted this control by passing the Printing Presses and Publishing Act,[62] and further amendments to the Police Act made it practically impossible to hold any political meeting, let alone a rally, without a police permit.

The Mahathir administration justified its use of the ISA against Muslim groups by saying such measures were necessary for "upholding the faith of Muslims in Malaysia [untuk mempertahankan aqidah orang Islam di Malaysia], as well as to safeguard the integrity and faith of Muslim citizens in Malaysia."[63] The government used the ISA on several occasions to curtail the activities of a number of Islamic groups and followers of dakwah. Mahathir explicitly pointed out that for Malaysians to be protected, the government had to limit extremism; where necessary, the government used this rationale to justify curbs on PAS activities.[64] This explanation was articulated by Malaysia's deputy minister of information, who announced that "ISA would be used to detain those who promote religious fanaticism among Muslims."[65] This comment was made in reference to several PAS leaders who were suspected of fanning the embers of religious fanaticism among the party's members. The logic here was simple enough: PAS was targeted for "religious fanaticism," and because state authorities describe fanaticism as a "deviation" of faith and a threat to national security, PAS leaders can and should be detained under the ISA. PAS members were detained during Operation Lallang and at the height of the *Reformasi* movement in the late 1990s, when they participated in street protests against the sacking of former deputy prime minister Anwar Ibrahim.[66]

Another Islamic group that fell victim to the Mahathir administration's strong-arm Islamization was *Al Arqam*, which the government perceived as a potential threat to Mahathir's Islamist project. Mahathir's repression of *Al Arqam* was initially informed by an abiding concern with extremism.[67] Yet, despite the government's suspicions that the organization was recruiting and training militants, the primary case against *Al Arqam* was the belief that the group was "deviationist" in its Islamic ideology.[68] At the height of its popularity, the *Al Arqam* movement boasted more than ten thousand male members, causing even greater alarm to the administration.[69]

The threat that *Al Arqam* posed to the state stemmed from how it was seen as a community of Muslims who pledged unyielding loyalty to a charismatic leader. Reminiscent of the People's Temple cult active in the United States and Guyana in the 1970s, *Al Arqam* members chose to live apart from mainstream Malaysian society in a number of self-sufficient communes. Because of the sheer size of its membership and their allegiance and absolute devotion to their leader, *Al Arqam* represented a "significant potential power base that could pose a threat to national security."[70] With little evidence that *Al Arqam* was posing an explicit security or political threat, the Malaysian government was compelled to contrive a case against Ashaari, the movement's leader, when he purportedly made claims that he was a prophet and had had visions of the Prophet Muhammad. As a result, *Al Arqam* was branded as "deviant," a *fatwa* was issued against it, and Ashaari was arrested with several followers under the ISA. It is interesting to note that they were not arrested for offenses against the *shari'a*, as one might have expected, but for threatening national security, despite the glaring lack of hard evidence for that charge. The organization was disbanded in 1995.

Al Arqam's open denigration of several aspects of Mahathir's Islamization policies further contributed to its demise. For instance, *Al Arqam* rejected the government's rural development programs as incompatible with Islamic principles. This criticism, taken together with the expansion of the movement's

activities, was viewed as a substantive challenge to the government's Islamization narrative. Consequently, Mahathir believed it was imperative for his
government to take "sudden and severe" action to remove a competitor and
"preserve the sovereignty of the state."[71] After moving against *Al Arqam*, the
Minister for Islamic Affairs in the prime minister's department escalated matters by issuing a blanket warning that the government would also arrest lecturers and politicians "if they continue with [deviant] activities that threaten to
disunite Muslims in the country."[72] As the *Al Arqam* episode demonstrated,
at the heart of the issue of policing Islamization lay the question of the right
to interpret Islam as well as the legitimacy of sources of such interpretations.
This episode further suggests, as chapter 5 will elaborate, that religiosity that
resisted or challenged state-defined Islamism has been curbed under the veil
of a national security discourse, which in turn allows secular instruments of
political domination to be employed in the name of "national security" to coun-
teract perceived threats to the state's Islamization agenda and challenges to its
popularity among the Muslim community.

Shari'a and Civil Law: The *Hudud* Controversy in Terengganu

The question of Islamic law and its role in governing society is a major component of any Islamization campaign. Thus, it is not surprising that Mahathir's
tenure as prime minister was marked by several controversial and high-profile
debates over Islamic legislation. These debates were indicative of the intensification of Islamization in Mahathir's Malaysia, and the manner in which
they were or were not resolved reveals their implications for the contours of
Islamism.

According to many Malaysian Muslims, Islamization is incomplete without implementation of the full *shari'a* and particularly of the *hudud* penal code
that governs a litany of crimes in Islam.[73] Implicit in this perspective is a contention that Islamic law should not be confined to the private sphere; instead,
it should extend into the public domain of common law, including criminal,
administrative, and constitutional law. The more extreme proponents of the
full *shari'a* have argued that in order to avoid accusations of "dualism and discrimination," *shari'a* should be a source of common law for both Muslims
and non-Muslims in Malaysia.[74] Those who share this perspective—most, but
not all, of whom are aligned or affiliated with PAS—tend also to be critical
of UMNO's Islamization campaign. To them, the government's reluctance to
implement *shari'a* in its entirety means that its campaign sought to only pursue a kind of "pseudo-Islamization" or Islamization in form rather than in
substance. In response to this criticism, Mahathir has defended the position of
his administration by arguing that it was not practical for *hudud* to be implemented in multiethnic, multireligious Malaysia.[75] Under the weight of popular

pressures, issues of Islamic law and *hudud* have become an arena of heated contest between UMNO and PAS, despite the fact that the positions held by both parties are closer than either would be prepared to concede.

Since 1990, when PAS was returned to power in the state of Kelantan, it began presenting draft proposals to Parliament for the introduction of *hudud* law in Kelantan. The PAS-controlled Kelantan State Assembly managed to pass an enactment of *hudud* that was supported by all thirty-six members of the State Assembly and was thus unanimously adopted in November 1993. The enactment, however, was rejected by the federal government when it was submitted for ratification.[76] The implementation of the enactment faced two major constitutional problems. First, in Malaysia's system of federalism, any motion adopted at the state level requires ratification by a two-thirds parliamentary majority before it can come into force. In this case, given UMNO's domination of the federal Parliament, it is hardly a surprise that PAS was not able to secure ratification. Second, the implementation of *hudud* required enforcement powers that state authorities did not possess, because official policing powers were vested only in federal authorities. Aside from these two constitutional constraints, PAS's attempt to implement *hudud* was also attacked by Mahathir himself: "A woman who has been raped, and is unable to produce four witnesses, would not be able to have the rapist punished even if she knows who he is. . . . On the other hand, if she were to have a child as a result, she would be guilty of *zina* [adultery] and could be punished by stoning to death. By no stretch of the imagination can this be considered justice."[77]

Mahathir's tendency to openly question Islamic jurisprudence and contravene Islamic scholars, despite his lack of the requisite religious qualifications (he is not an Islamic scholar), has led to tense relations with *muftis*, many appointed by his own UMNO-led federal government, over interpretations of Islamic teaching and the enforcement of Islamic law. This tension underscored the controversy surrounding the arrest under the Selangor Islamic Criminal Enactment of 1995 of three Malay women for participating in a beauty contest in June 1997. This episode was quickly followed by another arrest of two women in Federal Territory under similar legislation. Meanwhile, scheduled public concerts of local music groups were banned because they were deemed "un-Islamic." In the aftermath of the arrests, calls by Mahathir and his then-deputy Anwar Ibrahim for restraint on the part of state religious officials when enforcing *shari'a* were publicly rebuffed by Selangor *mufti* Ishak Baharuddin, who retorted that "if we regard everything as extreme, then things will be easier, then no enforcement can be conducted. . . . If something is wrong, it is wrong. If a beauty contest is wrong, it is wrong."[78] A surprisingly large number of Malays supported the actions of the Selangor State Religious Department in detaining the women.[79] This incident was not reported on by the mainstream media. As for Ishak, after crossing swords with Mahathir he found his position as *mufti* unrenewed when his tenure expired, and upon retirement he joined PAS.

The most contentious aspect of *hudud* law is the enforcement of the so-called *hudud* punishments. For instance, according to strict interpretations of the law, those found guilty of certain offenses, such as adultery, armed robbery and apostasy, are required to be subjected to punishments including flogging, mutilation of limbs by amputation, stoning to death, and crucifixion. In addition to this, *hudud* offenses also include *qisas* and *ta'zirat*, which becomes applicable when evidence in *hudud* and *qisas* cases are inadequate or other conditions are not met.[80] While one could argue that these extreme measures are a clear violation of human rights—especially sections 12(3) and 41(1) of the Kelantan *Shari'a* Criminal Code II Enactment 1993, which discriminate against women in the matter of giving evidence in a court of law and which contravene Article 8(2) of the constitution, guaranteeing equality of the sexes—its supporters would reply that these *hudud* punishments are in fact a key component of the implementation of the full *shari'a*. In the wake of these developments in Kelantan, the question of *hudud* surfaced again in Terengganu, when PAS attempted to implement the Islamic penal code after it wrested the state from UMNO in 1999.

According to PAS logic, because *hudud* law is divine law, there should be no question about its implementation, particularly in a country that claims to be Islamic. PAS considers it a matter of duty, obligation, and responsibility to ensure that *hudud* is enacted, implemented, and enshrined in the constitution as federal law. In fact, PAS argues that *hudud* is needed more than ever as a deterrent against the proliferation of social problems associated with development and modernization in Malaysia. PAS's strategy has been to use its strongholds in Kelantan and Terengganu (before it lost Terengganu to UMNO in the 2004 general election) as model "Islamic" states to demonstrate the efficacy of the PAS vision of a clean, efficient, corruption-free administration that adheres to Islamic teachings and principles. To soothe non-Muslim nerves regarding the Islamic state, PAS has also taken steps to reassure them that they will not be subjected to *hudud* legislation and punishment.

While the PAS position on *hudud* appears to enjoy widespread popular support in Kelantan, Terengganu provided a different context in which to test the acceptability of its model of governance. Given this state's substantial offshore oil reserves, it can be surmised that economic development, and in particular access to the state's largesse, would be the primary lens through which Terengganu state politics are assessed. This was corroborated when the UMNO-controlled federal government attempted to thwart PAS's aspirations toward economic reform and Islamic development by stopping royalty payments to Terengganu after the PAS state government assumed office. This move effectively cut Terengganu's annual budget by 80 percent.[81]

After its surprise performance in the 1999 elections, which saw it win control of the Terengganu state government (in addition to its vice-like grip on Kelantan), PAS introduced the *Hudud* bill on 8 July 2002 in the newly configured state legislature, where PAS controlled twenty-eight of the thirty-two seats.[82] The bill would only apply to Muslims above the age of eighteen in Terengganu, and non-Muslims had the option to chose whether or not to be covered by it.[83] When votes on the bill were cast and counted, all twenty-eight PAS members predictably voted for it. What was interesting was the voting pattern of the four UMNO asesmblymen, all of whom chose to abstain rather than oppose the bill. Explaining the decision to abstain, one of the four UMNO legislators, Rosol Wahid, admitted: "UMNO legislators didn't vote against the bill outright so that the fundamentalists could not brand them as being bad Muslims."[84]

Clearly, the issue of credibility loomed large in the eyes of the Muslim electorate, not to mention the legislators involved in the issue of the *Hudud* bill. Rosol said that despite their vote to abstain, the four UMNO assembly-men had in fact vigorously objected to the bill during the debates that tran-spired; they saw it as nothing more than politically motivated machinations on the part of PAS, aimed at burnishing its Islamic credentials in order to further enhance its popularity.[85] Abdul Hamid Othman, minister of Islamic Affairs in the prime minister's department, responded that the federal govern-ment had rejected PAS's *hudud* laws because "several sections contradicted Islam. . . . PAS only listed six *hudud* offences while the religion says there were seven. . . . *Hudud* laws are applicable to all Malaysians but PAS says non-Muslims can choose to opt out."[86] Elsewhere, however, it was reported that UMNO leaders "upheld the argument that the treatment of non-Muslims under this 'cruel' law was their utmost concern."[87] What counts here are the grounds of UMNO's rejection of the *hudud* legislation proposed by PAS. First, *hudud* was rejected on the grounds of intent, where UMNO disparaged PAS's initiative as a blatant attempt to enhance the party's popularity. More inter-esting, though, was UMNO's rejection of the bill on the grounds of content. Based on Abdul Hamid's comments, it seemed UMNO was implying that PAS was "not Islamic enough" in how it aimed to implement *hudud*. As a later chapter will elaborate, this criticism would take on greater significance when Terengganu returned to the UMNO fold, and UMNO inherited the state's *hudud* legislation.

Returning to the reluctance of the four UMNO assemblymen to directly oppose the *Hudud* bill in 2002, it was clear that it was equally politically mo-tivated. Just as Islamic credentials were at stake in the case of the PAS as-semblymen, they were equally at stake for the UMNO representatives, who most likely skirted the issue so as not to raise doubts of their commitment to Islam, doubts that almost certainly would have been sown if they had publicly opposed the bill.[88] Some observers have asserted that UMNO was at fault for pressuring PAS into introducing *hudud* law in a hurry, because "UMNO went around telling the Malays that even though PAS has been in power for more than ten years—three elections—in Kelantan, they are still unable to intro-duce the *hudud* law there. UMNO kept on saying that PAS is not sincere about introducing the *hudud* law."[89] According to this logic, PAS had little choice. If the party had delayed formulation of *hudud* in Terengganu, they would have proved UMNO right. Alternatively, formulating it as they did so soon after the electoral victory may have proved UMNO wrong, but it also forced PAS to raise the stakes in the Islamization race.

Despite securing the support of Sultan Mizan Zainal Abidin, the sultan of Terengganu and guardian of religious affairs in the state, PAS attempts to introduce *hudud* legislation met with several obstacles. First, several changes had to be made to the law in response to criticism by women's groups such as Sisters in Islam (SIS), who felt that the proposed law discriminated against women. Major amendments had to be made in the sections on *zina* (illicit sex—an accusation that placed the burden of proof on the female accuser, who had to provide four male witnesses of good character to substantiate her accusation) and *qazaf* (accusation of *zina* without witnesses).[90] For instance, under *qazaf*, which carries a penalty of ninety lashes, a woman who cries rape without having the requisite evidence would instead be found guilty of *qazaf*. In this manner, the harsh punishment meted out for "false evidence" serves as a deterrent to rape victims who might otherwise step forward to report the crime.[91] Another example that provoked protest was the matter of unmarried pregnancies. Even if a woman was pregnant as a result of being raped, her pregnancy would be deemed evidence of *zina*. For an unmarried offender, *zina* carries a punishment of 100 lashes and a year's jail; for married offenders, the penalty is death by stoning.

It is worth noting here that attempts to amend *hudud* law did little to assuage apprehension on the part of its detractors. In particular, vocal Muslim women remained critical. Zainah Anwar, an activist from SIS, exemplified this mood when she remarked that while PAS ideologues claimed to belong to the Shafi'i school of thought, which she suggests puts forward an "enlightened" opinion on the matter of *hudud*, the party's religious leadership instead preferred to pursue the harsher Maliki opinion by codifying *hudud* law.[92] Yet when a Maliki opinion on any particular matter proved more advantageous to women, PAS jurists, according to Zainah, would proclaim that it could not be accepted because "we are Shafi'i and we must follow Shafi'i rulings."[93] Put differently, Zainah alleged that PAS exercised double standards and that it systemically and deliberately discriminated against women.

Second, because UMNO controlled the federal Parliament, PAS would have a difficult time getting *hudud* law to be implemented as an amendment to the constitution. Though *hudud* could be passed at the state level, as was the case in PAS-controlled Terengganu, it could not secure the requisite two-thirds majority in the *Barisan Nasional*–dominated and UMNO-dominated Parliament for ratification. For this reason, the attorney general's office, the police, and the prisons—all institutions controlled by the federal government—made clear that they would not enforce the *shari'a* criminal enactments.[94] The police chief in Terengganu further announced that his officers would not enforce proposed *hudud* laws, as the federal constitution stipulates that Acts of Parliament take precedence over state laws.[95] In other words, when it comes to *hudud* law and punishment, the Malaysian police, which is a federal institution and hence possesses powers of enforcement, is governed by federal legislation and not state law.[96]

Third, there was the abiding issue of non-Muslims who harbored concerns that *hudud* law might eventually be applied to them as well, despite assurances to the contrary from PAS leaders. Non-Muslims worried that their rights to freedom of religion, enshrined in the federal constitution, would be threatened if *hudud* law became a reality. In response, PAS has on several occasions clarified that *hudud* law would not be extended to non-Muslims. Moreover, Abdul Hadi Awang, the former *Menteri Besar* of Terengganu and the current president of PAS, indicated that the party was considering amending its constitution to "appoint a non-Muslim Chinese as a people's representative" to address these concerns regarding *shari'a* and *hudud*.[97] Despite this gesture, skepticism has remained strong in non-Muslim circles. The PAS cause was made even more arduous when Mahathir publicly warned the people that the fundamentalists would "twist" the tolerant teachings of Islam and that the PAS attempt to introduce *hudud* law in Terengganu was an attempt to "hoodwink" Malays as well as non-Muslims.[98]

Additionally, the PAS position on *hudud* has to be viewed against the larger context of the party's policies and positions on issues such as the shutting down of bars and liquor outlets, the ban on gambling, and wide-ranging restrictions on socializing between the sexes.[99] The ban on bars and liquor outlets had a negative effect on the small but influential Chinese business community in Terengganu, evidently affecting "productivity levels" in the state. In addition to this, the Terengganu state government had also considered rules outlawing bikinis from beaches, though tourism was a pillar of the local economy.

In terms of concrete policies, the Terengganu experiment drew attention to the fairly strong constraints on PAS's bid to offer an alternative mode of Islamic governance in contrast to that of UMNO. Under earlier UMNO-led administrations, a policy of *Wawasan Sihat* (Healthy Vision) had been put in place in Terengganu with the explicit aim of creating the world's first "Islamic civil society" based on rapid industrial growth, a sustainable economy, and a low rate of poverty.[100] The 1999 elections were doubtless a damning indictment of the UMNO-led administration in the state, but given the PAS state government's difficulties in formulating and implementing *hudud* legislation, not to mention the party's eventual electoral defeat in 2004, the "Islamic experiment" of PAS unfortunately was not the panacea that popular opinion in Terengganu was hoping for.

To be fair, PAS has, as suggested earlier, tried to influence non-Malay perceptions of the party by demonstrating some flexibility on questions of *shari'a, hudud,* and the Islamic state.[101] For example, Abdul Hadi has assured individual states that they can exercise prerogative on matters concerning the Islamic state should PAS come to power.[102] This openness was again reflected in the enunciation of a two-pronged strategy for the 2004 elections, in which the Islamic state issue would only feature in PAS's campaign in the northern states.[103] At other times, Abdul Hadi has also attempted to reassure non-Muslims of their place in a theocratic state.[104] There have also been occasions when PAS appeared more accommodating toward non-Muslims. When Terengganu was under PAS rule, for example, the state government overturned existing policy that prevented Christians from building a church and prevented members of the ethnic Chinese community from engaging in its traditional pig-rearing activities.[105] The significance of these gestures is profoundly ironic, for, as Patricia Martinez observed, "It is perhaps significant that in their fidelity to the concept of an Islamic state, it is the party that represents political Islam in Malaysia [PAS] that has given non-Muslims more rights in fundamental issues, even as it has taken away others such as drinking alcohol in public and closing down unisex hair salons."[106]

These caveats, though, were not sufficient to exculpate PAS, and on balance developments in Terengganu under the PAS administration served to raise further concerns among the general public about the party's fundamentalist posturing and its pursuit of an Islamic state. This concern was made demonstrably clear at the 2004 general election, when UMNO was returned to power in Terengganu. Riding on the crest of their electoral triumph, UMNO leaders held a party convention titled "Toward Zero Opposition" (25–26 February 2005) and announced their intentions to wipe PAS off the political landscape completely.[107] The party was no doubt emboldened by the fact that its landslide victory in Terengganu was significant beyond the number of seats won or lost, for a large number of PAS ideological leaders hail from Terengganu, and most of them were defeated in the 2004 election.

Apostasy Legislation

The question of apostates (*murtad*)—Muslims who leave the faith—is an issue that has reverberated across the Malaysian social-political terrain at multiple levels, generating tension in Malaysia's multireligious fabric between Muslims and non-Muslims and escalating UMNO-PAS competition over the definition of *aqidah* (principles of the faith). The apostasy issue has also caused friction within UMNO and the government itself between those who favor hardline fundamentalist positions on the issue and their more accommodating counterparts. UMNO parliamentarians have reproved the government for appearing to be crippled by the PAS charge that "UMNO could not be regarded as Islamic as it provided no punishment for those who left Islam and yet would fine a citizen RM500 just for throwing a cigarette butt on the market floor."[108]

On the other hand, PAS has been unequivocal in its position on the issue. In his capacity as *Menteri Besar,* Abdul Hadi proposed a bill in Parliament to make apostasy a categorical offense punishable by death. To him, the call for the death penalty was legitimate, for it was based on a *hadith* that called on believers to "kill whomever changes his religion."[109] PAS had already attempted to introduce the death penalty for apostasy in *hudud* law at the state level in Terengganu, but, as discussed earlier, the party was unsuccessful in securing the requisite parliamentary approval.

Zainah Anwar makes the case that there are essentially three traditional juristic opinions on the punishment for apostasy. First is the orthodox view of death to all apostates; second is the opinion that prescribes the death penalty only in cases where apostasy is accompanied by rebellion against the community and its legitimate leadership; and third is the view that even though apostasy is a great sin, it is not a capital offense in Islam and hence warrants no punishment.[110] The PAS president appeared in this regard to subscribe to the most extreme juristic opinion: death to all who leave Islam.

The most recent controversy that has sparked a heated national debate over apostasy is the deceptively straightforward case of Lina Joy. The case revolves around a woman formerly named Azalina Jailani, a convert to Christianity who changed her name to Lina Joy in 1998. Since then, Joy has been attempting to remove the religious designation of "Islam" from her personal identity card.[111] Her application was rejected by the National Registration Department on the grounds that she had to furnish certification from the *Shari'a* Court that officially declared her an apostate before such a change could be made. The Federal Territories *Shari'a* Court, which she consulted in the issue, refused her request to leave the religion. Joy's appeal to the lower courts against the decision of the *Shari'a* Court in 2001 was likewise dismissed on grounds that civil courts had no jurisdiction over matters concerning the Islamic religion. Joy appealed the *Shari'a* Court decision to the Federal Court on constitutional grounds, thereby setting the stage for a watershed decision with grave ramifications.

Predictably, the Lina Joy case elicited sharp responses from key political actors. The religious leadership of PAS maintained categorically that jurisdiction over this case lay squarely with the *Shari'a* Court, and moreover that the court should not grant apostate status, as that would entail the death penalty according to the Qur'an.[112] Privately, however, some *ulama* did say that given her insistence on changing her religion and her conversion to Christianity, Lina Joy's case was a moot point, as she was already "lost to Islam."[113] Similarly, while some more orthodox UMNO *ulama* spoke equally stridently of the sanctity of the *Shari'a* Court, others have been more prepared to countenance Joy's act of leaving Islam as one of personal choice, albeit one that should remain in the private realm. They further intimate that apostates should refrain from using their case to challenge the delicate balance between the constitution and the *shari'a*.

On 30 May 2007 the Malaysian Federal Court finally made a much-awaited decision regarding the Lina Joy apostasy case. In a landmark pronouncement that will likely reverberate across the Malaysian social-political landscape for a long time to come, the Federal Court ruled two to one to dismiss Lina Joy's appeal of the earlier High Court decision. The panel concluded that only an Islamic *shari'a* tribunal could certify her renunciation of Islam and the legitimacy of her conversion. In the eyes of the Malaysian judicial system, Lina Joy remains a Muslim despite her public renunciation of the faith (by virtue of her baptism into the Christian religion) many years ago. In addition, the decision established a legal precedent that apostasy matters lay in the jurisdiction of state *shari'a* courts.

The debate over apostasy lent itself to greater controversy because of the multicultural and multireligious nature of Malaysian society. Political expediency, coupled with a concern for the alleged proliferation of apostasy cases over the past few years, has forced the UMNO-led government's hand and pressured the state into engaging in this difficult debate.[114] JAKIM stood at the forefront of the state's response by suggesting the possibility of a parliamentary bill on apostasy in 1998, the contents of which were never fully fleshed out. Then legislation was enacted that levied punishment in the form of a RM5000 fine or a three-year jail term, or both, for the Islamic offense of *murtad*.[115] These laws also clarified Article 11(4) of the federal constitution, which forbade adherents of other faiths to proselytize to Muslims in Malaysia.[116] In sum, this provision permits states to punish attempts by non-Muslims to proselytize to Muslims by outlawing the propagation of any non-Muslim religious doctrine or belief among persons professing the religion of Islam. In response to concerns raised by non-Muslims who were alarmed at the discriminatory tenor of the clause, Abdul Hamid described Article 11(4) as a "preventive measure" against apostasy, intended less to punish than to rehabilitate. Privately, however, notable Islamic figures who supported apostasy laws have argued that their main purpose was to address the problems particularly surrounding Muslim converts—non-Malay Muslims who for various reasons revert back to their previous religion or renounce Islam by way of a statutory declaration.[117]

According to the legislation proposed by UMNO for the "crime" of apostasy, those convicted would also be forced to undergo compulsory rehabilitation at specially created centers. Recalcitrant detainees at the end of the detention period will be officially declared *murtad* by the *shari'a* court and released from the faith. This rehabilitation program has come under heavy criticism from civil society groups for undermining the constitutionally guaranteed right to freedom of religion. In the UMNO-controlled state of Perlis, matters were taken further when the Perlis state legislature passed the Islamiah Qidah

Protection (State of Perlis) Bill 2000 (alternatively known as the Islamic Faith Bill 2000). According to clause 7 of the bill, evidence of an attempt to change *aqidah* by a Muslim would be met by a summons to appear before the *shari'a* court.[118] The bill further allows for *shari'a* courts to prosecute deviationist Islamic teachers and detain offenders in *aqidah* rehabilitation centers for up to a year. Predictably, the Perlis bill caused considerable consternation among the Muslim community for how it evidently criminalized the act of religious conversion, and various petitions were submitted to the government-appointed Human Rights Commission expressing concern. In response, notwithstanding the fact that it was state law, the federal government announced that the legislation would be considered further before implementation.[119]

This apostasy bill has clearly signaled a significant escalation of Islamist discourse and politicking during Mahathir's tenure, an escalation that had undoubtedly been facilitated by his policy of Islamization, regardless of whether he had anything to do with the Perlis decisions. Measures such as apostasy legislation have allowed the UMNO-led government to define, protect, and perpetuate its narrative of Islamism while shaping the parameters of Islamist discourse in a manner that not only bolsters its credibility and legitimacy as an Islamic government but also undercuts its primary political opponent: PAS.

Controversial initiatives surrounding apostasy sit alongside a range of other policies that have further expanded the state's control over religious institutions. Traditionally the sphere of local authorities, state religious departments now enjoy powers of appointment of *imam* and mosque committees, thereby perpetuating incumbent rule through the selection of UMNO supporters for these positions. By the same token, known opposition activists and sympathizers have either been removed or have not been rehired upon completion of their contracts, as was the case with the former *mufti* of Selangor, cited earlier, and the *imam* of the Damansara Utama Mujahidin Mosque. Sermons (*khutbah*), too, are prepared by the state religious departments and distributed to all the mosques in the state. The result of this has been the proliferation of fundamentalist Islamic state legislation that has criminalized opposition to *fatwa*, even if these *fatwa* contravened the freedom of religion and right to free speech guaranteed in the constitution, through the vehicle of the state.[120]

Even as debates over Islamic law raged in political and legal arenas, the bureaucratization of Islam under the UMNO government continued unabated. In fact, against the backdrop of heated debate over apostasy, two new government bodies—the National Islamic Action Council and the Malaysian Islamic Welfare Council—were added to the slew of state-sponsored Islamic institutions whose purpose was to propagate UMNO's version of Islam to the Malaysian people.[121] Despite concerns expressed from time to time by Malaysian leaders about the inordinate number of Islamic studies graduates in Malaysia, federal and state bureaucracies have followed a policy of preference for applicants with strong religious backgrounds. A large proportion of funds earmarked for state religious departments continue to be allocated as government scholarships to Islamic tertiary institutions, both local and foreign. The Malaysian cabinet even attempted to enact a bill to make the study of Islamic civilizations a compulsory component of undergraduate education.[122] Debates have also surfaced over revelations that students in private Christian mission schools have been forced to recite Islamic prayers, and there has apparently been an alarming increase of state-level religious authorities exercising Islamic-style checks on non-Muslim social activities in states such as Perak and Selangor.

Other instances of state-sanctioned Islamization policies include the requirement of consent of Muslim neighbors before applying for or renewing dog licenses in Johore Bahru, the ban on sale of pork in open-air markets in Kajang, the removal of liquor and beer advertisements in Selangor, and the moral policing by the Ipoh Municipality and Kuala Lumpur City Council that resulted in the arrest of couples for holding hands in public. In September 2002, at a seminar organized by the Selangor state government, titled *Understanding Malaysia as an Islamic State*, UMNO state officials proposed constitutional amendments that would declare the Qur'an and *sunnah* to be sources of federal law.[123] Whether deliberate or otherwise, UMNO's bureaucratization of Islam has, in effect, put in place the infrastructure of an Islamic state run by "state-sponsored firebrands" and a Muslim intelligentsia sympathetic to the government.[124]

Structural Conundrums

The controversies over *hudud* law in Terengganu and apostasy law in Perlis amplify unresolved structural tensions that exist in Malaysia concerning the question of jurisdiction and enforcement powers over alleged transgressions of a religious nature. These tensions manifest themselves at two levels. In the first instance, confusion is borne of a system of legal governance, at times hybridized and at times parallel, built into the Malaysian constitution and reinforced by the system of federalism, leading to a dispersal of power on the issue of the formulation of Islamic law. Equally confounding is the perplexing dynamic that defines the relationship between civil and Islamic law.

Individual states have historically enjoyed the prerogative to formulate laws through their respective religious departments (*Jabatan Agama*) and *shari'a* courts on matters pertaining to religion.[125] This has led to the observation that "those who constitute Islam in each state—the *ulama*, religious department officials, the Sultan, and *shari'a* court officials—have considerable power over how Islam evolves in Malaysia."[126] Accordingly, the Malaysian constitution lists in Schedule 9, List II the specific areas where state authorities have jurisdiction: Islamic personal and family law, *waqf* (foundations) and the regulation of Islamic charities and trusts, *zakat* and *fitrah* (tithes), mosques and other places of public worship, creation and punishment of offenses perpetrated by Muslims "against the precepts of Islam" except with regard to matters in the federal list, the constitution and procedure of *shari'a* courts, and control of doctrines and beliefs. As a pointed measure of how pervasive this system of state management of religious affairs is, consider the fact that aside from Sarawak, Islam is the official religion in all states. Indeed, in a striking demonstration of the potential influence of state religious authority over political affairs, the Council of Rulers, a body consisting of Malaysia's nine hereditary sultans, rejected a recommendation (likely politically motivated) by the National Fatwa Council for the term "Islam" to be banned from the nomenclature of political parties (namely, PAS).

While the freedom that state governments enjoy to formulate Islamic legislation is not insignificant, in practice their authority over how Islam is interpreted and practiced is often far more ambiguous. A major consideration is the fact that Malaysia's federal system of governance has meant that though states are empowered to formulate religious laws, these formulations have to be ratified by the federal Parliament in order to be codified as legally binding and enforced. In this connection, the question of criminal law and attendant punishment has proven particularly delicate and complicated. Because crime falls within the jurisdiction of the federal government, it follows that criminal law procedures, be they in accordance with civil law or *shari'a*, would come under the federal government's purview even when there are state religious laws governing such actions. Bearing in mind the issue of *hudud* laws in Kelantan and Terengganu discussed earlier, the complications and contradictions of this duality should already be abundantly clear.

The question of the "policing" of social activities by state religious authorities has taken on a decidedly political hue as well, particularly in the way that non-Muslims appear to be subject to standards set by Islamist state administrations. Consider, for instance, a recent case when a furor broke out over morality laws after state authorities ruled that under local bylaws, Kuala Lumpur's City Hall could prosecute a young ethnic Chinese couple for engaging in "indecent activity" in a city park.[127] This was purportedly based on the argument that "kissing and hugging [the "crimes" that were committed by the Chinese couple] was not the norm for Malaysians or other Asians and was only acceptable by Western moral standard."[128] This case echoed a similar one that occurred several years earlier, where Ipoh City Council officials issued summonses to couples (Muslim and non-Muslim) for holding hands or simply walking alongside each other in public parks.[129] Testifying to the clash of perspectives, the young Chinese couple was eventually charged by the state government, but JAKIM, which represents the federal government, insisted that "only Muslims will be charged in court under *shari'a* law since kissing and hugging are against Islamic teachings."[130]

The state-federal dichotomy in Islamic law further overlaps with another parallel system of legislation: civil law and *shari'a* law governing matters pertaining to the personal lives of Muslims. At the heart of the tension between these two systems of legislation is what Salbiah Ahmad observes to be "no right of appeal from the state *shari'a* courts to the federal civil courts. There is no power of judicial review by the Federal High Court over the state *Shari'a* Court."[131] This is not to imply absolute autonomy for the *shari'a* court, however, as there are delineated limits to the sphere of the jurisdiction of Islamic law. Nevertheless, the conflict that arises from this parallel jurisdiction over religious matters should be evident, not only in the case of Lina Joy, but also in the controversy surrounding the burial of Moorthy Maniam, the national hero who was the first Malaysian to scale Mount Everest. Moorthy passed away in December 2005, and his Hindu wife challenged the Muslim burial of her husband, who, according to the *shari'a* court, had converted to Islam before he passed away and hence was to be buried as a Muslim.[132] When the case was brought to the Kuala Lumpur High Court, it ruled on 28 December 2005 that it had no right to intervene in a matter that was in the *shari'a* court's jurisdiction.[133] Moorthy was thus buried as a Muslim despite his wife's protestations. From the perspective of non-Muslims in Malaysia, cases such as these proved unnerving, not only for the evident "flaws" associated with this diarchic court system but also because neither non-Muslim party had any recourse to civil authorities, which in any case were clearly cautious about challenging the authority of the *shari'a* courts. The legal framework that is brought to bear on apostasy cases in Malaysia has been cogently summarized thus:

> Only the state *shari'a* court is empowered to deliberate and declare on the apostasy, until such a time the application for conversion out of Islam has been made, heard and disposed of in the state *shari'a* court, the plaintiff is to all intents and purposes, a Muslim. In such a case, the High Court has decided that it has no jurisdiction over such a Muslim who is seeking a declaration as to a change in status.[134]

Few members of Malaysia's judiciary system would be prepared to risk being seen to be complicit in facilitating the grave sin of renouncing Islam in the current heated atmosphere in Malaysia, particularly if they were Muslim. Given that civil courts have ruled that only the *shari'a* courts can declare a person to be a non-Muslim, while *shari'a* courts upholding Islamic law are clearly reluctant to declare people apostates, the net result is a tense stalemate that ultimately disadvantages the individual seeking to change his or her religion as a matter of personal faith and belief.

At the heart of the civil law–*shari'a* controversy lies Article 121 1(A), which was introduced in 1988 via constitutional amendment and which stipulated that federal high courts "shall have no jurisdiction in respect of any matter within the jurisdiction of the *shari'a* courts." In effect, Article 121 1(A) enunciates a parallel judicial system between civil and *shari'a* courts in which the jurisdiction of *shari'a* courts is protected from civil court interference. The system is designed to prevent parties from appealing the decision of one court, usually the *shari'a* court, to the other. However, the problem may lie less with the parallel nature of this system than with the fact that the system itself is in effect a hybrid one and thus highly ambiguous. While criminal law falls into federal jurisdiction, the constitution assigns power to create and punish offenses against the precepts of Islam through Schedule 9, List II, Item 1. Shad Faruqi suggests that in effect, the constitution "assigns the entire field of criminal law and procedure to the federal parliament without specifying the areas permitted to the states [as would be implied in the reference to Schedule 9, List II]."[135] As such, the ambiguous nature of the constitution has opened the way for state religious authorities to interpret their jurisdiction expansively, which most have consequently done.

Islamic leaders from both the state and opposition parties share a similar conviction that all Muslims must be ruled under the *shari'a*, especially on confessional issues. In the case of apostasy, however, matters are somewhat more complicated. This complication has both legal and social dimensions. Legally, the fact that apostasy deals with an individual's profession of faith has led some to argue that faith is not something that can be imposed. To them, the logic is clear: the very nature of apostasy is that a person no longer professes Islam, even if he or she continues to be identified officially as a Muslim. Hence, such people should not be considered Muslims and should be allowed to leave the religion. From this perspective, the issue is at heart one of freedom of religion. Islamic legal tradition appears to view such matters differently. Describing this dichotomy, Salbiah Ahmad said, "Muslims may be subjected to a *fiqh* principle adopted/selected in the state Islamic law which may be contrary to traditional *fiqh* literature or human rights principles. . . . The legislated *fiqh* principle fails to recognize that freedom of religion means freedom from coercion to become Muslim or to leave Islam."[136] In other words, freedom of religion does not supersede Islamic law.

Observers often are led to believe that the parameters of Muslim politics in Malaysia are clearcut. At one end lies PAS, the Islamist opposition that demands that public space in Malaysia be governed by *shari'a*; at the other, UMNO, a "secularist" Muslim government that is apparently prepared to curtail Islamism and keep religion in the sphere of the private. Nothing could be further from the truth. With regard to apostasy, for instance, the congruence of opinions between UMNO and PAS is striking. Just as the track record of PAS is far more checkered than its strident Islamism of the early 1980s would admit, Islamist tendencies run deep in the "secularist" UMNO party as well. This trend was particularly pronounced during the administration of Mahathir Mohamad, when many features of a conservative and orthodox Islamic government were put in place even as PAS vacillated with its own visions of models of governance, and continued under his successor, Abdullah Badawi. There are many unresolved questions about how far state and federal governments are prepared to push the possibilities for Islamic governance in the context of Malaysia's multicultural social landscape, underscoring the fact that neither state nor federal authorities, nor civil or religious authorities, have been able to reconcile the blatantly contradictory policies and the obvious discrimination that appear to be inherent in both UMNO's and PAS's vision of Islamic governance in Malaysia.

3

Reconstructing and
Reinforcing Islamism

By the mid-1990s, scholars of political Islam claimed that "major changes taking place beneath the surface suggest that a transition is being made to a less arbitrary, exclusive and authoritarian rule" across the Muslim world, which would herald a new era and a new approach to issues of pluralism, participation, and social justice, all within distinctly Islamist democratic frameworks.[1] In Malaysia it would be PAS, the Islamist political opposition reeling from a comprehensive electoral defeat in 1986 and consequently forced to reimagine itself, that would exemplify this new political atmosphere as it shifted its rhetoric and recalibrated its political strategies from strident and uncompromising commitment to the Islamic state to a more inclusivist agenda of justice, democracy, and socioeconomic reform in the 1990s.

As PAS teetered on the brink of political irrelevance after 1986, the party underwent a period of introspection from which it reemerged to embrace political reform. This shift was engineered by a new leadership that fashioned Islam into an identity and voice of dissidence not only for the Malay-Muslim community but for Malaysia at large. The 1986 debacle was also significant because a number of party leaders critical of the narrow and exclusivist turn that PAS had taken after 1982 left the party, either joining UMNO or forming smaller, fringe parties.[2] For those who stayed, the realization set in that new strategies were desperately required if the party was to remain relevant to the Malaysian political scene. The renovation of party strategy began in earnest. One method PAS leaders used to distinguish themselves from UMNO was to play the hand of social welfarism and launch a critique of personal aggrandizement through political office. This approach proved timely, as UMNO was beginning to come under pressure from revelations of money politics involving several of its politicians.

This antithesis was expressed in the public and private personas of PAS leaders, which contrasted sharply with those of UMNO leaders and had an undeniable impact on public perception, particularly in the 1990s, when UMNO politicians unabashedly paraded the material benefits accrued from links with business interests during the Mahathir era of economic development and industrialization. The simple and approachable lifestyles of PAS leaders have been widely documented and contributed significantly to the reinvigoration of the party, while the PAS social-economic agenda of redistribution and social collectivism was more appealing than the scandals and accusations of corruption that were plaguing UMNO.[3] PAS reconstructed Islam as a counterhegemonic discourse against the stratification, social dislocation, and alienation of Malaysian society brought about by the Mahathir government's modernization and urbanization drive, including the corruption and money politics that came along with it.

Ironically, one of the earliest and clearest indications that PAS was repositioning itself as a reformist political party was its attempt to look beyond the traditional politics of ethnic representation. The Islamization of its political agenda notwithstanding, UMNO continued to see its purpose as the defense of Malay ethnic identity, into which Islam is subsumed. Since its ideological shift in 1982, PAS had already begun to attempt a turn away from the parochialism of the Malay nationalist agenda by arguing that the universalism of Islam rejects UMNO's narrow ethnic chauvinism. This move would gather strength in the 1990s as the reformist agenda, which transcended race and ethnicity, took hold in Malaysia. Again, developments in PAS-ruled Terengganu were instructive as the litmus test. As the previous chapter noted, after forming the Terengganu state government in December 1999, the PAS administration overturned the previous UMNO state government's moratorium on the release of land for the purpose of erecting non-Muslim places of worship and permitted the reintroduction of pig-rearing among the Chinese community. In a direct challenge to UMNO's script of Malay supremacy, PAS had criticized the NEP as an example of "ethnic chauvinism" and constantly stressed Islam's recognition of equality among races.[4] PAS responded to UMNO's calls for "Malay unity talks" after 1999 by calling instead for "Malaysian unity talks," shedding further light on an important but overlooked feature of PAS's emerging brand of Islamic politics in Malaysia.

While the tone of popular discussions in media chatrooms and blog commentaries indicates that a discerning non-Muslim community requires more convincing before they accept PAS's gestures as genuine, this perspective has nevertheless given PAS some leverage over UMNO in terms of the palatability of Malay dominance among non-Muslims.[5] It is instructive to note the support that PAS has among its Chinese constituents in Kelantan, the very minorities who would conceivably be "oppressed" in an Islamic state. At a pre-election *ceramah* at a Chinese temple in predominantly middle-class Taman Lima Manis in Kota Bharu (Kelantan) on 6 March 2008, the hundred or so ethnic Chinese in attendance were overwhelmingly supportive of PAS. One attendee said, "PAS is not as bad as they are made out to be in the media. PAS does not play race politics and respects non-Muslims, unlike UMNO. . . . There is hardly any crime in this Islamic state compared to other states."[6] Consider too the following excerpt from a blog posting of an ethnic Chinese resident of Kelantan:

> During BN's [*Barisan Nasional*'s] tenure [in Kelantan], pork sellers in the Chinese market were harassed daily. They were confined to a small inconspicuous space where pork could be sold hidden from public view. There was conditional and restricted time when pork could be sold. When PAS took over the government in 1990, they improved the Chinese market and pork was sold without any restrictions. In short they were not harassed. Again, during BN's tenure, Chinese could not buy houses built on Malay reservation land. Since most of the land came under the purview of Malay reservation, most Kelantan Chinese could not own a home. But all this changed when PAS came to power. . . . It was [also] under PAS rule that a prominent land in Jalan Hamzah was approved for the Hindus to build a temple when the same approval was rejected by BN four times before.[7]

Accommodationist Politics—PAS Style

Above all it was Ustaz Fadzil Noor, who replaced the ailing Yusof Rawa as PAS president in 1989, who set in motion this process of renovation in the Islamist opposition party. If Farish Noor is right in his observation that as a result of "the conflation of PAS with 'authentic Islam' during Ustaz Yusof Rawa's time . . . PAS became identified by its ideology rather than its leaders," then Fadzil Noor's tenure would mark a return to personality-centered leadership yet again, but one that was discernibly more accommodationist than the narrow fundamentalism of the early Yusof Rawa years.[8]

Despite the fact that he was himself once a member of the Young Turk *ulama* faction that wrested power from the party's previous coterie of ethno-nationalist leaders in 1982, Fadzil Noor's leadership of PAS heralded more concerted attempts to shift the party away from the scripturalist and uncompromising Islamist image that had accompanied the party since 1986. This transformation was captured in Fadzil's rearticulation of the party's image, away from being the "party of Allah" to a new image of "progress with Islam."[9] The notion of "progress" here is suggestive of an alignment of the PAS agenda with notions of egalitarianism, transparency, and good governance. Far from

the parochial fundamentalist party tag that the mainstream media often bestowed upon it, Fadzil demonstrated an acute awareness of the terrain upon
which PAS had to operate and the context in which the party's struggle had
to be reframed. This awareness was illustrated in many of his speeches. In a
party address titled "Islamic Governance and Democracy in the 21st Century,"
for instance, Fadzil warned the party that "the phenomenon of globalization
today has brought new meaning to processes of democratization, fundamental
freedoms and human rights, and civil liberties. . . . Human civilization today
is sensitive to issues of tyranny, meritocracy, justice, minority rights, gender,
and women's rights, particularly in complex plural societies."[10] In response to
this sensitivity, he exhorted his compatriots to lead a social movement "towards
the struggle for the rights and justice for all citizens regardless of their religion
or race."[11] This aim was welcomed in other quarters within the party. A major
supporter of Fadzil's agenda of reform was PAS deputy president Nasharuddin
Mat Isa, who noted in response to queries about the conservative image of PAS
that "the party culture was the result of the culture of the society in which it existed. But society has changed. And so we have to change in order to be relevant
to the environment in which we operate."[12]

To lend weight to this language of reform, political strategy was centered
more explicitly on "*rakyat*" (common folk) issues of income disparity, housing,
land allocation, and education, in particular the popular *Sekolah Agama Rakyat*
(Private Religious Schools) of northern Malaysia, which had been victimized by
the federal government's withdrawal of funds when the government accused
them first of spawning militants and then of militant agitation. These issues
played well with the largely rural Malay electorate in northern Malaysia, thereby
ensuring a steady pool of support for PAS.

In addition to this shift away from doctrinaire politics, there were two more
components of Fadzil Noor's strategy to repackage PAS. First, Fadzil oversaw
the transformation of the complexion of party membership. We will recall that
PAS had traditionally been a rural-based party built around religious leaders and
teachers. The 1980s saw this configuration supplemented with a clerical leadership of *ulama* that took the party down the path of ideological conservatism. The
1990s, however (and particularly the late 1990s), witnessed an influx of urban,
middle-class, Western-educated professionals into PAS, even though religious
teachers and scholars remained at the core of the party. These professionals and
intellectuals were actively courted in light of the party's desire to adjust to contemporary realities. Equally at home with Islamic precepts and with Western
discourses on modernity and capitalism, many of these professionals possessed
reformist credentials and rose quickly to assume leadership positions in the
party's Central Working Committee. From there they would prove instrumental
to Fadzil's mainstreaming strategy to transform the image of PAS.

It is important to note that this influx was facilitated by the political upheaval stemming from the Asian financial crisis and Prime Minister Mahathir's

unceremonious dismissal of Anwar Ibrahim in 1998, an event that drove scores of disgruntled Malaysians (including erstwhile UMNO activists) into the orbit of opposition politics. PAS was undoubtedly the chief beneficiary of this fallout, as its membership increased from four hundred thousand to one million in 1998 alone, at the height of the reform movement. Likewise, subscription to the PAS magazine *Harakah* increased from fifty thousand to 380,000 per issue during this period, more than the weekly subscription to all the government-linked New Straits Times Group print media combined. Cognizant of the groundswell of unhappiness caused by the government's treatment of Anwar and revelations of corruption and cronyism in the Malaysian political economy at the height of the Asian financial crisis, PAS members leveraged the narrative of reform, justice, and democracy to great effect by portraying themselves as Islamo-democrats.

Second, it was under Fadzil's leadership that PAS involved itself in a direct coalition with non-Muslim opposition parties for the first time in the party's history. He oversaw PAS's participation in the *Barisan Alternatif* (Alternative Front).[13] Prior to that, PAS under Fadzil Noor was also part of the *Angkatan Perpaduan Ummah*, an Islam-based coalition that indirectly worked with the Chinese-dominated Democratic Action Party (DAP) during the 1990 general elections.[14] Given popular perceptions that PAS was a doctrinaire Islamist opposition party, the party leadership's decision to join the *Barisan Alternatif* mystified both sympathizers and detractors. Responding to queries about this groundbreaking decision, Fadzil duly appropriated egalitarian principles to explain the move: "Our aim is very clear. It is to deny the government the power it has today and to bring back justice. The struggle for justice is not only for the Malays, not only for the Muslims, but for all Malaysians."[15]

Beneath the veneer of cordiality and camaraderie among opposition ranks, however, the decision to participate in an opposition coalition with non-Muslims was one that the leadership of PAS did not take lightly, making it all the more significant. For starters, Mustapha Ali, vice-president of PAS, made clear that the Islamist party's participation in any coalition movement was contingent on the maintenance and implementation of its own agenda.[16] Nik Aziz Nik Mat, *Musyidul 'Am* of the party, also stressed repeatedly that cooperation with non-Muslims did not prejudice the party's ultimate objective of the establishment of an Islamic state, and it was toward this end that the party continued to strive, even within the ambit of coalition politics. Largely because of this, PAS continued to be held at arm's length by many non-Muslims, despite these attempts to revamp its image. On the matter of the uneasy relations with non-Muslims, there were additional structural impediments to the improvement of these ties. For instance, PAS membership remained the exclusive preserve of Muslims; non-Muslims can at best be accorded associate membership status.[17] Likewise, the party leadership continued to grapple with the freighted question of the place of non-Muslims in an Islamic state.

A particularly pressing problem for PAS was the party's commitment to the implementation of *hudud*, which non-Muslims had never accepted. This provided ammunition for UMNO leaders to attack the fundamentalist credentials of PAS. By leveraging its control of a variety of information outlets, UMNO has managed to sustain, if not heighten, non-Muslim suspicions of the Islamist opposition merely by alerting them to PAS's alleged unstinting commitment to *hudud*.

For their part, some PAS leaders have sought to rationalize *hudud* from a moral perspective, arguing that *hudud* is more than a mere penal code; it is a body of moral and ethical codes that is increasingly necessary to confront the social ills that plague Malaysia today.[18] This argument does little to convince non-Muslims, not to mention Muslims apprehensive of the rigid enforcement of *hudud* in contemporary Malaysia. A satisfactory formula for the status of non-Muslims in a PAS-ruled national polity remains elusive, despite the publication of an Islamic State blueprint and various attempts to reach out to these constituencies. *Hudud* aside, there is no denying that inasmuch as the Malay community was concerned, it was becoming clear that PAS was reaching beyond its traditional bastion of support (namely the religious establishment and the rural Malay constituency in the northern Malay-dominated states) and increasing its appeal to the educated Malay middle class.

The discursive and ideational shift described above reaped immediate dividends for PAS when, with the help of UMNO dissidents who had coalesced into *Semangat '46*, they trounced UMNO to regain the state of Kelantan at the 1990 general election.[19] The success in Kelantan owed much to the problems that had surfaced within UMNO several years earlier and which culminated in an unprecedented party crisis and split. Even so, observers have argued that the revival of PAS's popularity in Kelantan in particular, and in the northern states during the 1990s in general, can be attributed at least in part to the introduction of a policy of Islamic social welfarism, which was later articulated in a simple but effective mantra of a "caring society" in 1990 and as "Progress with Islam" in 1995.[20] Notwithstanding these developments, it was at the 1999 Malaysian general election that the political fortunes of PAS reached its apex, when the party's decade-long effort to recalibrate political strategies and sow seeds of Islamist reform dovetailed with the popular mood of resentment toward the Mahathir administration. A large harvest awaited PAS as this combination of design and circumstance quickly translated into substantial political gains.

The *Reformasi* Watershed of 1999

The formerly tranquil domestic political scene in Malaysia through the 1990s was rudely interrupted by a string of events that began with the regionwide financial crisis and culminated in the birth of a reform movement and a shocking electoral setback for the incumbent government.

In 1997, several years of strong economic growth rates across East Asia ground to a halt when the value of regional currencies plunged to alarming depths. This meltdown had major political ramifications, bringing down several regional governments, notably in Indonesia, Thailand, and South Korea. While Mahathir remained defiant in his defense of the ringgit, policies undertaken by his administration soon revealed fundamental differences of opinion within the government. These differences were expressed most vividly in a widening rift between Mahathir and his deputy Anwar Ibrahim, resulting in the latter's ignominious dismissal from office in September 1998. Anwar's removal was the catalyst for a reform movement already brewing in the wake of revelations of corruption and cronyism that surfaced as the Malaysian economy struggled to regain its footing. UMNO suffered a major blow as the dismissal of Anwar was met with an exodus of its rank and file to the newly formed *Keadilan* (*Parti Keadilan Rakyat* or People's Justice Party), the reform party headed by Anwar's wife, Dr. Wan Azizah—and, more significantly, to PAS. With a general election looming, matters indeed looked to be taking a turn for the worst for UMNO and the *Barisan* coalition.

By the 1999 elections, PAS had fashioned Islam into a voice of dissidence for a Malay-Muslim community disenchanted with the authoritarian trends and excesses of UMNO, the *Barisan Nasional*, and the Mahathir administration, in much the same way that earlier permutations of the party had subsumed Islam into Malay nationalism.[21] Capitalizing on widespread discontent among the Malay population with the dismissal, incarceration, ill-treatment, and questionable conviction of Anwar for corruption and sexual misconduct, PAS deliberately downplayed its Islamic state agenda, with the exception of its manifestos for Kelantan and Terengganu, and chose to focus on broader concerns of social justice, civil society, and good and honest government.[22] Testifying to the monumental nature of this shift, even the usually indomitable Nik Aziz openly declared on the campaign trail that PAS had agreed to the exclusion of its Islamic state objective from the constitution of the *Barisan Alternatif*.[23] Aside from its participation in the opposition coalition, PAS also entered into its first cooperation with NGOs that agitated for change in the country.

By the time the dust of electoral campaigning settled, it was evident that the agenda of reform had enabled PAS to make a major dent in UMNO's erstwhile dominance among the Malay-Muslim electorate. In its best performance ever at the time in a national election, the Islamist opposition captured two state legislatures on its way to a total of twenty-seven parliamentary and ninety-eight state seats. Not only was the magnitude of victory huge by the standards of Malaysian oppositional politics; the results of the elections were of further significance for PAS on several fronts. First, it not only vindicated PAS's new strategy, but it appeared to portend a new era of Malaysian politics in which its brand of new Islamism (or as some would have it, "post-Islamism") could conceivably pose a major challenge to UMNO dominance. Furthermore, it appeared that the PAS strategy of collaboration with non-Muslim parties was vindicated, as its cooperation with DAP did not lead to an erosion of support from its core Muslim electorate.[24] The increasing number of middle-class Malays who threw their support behind PAS, despite residual reservations regarding some of the more fundamentalist aspects of the party's philosophy, further testified to this change.[25] Second, the 1999 elections demonstrated the dynamism and vivacity of civil society activism in Malaysia, illustrating their increasingly critical role in framing and articulating mainstream political issues. As will be evident in the next chapter, it is this very activism that has spurred civil society groups, both Muslim and non-Muslim, to engage with the discourse of Islamism in Malaysia over the last decade or so in a manner that at least attempts to take it beyond the boundaries of mainstream partisan politics and the proverbial "Islamization race."

Tellingly, though, within PAS itself interpretations of the 1999 results varied. Despite the fact that the Islamic state agenda was deliberately muted during campaigning, some within the party, not least the conservative *ulama*, were firmly convinced that the PAS triumph indicated that Malaysia had warmed to the idea of Islamic government. Others, however, were more circumspect and were keenly aware that it was highly likely that the success of PAS owed more to enthusiasm for political, economic, and social reform in Malaysia and fallout from the Anwar issue than any concrete endorsement of PAS policies, to say nothing of the Islamic state. In hindsight, it is clear that those holding the latter opinion were in the minority, or at least were not holding major positions in the *ulama*-centered policy structure that would allow them to dictate the trajectory of the party. PAS's success in 1999 injected a large dose of confidence into the Islamist opposition party. The belief that the time was ripe for PAS to press its Islamic state agenda permeated party ranks in earnest, finding expression in increasing demands from several segments within the party for the leadership to finally put on paper its ambiguous ideas for an Islamic state in Malaysia. The question that remained was: what sort of Islamic state would PAS present to the Malaysian people?

Regardless of the bullish mood within PAS toward the Islamic state or the concerns among the more circumspect about what kind of Islamic state would be acceptable to Malaysians, what eventually lit the fuse on the party's internal debates on the matter, to the point where party leaders felt compelled to formalize and announce an Islamic state blueprint, was a statement made by Mahathir himself. Paradoxically, notwithstanding PAS's incessant saber-rattling over the need for an Islamic state in Malaysia, it was ultimately pressure from UMNO that forced the party to come out with clear details of what its vision of Islamic government entailed.

Articulating and Mainstreaming the Islamic State

The discourse of Islamism centers heavily, albeit not necessarily solely, on the concept of the Islamic state. Indeed, the question of the form and relevance of a polity ruled according to injunctions distilled from the Qur'an, *sunna*, and earlier traditions of Muslim governance lies at the heart of "political" Islam. This debate over what exactly constitutes an Islamic state, and whether such an entity is viable in the contemporary era defined by globalization and pluralism, continues to rage across the Muslim world, not merely in intellectual discourse, but also in everyday political exchange. The situation in Malaysia is no different in this regard, where debates on the feasibility and extent of an Islamic state continue. In countries such as Indonesia, Morocco, Turkey, and Egypt, a major facet of the debate centers on whether an Islamic state is a realistic option for the organization of politics in contemporary Muslim societies, but in Malaysia the debate's parameters and terms of reference have begun to deviate from this convention. Indeed, given that both major Muslim parties in Malaysia, including the lead party in the incumbent coalition government, have appropriated the Islamic state concept (despite its ambiguities) and are using it to define and anchor their respective political projects, the question of whether the Islamic state is a relevant organizing principle has become a moot point insofar as mainstream political discourse in Muslim circles today is concerned. Rather, the debate in Malaysia centers on just what kind of Islamic state Malaysia is or should be, and who has the right to define this.

While the establishment of an Islamic state has been on the PAS political agenda since the party's formation, it was only since the early 1980s, when *ulama* became a major force in the party and started influencing its trajectory, that this rhetoric gained considerable momentum with its articulation as a major policy priority. According to Yusof Rawa, the first *ulama* president of PAS, the Islamic state would be a natural outcome of leadership by *ulama* and Muslim intellectuals, who were tasked first and foremost with the responsibility of "overseeing the welfare of the Muslim community and keeping abreast with their spiritual needs, and to strengthen their faith."[26] Nevertheless, despite its strident rhetoric on the need for an Islamic state, PAS had for many years been criticized for not stating explicitly what an Islamic state would entail in terms of governance.[27] In defense of this ambivalence, Yusof Rawa retorted that "to us, it is not practical to go into details of what we want to do in an Islamic state. If they want to see we operate it well, they must elect us. They owe to God something if their vote deprived us to govern the Islamic state. All operational aspects of how and when to do certain things or launch certain policies can be taken up later when we do have the Islamic state."[28]

For a long time, this ambiguity defined the party's official response to queries regarding its vision for the Islamic state in Malaysia. Aside from conceptual difficulties that confronted PAS leaders when prodded to elaborate on the concept, there were also pragmatic reasons why PAS had resisted this pressure that emanated both from within as well as outside the party. First, the demographic configuration of Malaysia and constitutional realities meant that the prospects for the formal establishment of an Islamic state remained very slim. Malaysia has always had a significant non-Muslim minority that has been circumspect toward PAS and the idea of an Islamic state, and any formal institutionalization of the Islamic state would require constitutional changes that, given the dominance of the incumbent coalition government in the federal legislature, make it a nonstarter, at least insofar as the PAS version is concerned. Second, the vagueness of the Islamic state has served as an important political tool for PAS in its rhetorical battles against UMNO. Even without specifying what was meant when they issued their clarion call for the establishment of the Islamic state, PAS leaders managed to use this ambiguity to secure the moral high ground in political tussles with UMNO over government policies. All PAS had to do was to utter the simple yet effective refrain that the latter's positions on governance were "un-Islamic" because they did not accord with the strictures of Islamic government, however that was defined. This position of "strategic ambiguity" soon started to shift when PAS leaders interpreted their 1999 electoral success as a mandate to press the PAS agenda for the formation of an Islamic state in Malaysia.

To reiterate an important point, it is ironic that it was UMNO, and not PAS, that took the debate over the Islamic state to a higher plane. Malaysia's political discourse concerning the Islamic state took on greater urgency when Mahathir, in a move that took many by surprise, made the controversial proclamation on 29 September 2001 that Malaysia was already an Islamic state. While detractors were quick to dismiss Mahathir's statement as little more than a gambit, it was in effect the culmination of a number of low-key but significant government-initiated discussions on the Islamic state in the present Malaysian context, resulting in the conclusion, reached by a number of state-linked *ulama*, that Malaysia already possessed the qualities of an Islamic state.[29] Sure enough, shortly after Mahathir's announcement, the government moved to publish a booklet justifying the Prime Minister's claim.[30]

From a historical standpoint, Mahathir's pronouncement departed fundamentally from the stance of Malaysia's first prime minister and former UMNO president Tunku Abdul Rahman, who famously countered pressures for the formation of an Islamic state in Malaya in the 1950s with his oft-quoted riposte that such a move would entail "the drowning of every non-Muslim in Malaya." Despite the fact that Mahathir had on previous occasions described Malaysia as an "Islamic country," his pronouncement that the country was already an Islamic state marked a fundamental shift in Malaysia's discursive politics of

Islamism.[31] Mahathir's statement drew a vehement reply from non-Muslims, including the ethnic-Chinese opposition. These non-Muslim sentiments are encapsulated in the following excerpt, translated from Mandarin, from remarks made by a senior leader of the DAP in response to the Islamic state debate:

> The debate on the Islamic state must be extended to the whole civil society and the motion should be whether Malaysia should become an Islamic state rather than focusing on the kind of Islamic state Malaysia is. The federal constitution of Malaysia as laid down by our forefathers clearly stated that Malaysia is a secular country, so Mahathir's statement that Malaysia is an Islamic state violates the spirit of the constitution as formerly laid. . . . The establishment of an Islamic state will mean the subversion of the secular laws to make way for Islamic laws. Non-Muslims will then be reduced to the status of "second-class citizens," and the space for religious freedom, democracy, women's rights, and education will be subsequently reduced. Malaysian society will also be further polarized and segmented into the Muslim and non-Muslim communities. The issue of whether Malaysia is an Islamic state should be decided by all citizens rather than by one person or one political party.[32]

While Mahathir might have hoped to truncate the Islamic state debate with this declaration, he had instead precipitated its intensification. Through its president's pronouncement, UMNO effectively browbeat PAS to react and articulate its own conceptions of a functional Islamic state.[33] It did not take long for the Islamist opposition to pick up the gauntlet.

Because of Mahathir's announcement and challenge, PAS's own deliberations on the Islamic state gained momentum.[34] It is important to consider how significant this move to revisit the Islamic state concept was for PAS. Given that the party's success of 1999 was achieved by muting the Islamic state agenda, it certainly seemed counterintuitive for the party to return to this issue at this particular juncture. As suggested above, the move was in part a reaction to pressure from both outside and within the party. Not only did Mahathir's announcement force PAS to attempt to reclaim its Islamist credentials; within the party there were those, especially among the conservative *ulama*, who also interpreted the 1999 success as precisely the signal they had been waiting for, the signal to return the Islamic state to the PAS agenda. In addition, the events of September 11 and its aftermath had drawn attention to the Islamic credentials of Muslim leaders in a way that forced them to either reassert or reinvent themselves.

This initiative to rearticulate the PAS Islamic state concept was led by Fadzil Noor. The project was driven by the party's Central Working Committee, and the research team tasked with undertaking this study, known as the Islamic State Memorandum Panel (*Panel Memorandum Negara Islam*), consisted of Zulkefly Ahmad, the director of the PAS Research Center and a doctorate in toxicology from Imperial College, London; Kamarudin Jaffar, a public intellectual and former director of the *Institut Kajian Dasar* (Institute of Policy Studies), which was aligned with Anwar Ibrahim, and later secretary-general of PAS; and Husam Musa, an economics graduate from Universiti Malaya and party vice-president. The research team made several working visits to the United Kingdom in hopes of establishing key terms of reference for Islamic governance in a modern, developed, pluralistic society.[35] Significantly, none of the key members of the team were *ulama*. In point of fact, major *ulama* figures such as Harun Din, Abdul Hadi and Nik Aziz were detached from the process at this stage, and it was not until after several drafts of the Islamic state document were prepared that the *ulama*-populated *Majlis Shura* began to weigh in on the process.[36]

The PAS study on the Islamic state resulted in the production of four consecutive drafts of an Islamic state blueprint over a period of approximately eighteen months. While the first two drafts remain in limited circulation within party leadership circles, the penultimate draft was made public by way of an introduction of its key points by Fadzil Noor to the party rank and file at the 2002 PAS Muktamar.[37] The speech was titled "PAS Memorandum to the Malaysian People: The Understanding of Islamic Rule in the Context of 15th Hijrah/21st Century Democracy" ("*Memorandum PAS kepada Rakyat Malaysia: Penghayatan Pemerintahan Islam Dalam Demokrasi Abad ke-15H/21M*"). Because a full review and analysis of all four drafts is beyond the scope of this book, the following discussion sets out the key features of two versions that were actually presented in public and which merit closer investigation, beginning with the principles of the PAS Islamic state document introduced by Fadzil, which was the first detailed attempt by the *ulama*-led PAS to formally articulate its vision for Malaysia.

PAS Memorandum to the Malaysian People: The
Understanding of Islamic Rule in the Context
of 15th Hijrah/21st Century Democracy

The memorandum was essentially divided into five parts: (1) Introduction, (2) Preliminary Observations, (3) The Understanding of Islamic Rule in the 15th Hijrah/21st Century Democracy, (4) Definitive Characteristics of an Islamic State, and (5) Policies of the Islamic State.

The memorandum began with the standard declaration that Islam is both religion and *ad-din* ("a way of life") and that with the Qur'an Muslims have already been given sufficient "direction and guidance to regulate their life, and to live in a society and a state."[38] It proceeded to stress that the PAS struggle to emphasize Islam in governance has been consistent since the party's formation in 1951 and rests on the core principles of the party constitution, particularly those found in Chapter 5, Articles i and ii, which declared:

i. This struggle was necessary in Malaysia to create a society and government that implemented Islamic values and law towards the blessings of Allah;

ii. To defend Islam and the independence and sovereignty of the state.

The memorandum rejected UMNO's declaration that Malaysia was already an Islamic state by warning that such proclamations "should not be an outcome of desperation on the part of the ruling party to attract support from Muslims."[39] The authors of the memorandum further established the reformist credentials of PAS by arguing that since the tenth general election (in 1999), PAS had staunchly opposed tyranny, abuse of power, and UMNO excesses, all of which had worked to undermine the peoples' trust in the incumbent government. It reiterated its commitment to the *Barisan Alternatif* and suggested that the concept of "*Negara Islam*" (Islamic State) would bring the reform agenda to fruition and would "bring justice and prosperity to all people regardless of religion, ethnicity, and culture."[40] This commitment included the implementation of Islamic law (*Perundangan Islam*), which was the obligation of all Muslim governments toward all their citizens, as stated in the Qur'an.

The second part of the memorandum set out three caveats to PAS's pursuit of the Islamic state objective. First, it clarified that the party was not interested in semantics and hence was not bound by the term "Islamic state." What mattered more, according to the authors, was "substance rather than form." Second, the authors conceded that the 21st century provided a "new reality" and that there was a need to properly contextualize the Islamic state concept accordingly. Finally, the authors addressed non-Muslims, assuring them that their concerns had not been marginalized in the conceptualization of the memorandum. Interestingly, the authors conceded the difficulty of surmounting the perceptions of certain Islamic terms as "exclusivist." The attempted conciliatory tone was also present in the president's preamble, wherein Fadzil noted that "contemporary human civilization is sensitive to issues such as tyranny, meritocracy, justice, minority rights, women's rights in a plural society," and that "PAS is seen as the leader of the current move to awaken the public and to struggle for rights and justice for all peoples, religions, and cultures."[41]

The third segment of the memorandum presented a brief exposition on the contemporary context of those who championed the Islamic state. Specifically, the authors addressed criticisms that Islam was incompatible with democracy by retorting that Islam had historically always struggled against imperialism, dictatorship, and authoritarianism.[42]

The fourth segment of the memorandum set out core principles underlying the Islamic state as envisaged by PAS. These were *Madani* Society (Civil Society), Equality, Sovereignty of Law based on *shari'a*, Justice, Respect, Welfare,
Dynamism, and Innovation. The memorandum reiterated the points that the
establishment of an Islamic government was an obligation for Muslims and
that this form of government will emphasize a *Madani* society and a *Hadhari*
state, equality, law, justice, development, welfare, and a dynamic and innovative
political system based on consensus and democracy.

The importance of the memorandum reached beyond the fact that it was
the first formal articulation of the PAS vision of an Islamic state for Malaysia. First, as a formal articulation of the PAS vision, the memorandum was
avowedly political and in this respect was at least partly framed against the
backdrop of the UMNO-PAS rivalry. This was clearly captured in the thinly
veiled reference to Mahathir's declaration that Malaysia was already an Islamic
state, which effectively served as the memorandum's point of entry. Second, in
light of longstanding academic debates regarding the compatibility of Islam
with democratic principles, the memorandum attempted to reiterate PAS's
commitment to democracy. For example, the memorandum stated that in
pressing its cause, PAS "has never employed violent measures against democracy."[43] The party also reaffirmed its commitment to Malaysia's parliamentary
democracy.[44] In addition, the authors also sought to stress the democratic
and reformist nature of Islam by arguing that it always stood in opposition to
tyranny and authoritarianism. In the same vein, the memorandum stressed
the protection of individual rights and minority rights in the Islamic state.[45]
Third, mindful of the context of religious pluralism in Malaysia, much emphasis was also given to recognizing the needs and concerns of non-Muslims.
The point to stress here is that, clearly conscious of criticisms regarding the
party's perceived insensitivity toward non-Muslims, the PAS memorandum
was replete with references to the protection of minority rights and the party's
commitment to pluralism, including a curious plea for non-Muslims to understand the limitations of Islamic terminology.[46] Fourth, the memorandum
emphasized the reformist credentials of PAS. In a clear attempt to gain greater
currency by riding the waves of reform, the document liberally engaged the
language of the reform movement by repeatedly referencing the themes of
justice, equality, welfare, rights, and democracy, laboring to relate them to the
Islamic state.

Equally conspicuous, though, were the evident silences in the memorandum. Given the close association of the Islamic state with law, it is curious to
note that *shari'a* was mentioned merely twice in the entire document, once in
relation to the obligation of Muslims and on another occasion with reference to
the legal framework of an Islamic state. Furthermore, the *hudud* and *qisas* penal
legislation, which lay at the heart of nationwide debates over the implementation of *shari'a*, were not mentioned at all, even though such laws had already

been formulated by PAS-led state legislatures for the states of Kelantan and Terengganu.

The memorandum was presented to the party on the occasion of the May 2002 Muktamar. The principles behind the memorandum, however, had been enunciated several months earlier, when Fadzil delivered a speech (bearing the same title as the memorandum) at a party convention in October 2001, outlining the challenges to Islam posed by existing societal and political norms, the importance of reconciling Islamism with these contemporary contexts, and the need to stress adherence to democracy, human rights, and social justice, principles that he argued were inherent in Islamism. The speech ended with Fadzil's hope that "the foundations and practical suggestions that have been proposed [in the speech, and later elaborated in the memorandum] would be studied and internalized."[47] In response to queries about the conciliatory tone expressed in the party's attempt to rearticulate its agenda, Nasharuddin answered:

> The establishment of the [Islamic] state as such is part of our struggle. This process of 'repackaging' is part of an effort to offer those principles in accordance with the changing of time, situation and the condition of the country. What is being read in the media, especially the Malaysian media, does not really represent the position of PAS on many issues.[48]

Soon after the assembly however, speculation was rife that the party's religious leadership harbored reservations about the memorandum in its current form and were planning to replace Fadzil and rewrite the memorandum.[49] Among other things, the conservatives among the *ulama* were opposed to the dilution of *shari'a* and *hudud,* on the one hand, and excessive references to Western concepts such as democracy on the other. The plans to replace Fadzil, however, were soon superseded by events. Fadzil Noor failed to recover from heart surgery and passed away in June 2002, soon after presenting the controversial draft memorandum to the party. Fadzil's death, along with the American government's decision to launch attacks against the Taliban regime in Afghanistan (a decision that was widely unpopular in Malaysia), paved the way for conservatives to reassert their influence and rescript the party's Islamic state initiative. In certain respects, these changes in circumstance portended a return to the uncompromising stand on certain issues that characterized earlier permutations of the party.[50]

The 49th PAS Muktamar

There is often a tendency to assume that *ulama* have outlooks and perspectives that are generally conservative, dogmatic, and narrow in their understanding of the world. In the case of Malaysia, this appears to have been the case in the early 1980s, when *ulama* leadership was introduced into PAS, and the trajectory of the party subsequently traversed a conservative fundamentalist path, at least until the late 1980s. However, a full picture of the character of *ulama* leadership is likely to be far more complex, and a dichotomy that unproblematically sets up *ulama* political leadership as the structural antithesis to "moderate" and "progressive" politics might well be a false one, particularly given that such dichotomies are ultimately issue-specific.

One should remember that the progenitor of the mood of reform within PAS in the 1990s, and the man who oversaw the recalibration of the party's political rhetoric in its battle against UMNO, was the late president Fadzil Noor, who was a member of the infamous *ulama* class of 1982 and who is also often mentioned in the same breath with Abdul Hadi Awang, his fiery fundamentalist Islamist successor. Likewise, among the new generation of reformists in the party are Nasharuddin Mat Isa and Idris Ahmad, both *ulama*, while 1982 stalwart Muhammad Sabu (who, though not an *ulama*, is nevertheless seen as a conservative) is believed to have supported Nasharuddin's candidacy for deputy president. On the other hand, non-*ulama* leaders generally associated with the "professionals," "moderates," or "reformists" in recent years have also been known to adopt hardened, uncompromising, "fundamentalist" positions on issues such as apostasy, moral policing, and interfaith dialogue. This is true not only of PAS but also of UMNO, particularly among the membership of the youth wings in both parties.

Bearing in mind the difficulties associated with any attempt to construct reductionist typologies, the events of the 2003 PAS Muktamar were telling because the conference witnessed the installation of a narrower, more conservative leadership within the party. The 49th Muktamar of PAS, held in September 2003, was noteworthy on a number of counts. First, the Muktamar confirmed Terengganu *Mentri Besar* and cleric Abdul Hadi Awang (articulator of the infamous *Amanat Haji Hadi*, discussed in chapter 1) as president and elected another conservative *ulama*, Hasan Shukri, as deputy president. Given the ideological predilections of both Abdul Hadi and Hasan, it was widely acknowledged that their appointment marked a return to a narrower, more conservative brand of Islamist leadership. Hasan Shukri's election was also notable because it was the result of the first open contest for the post of deputy president in twenty years. In this contest, Ustaz Hasan easily defeated Mustapha Ali, a lawyer and the deputy *Mentri Besar* of Terengganu, who remained a vice-president. Harun Din, another well-respected *ulama* who was widely expected to win when his candidacy for deputy president was initially announced, withdrew at the very last minute.

Equally notable during this Muktamar was the return to the virulent religiopolitical discourse that had defined the UMNO-PAS struggle in the 1980s. Abdul Hadi set this tone for the meeting when he proclaimed in his opening address that UMNO "are planning to deny us victory but Allah is with us as long as we uphold Islam," and "our mission is not to win, our mission is to save souls." Shorn of poetic polemics and melodramatic hype, the PAS Muktamar signaled that the self-professed Islamic party was in fact an archetypical political party preparing to engage in a battle for the here and now. The PAS leadership made plain their political ambitions at the meeting, publicly expressing their confidence that they would retain the state assemblies of Terengganu and Kelantan. Many also expressed their belief that Kedah would be next to fall and that a significant dent could even be made in Johore, the bastion of UMNO support.[51] Clearly, PAS was confident regarding their religious appeal, and they were sure that this refocus on conservative and uncompromising Islamism would help enhance the party's legitimacy, resulting in further gains at the next elections.

Yet there were indications that some party members were also looking to balance, if not restrain, fundamentalist *ulama* rule. Mustapha's candidacy indicated that the party had become more receptive to the prospect of non-*ulama* assuming major leadership positions.[52] This development is even more striking given that all candidates for party elections (initially fourteen, nominated by the divisions) had been gathered for a private caucus on 4 September with Nik Aziz and Abdul Hadi, at which they were discouraged from having an open contest.[53] More important, a cohort of younger, reform-minded professionals had either won positions of leadership (in the Central Working Committee) or were identified as possessing the potential to assume leadership roles in the party in the near future. This cohort had already been gradually making their voices heard on the sidelines of party conventions and assemblies, and it would only be a matter of time before they began to assert a more significant presence.

These subterranean developments at the Muktamar revealed fractures within the party that gradually deepened over the next few years. For the time being, however, it was the conservatives who had regained the initiative, and they were intent on pressing it home. One of the earliest and clearest manifestations of this turn to conservatism was the redrafting of the PAS memorandum on an Islamic state, spearheaded by the party president himself and other *ulama*. In time, the PAS memorandum would resurface, but this time as the PAS Islamic State Document, revised by the conservative clerics and released as the official PAS Islamic state blueprint on 12 November 2003.[54]

The PAS Islamic State Document

In the Preface of the Islamic State Document, President Abdul Hadi made clear that "establishing an Islamic Government is as important as establishing the other daily rituals of Islam." He proceeded to rationalize this comparison by suggesting that "since the successful implementation of the obligatory

injunction of 'enjoining good and forbidding vice' and the entire good governance, is dependent on the acquiring of executive power, thus the establishment
of the Islamic state has become obligatory."[55] The document further made clear
that PAS saw its administrations in Kelantan and Terengganu as "Islam in real
practice of government and governance."[56]

The document proper began with an Introduction similar to that in the earlier memorandum, setting out the historical and doctrinal premises of the PAS
struggle for an Islamic state. The second section, titled "The Conception of an
Islamic State," stipulated various characteristics of such a polity. While most of
these characteristics echoed the earlier version, the document tellingly declared
that "the implementation of *shari'a*, *hudud* being part of it, provides the much
required peace and security as crime would be reduced to its minimum."[57] Following this, the document proceeded to stress the "supremacy of law" as a key
principle of Islamic government: "The determining characteristic of an Islamic
state is its total commitment and will to see that the *shari'a* is codified into law
of the land. . . . Allah has ordained the leaders of Islamic society to implement
what He has revealed and prohibits them to take recourse to other sources of
law."[58] On the matter of the penal code, the document noted that "only the Muslim members of the state are subjected to the *shari'a* penal code [*hudud*, *qisas*,
and *ta'zir*]. The non-Muslim members are given the options of either being
subjected to the same penal code or to be subjected to the current penal code of
the land."[59] As to the interpretation of law, it said that "where there exists clear
injunctions and verses pertaining to the issue no *ijtihad* [informed reasoning] is
required except as to conduct *shura* [consultation] in matters that relate to its
implementation within a certain context."[60] The final two sections of the document elucidated "Main Characteristics of an Islamic State" and "General Policies of an Islamic State," and save for a few innocuous points, they essentially
replicate parallel sections of the earlier memorandum.

In assessing the document and comparing it with the memorandum, perhaps most striking is the primacy of *shari'a* and its punitive component, *hudud*,
in the document. While *shari'a* was mentioned only twice in the memorandum,
in the document it was referred to on multiple occasions, at times categorically. Moreover, several of these references related specifically to its penal code,
something not articulated in the memorandum at all. With regard to individual
freedoms and rights, the document said that "the freedom and rights of the citizens especially enjoined by the Universal Declaration of Human Rights are not
only enjoined but are also protected by the Islamic state. It must not however
contravene the provision of *shari'a*."[61] The document declared that under the
PAS Islamic state, "citizens are free to conduct their economic activities," but
these activities have to be conducted "within the ambit of the *shari'a*."[62] Moreover, while "healthy competition" between men and women will be encouraged,
this too must fall "within the limits of the *shari'a*."[63] The document gave the
shari'a such weight that it could only amplify further the tension within PAS's

brand of Islamism that already existed between theocracy and universalism, working to effectively reify non-Muslim concerns even as the party's leadership attempted to endear itself to this constituency.

Beyond this, it is also notable that the term democracy was entirely absent from the document. Instead, the document introduced the concept of "parliamentary *shura*" in place of "parliamentary democracy," a term that appeared frequently in the earlier memorandum. Likewise, the punitive character of the PAS Islamic state and the interpretation of the *shari'a* (primarily its proposed implementation of *hudud, qisas,* and *ta'zir*) were never far from the document's surface. This was made clear where it was suggested that "man-made laws have proven a failure in ensuring the security and dignity of the human race."[64] Further, in stark contrast to the earlier memorandum, where *ijtihad* at least appeared to be an important precept of a "dynamic and innovative government," in the document the practice of *ijtihad* would be markedly restricted and would be subject to *shura.* While conciliatory in principle, in the context of an *ulama*-led government it is clear that such *shura* is likely to reinforce clerical hegemony.

The point here is that the formulation and implementation of laws based on the *shari'a* as envisaged in the document did not appear to be premised on the traditional model of Islamic scholasticism anchored in several jurisprudential traditions, but instead was the sole prerogative of the Islamic state. In other words, law would not create and govern the state; the state would instead create the law. This approach differs markedly from a number of Malaysian Islamist civil society groups such as ABIM and JIM, or even *Hizbut Tahrir,* who have maintained that an Islamic society has to be fostered, cultivated, and nourished before a genuine Islamic state can materialize. In contrast, the PAS Islamic State Document suggests that the Islamic state will create the Islamic society, not the other way around.

Prospects for debate on the implementation of *shari'a* among Muslims were effectively circumscribed on the premise that "any attempt to say that it [the document] is not just, is tantamount to saying that Allah is unjust in his injunction. The option is actually divinely derived and it is not an option provided by PAS. Any contention in this regards, amounts to contesting the divine wisdom."[65]

Islam Hadhari

Predictably, the release of the PAS Islamic State Document elicited heated responses in many quarters. Civil society groups took umbrage at its legalistic and proscriptive tone, while UMNO attacked it as nothing more than a political gimmick in preparation for a forthcoming election. UMNO's response was to ratchet up the Islamization race further with its own list of principles for Islamic governance. These principles took the form of *Islam Hadhari* (Islamic Civilization), the latest addition to the litany of Islamic terms in Malaysian politics.

The Abdullah administration made *Islam Hadhari* a major component of its campaign platform for the 2004 general election, the first of Abdullah Badawi's tenure as prime minister. *Islam Hadhari* was created by a committee comprising Nakhaie Ahmad (a former *ulama* stalwart of PAS who defected to UMNO), Mustapha Mohamed (Kelantan UMNO liaison chief), and Abdul Hamid Othman (then minister-in-charge of Islamic Affairs). Abdullah Zin, minister in the prime minister's office, was tasked with implementing its principles. *Islam Hadhari* was purportedly an adaptation of the thought of Ibn Khaldun, the fourteenth-century Muslim historian and sociologist. The concept itself consists of ten lofty principles:

1. Faith and piety in Allah
2. A just and trustworthy government
3. A free and independent people
4. Mastery of knowledge
5. Balanced and comprehensive economic development
6. A good quality of life
7. Protection of the rights of minority groups and women
8. Cultural and moral integrity
9. Protection of the environment
10. Strong defense capabilities

While the term was already being bandied about in 2003 and was employed as an election tool in March 2004, it was only at the UMNO General Assembly on 23 September 2004 that party president Abdullah Badawi elaborated in greater detail on his vision of *Islam Hadhari*. He articulated the concept in a manner that resonated with the Malay community's struggle for independence and development. In Abdullah's words, *Islam Hadhari*

> is an approach that emphasizes development, consistent with the tenets of Islam, and is focused on enhancing the quality of life. It aims to achieve this through the mastery of knowledge and the development of the individual and the nation. In addition, through the implementation of a dynamic economic, trading and financial system, it aims to achieve an integrated and balanced development that creates a knowledgeable and pious people who hold fast to noble values and are honest, trustworthy and prepared to take on global challenges.[66]

To Abdullah's mind, such a balanced development would produce an *umma* or community of knowledgeable and pious people with noble values, a people who would be able to take on challenges of modernization without compromising religious belief and praxis. *Islam Hadhari*, as later explained in a sixty-page document drafted and published by the government, further stressed the centrality of knowledge in Islam along with the virtues of hard work, honesty, good administration, efficiency, tolerance, and open-mindedness. Several committees were subsequently established to elucidate and spread the *Islam Hadhari* message throughout Malaysia, and state-appointed *imam* were instructed to preach it during Friday sermons. A *Yayasan Islam Hadhari* (*Islam Hadhari* Foundation) was established under the patronage of the prime minister to further flesh out the meaning and content of the concept.

In some respects, *Islam Hadhari* appeared to derive from earlier UMNO attempts to inspire an Islamic culture of reform. At the heart of *Islam Hadhari*, as its progenitor Abdullah himself has claimed on numerous occasions, was attitudinal change. *Islam Hadhari* was an attempt to inspire a shift in outlook and worldview on the part of the Malay-Muslim population that would in turn spur them to greater economic and scientific achievements. In other words, in order to launch Malaysia forward, Abdullah had taken a step back to the ideas of Ibn Khaldun. Yet, as an intellectual blueprint for Islamic modernism, the principles behind *Islam Hadhari* were hardly new. For those who have been following Malaysian politics, Abdullah's idea of *Islam Hadhari* bears an uncanny similarity to what Mahathir had sought to accomplish for the better part of his twenty-two-year tenure as prime minister and UMNO president: a distinctly Islamic brand of modernization and industrialization built on a Qur'an-sanctioned work ethic, albeit without the allusions to Islamic philosophers of the past.

However, *Islam Hadhari* resonated most with Anwar Ibrahim's ideas. In 1996, deputy prime minister Anwar Ibrahim sought to capitalize on the overall heightened Muslim consciousness and his own personal popularity by manufacturing a new and captivating organizing principle for a pluralistic society based on Islamized precepts of democracy, good governance, inclusivity, and civil relations among ethnic groups. The principles Anwar had in mind would fundamentally restructure Malaysia's hitherto communally oriented sociopolitical landscape. He created the catchphrase "*Masyarakat Madani*" (Civil Society) to describe such a society, and the concept was presented as a polity where God had endowed individuals with rights that were to be recognized, respected, and protected by the state, and where democratic principles were to be enshrined. As Anwar himself said, "Only the fostering of a genuine civil society or *Masyarakat Madani*, a critical component to the establishment of democracy, can assure the path of sustained growth including economic, social, and political."[67] The concept of *Masyarakat Madani*, as Anwar imagined it, was anchored on the notion of *keadilan sosial* (social justice). Through the efforts of his *Institut Kajian Dasar* (Institute of Policy Studies), *Masyarakat Madani, keadilan sosial,* and Anwar's attendant call for intercivilizational dialogue (which underpinned his 1996 compendium of speeches, published under the title *Asian Renaissance*) soon became the focus of trendy intellectualism. Road shows, seminars, and conferences were held throughout the country to promote the concept and reach out across ethnic and class schisms.

Anwar's *Masyarakat Madani* concept met with a mixed reception. On the one hand, critics assailed *Masyarakat Madani* as merely an extension of Anwar's ambition and brand of leadership as he prepared for an eventual leadership succession. After all, Anwar was slated to be Mahathir's successor and was building on his reputation as an activist and modernist Muslim leader, dating from his ABIM days. As a matter of fact, by that time Anwar was already widely seen as a popular Muslim intellectual and the personification of all that was progressive and modern about the government's Islamization program. Anwar was known to have been an avid follower of the teachings of Yusuf Qaradawi, the dean of Islamic law at Qatar University, who popularized the application of *Al halal wal haram fil Islam* (the lawful and prohibited acts in Islam) as the basis of Islamic legal scholarship and who is generally associated with a narrow approach to Islam and the Islamic state that focuses on punitive sanctions. Yusuf was also chancellor of the International Islamic University of Malaysia.[68]

Regardless of whether it was driven by instrumentalist motivations or self-aggrandizement, *Masyarakat Madani* did contain some remarkable ideas that sought to transcend the communal structure of society and politics in Malaysia. Concepts such as democracy and human rights, long rejected by the Malaysian establishment under Mahathir as Western imports, stood at the forefront of Anwar's discourse on the future of the Malaysian polity. However, *Masyarakat Madani* died a premature death with Anwar's removal from office. It does appear, though, that the concept, or at least elements of it, may have been reborn in a different guise and under a different regime.

When the concept of *Islam Hadhari* was presented as a major instrument of reform by the Abdullah administration, it served as a reply to the PAS Islamic state while also enhancing Malaysia's prestige as the preeminent moderate and progressive Muslim state. The *Islam Hadhari* concept has been celebrated as the "right" approach to reform in the Islamic world, and it has won endorsement from Western governments and from the Organization of Islamic Conferences. Notwithstanding these felicitations, *Islam Hadhari* demands closer scrutiny against the backdrop of broader and deeper processes of Islamization.

Much like the PAS memorandum or the Islamic State Document, *Islam Hadhari* was primarily an instrument of elite political posturing. It operated as a top-down phenomenon; not unlike his predecessor, Abdullah attempted to carry Malay-Muslims across the threshold into modernity on the shoulders of his imagination, not to mention his creative phraseology. Be that as it may, there are several flaws in the logic of *Islam Hadhari* that would fundamentally hamper its efficacy as the definitive paradigm for "progressive" Muslim politics in Malaysia, notwithstanding the politically motivated criticisms leveled at it by PAS. First, by enunciating "Faith and Piety in Allah" as its opening tenet, *Islam Hadhari* paradoxically constricts the very space for civil and plural discourse that it purports to open, thereby launching Islamist politics in Malaysia to new levels of intensity and exclusivism. The reference made to "Allah" is a considerable shift from the *Rukunnegara*, which had as its first principle "Belief in God." By this token, *Islam Hadhari* effectively narrows the national discourse to an Islamic one.

Second, when Abdullah announced in his presidential address at the 2004 UMNO General Assembly that "*Islam Hadhari* is complete and comprehensive, with an emphasis on the development of the economy and civilization, capable of building Malay competitiveness" and that "the glorious heritage of the Islamic civilization in all its aspects must be used as a reference in order to become the source of inspiration for the Malay race to prosper," what he effectively did was leverage yet again a fundamental, longstanding issue in Malaysian politics: the specter of Malay-Muslim primacy.[69] This phrasing demonstrates the intensification of the process of Islamization that has captivated Malay-Muslim politicians and to which Abdullah Badawi is not immune. As some have presciently observed, "to suggest that race can be the basis of politics, or more bizarre still the politics of *Islam Hadhari*, is a contradiction as embarrassing as a socialist party trying to promote capitalism."[70] Indeed, while the champions of *Islam Hadhari* paid lip service to the protection of "rights of minority groups," the concept's efficacy was ultimately hampered by the baggage of race and communalism. It is noteworthy how the "lessons" of *Islam Hadhari* were all but lost at the 2005 and 2006 UMNO general assemblies, as racial politics reared its head yet again when UMNO Youth leaders reminded non-Malays that they were recipients of Malay-Muslim goodwill that permitted them to merely *"menumpang"* (temporarily reside) on Malaysian soil, even as others called for the reinstatement of the thirty year-old NEP. Despite Abdullah's claim that *Islam Hadhari* was for every Malaysian, there was very little in the enunciation of the concept that spoke to the concerns of non-Muslims, who continued to be marginalized even as the discourse of Islamism intensified.

Third, the notions of democracy and human rights were also absent from the exposition of *Islam Hadhari*, perhaps even more conspicuously so when compared to the two PAS documents discussed earlier. Commentators have been quick to note that *Islam Hadhari* remains silent on such pressing issues as civil liberties, human rights, and corruption;[71] nor has *Islam Hadhari* much to say about the constant policing of Islamic discourse and practice in Malaysia, which has caused much consternation for Muslims and non-Muslims alike.

Finally, while most will have little disagreement with the principles underlying *Islam Hadhari* as articulated by Abdullah, fundamental questions of operationalization remain. Not unlike the PAS memorandum and Islamic State Document, Abdullah's *Islam Hadhari* is so nebulous as to do little more than provide general principles drawn from classical Islamic sources. In fact, while the respective PAS models of the Islamic state did attempt to identify broad areas of government policies that needed to reflect these principles (interspersed with verses from the Qur'an), even this was lacking in *Islam Hadhari*.[72] The absence of a clear strategy of implementation was strikingly evident in the concept's deafening silence on everyday challenges such as the controversial matter of moral policing.

These shortcomings, however, did not prevent *Islam Hadhari* from serving as the centerpiece of the Abdullah administration's political strategy, allowing UMNO to present an alternative model to the Islamic state articulated by PAS as the protracted competition between the two Islamist parties escalated. The immediate appeal of *Islam Hadhari* lay in the fact that Abdullah managed to express the religious character of ongoing policies carried over from the previous government in readily identifiable and catchy Islamic terminology. This strategy would reap dividends for the incumbent administration at the 2004 general elections.

The 2004 General Elections

The results of the 2004 elections were in many respects a major reversal of 1999. At first glance, the PAS performance was dismal, particularly given the fact established earlier that PAS leaders were confident of making further inroads into UMNO strongholds. Instead, the party lost the state of Terengganu and came close to losing control of the Kelantan state legislature as well. What was worse, its representation in the federal Parliament was whittled down from twenty-seven seats to a mere six. *Keadilan*'s association with PAS also proved costly: it lost all but one of its parliamentary seats.

While a range of factors accounted for the poor performance of PAS, the consensus among most observers was that the results were an outright rejection of the party's Islamic State Document released several months earlier. PAS leaders too have reached this conclusion, along with the fact that the elections were effectively a triumph for *Islam Hadhari*, regardless of its conceptual ambiguities and the efforts of PAS *ulama* to discredit it as a new school of Islamic thought that was in fact an illegitimate innovation.[73]

The *Barisan Nasional*'s landslide victory was greeted with accolades by the international media and analysts, who lauded it as the roll-back of Islamism and the resurgence of moderation and secularism in the crucial arena of Malay-Muslim politics in Malaysia.[74] This "mandate for moderation," as the election result was called by CNN, was celebrated as "a good precedent for the Muslim world." ChannelNewsAsia, a major regional news network, further opined that the election results were "an overwhelming mandate for its [UMNO's] secular rule in one of the world's most developed Muslim states."[75] Elsewhere, it was reported that "Abdullah Badawi handed the fundamentalist Pan-Malaysian Islamic Party, or PAS, one of its worst-ever defeats in last week's elections by touting a modern, progressive Islam. His ruling coalition now controls eleven of the country's twelve states, and seems to have quashed the idea that radical Islam was infiltrating the politics of Southeast Asia."[76] Taken together, two things are immediately clear from these pronouncements: first, many observers viewed Islam as a determining factor in the elections; second, the election results were a triumph for UMNO's brand of "progressive" Islam over the "fundamentalist" opposition.

The *Barisan* coalition's success was primarily attributed to the Abdullah administration's successful co-optation of the *"reformasi"* language and agenda of pluralism, openness, and reform. The *Barisan* cause, however, was also undoubtedly assisted by the introduction of prominent and popular candidates with strong Islamic credentials on the *Barisan* ticket.[77] Some of the more prominent personalities included Pirdaus Ismail, former *imam* of the national mosque, and Dr. Mashitah Ibrahim, a young university lecturer and Islamic television personality. Yet despite UMNO attempts to outflank PAS with its own slate of Islamic candidates, what escaped most analysts was the fact that popular support for the Islamist opposition actually increased marginally, from 15 percent in 1999 to 15.6 percent. As far as the party's grassroots popularity was concerned, the results contradicted proclamations of a "scaling back" of the PAS tide.[78]

More important, while many have been sanguine about the prospects of "moderate" Islam following this electoral success, developments since March 2004 suggest that a fundamentally conservative brand of exclusivist Islam continues to hold sway in Malaysia under an UMNO-led government. A number of developments, particularly the amplified debates over apostasy and the status of constitutional rights, have already been discussed in detail. In terms of the Islamist tendencies of UMNO and the Abdullah administration, the efforts of Terengganu's UMNO-controlled state legislature to deal with *shari'a* and *hudud* legislation formulated by previous PAS administrations should provide some revealing insights.

Observers have identified *hudud* legislation in Terengganu as a "problem" that UMNO has inherited from PAS.[79] They suggest that any inability on the part of UMNO to rescind the PAS-formulated laws can be explained by the fact that the political costs in terms of the potential loss of Malay-Muslim support may be too great for UMNO to bear in a state where its margins of victory in many constituencies during the 2004 elections were razor-thin. There is certainly more than a modicum of truth behind this assumption, given the intense political rivalry between UMNO and PAS for Malay-Muslim votes. Be that as it may, this assumption first presupposes a desire on the part of UMNO to overturn these laws, when in fact there may well be deeper undercurrents at work that would inform a range of UMNO responses to the situation in Terengganu.

Upon defeating PAS in Terengganu, a victory that also included the defeat of PAS president Abdul Hadi in his parliamentary seat, UMNO's new

Terengganu leadership, led by *Menteri Besar* Idris Jusoh, began to work hard to ensure that "federal funds are delivered fast to boost economic development and provide jobs."[80] On the question of the Islamic state in Terengganu, Idris was quick to assert UMNO's position on the matter when, in an interview with the *New Straits Times* on 20 March 2006, he promptly declared: "Terengganu has always been an Islamic state."[81] Idris further noted that insofar as *hudud* was concerned, UMNO would be prepared to implement it "when we think we are ready."[82] Commenting on the Islamic legislation enacted by PAS, state religious leaders and UMNO politicians intimated that the Terengganu *hudud* and *qisas* bill could not be supported—not because UMNO was resistant to the implementation of the Islamic penal code in contemporary Malaysia, but because the PAS-sponsored bills were "not comprehensive enough and had to cover further aspects of *hudud*."[83]

This perspective on the Islamic penal code has been expressed on other occasions by government-linked religious leaders. For instance, Wan Zahidi maintained that it was the government's responsibility to ensure that all features of *shari'a*, including the penal codes, were implemented.[84] This lent credence to Nakhaie Ahmad's earlier argument that the Islamic penal code should eventually be incorporated in government initiatives on Islam, thereby making his contention relevant to subsequent pronouncements, such as Mahathir's Islamic state or Abdullah's *Islam Hadhari*.[85] Faisal Haji Othman further suggested that while the Malaysian government could delay the implementation of *hudud* based on the principle of *tadaruj* (evolutionary stages), the failure of Muslims to subscribe to Islamic criminal laws was tantamount to rejecting the basic beliefs of Islam.[86] These opinions all but undermine the received wisdom that speaks of UMNO's credentials as "moderate," "secular," or "progressive."

In essence then, the question of repealing the PAS enactments was clearly a nonstarter for UMNO. At best, one can argue that *hudud* is not an immediate priority for UMNO. Idris Jusoh said as much when he argued that, while UMNO believes in *hudud* as part of Islamic Jurisprudence or *fiqh al alawat*, for the Terengganu administration the immediate challenge was to prioritize the organization of society, and this meant that the party was to focus on "education, poverty, and the mindset one has on Islam."[87] UMNO has carefully employed deliberately ambiguous rhetoric to avoid being seen as denouncing Islamic law or as embracing a narrow and conservative brand of Islamism. In Terengganu, this translated into a number of initiatives that worked to turn attention away from the contentious issue of *hudud*. These included plans to invest in a RM200 million *Taman Tamadun Islam* (Islamic Civilization Theme Park) and Majid Kristal (Crystal Mosque), which would purportedly rank alongside Masjid Al Haram in Mecca, Al Nabawi in Medina, Al Aqsa in Jerusalem, and Alhambra in Spain as a major monument to the "glory of Islam."[88] Besides *hudud*, the new UMNO state administration also had to deal with other aspects of "everyday policing" inherited from PAS. For instance, while UMNO did not legislate for a formal dress code for women, the state government did encourage them to "cover up what needs to be covered."[89] Similarly, while upmarket karaoke lounges banned by PAS resurfaced after UMNO's victory, liquor was still banned.

UMNO's initiatives in Terengganu had a very definite strategic logic to them. Having returned to power in Terengganu, UMNO eyes were now trained on Kelantan, the last PAS stronghold in Malaysia. As a beachhead for its move into Kelantan, Terengganu was to exemplify the potential that Abdullah's *Islam Hadhari* agenda held for the creation of a model of Islamic government that married religious doctrine with development and modernization.[90]

Reinventing PAS?

Given the assertion that Malaysian elections have always been "a convenient and effective way of assessing the significance of religion," 2004 was instructive of the fact that while Islam continues to be a major theme in Malaysian politics and the major Malay-Muslim parties continue to mobilize Islamic symbols and ideas for the instrumental purposes of increasing political support, Islam's resonance is often linked to the pressing social, political, and economic issues of the day, and the extent to which these issues are perceived to be specifically addressed by the Islamic agendas of the respective parties.[91] Thus, while observers and media sources were quick to claim (with the privilege of hindsight, it should be added) in the aftermath of the 2004 election that UMNO's landslide victory meant that the Malay-Muslim population had roundly rejected the fundamentalist platform of PAS, in point of fact their observations derived more from the fact that the appeal of a reform-minded PAS had been negated by certain PAS leaders who accentuated and perpetuated the image of the party as one that espoused antiquated and essentialist ideas, such as the notion that women are the source of evil because of their "sexy clothes."[92] The shortcomings of the PAS Islamic agenda were further magnified by the fact that the Abdullah Badawi administration had effectively hijacked, at least in rhetoric, what had been its more persuasive themes—social justice and distributive equality.

Since the presidency of PAS passed into the hands of Abdul Hadi upon Fadzil Noor's untimely passing, the doctrinaire approach to opposition Islamist politics had apparently regained a foothold in the party. This shift consequently upstaged the emerging role of Islam as a voice of dissidence in Malaysian politics that Fadzil and his reformist followers had nurtured, and the fundamentalist agenda of the new coterie of senior leaders, exemplified in their campaign platform based on the Islamic State Document, took over. Not surprisingly, this shift has generated tensions within the party between the more moderate professionals that flocked to the party in the late 1990s and the conservatives among the *ulama* leadership. These tensions had already surfaced before the elections, when moderates who spearheaded the first draft of the Islamic State memorandum were eventually sidelined in the process as conservatives moved to revise the document.

In the PAS election postmortem *Munaqashah* (special convention) that followed the 2004 debacle, crestfallen party leaders were in a contemplative mood and quickly conceded that while their comprehensive defeat was partly attributable to electoral irregularities and the *Barisan Nasional's* powers of incumbency, the party itself was culpable, as it had not done enough to win the support of three key constituencies—non-Muslims, youths, and neutrals. Beyond that, the Islamic State Document was also acknowledged to have been a major weight on the party. The leadership of the conservative *ulama* came under heavy scrutiny at this time, not least from a younger generation of reformists who began to openly express their frustration and disappointment with the old guard's lack of vision.

Events that transpired at the PAS Muktamar in 2005 gave further impetus to this mood of change. Leading the way was a new generation of Young Turks from the youth movement. In his opening address at the 2005 PAS Youth Assembly, youth leader Salahuddin Ayub said that the *Majlis Shura* had failed to live up to party expectations and that "the council should not only give religious guidance on issues affecting women and ties with non-Muslims. It must also provide guidance on other issues like banking, science, and technology, so that its presence can be felt more."[93] Others were even more caustic in their criticisms of the conservative *ulama*. Mujahid Yusof Rawa, son of former PAS president Yusof Rawa and a senior leader in the PAS youth movement, took umbrage with decision-making in the *Majlis Shura*. In an extensive interview with alternative news source *Malaysiakini*, Mujahid stressed *fiqh* (Islamic jurisprudence) in his assessment of the need for change in the party because "in PAS, most decisions are made by the *Majlis Shura*. So how did the *Shura* make the decision? Do they base their understanding [in making the decision] on *fiqh* as we understand it? . . . Because *fiqh* is very wide."[94] Reformists further questioned the *ulama* fixation on the Islamic state, with many saying that it should not be an immediate objective for the party and that the focus should rightly center on democracy and the fight for justice and against corruption. In this vein, others have called for a return to the spirit of the *Barisan Alternatif* manifesto of 1999 that underpinned the opposition coalition.

Given that party elections were scheduled for the 2005 Muktamar, displeasure with the old guard soon translated into major changes in party leadership. Most significant among these changes was the rise of Nasharuddin Mat Isa, a law graduate who had studied in Lucknow and Glasgow and who was a surprise eleventh-hour candidate for the party deputy presidency. Nasharuddin, a popular moderate among younger party circles, defeated incumbent

Hasan Shukri as well as Abdul Halim, favored by Nik Aziz, in a three-way contest for the deputy presidency. Husam Musa, an economist, also won the highest number of votes as one of three elected vice-presidents, of whom none were *ulama*. Reformists also captured key posts in the party Central Working Committee.

Just as reformists gradually reemerged in the party, there were equally telling countercurrents that indicated the resilience of conservative elements in the PAS leadership. These, in turn, attest to the complicated politicking within the Islamist opposition party, suggesting that it is unwise to assume that the reformists have conclusively regained the initiative. Nasharuddin's victory was arguably only secured because the popular deputy *Musyidul 'Am*, Harun Din, declined to be considered for the deputy presidency for health reasons. Likewise, when the PAS rank and file was presented with its first female candidate for a vice-presidential post in the form of Dr. Siti Mariah Mahmud, a British-trained physician who was personally endorsed by Nik Aziz, she was decisively rejected.

It is also notable that the PAS elections took place against the backdrop of an eye-opening attempt to transform the structure of the party in a way that would have cemented *ulama* rule. In December 2004, Harun Din presented a paper titled *"Kepimpinan Ulamak Di Era Cabaran Baru"* (*Ulama* Leadership in a Challenging New Era) at a PAS convention that proposed to have the party president and deputy president made automatic members of the *Majlis Shura* rather than having to be part of a formal election process, as is presently the case. The paper further proposed a separate secretariat and party workers for the *Majlis Shura*, ostensibly for the purpose of monitoring and coordinating grassroots activism in the party. Given the fact that under the prevailing system members of the *Majlis Shura* must be *ulama*, the proposal raised concerns that it was a step toward a constitutional amendment that would eventually restrict the presidency and deputy presidency to the *ulama*.[95]

There were further indications of resilient trends of conservatism even within the so-called reformist professional camp. For instance, when the Malaysian Bar Council moved to convene a national conference to discuss the possibility of establishing a national interfaith commission, PAS Youth stridently protested this move, deeming it a threat to the sensitivities of Muslims and Islam. The opposition party also withdrew its representatives on the parliamentary human rights caucus in protest of the latter's support for an NGO campaign against moral policing. These apparent contradictions betray a deeper impasse for the party, for even as reformists among its ranks continue to stridently defend the party by arguing that the media consistently "misrepresents" it, this response has nevertheless been compromised to some extent by the party's inability to put forth a coherent position on a number of contentious issues. This ambiguity rehearsed itself in 2007, when the party went to the polls to select a new leadership.

53rd PAS Muktamar

The 53rd PAS Muktamar was held 1–3 June 2007 in Kota Bahru, Kelantan, and proved to be as tense as some of their more recent meetings. This time, the contest for senior leadership was discernibly more animated because it was seen as a test of whether the rebranding and repackaging efforts of Nasharuddin's reformist group could be sustained, or whether the conservative *ulama* would return to prominence in the upper echelons of the party. Against this backdrop, the results were inconclusive and failed to give a clear mandate either to the conservative *ulama* or the reformist professionals.

Prior to the election proper, talk along the sidelines of the meeting was that there would be a swing back to religious conservatism. Chief among the criticisms of the reformist faction was its failure to defend the state seat in Pengkalan Pasir, Kelantan, which it lost to UMNO in a December 2005 by-election. Because this byelection was the first major political contest for the reformists in the post-Fadzil Noor era, some within the party viewed the result as something of a failure. At the *Muktamar*, recrimination came not only in the form of murmurings on the sidelines but also through conservative victories in major posts in the *Dewan Muslimat* (Women's Wing) and PAS Youth in their respective elections on 2 June, a day before the main party elections. Results of contests for senior party positions the following day, however, reinforced the ambiguity that has come to define the present state of the party. Conservative *ulama* won a significant number of seats in the party's thirty-five-member Central Executive Committee (of which eighteen seats consist of elected members), while Ahmad Awang, former head of the *Dewan Ulama* (*Ulama* Council), won the third-highest number of votes in the course of securing one of the three party vice-presidencies. That meant, however, that reformists managed to secure the other two posts. Moreover, Nasharuddin Mat Isa, the moderate *ulama* leader of the party reformists, also comfortably defended his position against the challenge of Harun Taib, outgoing head of *Dewan Ulama*.

Several observations can be drawn from these results. First, the results indicate that *ulama* remain an important group within the party. This was most clearly illustrated when Ahmad Awang broke the professionals' grip over the vice-presidencies. The meeting also witnessed the election of another conservative, Daud Iraqi, as leader of the *Dewan Ulama*, and the reappointment of Abdul Hadi Awang as president. The continued relevance of the conservatives in the party was further reflected in the speeches of some delegates and murmurings along the sidelines of the meeting that betrayed a latent discomfort with how reformists have conducted party affairs. For instance, some criticized the reformists' decision to build a posh new party headquarters building in downtown Kuala Lumpur as part of their broader agenda of retooling the party's image and reaching out to urban Muslims, saying the expense and display were an unnecessary opulence. Ordinary members further expressed discomfort with the apparently extravagant lifestyles of some among the reformist professionals, whose penchant for grand living quarters, luxury cars, and executive air travel stood in stark contrast to the legendary austere lifestyles of conservative stalwarts such as Abdul Hadi and Nik Aziz.[96] These reactions to the reformists indicated the party's reluctance to shift too far from its *ulama* center. This being the case, the terms of reference for PAS's longstanding contest with UMNO for the hearts, minds, and votes of Malaysia's Malay-Muslim electorate is likely to continue to take religious forms.

The strength of the conservative presence at the meeting and the polls, however, should not detract from the fact that at the end of the day, major figures associated with the reformists such as Nasharuddin, Husam Musa, and Muhammad Sabu were retained in the top echelon of the party's leadership. Clearly, any misgivings about the reformists were balanced with a realization that their role remained pertinent insofar as the party's broader political ambitions were concerned. The results also indicated how the reform agenda of PAS, put in place by the late Ustaz Fadzil Noor in the wake of the *Reformasi* movment of the late 1990s, continues to enjoy support in the party. The reformist agenda influences the party's strategies for how PAS should position itself to defend its northern Malay heartland from the UMNO onslaught and to expand its footprint at the national level. Even conservative leaders, such as party president Abdul Hadi, are acutely aware of this challenge, which is why he has assured members of the Malaysian opposition that PAS will not base its campaign for the next general election on the Islamic state.[97] The inconclusive nature of the results alerted some leaders to the need for party cohesion and unity. This attitude was exemplified in a call by outgoing vice-president Hassan Ali to the *ulama* leadership to "make clear their policy for PAS and Malaysia so as to diffuse the tension in PAS between *ulama* and professionals [reformists]."[98]

The Non-Muslim Conundrum

Notwithstanding the various attempts by UMNO and PAS to explicate their respective conceptualizations of how Islam should serve as an ordering principle for national affairs, it should be clear by now that the challenge for both has consistently been how to balance this objective with the concerns of an increasingly apprehensive non-Muslim minority.

During its immediate postindependence years, the political commissars of postcolonial Malaysia made the management of interethnic and inter-religious ties key priorities for the new administration. Underlying the crafting of a social compact to that end was the belief on the part of the UMNO-led ruling government that peaceful coexistence between ethnic groups should be premised on the recognition of the special rights of the *bumiputras* ("sons of the soil"), a term that refers to Malays and indigenous peoples.[99] On the matter of religion, though, the conservative Malay elite of UMNO who inherited the colonial government were cautious about employing it as a catalyst for the mass political mobilization of the Malays, and a secular approach to politics was generally favored, which led to the breakaway of the party's religious wing and the formation of PAS. In May 1958, in response to legislative council member Yahya bin Haji Wan Mohamed's statement that "we have been officially recognized as an Islamic state," Tunku Abdul Rahman replied, "I would like to make it clear that this country is not an Islamic State as it is generally understood; we merely provide that Islam shall be the official religion of the State."[100] On the role of Islam in affairs of state, the consensus of the UMNO-led Alliance Party, predecessor of the current *Barisan Nasional* government, was that "the intention in making Islam the official religion of the Federation was primarily for ceremonial purposes, for instance to enable prayers to be offered in the Islamic way on official occasions such as the installation of the *Yang di-Pertuan Agong* [King of Malaysia], Merdeka Day [Independence Day], and similar occasions."[101]

The government's reliance on the political support of the Malay majority and its dependence on the economic clout, enterprise, and labor of the Chinese and Indian minorities demanded that the chosen model of national development balance the respective interests of all the communities involved. The negotiation that followed resulted in several clauses being added to the Malaysian constitution to assuage both camps. Hence, for instance, Article 153 guaranteed special rights to the Malays in education, business, and public service, and guaranteed further that these rights were to be safeguarded by the *Yang di-Pertuan Agong*, while Article 11 pledged that all Malaysians, including Muslims, would enjoy religious freedom. Not long after it was designed, however, this postindependence social compact came under significant strain as Malay-Muslim discontent over the economic and political influence of the Chinese minority deepened. Simmering beneath the surface for the first decade of independence, this discontent eventually spilled over on 13 May 1969, when racial riots broke out.[102]

The May 1969 riots sparked a chain of events that, combined with other factors, gradually set Malaysia down a path to Islamization. Given that the riots were traced to Malay-Muslim unhappiness toward their socioeconomic position, the NEP (New Economic Policy) was formulated to enshrine affirmative-action policies for the *bumiputra*, of whom the Malays were the majority. While seemingly egalitarian in theory, the NEP's declared objective of eradicating poverty and its linkage of ethnicity with economic function were in fact rooted in the UMNO-led government's desire to accord greater economic and political privilege to the Malay community. By this token, the NEP further polarized Malaysian society along ethnoreligious lines. This effect was certainly apparent to non-Muslims, who saw that the guarantees of Malay special rights contained in the constitution and the NEP cemented the concept of *Ketuanan*

Melayu (Malay supremacy) and effectively relegated non-Muslims to the status of second-class citizens. The Seditions Act was introduced in 1970 to further marginalize non-Muslim interests by criminalizing public questioning of the special rights of Malay-Muslims under the Malaysian constitution. In this way, the stage for Islamization had effectively been set, for with the increased salience of Islam to Malay identity and politics in the 1980s, the culture of affirmative action helped to create a potentially combustible situation in which religion easily replaced ethnicity as the catalyst for the further polarization of Malaysian society and marginalization of Malaysians of minority faiths.

The intensification of Islamist discourse and praxis in Malaysia and the changing boundaries of its political terrain wrought by the amplification of the Islamic state debate between UMNO and PAS indicated a major shift in the traditional role of Islam in Malaysian politics. These changes have predictably been met with much consternation in the non-Muslim community. This mood was succinctly captured in the following observation: "The Islamization race which began in earnest in the 1980s and 1990s was unique in its apparent disregard for alternative viewpoints and beliefs. Thus it came to pass that the whole Islamization project has managed to sideline the sensitivities and reservations of the non-Muslims in the country."[103]

Since PAS came to power in Kelantan in 1990, the specter of Islamization in the form of strict Islamic legislation, particularly *hudud*, heightened the suspicions of Malaysia's non-Muslim minorities and compromised attempts at tactical cooperation with non-Muslim opposition parties, primarily the DAP. These concerns were fueled by pronouncements, purportedly made by party leaders, that Islamic law would cover all residents of Kelantan, "regardless of religious or ethnic origin."[104] In addition, even as PAS found itself mired in heated debates over the constitutionality of its formulation of *hudud* and *qisas* policies at the level of high discursive politics, on the ground in Kelantan and Terengganu the party was enacting general Islamic laws pertinent to everyday life, to which non-Muslims residing under PAS jurisdiction were purportedly held. These included the introduction of gender segregation in public places, restrictions on live entertainment, bans on gambling, and in some instances the enforcement of the Muslim headdress upon non-Muslim students attending state schools. Concomitantly, PAS's electoral success in 1999 and its corresponding political aspirations to govern the country only served to strengthen non-Muslim apprehension and placed severe stress on the party's attempt to project a more moderate image.

In fairness, there is probably some disconnect between the opinions of PAS held by non-Muslims outside Kelantan and those of non-Muslims actually residing under the PAS administration in Kelantan. PAS leaders have tried to assuage non-Muslim fear of the party's Islamist agenda, and the reformists have been especially quick to play down the categorical nature of the Islamic state. For instance, Nasharuddin Mat Isa has insisted on several occasions that

PAS will not unilaterally establish a theocratic state, because "responsibility of leadership must be derived from a mandate through consent of citizens."[105] Furthermore, when questioned by the media, party leaders have been quick to deny that the Islamic law they envisage for their vision of Islamic government will apply to non-Muslims.

Though these gestures were certainly more than mere window dressing, at a deeper level the party's wavering between its Islamic state ambitions on the one hand and its egalitarian principles on the other speaks to the difficult relationship that PAS has long had with Malaysia's non-Muslim population, to say nothing of possible inherent inconsistencies within Islamic thought in the party itself. Notably, party leadership continues to labor over the rudimentary question of having non-Muslims as PAS members. The party has created several Kelab Penyokong PAS (PAS Supporters' Clubs), and, rather peculiarly, has openly discussed the possibility of non-Muslims contesting elections on PAS tickets without necessarily being official members. PAS has also attempted to build a "multicultural" mosque in Kelantan to reflect the variety of influences on Malaysia's Islamic culture.[106] Still, courting non-Muslims remains a challenging task for the party, as indicated by the negligible membership of their supporters' clubs.[107] Even PAS's non-Muslim sympathizers have felt the need to alert the party leadership to the realities confronting them in terms of winning non-Muslim support and endorsement. Such was the subtext of Kelab Penyokong PAS chairman Hu Pang Chua's public call for the party's leadership to "explain their vision for Islam in Malaysia" clearly to Malaysia's ethnic and religious minorities in a way that does not threaten to marginalize them.[108]

Underlying this constraint is the fact that the party's deliberation on matters pertaining to non-Muslim membership in PAS suffers from an epistemological paradox. PAS leaders would do well to ask themselves what conceivable impetus would drive non-Muslims to join or support PAS. Save for the occasional rant against UMNO's pro-Malay bias, which PAS leaders criticize as ass-abiyah (tribalism), the party has offered little in the way of alternative policies or concessions that meet the immediate needs of non-Muslims. When PAS was in control of the state legislatures in Terengganu and Kelantan, it did overturn some rather dogmatic UMNO policies, which endeared the party to some segments of the non-Muslim community in these states. In the larger scheme of things, however, the party's continued inability to reconcile its unstinting pursuit of the Islamic state objective in national politics with non-Muslim concerns continues to overshadow any conciliatory gestures it might devise. The fact that the party's Islamic State Document was conspicuously thin on information regarding where non-Muslims stand in an Islamic state, or how their rights and interests would be protected or advanced under PAS leadership, will only further deepen this apprehension.

Circumstances for UMNO are no less somber. Non-Muslims are today more conscious than ever of issues such as freedom of religious worship and expression, their position within the fabric of Malaysian society, and the nature of governance in Malaysia. In the context of the rise of Islamization in Malaysia, it is the question of marginalization that lies at the heart of non-Muslim apprehension regarding these trends. By this token, the recent slew of government policies and statements highlighted in the previous chapter, not to mention the continuation of moral policing by state religious authorities that have on occasion penalized non-Muslims as well, has served only to frustrate religious minorities. This sense of marginalization and incapacity on the part of Malaysians of minority faiths has also been carried over into parliamentary debates. For example, on 11 July 2005 Jerai member of Parliament Badruddin bin Amiruldin declared in the *Dewan Rakyat* House of Parliament that "Malaysia ini negara Islam" (Malaysia is an Islamic state), and in animated fashion warned non-Muslim detractors, "You tidak suka, you keluar dari Malaysia!" (You don't like it, you get out of Malaysia!) Despite protestations from non-Muslim MPs from both the ruling coalition and the opposition, Badruddin did not retract his statement, and his provocation went unpunished. Indeed, the fact that a subsequent motion to refer him to the House Committee of Privileges was later rejected by majority vote made the episode all the more galling for non-Muslims.[109]

Pressures of expediency led the non-Muslim parties of the *Barisan* coalition to publicly support Mahathir's September 29 Islamic state declaration. Some rationalized that it was by far the more desirable Islamic "option" when compared to the PAS version of an Islamic state.[110] This move to rally behind UMNO and Mahathir barely veiled the concern that these groups had for the intensification of Islamist discourse. This concern led to a number of closed-door dialogue sessions with members of the UMNO religious elite as well as Muslim and non-Muslim NGOs to discuss the full spectrum of implications for Malaysia's pluralistic society that might flow from Mahathir's announcement. Unlike *Barisan* component parties, the non-Muslim opposition was predictably more impassioned in their rejoinder to UMNO. The DAP was particularly swift in its response, launching a "say no to 929" public awareness campaign in response to the declaration and arguing that Mahathir had fundamentally contravened the 1957 Merdeka constitution, the Alliance "Social Contract," and the 1963 Malaysia Agreement.[111]

The tension within the *Barisan* over the government's apparent endorsement of restrictive policies toward non-Muslims escalated when, in response to apostasy cases (particularly the cases of Lina Joy and Moorthy Maniam, discussed earlier), nine non-Muslim cabinet ministers broke tradition and presented a memorandum to Prime Minister Abdullah Badawi calling for a review of Article 121 (1A) of the federal constitution, which states that civil courts shall have no jurisdiction with respect to any matter within the jurisdiction of *shari'a* courts. This unprecedented act followed protests by the religious and legal bureaus of the Malaysian Chinese Association (MCA). While the memorandum was promptly withdrawn after Abdullah voiced displeasure at this move in a private meeting with five of the nine ministers, it was an extraordinary (and very public) indication of rifts within the government coalition over a matter of religion.[112]

The fallout from the decisions on these recent apostasy cases—where the federal court ruled that it had no jurisdiction over the rights of Muslims to leave their faith and that jurisdiction over such matters lay with the *shari'a* court— was further aggravated by yet another claim by a senior statesman, Deputy Prime Minister Najib Tun Razak, that Malaysia is an "Islamic state." On 17 July 2007, Najib revived Mahathir's controversial comments by suggesting on the occasion of the International Conference on the Role of Islamic States in a Globalized World, organized by IKIM, that Malaysia was an Islamic state and was not a "secular nation" according to the Western definition of "secular," because Malaysia's governance was based on Islamic principles.[113]

Najib's remarks provoked another cycle of heated responses from a range of civil society groups and political parties. So controversial were Najib's remarks that the MCA, smarting from earlier accusations of impotence in the wake of UMNO's unrelenting assertion of Islamist principles and Mahathir's own announcement, ventured a rare public refutation of UMNO's political statement that Malaysia was an Islamic state. MCA secretary-general Ong Ka Chuan pointed out that according to the Reid Commission of 1957, the Cobbold Commission of 1963, and a Supreme Court precedent from 1988, "a secular state is the foundation of the formation of Malaya and this consensus was made by our forefathers."[114] Ong's remarks elicited a stern rebuke from UMNO Youth chief Hishammuddin Hussein, who warned MCA not to make statements about Malaysia being a secular state, to which MCA Youth responded with a broadside of its own that UMNO leaders should not be making statements about Malaysia being an Islamic state without prior consultations with its coalition allies.[115] Often criticized by the Chinese electorate for excessive obeisance to UMNO, and still smarting from attacks against its earlier attempts to "justify" Mahathir's Islamic state announcement, MCA's stand indicated the tense nature of relations within the *Barisan* coalition under the weight of Islamization. Nonetheless, the party was still lambasted by cynical critics who alleged that such public refute of the actions of UMNO was too little, too late.[116]

The deputy prime minister's remarks also elicited strong responses from non-Muslim civil society groups. Bishop Paul Tan, chairman of the Christian Federation of Malaysia, issued a press statement claiming that the use of the term "Islamic state" is unacceptable to Malaysians of minority faiths for three reasons. First, the term is not used in the federal constitution; second, Malaysia's "founding fathers" never intended the country to be an Islamic state; third, non-Muslim coalition parties that make up the ruling government never consented to, nor officially endorsed, the term "Islamic state" to describe the country.[117] Tan appealed to Najib to retract his remarks and to refrain from undermining the founding fathers' supposed agreement on the secular nature of the country.[118] A. Vaithilingam, president of the Malaysian Consultative Council for Buddhism, Christianity, Hinduism, and Sikhism (MCCBCHS), also released a press statement on the same day rejecting Najib's claims. He stated:

> The MCCBCHS is firmly of the view that Malaysia remains a secular country as it was intended to be from Merdeka. . . . We urge the government, the judiciary and all Malaysians to respect the social contract which was formulated in 1957 and reaffirmed in 1963 and object most strongly to attempts by the government and the judiciary to change the status quo surreptitiously, thereby jeopardizing the democratic freedoms of all Malaysians.[119]

The Council of Churches of Malaysia interpreted Najib's claim as a bid to provoke racial tension. It issued a statement saying, "We appeal to the government in general and to the Deputy Prime Minister in particular, to refrain from using 'Islamic state' as an official description of the country to stir up racial tension."[120] Opposition political parties also weighed in with their criticisms. Anwar Ibrahim accused Najib of making a statement "calculated for political mileage."[121] Despite a directive issued by the Home Ministry for all mainstream media to stop publishing further comments on Najib's "Islamic state" remarks, the DAP organized a forum titled "No Debate on Islamic State?" on 25 July 2007 for the purpose of discussing constitutional rights and religious freedoms.[122]

Najib's declaration sharpened sensitivities, given that it followed in the wake of a spike in reports of Hindu temples, Taoist shrines, and Christian churches being allegedly demolished by the Malaysian authorities. Noticeably, the mainstream national press has been silent on these issues, and it has been the alternative media on the Internet, such as www.Malaysiakini.com, www.mt.m2day.org, www.malaysia.net, and *Harakah*, that have been reporting these occurrences. In July 2006, *Asia Times*, a Hong Kong–based Internet-only news and commentary publication, reported a series of temple demolitions in Malaysia.[123] It noted the demolishment of the Hindu Malaimel Sri Selva Kaliamman Temple, which was situated in Kuala Lumpur and was more than a century old, by Malaysian authorities despite angry protests.[124] Similar fates befell temples such as the Kuil Shri Maha Mariamman Temple, built in Selangor circa 1899, and the sixty-five-year-old Shri Ayyanar Sathiswary Temple.[125] The report noted that the Malaysian government justified the demolition of these temples as the removal of "illegal structures" that were not properly registered.[126] This contrasted starkly with the situation in Kelantan, where the opposition PAS government had provided a one-acre plot of prime land in Kota Bharu for the rebuilding of the Sri Maha Mariamman Temple. The perception of a systemic government-endorsed plan of "temple cleansing" in Malaysia has led the Hindu Rights Action Force, a conglomeration of thirty Hindu groups, to write a petition to Prime Minister Abdullah Badawi.[127] The petition, and a concomitant request for a meeting with Abdullah, was rejected.

The activism of non-Muslim political parties and civil society groups in response to these perceived contraventions of their rights as minorities elicited an equally passionate reaction from Muslim organizations, PAS, and even the Abdullah administration. A recurrent target of Muslim protests was the Article 11 Coalition. This initiative was led by the Malaysian Bar Council and "Article 11," a consortium of fourteen NGOs that sought to "reaffirm the supremacy of the constitution" and defend fundamental rights for all Malaysians "regardless of religion, race, descent, place of birth or gender."[128] This consortium included not only non-Muslim groups but also Muslim organizations of a discernibly moderate nature that defended freedom of religion and opposed the clampdown by state religious authorities on fringe Islamic groups, such as the Sky Kingdom cult, which preached the synthesis of Islam with other religions.[129] A public forum to address the issue of religious freedom organized by the Article 11 Coalition and human rights group *Aliran*, scheduled to be held on 11 May 2006, was stopped by police after a demonstration by two hundred protestors purporting to "defend the sanctity of Islam."

Similar forums in June and July were also met with angry public protests, most likely orchestrated by Islamist groups. The Article 11 Coalition was further condemned as "enemies of Islam" by PAS, which supported the protest. At the party's Muktamar in 2006, PAS Youth submitted resolutions for the party's leadership to approach the Council of Rulers, which oversees Islamic affairs in Malaysia, to discuss actions that could be taken against "those quarters that seek to challenge the authority of Islam and the *shari'a* courts in the country."[130] The Muslim NGO coalition, PEMBELA, responded with its own signature campaign for a memorandum to the prime minister that categorically opposed the Article 11 Coalition and called upon the Abdullah administration to defend the special place of Islam in the federal constitution.[131] Another anti–Article 11 Muslim coalition, the Anti-Interfaith Commission Body, issued a press statement condemning the coalition as "an enemy of Allah" and warned of "bigger risks" in the future.[132]

For the non-Muslim cause, the response from the incumbent Abdullah government inspired little confidence. In response to increasingly heated debates, the Abdullah administration imposed a moratorium on media discussions on Article 11 on the grounds of sensitivity. In a veiled threat, the prime minister further warned the Article 11 Coalition not to "force the government to take action," thereby implying the government's tacit endorsement of PEMBELA's position that the Article 11 Coalition was not merely challenging Muslim interpretations of the law and constitution but was challenging Islam itself.[133] This response essentially carried over from the government's reluctance to support the formation of an interfaith commission for the same reason. Indicative of the volatility of the state of affairs, death threats were made against Malik Imtiaz Sarwar, a human rights lawyer and Article 11 activist, for representing Lina Joy and supporting the Article 11 Coalition. While these death threats were condemned by non-Muslim NGOs as well as major Muslim civil society groups, they demonstrate the alarming implications that flow from the intensification of discourse over the issue of Islamic law and non-Muslim rights.

Even while debates rage as the Islamization bandwagon rolls on in Malaysia, it is in the wake of intensified UMNO-PAS competition to "out-Islam" each other, the deepening of religious conservatism in Malaysian society in general, and the constriction of religiopolitical space in Malaysia that the emergence and assertion of alternative spaces and perspectives on how Islam can and should order Malaysian politics and society has taken on greater urgency over the past decade. It is to this question of alternative voices and how they specifically sought to either shape or inflect the discourses and debates on Islamism and Islamization that the book now turns.

4

"Popular" Political Islam

Representations and Discourses

It is clear that the 1980s were a major watershed for Malaysia insofar as the invigoration of the Islamic factor in mainstream politics and the bureaucratization of Islam are concerned. The changing complexion of PAS and the Mahathir administration's systematic Islamization of the Malaysian administrative apparatus catapulted social consciousness and political discourse to a new, more Islamic plane. The intensification of UMNO–PAS competition by referencing credibility and legitimacy to Islam was an immediate outcome of this process; but a parallel Islamic discourse rooted in an increasingly vibrant civil society sphere that encompassed NGOs as well as alternative expressions of Islamic consciousness, namely alternative media sources beyond the mainstream government-controlled outlets, and the Internet, also emerged to add to the complexion of Malaysian politics. Concomitantly, even as the heavily contested politics of UMNO and PAS began to converge, a parallel form of civic activism was emerging, which coalesced around not only political parties but also professional organizations, civil society organizations, educational institutions, and religious institutions. This parallel discourse aimed to carve out an expansion of the discursive terrain of politics. Particularly significant here are the religiously inspired components of this civic activism, both Islamic and non-Islamic, and their contribution to the shaping of Islamist narratives and Islamization trends in Malaysia.

In their groundbreaking research on civil society groups in Malaysia, Weiss and Saliha have observed that such groups "began with more of a focus on service delivery, then evolved toward issue advocacy."[1] Events have since confirmed the conclusions of scholars who argued for the importance of civil society organizations and movements in the (democratic) political process, as Malaysia witnessed the proliferation of organizations that contributed to the process of negotiating and refining the Islam agenda.[2] As a result, what materialized in Malaysia was an increasingly vibrant civil society that has sought to engage and affect the identity and structure of the Malaysian state in relation to the role of Islam. Components of this civil society strive to either contest or supplement the claims of mainstream Islamist political parties to speak for Islam on a range of issues.

A cursory survey indicates that NGO activism in Malaysia has usually peaked during periods of major social upheaval that occurred on an otherwise comparatively tranquil sociocultural landscape. Hence, just as the emergence of the *dakwah* phenomenon of the early 1970s spawned a number of Islamist NGOs such as ABIM and *Al Arqam*, the *Reformasi* movement of the late 1990s precipitated the emergence of a new generation of civil society groups such as *Jemaah Islah Malaysia* (JIM) and Sisters in Islam (SIS) and the rejuvenation of more established groups. In recent years, the issues of apostasy, religious freedom, and the sanctity of the *shari'a* have sparked yet another round of NGO political and discursive activism that has challenged the hegemony of the state as well as the policies of the opposition PAS. Muslim and non-Muslim groups spanning the political spectrum have weighed in on the discourse and debate on Islamization in Malaysia. In their own way, these groups speak to, for, and against the positions and policies of both UMNO and PAS, at times forcing these mainstream parties to negotiate their politics and recalibrate their narratives. Describing the impact of these (relatively) new actors on the Malaysian political scene, Clive Kessler observed:

> These INGOs [Islamic NGOs] and the Islamic civil society that they generate and sustain have not simply emerged as a rival or parallel form of "parapolitical activity" but have now become the dominant force in Malaysian public life, in the life of "active citizenship" such as it manages, and is permitted, to thrive in Malaysia in its fiftieth post-*merdeka* year. The impetus that they express projects itself within both UMNO and PAS, straddles the old UMNO/PAS ideological divide, and is beginning to set important policy and political terms to both the main Malay-backed parties.[3]

By this token, the impact of the rise of Islamic NGOs and civil society movements is a phenomenon that warrants much closer attention than extant literature has given it in the study of Muslim politics in Malaysia, particularly in terms of its relation to mainstream political issues and party politics.

Angkatan Belia Islam Malaysia (Malaysian Islamic Youth Movement, or ABIM)

The most prominent, influential, and widely studied Islamist civil society movement in Malaysia, arguably the archetype for later movements, is ABIM. Formed in August 1971, ABIM was established around major tertiary student organizations such as *Persatuan Bahasa Melayu Universiti Malaya* (University of Malaya Malay Language Society) and *Persatuan Kebangsaan Pelajar-Pelajar Islam Malaysia* (National Union of Malaysian Muslim Students), and it is possibly the largest and most organized civil society movement in Malaysia. The arrival of ABIM on the Malaysian scene was profoundly significant, as it signaled the beginnings of a shift in the constellation of Malay-Muslim politics. Given its urban base and vocal presence in tertiary education institutions, mostly among students pursuing secular education, ABIM challenged the traditional bastions of Malay-Muslim leadership that had revolved around *ulama* and *tok guru*, long seen as leaders of rural communities.

Under the charismatic leadership of Anwar Ibrahim and inspired by the intellectual works of the Pakistani Islamist scholar Maulana Abu Ala Mawdudi, ABIM propounded a vision of postcolonial Islamic society that was grounded on strict interpretations of the Qur'an and *hadith* but was nevertheless also reconcilable with modernity as exemplified by the pursuit of scientific and technological progress. As Saliha Hassan observed, "among INGOs, ABIM's discourse was the loudest and best informed. The group debated, explained and challenged the state on key issues such as the character of an Islamic state and Islamic leadership, Islamic education and the Islamic way of life, and Malaysia's involvement in international politics as part of the global Muslim brotherhood."[4] ABIM laid claim to an Ikhwani pedigree as it shared in the modernist agendas of established anticolonial transnational Islamist movements such as the Pakistan-based *Jamaat-e-Islami* and the *Ikhwanul Muslimim*, both of which were stridently opposed to colonialism and secular nationalism.[5]

Throughout the 1970s, ABIM proved immensely popular among the educated Malay-Muslim population, which found itself caught up in the throes of the global Islamic revival, and the movement grew rapidly, with branches sprouting across Malaysia.[6] While ABIM's popularity is often attributed to Anwar, it should be recalled that his compatriots in leadership at that time were Fadzil Noor and Abdul Hadi Awang, both eventual presidents of PAS who held their own in terms of influence and gravitas. As an Islamist civil society organization, ABIM cut its teeth as a vehement critic of the ruling government. In particular, ABIM leaders regularly questioned the religiosity of UMNO and its leaders, routinely taking them to task for not being "Islamic enough" in their formulation and implementation of national policies. Yet in a demonstration of its nonpartisan credentials, ABIM was equally critical of PAS at times, especially when PAS made the fateful decision to join the ruling coalition in 1974. The most dramatic and high-profile example of ABIM's political activism took place in 1974, when Anwar Ibrahim and card-carrying activists such as Kamarulzaman Yaacob, Syed Husin Ali, Ibrahim Ali, Kamal Selamat, and Adi Satria were imprisoned under the ISA for leading demonstrations in support of poor Malay farmers in Baling, Kedah, who were being forced off their land by state authorities with minimal compensation.[7]

Despite an initial reluctance to engage in partisan politics, ABIM was viewed by both Muslim parties as a valuable ally by virtue of its popularity and influence. Anwar's credentials as an Islamist, nationalist, and socialist, not to mention his charisma, were particularly appealing to PAS. This led to efforts on the part of the Islamist opposition to court ABIM after Anwar's release from detention in 1975, as prospects of a formidable ABIM-PAS alliance loomed on the horizon of Malay-Muslim politics. In fact, ABIM had by then become a place of refuge for numerous members of PAS disillusioned with the party's decision to join the coalition government in the mid-1970s. When PAS subsequently left the coalition, ABIM openly campaigned for the Islamist opposition in the 1978 general election. While Anwar himself resisted PAS overtures, several of his contemporaries, primarily Fadzil Noor, Abdul Hadi Awang, Syed Ibrahim, and Nakhaie Ahmad, found themselves gravitating toward opposition politics. They soon swelled the ranks of PAS, and many of them ran in the 1978 general election on a PAS ticket.

Despite the fact that ABIM and PAS saw eye to eye on a number of matters, thereby suggesting a natural congruence between the two organizations, fundamental differences surfaced in 1982 when the *ulama*-led Islamic state agenda of the reformed PAS conflicted with the "bottom-up" transformation of the sociopolitical system of Malaysia envisaged by ABIM, whose leaders were mostly educated in secular institutions. While ABIM was committed to the formation of an Islamic state in Malaysia, this objective was seen more as a long-term one than something to be realized in the immediate future.[8] ABIM leaders viewed the overt focus on the Islamic state as an unnecessary distraction, given that it was not an immediate priority for the educated Malay middle class, ABIM's largest constituency.[9]

As ABIM activism was anchored by the leadership of Anwar, Fadzil, and Abdul Hadi, so the departure of this triumvirate to UMNO and PAS sparked an exodus of more radical (by which is meant politicized) elements in the movement. This outcome dulled ABIM's political edges, forcing a retreat into political quietism.[10] Under the leadership of a succession of moderate centrist leaders such as Sidek Fadzil, ABIM's activities were largely confined to *usrah* (discussion groups) and forums that addressed issues such as human rights, Islamic values, and democracy, but in a manner that lacked the political activism that had defined the movement's earlier incarnation. While the occasional demonstration was staged, they were of a much smaller scale compared to the height of ABIM activism in the 1970s and were usually confined to campus issues. Controversial members who espoused potentially radical agendas (e.g., Ahmad Lutfi Othman) were expelled from the movement. The loss of ABIM's political edge led former president Ahmad Azzam to say that "our [ABIM's] biggest problem is trying to rekindle a sense of purpose and idealism amongst the young. After two generations of struggle, the third generation now seems indifferent and complacent. They want the easy way out to get to the top without having to struggle."[11]

This self-criticism would prove portentous of a new phase of Islamist activism for ABIM. The movement was rejuvenated when it participated in the national reform movement, known as *Reformasi*, in protest against the government's abuse of power by incarcerating its former leader, Anwar Ibrahim. ABIM was also instrumental in the formation of *Keadilan*, the political party that sprang from this reform movement, furnishing it with leaders and activists.[12] As a consequence of this reinvigoration, several ABIM leaders and Anwar loyalists were detained under the ISA for various periods at the height of the *Reformasi* protests against the government in the late 1990s. These included then-president Ahmad Azzam Abdul Rahman, deputies Abdul Halim Ismail and Mukhtar Redhuan, and secretary general Shaharuddin Baharuddin.

The resurgence of ABIM extended to its increasingly vocal defense of Malay-Muslim primacy in the wake of the activism of non-Muslim groups that sought to question the supremacy of Islam in Malaysia's legal and political constellations, despite a senior ABIM member's opinion that "Islam can coexist with any religion—that is the principle behind the faith. We concentrate on strengthening the community of Muslims. This doesn't mean that we simultaneously want to weaken others; we want to contribute to better understanding, but not to the secularization of the system."[13] ABIM has returned to the forefront of Malaysia's alternative NGO politics, this time not in the defense of the Malay language or identity, but of Islam; and to that end it has also fostered cooperation between Islamic NGOs across the ideological spectrum.

Pertubuhan-Pertubuhan Pembela Islam (Defenders of Islam, or PEMBELA)

On 16 July 2006, in the wake of the controversial apostasy case revolving around Lina Joy, ABIM spearheaded the formation of PEMBELA, a coalition group comprising seventy Islamic NGOs that consisted mostly of professionals, students, and Islamic clerics. According to statements that accompanied its formation, PEMBELA was formed to address the issue of apostasy among Muslims in Malaysia by defending the Islamic faith and its status as the official religion of Malaysia from legal challenges posed by apostate Muslims and non-Muslims. Illustrating the salience of this issue to Muslims in Malaysia in general, the membership of PEMBELA came from groups as diverse as ABIM, the Malaysian *Shari'a* Lawyers Association, the Muslim Professional Forum, *Jemaah Islah Malaysia, Peguam Pembela Islam, Wadah Percedasan Umat, Teras Pengupayaan Melayu*, and MUAFAKAT. As alluded to above, the formation of PEMBELA was a response to the questioning and challenging of the authority of the *shari'a* courts, and this new umbrella Islamist organization was intended to bring together a wide range of interest groups to defend the primacy of Islam.

In the wake of a number of legal cases challenging the rulings of the *shari'a* courts, PEMBELA sought to repel what it perceived as a "liberal tide sweeping the judiciary and viewed as a threat to Islam's position in the country."[14] PEMBELA activism involved a series of public forums on the need for Muslims to "defend their faith," and the group mobilized its network of *ulama* and religious experts to campaign against the use of civil courts by Muslims intent on denouncing Islam by being declared apostates. A group of lawyers spun off from PEMBELA to form "Lawyers in Defense of Islam," a movement dedicated to defending Islam from what it perceived as a series of legal attacks against the religion. Headed by a former president of the Bar, Zainur Zakaria, this movement said its main priority was to combat misconceptions of the status of Islam arising from recent court cases concerning apostasy and conversion to Islam.[15]

To formalize its advocacy work, PEMBELA has established a secretariat, developed an official Web site, and drafted petitions and statements on the question of apostasy. One of the first steps taken by PEMBELA immediately after its formation was a signature campaign against the activities of Muslim and non-Muslim groups that attempted to elevate Article 11 of the Malaysian constitution above Article 121 1(A), which codified the independence of *shari'a* courts from civil court interference in matters pertaining to religion. Second, seminars and forums focusing on *shari'a* have also been organized by PEMBELA in collaboration with the Malaysian Ulama Association with the aim of drawing attention to the need for Muslims to defend the Islamic faith in Malaysia.

While PEMBELA's strident position on apostasy could be deemed fundamentalist in certain respects, it is nevertheless important to note that the organization has at times also exercised fairly considerable restraint during heated public debates on issues touching race and religion, despite the fact that the adoption of a more radical position offered the prospect of increased popular support. For instance, while the organization has agitated against the actions of Lina Joy and clearly stands in opposition to the application of Article 11 to Muslims seeking to leave the religion, PEMBELA has also issued statements condemning intimidation and death threats made by cantankerous elements against a senior member of Lina Joy's legal team. Underlying this has been the leadership's position, as articulated by ABIM president and chairman of PEMBELA Yusri Mohamad, that "PEMBELA is willing to work together with all parties to hold briefing sessions and dialogues, including with non-Muslims and the government leaders so as to handle the apostasy issue and to strengthen the status of Islam in Malaysia."[16] Nevertheless, non-Muslim suspicions toward vocal and fundamentalist Muslim organizations such as PEMBELA continue to linger.

Persatuan Ulama Malaysia (Ulama Association of Malaysia, or PUM)

PUM was formed on 8 April 1972 at the Al-Malik Faisal Hall (on the grounds of the current International Islamic University) and was an outgrowth of *ulama* lobbying during the Islamic Economics Congress that year.[17] As a result of initial discussions between leading Malaysian *ulama*, it was agreed that the late Tan Sri Ahmad Ibrahim would become an advisor to PUM, the late Haji Nik Muhd Muhyiddin Haji Musa would be the president, and Dr. Mohd Zin Othman would be his deputy. Other prominent *ulama* who were part of PUM were Nakhaie Ahmad and Ghazali Abdullah. Aside from these heavyweight religious scholars, a number of whom were closely associated with UMNO, other leading figures involved in PUM included the late Fadzil Noor, Harun Din, Abdul Hamid Othman, and Taib Azamuddin. These leaders would subsequently move into mainstream politics as prominent *ulama* leaders in both UMNO and PAS.

Over the years, PUM has increasingly been identified with PAS, and the organization has gravitated into the orbit of the Islamist opposition on a number of issues. Many of the current leaders in PAS, such as Ahmad Awang and Ghani Shamsuddin, were involved in PUM. The current chairman of PUM, Haji Mohammad Saleh, while not a member of PAS, is nevertheless known to sympathize with the struggle and agenda of the Islamist opposition (his brother is actively involved in PAS). In terms of the objectives of PUM, Ghani, a prominent leader in PAS, has explained that PUM was formed to address a concern that *ulama* in the government service are often expected to subscribe to and endorse government positions. The formation of the association "is a mechanism to allow the *ulama* to voice their concern and disagreement without having to fear government prosecution."[18]

In 2002, PUM was at the forefront of attacks on several Malaysian writers and public intellectuals, including SIS executive director Zainah Anwar; academics Farish Noor, Kassim Ahmad, and Patricia Martinez; newspaper columnist Akbar Ali; and lawyer Malik Imtiaz Sarwar.[19] PUM *ulama* claimed that these individuals had written articles that "insulted" Islam, the Prophet Muhammad, and the institution of the *ulama*, and that legal action should thus be taken against them. Following this, PUM submitted a memorandum to the Council of Rulers questioning the authority of these scholars and activists to interpret the Qur'an and comment on the religion; the memorandum called for them to be prosecuted for their actions. To further instigate action against these individuals, PUM stirred public sentiments by releasing publicity material that roundly criticized them. They also released a publication on the issue to influence the Muslim public against these differing voices.[20] The pressure exerted by PUM succeeded in these activists and public intellectuals being effectively muzzled, if only for a time, when local newspapers stopped publishing their writings.[21] In an apparent endorsement of PUM's activism in "safeguarding" Islam, Zainuddin Maidin, parliamentary secretary of the Information Ministry, provocatively suggested that PUM's role should be to "question dubious decress or *fatwa* issued by so-called scholars and not restrict itself to writers who allegedly denigrate Islam, the Qur'an, and *hadith*."[22]

On other occasions, PUM has stood at the forefront of debates over legalistic interpretations of Islam. In the 1997 beauty pageant issue, PUM supported the Selangor religious authorities' arrest of Malay-Muslim contestants, and it supported the *Jabatan Agama Wilayah Persekutuan* (JAWI) arrests of Muslims at a night spot in February 2005. PUM was also vocal in its opposition to American military action in Afghanistan, arguing vehemently that it was a Judeo-Christian war against Islam and Muslims.[23] On other occasions, though, PUM has also sought to brandish reformist credentials. PUM actively supported the *Reformasi* movement that challenged the mistreatment of Anwar Ibrahim by the Malaysian government. This support was likely to have been as much a function of the close relationship that PUM leaders Ahmad Awang and Ghani Shamsuddin had with Anwar as of identification with a broader agenda of political change.

Jemaah Islah Malaysia (Malaysia Islamic Reform Society, or JIM)

JIM was officially formed on 27 July 1990 as an Islamic NGO. At present, the organization has a membership of 8,000, mostly professionals. It has an extensive national presence, with fourteen state and fifty-four provincial branches across Malaysia.[24] Propelled by its official mission of "Together Islam, Building Community," JIM has continued to expand its influence and presence through a range of welfare activities and *dakwah* institutes affiliated to it.[25] The leadership of JIM sees its calling as the preservation of Islamic principles as the pillars of Malaysia's development plan of Vision 2020.[26]

Being one of the larger and more organized Islamic NGOs in Malaysia, JIM is involved in a wide spectrum of advocacy activities. These range from educational and outreach programs for youth, women, and the poor to issuing statements reinforcing Islam's status as the official religion of the country.

Beyond local issues, JIM also actively publishes and comments on develop-ments in the broader Muslim world.

JIM projects itself as a professional, middle-class Muslim organization aspiring to a "moderate" and "progressive" application of Islam in the country, yet it also espouses views that uphold the Islamic state as the ultimate objective of all Muslim social-political activism and advocacy. This is made clear in its charter, which makes explicit reference to the Islamic state. This apparent di-chotomy between conservatism and modernism in the organization finds fur-ther expression in JIM's position on gender issues. Though JIM promotes the role of women in leadership, it also asserts that in the private sphere women are subordinate to men and require consent from male members of their fam-ily before they can actively participate in the public sphere. JIM's position on women's issues is all the more striking considering the size of its women's wing, which purportedly forms a majority of total membership in the organiza-tion and which has been noticeably proactive and vocal in articulating and de-fending the cause of women in Malaysia, albeit from an Islamic perspective.

Like most NGOs in Malaysia, JIM has on occasion articulated very resolute positions on political issues that dovetail with its causes. As part of its reform agenda, JIM threw its weight behind PAS in the formation of the Malaysian People's Movement for Justice in the buildup to the 1999 general election.[27] Today, it continues to actively participate in party politics in order to advance its Islamic agenda by explicitly aligning itself with the Anwar-inspired *Parti Keadilan Rakyat*.[28] JIM has also come forward to support PEMBELA against the perceived rising tide of apostasy in Malaysia. To that end, JIM activists have proven swift and resolute defenders of the status of Islam in Malaysia. For instance, JIM assailed the proposal for extending the operating hours of Kuala Lumpur's entertainment outlets, arguing that this would lead to more vices among the youth, like drugs and alcoholism, which are against Islam.[29]

JIM's initial support for PAS however, did not preclude open criticism of certain shortcomings of its brand of politics. For example, JIM was quick off the mark when PAS chief Abdul Hadi launched a personal attack on Prime Minister Abdullah Badawi in the heat of an election campaign in 2004. In a statement that was highly provocative, Abdul Hadi claimed that Abdullah was merely "playing to the gallery" when he led prayers during Ramadan be-cause the prime minister did not choose to be the *imam* at his own mother's funeral.[30] This remark was described by JIM president Zaid Kamaruddin as "hitting below the belt."[31] Metaphors aside, one could argue that Abdul Hadi's response was driven by a need to undermine Abdullah's Islamic credentials, which "denied the theocratic PAS the opportunity to take the religious high ground in the campaign."[32] Yet again, the episode demonstrated how PAS lead-ers are often forced to react to the Islamic initiatives of UMNO.

Despite its endorsement of the creation of an Islamic state in Malaysia and its alignment with certain political parties, leaders of JIM maintain that the organization prioritizes social welfare issues such as the creation of modern Islamic schools, running shelters for single teenaged mothers, and social and educational programs aimed at uplifting women, an area where JIM activism is noticeably strong.[33] JIM has been very active and outspoken on women's issues in Malaysia since its inception, attempting to reconcile and promote women's rights and advancement within the framework of Islam. For instance, JIM has issued statements urging all Malaysian men to play an active and effective role in the upbringing of their children, which it insisted was not the sole responsibility of women.[34] This was followed by a "Fatherhood Campaign" in Kelantan. In addition, Dr. Harlina Siraj, head of JIM's women's wing, has been an outspoken commentator on the issue of rape in Malaysia, calling upon men to play a greater role in preventing this crime. According to Dr. Harlina, "Rape is not just a women's issue—men must take responsibility because most rapists are men. They must take a stand and fight this scourge."[35] Given its stout activism on women's issues, it should not be surprising then that JIM's women's wing has been described as a "fundamentalist" Muslim women's organization that looks to develop "women leaders that are fundamental, contemporary and progressive."[36] The "fundamentalist" label should not detract from the fact that the profiles of JIM's female members vary not only in age but also vocation and class, from rural homemakers to well-educated professionals.

While JIM champions the rights of Muslim women in Malaysia, its interpretation of these "rights" differs markedly from those of other civil society movements, particularly SIS. This was conspicuously illustrated in the two organization's responses to the Islamic Family Law (Federal Territory) Amendment 2005, which among other things made polygamy easier for men and gave them a claim to a share of matrimonial assets upon remarriage.[37] While the law provoked an outcry from SIS, female JIM activists were more muted in their response, asking only that the *shari'a* court "implement existing laws with sensitivity to women, and for any ambiguity in the laws to be cleared up."[38] JIM was prepared to accept polygamy with the provision that "opinions of wives should be considered before deciding if their husbands can take a second spouse."[39] Similarly, when the Shah Alam Municipal Council penalized courting couples for hugging and kissing in public, most women's organizations in Malaysia opposed this ruling, but JIM's position was captured in the following comments of Dr. Harlina Siraj: "Islam clearly stated that except for immediate family members, it was not permissible for those of the opposite sex to hold hands, hug or kiss."[40] She added that "a return to traditional decency in expressing love would remove the need to check courting couples from indulging in a public show of affection."[41]

On other occasions, JIM leaders have been vocal in opposition to more conservative injunctions. For instance, when the PAS government in Kelantan sought to impose a RM50 fine on women who did not wear the head scarf to work, JIM criticized this policy as "too harsh" and "undemocratic."[42] It appears that insofar as the status of women is concerned, JIM's position has reflected a blend of progressive and conservative thinking that at times appears contradictory. The leadership of JIM sees no contradiction in its positions on specific issues, though it is clear that JIM did not have a consistent policy that applied across the entire gamut of gender issues.

JIM draws a large portion of its membership from Malaysia's overseas Malay student diaspora. Its popularity among student movements was born of JIM's engagement in what can be considered archetypal activism of modernist Islamic movements—the provision of education and health services for the Muslim community.[43] For instance, JIM established institutions such as the Raudhatus Sakinah Shelter in Selangor to "rehabilitate girls who were involved in prostitution and 'bohsia' activities which often resulted in teenage pregnancies."[44] In addition to this, JIM also targeted its publicity at youths when they launched a nationwide "Let's Enhance Positive Attitudes and Knowledge" (LEPAK) program to establish special "*lepak* [loitering] corners" at shopping malls that engaged youths so as to curtail the spread of negative influences by raising awareness of the consequences of involvement in illegal activities.[45]

Several observations can be made here about JIM's brand of activism. First, it is clear that while JIM is a politically active NGO, having lent its weight on different occasions to both the UMNO and the PAS cause, it cannot be said to be a partisan player. That is not to say that JIM has not been made to pay the price for supporting the "wrong" side. JIM's former president, Saari Sungip, was detained under the ISA in April 2001 after he was alleged to have joined *Keadilan* activists in a plot to overthrow the UMNO-led Malaysian government when the organization held demonstrations to mark the anniversary of Anwar Ibrahim's conviction on corruption charges in April 1999.

Second, despite its occasional use of strong language, JIM remains essentially a moderate Islamic NGO that is careful to avoid confrontations when it raises issues of concern. One could argue that after the arrest of Saari Sungip, JIM adopted a more carefully calibrated approach in order not to run afoul of the state. Finally, while it agitates for women's rights, this has been done in a fashion that, at least to the minds of the JIM leadership, can be reconciled with the teachings of Islam as they understand it. Female members of JIM keep clear of secular feminist discourses and organizations even as they agitate for more rights. This is necessary for JIM simply because its consultative agenda suggests that its overall aim is to integrate rather than segregate gender interests within the larger rubric of Islamization, where "Muslim women advocated the principle of gender complementarity rather than equality."[46]

Sisters in Islam (SIS)

Established in 1988 and registered in 1993 as an NGO, SIS is an organization of women professionals who are committed to promoting the rights of women within the framework of Islam. From its beginnings as a research and advocacy group focusing on the legal aspects of women's rights under Islamic law, SIS has expanded its field of interest to deal with issues of democracy and fundamental liberties. As an advocacy group, SIS has actively and vocally taken public positions on critical issues such as freedom of religion and freedom of expression.[47]

Against the backdrop of Mahathir's Islamization project, which expanded the jurisdiction of *shari'a* laws, a major motivation for SIS has been growing concern over numerous complaints from Muslim women about the injustices of the *shari'a* court system and the administration of Islamic family law to which they were subjected. This is ironic given the fact that Malaysia once had the most progressive Islamic family law in the Muslim world, when it was first codified in 1984.[48] According to SIS, Islamic family law and *shari'a* criminal legislation tended to discriminate against women when implemented and enforced in the Malaysian context.[49] This state of affairs drove SIS to position itself as an Islamic organization safeguarding women's rights even as Islamism accelerated and deepened under Mahathir's watch. SIS's work was not solely focused on checking the Islamist policies of the UMNO-led government and its repercussions on civil rights and liberties, particularly among women; SIS was equally concerned with the Islamist discourse of PAS and the attendant policies that were enacted in PAS-controlled states, such as the introduction of the *hudud* penal code.

Though small in terms of formal membership numbers compared to other organizations, SIS enjoys extensive media publicity disproportionate to its membership size and has managed to amplify its voice through the exertions of its members who write and speak extensively on the issues identified above. Still, one of its major handicaps is the fact that SIS remains primarily an urban group with little appeal outside of the Klang Valley, let alone in rural northern Malaysia. In addition, SIS has not been well-received by the religious establishment. Indeed, most Islamic leaders view them as a conglomeration of "brash" women with little knowledge of Islam and disparage their work as "anti-Islam, anti-God and anti-Qur'an."[50]

Because of SIS's uncompromising position on controversial issues such as apostasy, UMNO leaders have kept the organization at arm's length in their public statements, even if some express measured sympathy for the organization in private. PAS, in contrast, has been more blatant and deliberate in voicing its opposition to SIS, as have Islamist activists, state religious officials, and even elements in the mainstream media (particularly the Malay press), all of whom have openly criticized the organization. In most instances, SIS has been assailed for its liberal and feminist perspectives on Islamic issues. These detractors accuse SIS of trying to impose alien Western values on Muslims. In fact, PAS has constantly urged the government to investigate and take action against SIS for purportedly showing "disrespect" to Islam, fomenting disunity among the *ummah*, and creating disharmony in Malaysia.[51]

Under more adverse circumstances, SIS's tendency to adopt positions that challenge mainstream conservative orthodoxy has led to accusations that its members were "heretics" and "deviants," devoid of any religious credentials. These conservative orthodox scholars aver that arguments propounded by SIS are arrived at through unsystematic and questionable methodologies of *tafsir* (interpretation of the Qur'an). In addition to this, SIS is criticized for privileging logic, reason (*akal*), and reinterpretation (*ijtihad*) over classical exegesis and jurisprudential epistemologies. To such scholars, SIS has no right to speak about Islam because they do not hail from the male-dominated and paternalistic *ulama* class. Opposition to SIS is further compounded by the fact that many of its members do not wear the traditional Islamic head scarf, which is taken to mean that SIS is influenced not by Islam but by Western ideas and standards. As one critic somewhat facetiously put it, "*Sama lah pakai seluar pendek berdegar-degar cerita nak tegakkan shari'a* [It's like wearing shorts while trying to spread the word of God]."[52]

Despite its detractors, the presence of SIS on the Malaysian political landscape speaks to an underlying paradox that has resulted from the acceleration of Islamist discourse and praxis in Malaysia. While SIS struggles to be accepted as a legitimate voice for "Islam," especially in the eyes of the religious leadership and mainstream segments of Muslim society, the issues it has championed—namely, the rights of Muslim women in Malaysian society—have in fact resonated across the political and ideological spectrum. Indeed, this is an issue that even PAS has recognized and sought to address through its attempts to introduce women into positions of party leadership. To appreciate this apparent paradox, one first needs to understand that the Mahathir administration oversaw the introduction of several new *shari'a* laws and policies, as well as amendments to existing laws, that increasingly curtailed women's rights and fundamental liberties of citizens in a manner many would deem a contravention of human rights and democratic principles. In most of these instances, it has been SIS that has led the way in protesting these efforts to reverse the gains of women in Malaysia and curb the fundamental liberties of citizens in the name of Islam.

Amendments to Islamic Family Law

A major arena where SIS has been active is Islamic family law. Muslims in Malaysia are governed by Islamic family laws that establish rules for marriage, divorce, guardianship, and inheritance. Among other things, in the Malaysian context these laws endorse polygamy for men and allow for easier divorce procedures if initiated by males. Moreover, even if divorced women obtain custody of children, fathers retain guardianship and decision-making rights regardless of the terms of divorce. The Malaysian government has identified divorce as one of the most pressing challenges confronting Muslim society. This concern has been based on rather alarming statistics concerning the divorce rate among Malaysian Muslims: there were a total of 16,509 Muslim divorces in 2004, compared to 3,291 non-Muslim divorces.[53] SIS traces the root of the problem to unequal family laws legislated in the name of Islam that have made divorce an easy and appealing option for Muslim men.

Since the late 1980s, several states in Malaysia have begun amending family laws in a gender-biased direction that has further eroded the rights of Muslim women. One such amendment allows for a contracted polygamous marriage to be registered without the permission from the shari'a court. Whereas original Islamic family law in Malaysia prohibited this, the amendment allows it after payment of a token fine. This amendment led to a proliferation of illegal polygamous marriages entered into in southern Thailand, which is considered culturally and religiously coterminous with Northern Malaysia, or through illegal marriage syndicates operating in Malaysia. Such was the extent of this problem that in certain states there were three times more polygamous marriages entered into through these "alternative" channels than officially sanctioned ones.[54] Because mattters of Muslim personal and family law are governed by state religious authorities and not the federal government, the system has been easily abused by those seeking to skirt restrictions placed by specific states. Even if a given state government acts to place restrictions on polygamous marriages, Muslim men would have recourse to other states under the federal system for the registration of these marriages.

Besides promoting polygamy, these amendments also permit divorces to be approved outside of the shari'a court if it can be proven that the talaq (repudiation) requirement in Muslim divorce was met.[55] This was ironic given that the original intention of Islamic family law was to prevent unilateral declarations of divorce by irresponsible husbands without consent from the court. As a result of this amendment, the number of men who unilaterally divorced their wives outside the court was three times higher than those who applied for divorce through the court.[56] Sometimes women only discovered that they had been divorced by their husbands when they received notification from the shari'a court. Matters were aggravated further when a debate emerged as to whether the use of text messaging for divorce was permissible. Because of widespread protest, the federal government moved to enact rules that penalized men who divorced their wives this way.

On the other hand, women who initiated divorce, usually against a polygamous husband, found their cases delayed by shari'a courts that would only proceed if husbands were physically present at the hearings. In some cases trials have been delayed for more than a decade simply because husbands have not appeared in court, and wives have no other recourse, as there are no penalties for deliberate absence at *shari'a* hearings. One case involved a woman named Aida Melly Tan Abdullah who was left in "marital wilderness" for seven years because her abusive husband refused to grant her a divorce even after secretly taking a second wife.[57] Her lawyer had advised her to return to her husband, and it was only after Aida took it upon herself to study *shari'a* law in order to represent herself that she managed to obtain her divorce in October 2002 in a high-profile legal battle.

A legal victory such as Aida's is rare, and in any case, unlike landmark cases in civil law, such cases do not go on to set legal precedent. Muslim women continue to be discriminated against under the *shari'a* system, to the extent that it has become a "common perception among Muslim women that the *shari'a* court is sexist in its handling of divorce cases."[58] It is in this respect that SIS has actively lobbied for the *shari'a* court system to be upgraded and reformed so that Islamic family laws are in accordance with what they argue are core principles in the Qur'an—justice for women and children.

On 4 May 2003, Selangor Muslim family law was amended to tighten requirements for polygamy, declaring that all parties must be present in the *shari'a* court in an application for a polygamous marriage. However, because the wording in the amended article was written in a manner that suggested that any proposed polygamous marriage must be "just or necessary," instead of "just and necessary" as was previously the case, the amendment became open to interpretation. Thus, instead of tightening conditions for polygamy, the amended provision has had the opposite effect of further discriminating against Muslim women.[59] In the same amendment, which has come into force in almost all states in Malaysia (albeit with different variations), there was another provision that caused a furor among women's groups like SIS. The controversial provision permitted a husband to claim a share of his first wife's matrimonial assets if he wished to take another wife. Not only has this amendment made polygamy easier for men; it has made it more lucrative as well. As a result, it is now easier for Muslim men to take on additional wives without having to ensure they maintain their obligations to their existing wives. According to SIS, the amendment was so vague that a man could easily attempt to make a claim on his wife's personal property if he wished to. The problems this provision caused came to light in the case of Zaidah Rahman, who found her personal bank accounts frozen in Johore when her ex-husband sought a share of the matrimonial assets. Zaidah had to sell her jewelry to cover her daily expenses as the case lingered at the *shari'a* court. While this case was described by the UMNO-led state government as a "mistake" and "a misinterpretation of the law," it suggests that there are a considerable number of gray areas that can work against women.[60]

Anger about amendments to Islamic family law was to surface again when the UMNO-led government planned to formally introduce the Enactments of the Islamic Family Law (Federal Territory) Amendments 2005 in 2006. The Federal Territory, which comprises Kuala Lumpur, Putrajaya and Labuan, was the last to adopt the amendments. Following protests from a range of women's groups and politicians, the amendments have been shelved pending further changes. SIS urged the UMNO-led government to "review the language used in these amendments, which are alleged to contain elements of selective gender neutrality."[61] SIS appealed for the language to be tightened to convey a more concise meaning in order to avoid misinterpretation.

The organization also publishes a bulletin, *Baraza*, that articulates its agenda on the issue of Islamic family law, for which it sees the need to invoke *ijtihad* and allow for reinterpretation of sacred texts to adapt Muslim practices to modern contexts and needs, rather than having assumptions based on the belief that Islamic legal practice is expressed in a legal tradition consisting of a timeless set of injunctions.[62]

Shari'a *Criminal Offenses Act/Enactment*

Since 1994, most states in Malaysia have adopted the *Shari'a* Criminal Offenses Act/Enactment, which contains provisions that regulate the moral behavior of Muslims according to the "precept of Islam."[63] Under this Act/Enactment, *fatwa* issued by state *mufti* are given the automatic force of law without having to be scrutinized by the legislative process of civil courts, which involves debate in Parliament and respective state legislative assemblies. In similar fashion, aspects of the *Shari'a* Criminal Offenses Act/Enactment are also passed without debate at either the national Parliament or state assemblies. By way of this authority, any violation of the *fatwa* or effort to dispute or contradict the *fatwa* constitutes an offense. SIS leaders have criticized this as "theocratic dictatorship," whereby the word of the *mufti* becomes the word of law and only the *mufti* has the power to revoke or amend a *fatwa*.[64]

Matters take on greater urgency when this system is applied to punitive laws designed to regulate an individual's conscience, faith, and private lifestyle in the name of Islam, and when the laws are enforced through the policing activities of state religious authorities. Islamic authority in Malaysia has assumed a hegemonic hue by encroaching further into the private sphere of Muslims in ways that have spilled over into the lifestyles of non-Muslims. According to Zainah Anwar, these measures "support the pursuit of a 'moral' society in a literal and shallow way—by policing what people can wear and where, how and with whom they socialize in their leisure time."[65] According to SIS, implementation of this legislation has created "a climate that ran counter to the spirit of justice, equality, freedom and dignity as promoted in the Qur'an."[66]

This state of affairs has been further aggravated by the apparent overzealousness of state religious officials in "promoting good and preventing evil." In some instances, policing activities have roused public outrage because those arrested, and in particular women, have been shamed and humiliated. One such example, already mentioned in the previous chapter, was the arrest of three Muslim beauty pageant contestants by JAWI officials in July 1997 for "violating" Islamic codes on dress.[67] In the wake of this incident, SIS wrote to Prime Minister Mahathir raising concerns that the *Shari'a* Criminal Offenses Act/Enactment promoted unwarranted policing actions that impinged on individual privacy and rights. Similar circumstances surrounded the arrest of one hundred Muslim patrons of a nightclub by JAWI officials during a raid on 20 January 2005. These patrons, in particular the women, were allegedly treated like "juvenile delinquents" and subjected to verbal abuse and physical humiliation. Yet another instance of controversial policing and punishment was an incident in March 2003 in Kota Bharu, when a male and female student of a secondary school were lashed in public, apparently for the mere act of conversing in the school canteen.[68]

These incidents point to debates that continue to rage over legal definitions and guidelines for what constitutes decent or indecent and acceptable or unacceptable behavior in public, as well as the scope of religious authority to regulate and police such behavior. The fact that non-Muslim couples have been apprehended and charged by state religious authorities has resulted in a further deterioration of the situation and escalation of tension, especially when harsher punishments have been meted out to them than to Muslim couples, as was the case in several instances. Against this backdrop, SIS has contended that the state did not possess the legal or moral right to police personal choices and conduct of citizens.

SIS builds its case, at least in part, on conceptual grounds. In essence, it argues that in Muslim societies, *fatwa* never had and still do not have the automatic force of law. *Fatwa* function as theological and legal opinions given by *mufti* to enlighten and educate a Muslim public about Islam, and to assist them in managing their affairs in accordance with the *shari'a*.[69] In other words, *fatwa* act merely as a guide and not a legal directive that a government is obliged to enforce. Given that matters have taken a turn toward the direction of enforcement, SIS believes that it has a duty to enlarge the "public space" within Islam where women can "challenge, criticize and change" social and legal norms that they suggest were dictated not by the divine teachings of the Prophet but by fallible religious scholars.[70] This position has not endeared SIS to the religiolegal establishment or to the general Muslim population of Malaysia, who mostly remain deferential to traditional and orthodox religious authority.

Not surprisingly, SIS has been especially scathing in its attacks on PAS, which it admonished for having a "mindset frozen in medieval jurisprudence."[71] This view was articulated in response to the enactment of *hudud* laws by PAS-controlled state legislative assemblies in Kelantan in 1993 and Terengganu in 2002. To SIS, not only did this *hudud* code prescribe punishments that grossly contravened human rights (punishments extracted right out of the Qur'an and *sunna*, which include flogging, amputation of limbs, stoning to death, and crucifixion); the *hudud* specifically discriminated against women in a number of ways.[72] These included:

- Presumption of *zina* (adultery/illicit sex) by an unmarried woman if she is pregnant or has delivered a baby, even though she might have been raped
- Inadmissibility of women as eyewitnesses to rape
- Termination of marriage by a husband's accusation of *zina* against his wife (*al-li'an*), whether proven or not
- Implied endorsement of the view that *diyat* or compensation for death or injury to a woman should be half that for a man

SIS remains opposed to the PAS *Shari'a* Criminal Code because it is "unconstitutional and contravenes the principle of justice emphasized by Islam."[73] SIS has argued that "PAS's *hudud* was an infringement of international human rights standards because it provided forms of punishment that could be regarded as torture, or cruel, inhuman, or degrading treatment."[74] SIS has in fact challenged UMNO to take legal action against the respective PAS state governments for their *hudud* enactment under the *Shari'a* Criminal Code so as to "preserve, protect and defend the federal constitution."[75] As SIS's Nik Noriani puts it, PAS's *hudud* is a "man-made codification that is a distortion of God's law" and is "a complete contradiction of the Islamic justice system."[76] At the same time, SIS has slammed UMNO for not investing in either the machinery or the intellectual capital required to expand and deepen the more progressive elements of its Islamic leadership as a counterweight to fundamentalist Islamist forces both within the ruling party and PAS.[77]

SIS's advocacy activities include a weekly legal column in *Utusan Malaysia*, which was launched in 2002. Because *Utusan Malaysia* is one of the most popular newspapers in the country, the response to this column has been overwhelming as Malaysians, both men and women, seek its counsel on their rights and responsibilities under Islamic family law.[78] SIS also led the Article 11 Coalition to garner more than eighteen thousand signatures calling on the UMNO-led government to uphold the supremacy of the constitution and ensure constitutional protection for the right to freedom of worship for all Malaysians.[79] Despite its small number of active members, SIS has produced a wide range of literature and commentaries on issues it deems critical to the welfare of Muslim women in Malaysia. Some of its titles include *Islamic Family Law and Justice for Muslim Women, Islam and Polygamy,* and *Islam and Family Planning.* SIS also regularly organizes public lectures on contemporary Islamic issues, meetings that draw fairly large crowds, and runs a monthly training program on women's rights that is attended by human rights lawyers, young professionals, and university students, among others. Most important, SIS has started a weekly legal aid clinic that provides immediate legal counselling for Malaysians from all walks of life. Given SIS's particular interest in *shari'a* reform, it is not surprising that its legal clinic deals with an average of seven hundred *shari'a* court cases each year, the majority of which are women seeking divorce or child support.

By virtue of its credentials and activities, it is clear that SIS intends to plot an alternative Islamic agenda on a range of issues that impinge on individual rights while checking the rising conservatism in state and federal governance. To that end, it has not only challenged policies enacted by both state and federal governments; it has challenged the interpretation of religious scripture by traditional religious authorities as well. Predictably, the *ulama* have responded to this criticism by freezing SIS out of mainstream religiopolitical discourse. Given the sometimes heated nature of debates between SIS and conservative religious authorities, political leaders and government officials have mostly also chosen the path of caution when dealing with SIS, keeping them at arm's length so as not to antagonize the *ulama*. SIS has been further crippled by the gendered nature of mainstream religious discourse in Malaysia, which has in turn hampered prospects for its deeper penetration into society. To its credit, however, the organization has continued to actively question the statements and policies of religious authorities that it considers discriminatory.

Malaysian Consultative Council of Buddhism, Christianity, Hinduism, and Sikhism (MCCBCHS)

Challenging the religiopolitical agenda of both UMNO and PAS has not been the sole prerogative of Islamic NGOs and civil society organizations. Indeed, the demographic realities of Malaysia mean that any debate on Islamism will inevitably elicit responses from the non-Muslim community as well. This has certainly been the case in recent times, when the intensification of Islamist discourse and its increasingly hegemonic nature accelerated non-Muslims' concerns for their place in Malaysian society.

Officially registered as a society on 6 August 1983, the Malaysian Consultative Council of Buddhism, Christianity, Hinduism, and Sikhism (MCCBCHS) is an interfaith organization that seeks to enhance dialogue and cooperation not only among Buddhists, Christians, Hindus, and Sikhs, but also between these communities and Malaysia's majority Muslims. The work of the MCCBCHS took on great urgency in light of the rising tide of Islamism flowing from the Mahathir administration's Islamization initiatives and the intensification of Islamist discourse on the part of PAS, as it cast itself as the guardian of non-Muslim rights and interests. MCCBCHS currently has branches in Penang, Perak, Kelantan, Negeri Sembilan, Malacca, Johore, and Sarawak. While it does not enjoy major influence in the decision-making process within the UMNO-led government, as a representative of the interests of 40 percent of the population of Malaysia, the organization does wield a certain degree of leverage as a vocal pressure group.[80] The organization's immediate agenda is the expansion of interfaith cooperation and dialogue by creating awareness through the printing, publication, and distribution of journals, periodicals, leaflets, and books, as well as the organization of conferences and seminars. Another aspect of its advocacy work, and one that has on occasion provoked the ire of the government, has been active lobbying for non-Muslim rights in Malaysia.

Since its formation, the MCCBCHS has had an uneasy relationship with the Malaysian government, given that the government promotes a wide-ranging Islamic agenda. That said, the Malaysian government has also prudently decided to tacitly endorse the work of MCCBCHS inasmuch as its advocacy of dialogue is concerned, so long as it is pursued within the rubric of Malay-Muslim primacy. When Mahathir spoke at MCCBCHS's tenth-anniversary dinner in 1994 as prime minister, he established that "it is the duty of all Malaysians to try and perpetuate religious tolerance in the country, where problems are resolved not through violence but through discussions."[81] The MCCBCHS was cited as a specific example of this tolerance. Endorsing the work of MCCBCHS, Mahathir said that the "sensitivity toward the beliefs and practices of the different religions in the country has helped Malaysians come together in a multiracial, multireligious, multicultural and multilingual nation."[82] Mahathir added that "the government on its part will seriously examine the views and feedback from the various religions in the country and resolve any differences amicably."[83] Beyond this rhetoric, however, MCCBCHS's relations with the state have been strained as it has attempted to defend the interests of Malaysia's non-Muslim population in ways that have been perceived as challenges to Islam and to Malay-Muslim authority.

One such issue has been the matter of non-Muslim burial grounds and places of worship in Malaysia. While the federal government endorses freedom of worship, state governments have been rationing permits for the building of non-Muslim places of worship and the allocation of land for non-Muslim cemeteries, and there have been several instances when approvals for permits were stalled by various state administrations. In response, MCCBCHS protested the planned implementation of Ministry of Housing and Local Government guidelines governing non-Muslim places of worship in 1999.[84] Articulating their dissent, the organization's former president said, "Our council regrets the little consideration given for non-Muslim places of worship in local council structure plans. We also appeal to civil servants to have a better understanding of the needs of non-Muslims in settling issues."[85] Specifically, the MCCBCHS protested the discriminatory nature of some of the guidelines laid down by the ministry. These included different requirements for the approval of requests for allocation of land for the building of places of worship.[86] While these minimum guidelines were relaxed somewhat in 2000, authority for the approval of permits was vested with the Islamic councils of the various states, most of which were, for obvious reasons, reluctant to approve construction of non-Islamic religious structures. It was only after continued agitation on the part of MCCBCHS, and with the support of non-Muslim political parties, that the relevant authorities moved to lift stipulations requiring permits. In practice, however, obstacles remain, and some state authorities continue to stymie the construction of non-Muslim religious buildings.

MCCBCHS has been particularly robust and strident in its opposition to the *Shari'a* Criminal Code passed in the PAS-controlled Terengganu state legislature in 2002. To that end, MCCBCHS issued a statement to "reject any attempt to infringe on the human rights of Muslims and non-Muslims by subjecting them to injustices through the implementation of PAS's *hudud*."[87] MCCBCHS concern for these issues drew them into the mainstream political arena, and it pledged its support during the 1999 general election to the *Barisan Nasional* on the grounds that it was the "only coalition of parties that will ensure a liberal and accommodative policy on freedom of worship" and was prepared to "accept the reality of coexistence of a multiracial and multireligious community."[88] This pledge of support was not without repercussions. In particular, it was viewed in non-Muslim quarters of the *Barisan Alternatif* as detrimental to the opposition's cause for greater transparency and accountability. DAP secretary-general Lim Kit Siang expressed this view when he noted that the MCCBCHS pledge of support for *Barisan* would be a "major blow" for the DAP and the opposition parties and would probably be the "single biggest cause for the DAP to lose badly at the 1999 general elections."[89] Persistent pressure and lobbying by non-Muslim opposition parties eventually convinced MCCBCHS of the larger cause; the statement was retracted, and no further comments suggestive of political allegiances were made by its leaders.

Another controversial issue in which MCCBCHS found itself embroiled was that of religious identification. In 1999, Home Affairs minister Abdullah Badawi proposed that the new identity cards then being prepared for all Malaysians should indicate the carrier's religion. According to Abdullah, this feature was necessary to "help the authorities ascertain the religion of identity-card holders in critical cases such as family disputes over a person's religion when he dies."[90] At the same time, this would also "help prevent Muslims from masquerading as non-Muslims to patronize the casino at Genting Highlands or to avoid fasting during Ramadan."[91] In response to this initiative, which clearly had a policing dimension, MCCBCHS and other non-Muslim groups registered their objection by calling on the government to reconsider its decision to include one's religion on identity cards, for the simple reason that the mention of race or religion could engender "bias and discrimination."[92]

These groups described the initiative as a "step backward in the light of the prime minister's [Mahathir's] desire for national unity and *Bangsa Malaysia.*" MCCBCHS leaders observed that "while one can appreciate that one would be proud that his or her religion is mentioned in the identity card, the MCCBCHS is also concerned with the arbitrary methods used by the National Registration Department in identifying one's religion."[93] They were alluding to cases where, in the event of any confusion or dispute as to a particular person's religious confession, "evidence" provided by Islamic authorities was often considered more authoritative than that provided by non-Muslim religious institutions or leaders. Considering the outcome of the Lina Joy and Moorthy Maniam cases, MCCBCHS clearly had grounds for apprehension.

Interfaith Dialogue

Since 2001, MCCBCHS has been at the forefront of an effort emanating from the non-Muslim community to form an Inter-Religious Council (IRC) to encourage dialogue across religious boundaries. Together with several other organizations, this proposal aimed to strengthen ties between religious groups by fostering greater understanding and harmony through interfaith dialogues. Specifically, MCCBCHS wanted to forge an understanding with Muslim leaders through the IRC on sensitive matters such as religious conversion. In particular, it felt that the "proper procedures" regarding marriage, divorce, and child custody matters relating to converts to Islam needed to be clarified with Islamic clerics.[94] To their mind, there were "several gray areas in this matter, which has caused much emotional suffering and confusion for family members of converts," not to mention the strain that it put on intercommunal relations.[95]

In 2005, on the initiative of MCCBCHS and the Malaysian Bar Council's Human Rights Committee, a national interfaith conference was held in Bangi to discuss the formation of an Inter-Faith Commission of Malaysia (IFCM). This meeting was attended by more than two hundred representatives from more than fifty religious groups, political parties, and civil society organizations.[96] The meeting was boycotted by Muslim groups. Indeed, the polarized nature of the respective Muslim and non-Muslim positions on the matter of the IFCM was captured in the following intimations of Hermen Shastri, secretary-general of the Council of Churches of Malaysia: "Islam doesn't come into the MCCBCHS because they feel they are part of the government and hence set apart from others."[97] Following this conference, a draft bill to formalize the IFCM was considered but has since been shelved owing to strong opposition from Muslim groups and political leaders. Among the more outspoken critics was the Allied Coordinating Committee of Islamic NGOs (ACCIN), which objected to the IFCM proposal on the premise that "the constitutional right to practice one's religion does not extend to questioning the teachings of other religions."[98] It further asserted that "non-Muslims have no right to interfere in the teachings and practices of Islam, and intrafaith matters of any religion are for the followers of that religion."[99] In other words, the underlying fear was that the IFCM would encroach into, transgress upon, and interfere with Islam and the *shari'a*. On another occasion, ACCIN argued that "this [IFCM] would be a direct contravention of the letter and spirit of the social contract as enshrined in the federal constitution."[100] Clearly, ACCIN's criticisms were framed not only in terms of a defense of Islam; they also took constitutional overtones.

In recent times, MCCBCHS has been active in articulating and defending non-Muslim rights with regard to the dual system of civil court–*shari'a* court jurisdiction. Reacting to the civil court's apparent capitulation during the case of Moorthy Maniam, MCCBCHS criticized the way the case was managed, which it argued was based solely on "disputed verbal evidence" and was indicative of the fact that the "Islamic authorities are slowly but surely trying to enlarge the powers of the *shari'a* courts."[101] According to MCCBCHS's Rev. Wong Kim Kong, "We cannot allow a small group who are extreme in their views to dominate the nation's social and religious life. And if no action is taken by the government, then it might sow disharmony."[102] Similarly, current president Dr. K. Dhammananda said, "It is frightening that this sort of thing is happening in a multiracial country like Malaysia. This is the biggest seed of disunity that can be sown at this time."[103]

In an attempt to raise awareness of this issue, MCCBCHS held a nighttime vigil outside the Kuala Lumpur High Court during the proceedings of the Moorthy Maniam case. While only about twenty people attended, MCCBCHS was unfazed and further announced that they "intend to repeat it every night for six months."[104] MCCBCHS also wanted to emphasize that the case of Moorthy Maniam was not unique; it pointed to trends of Islamization that threatened the fundamental rights of non-Muslims in Malaysia. Some of the other cases mentioned included the 2005 case of Shamala Sathayaseelan, whose application to nullify the conversion of her two children to Islam by their converted father was rejected on the grounds that the High Court had no jurisdiction over religion,[105] and a case in Malacca when the family of a deceased firefighter was denied access to his estate on grounds that he had converted to Islam prior to his death without the family's knowledge. In the firefighter's case, it was only after the national media highlighted the wife's plight that the Islamic Religious Council of Malacca "donated" a house to the family of the deceased on "humanitarian grounds."[106] Summarizing the MCCBCHS's concern, its vice-president, Harcharan Singh, noted that "while [it has become clear] that the federal constitution stands as the supreme law of Malaysia, Article 11, which guarantees religious freedom, has been overridden by the *shari'a* court."[107] In addition, MCCBCHS said that the question of religious conversion should not be looked at as merely a religious issue but instead as a "social issue emerging out of a religious matter," because the entire episode raised questions of the law, the constitution, and human rights.[108]

Hizbut Tahrir Malaysia (HTM)

Despite the fact that its membership is gradually growing, *Hizbut Tahrir Malaysia* (HTM) remains one of the most secretive Islamist groups in Malaysia. HTM is part of the worldwide *Hizbut Tahrir* (HT) organization, which was first formed in 1953 in Jerusalem. HT has as its key aspiration a worldwide Muslim revival, with the ultimate aim of reviving the Islamic Caliphate. The first leader of HT, Syeikh Taqiuddin An-Nabhani, was a religious scholar, a graduate of al-Azhar University, and a judge at the *shari'a* court in Palestine. Currently, HT's key leadership is believed to be based in Jordan and the United Kingdom.

Over the years, the organization has spread around the world, including North Africa, Europe, the Middle East, and Asia. Its network is particularly strong in Central Asia.[109] In Southeast Asia, HT activism originated in Indonesia through the activities of graduates returning from universities in the United Kingdom and the Middle East. The organization subsequently spread to Malaysia in the late 1990s, both through graduates of U.K. universities and through their Indonesian counterparts.[110] Little is known about the activities and actual influence of HT Indonesia (HTI) on the Indonesian political scene, though anecdotal evidence suggests that given the more open nature of Indonesian society today, it is likely that HTI enjoys substantially more sociopolitical freedom than many of its counterpart organizations.[111]

To differentiate itself from other Islamic organizations, HTM states explicitly that it is not an academic, educational, or charity group but a bona fide political movement, though not necessarily a participant in electoral politics. Among its declared objectives are the revival of the Muslim world from its perceived current state of decline; the liberation of Muslims from the ideologies, systems, and laws of unbelievers; and the restoration of the Islamic Caliphate.[112] HTM members must be Muslims, regardless of their race and *mazhab* (school of Islamic jurisprudential thought). Women are allowed to be members of the movement, though activities and meetings are often segregated along gender lines. Unlike other Islamic groups in Malaysia, which essentially operate within the framework of a procedural democracy, HTM sees democracy as an ideology abhorred by Islam.[113] For HTM, the only way for Islam to be fully implemented is through an "Islamic Revolution."

In agitating for the reestablishment of the Caliphate, HTM claims that its vision accords with the Prophet Muhammad's methods of establishing the state of Medina. In essence, HTM looks to replicate the various stages of the Prophet's creation of the society and state in Medina by dividing its strategy into three stages. The first stage was one of "culturing," which entailed efforts to produce a mass base that subscribed to and supported the ideas and methods of the movement so as to strengthen HTM numerically. The second stage involves interaction with the *ummah* so it can establish an acute Islamic consciousness toward the affairs of life. This was to be accomplished by open and public *dakwah* on the part of HTM members. After tilling the ground in these two stages, the third and final stage would be the establishment of an Islamic government in the form of the revived Caliphate, which would implement Islam comprehensively in all spheres of society and carry the Islamic message to the world.[114] In the ideology of the movement, these three stages accorded with the work of the Prophet Muhammad, who had performed his *dakwah* quietly in Mecca during the first three years of his ministry, after which he started to engage authorities publicly, and eventually to assume authority, in Medina. The final stage of the prophet's ministry saw him conquer Mecca after securing the *nusrah* (political support) of key stakeholders and establishing the Caliphate.

What is notable about HTM's agitation for political change is the fact that it does not explicitly shun the use of violence. Indeed, in a recent HTM seminar, a speaker said that "Muslims should not be apologetic about the need for them to wage war and use violence if necessary in their pursuit to establish the Caliphate and uplift Islamic values and beliefs."[115] HTM clearly opposes democracy, arguing that the main features of democracy, such as capitalism and secularism, are anathema to Islam and Muslims.

For fear of persecution, during its formative years HTM utilized several front organizations, such as the Network of Intellectuals in the Malay World and various student organizations in local tertiary institutions. What is striking about HTM membership is its distinctly middle-class complexion; it comprises young professionals, academics, lawyers, teachers, and college students. According to its leaders, HTM membership stands at about three hundred nationwide. These members are spread across Malaysia, though most can be found in the states of Johore, Selangor, Pahang, Kelantan, Terengganu, Kedah, Penang, and Perak.[116]

Given its transnational nature, it is not surprising that the organization also maintains close links with the HT organization in the United Kingdom and with other HT chapters in the Muslim world. HTM produces a bimonthly pamphlet, *Sautun Nahdhah,* which is distributed in mosques and prayer halls around Malaysia by HTM members. *Sautun Nahdhah* features HTM's views about contemporary issues affecting Muslims in Malaysia and other parts of the world, and it publicizes upcoming events and activities organized by HTM.[117] HTM sees this as a form of acclimatization, a culturing process to generate awareness of and interest in its ideas among the Malaysian public. The party also utilizes its Web site, www.mykhilafah.com, to spread its message, and its members have surfaced in chat rooms and blogs such as www.bicaramuslim.com and www.miftahulasrar.multiply.com.

The party also organizes seminars on a regular basis, often held in different parts of the country. In such seminars, HTM senior members speak
in panels of two to three speakers. As speakers from other Muslim groups or
senior Malaysian religious scholars are also invited to speak in these forums,
it appears that HTM is prepared to be somewhat egalitarian in its approach
to discourses on Islam. Alternatively, it could also be that given HTM's position that most Islamist groups in fact contradict "true" Islamic teachings, these
non-HTM speakers are mostly invited as part of the effort to draw public interest to these forums. The seminars are often focused on local issues that resonate with potential participants and members, but they almost always lead to
discussions about the need to revive the Caliphate, which to HTM is a panacea
for the problems confronting contemporary Muslims.[118] These seminars serve
an important function as a conduit for outreach and interaction between the
organization and the general public. Participants who seem to be more interested in the issues discussed will then be invited to join the group's *halaqahs*
(discussion circles). The *halaqahs*, held on a weekly basis, are meant to identify
the key members of the group and to indoctrinate potential recruits. HTM is
extremely careful about selecting its members and often refer to its adherents
as "supporters" rather than as full-fledged members. The key difference between a member and a supporter is that a member can communicate with the
higher echelon of the HT leadership in other parts of the world, while a supporter does not enjoy such access.

It is still too early to assess the impact of HTM in Malaysian politics. However, its rate of expansion, together with the fact that it has been able to capture
the interest of highly educated people, indicates that HTM may be a group to
watch.[119] Its seemingly radical yet nonviolent message—despite the fact that
it has not explicitly disavowed the use of violence—may strike a chord with
the younger segments of Malaysian society, especially those who are growing
increasingly disillusioned with mainstream political parties like UMNO and
PAS, or with civil society groups such as JIM and ABIM, which are sometimes criticized by more radical elements as being slow to Islamize Malaysian
society.

Already, PAS is beginning to feel the heat from the emergence of HTM, as
some of its members have left the party to become members of HTM.[120] One of
these members said he quit PAS because he was never really comfortable with
PAS's support for democracy, and he felt that HTM advocated "a more Islamic
approach."[121] HTM also appears to be having some impact among students in
various tertiary institutions. The organization has been able to draw from the
wells of student alumni associations, particularly former members of Islamic
student groups affiliated with PAS.[122]

Some members of PAS believe that UMNO permitted groups like HTM
to operate freely because UMNO sees such groups as potential spoilers that
are more likely to dampen popular support for PAS than for UMNO.[123] At the

same time, however, HTM claims that they are now under surveillance by the Malaysian government. This was openly acknowledged by an HTM speaker at an HTM seminar organized in Kuala Lumpur when he included the Malaysian Special Branch officers who were present in the audience in his list of salutations.[124] This possibility cannot be dismissed, as HT ideology in general tends to reject mainstream political systems and explicitly articulates intentions to overthrow them. Little is known at this stage about how HTM is perceived by UMNO, although HTM is unlikely to supplant the dominant Islamic groups in Malaysia anytime soon. That said, one should keep in mind that fringe groups, such as the Islamic Revolutionary in the 1980s and *Al Arqam* in the 1990s, have at time surfaced in Malaysia to challenge the dominance of mainstream Islamic groups.

Cyberpolitics and Popular Discourses

While civil society groups essentially represent popular discourse in its more organized and mobilized form, in Malaysia cyberspace and various alternative media sources have opened new outlets and pathways of political expression and have emerged as a major alternative arena of popular discourse that take debates over Islamism deeper into Malaysian society.[125] Driven primarily by the controversies surrounding various judicial rulings on the matter of apostasy, declarations by Malay-Muslim political leaders about the status of Malaysia as an Islamic state, and the government's seeming intolerance of open debate that touches on the "sensitive" issue of Malay-Muslim rights and primacy, these new avenues are playing an increasingly vital role in the Malaysian political scene by providing a forum for contrarian views. Of special interest is the emergence of weblogs (henceforth referred to as blogs), chat rooms, and listserves that socially (re)construct agendas and provide interpretive frames as a focal point, contributing to the shaping and constraining of larger political debate.[126]

　　Despite some exceptions to the rule, it can be argued that in general one will find, in the increasingly intense discursive arena of cyberspace, a discernible schism between the opinions and perspectives proffered by Malay-language blogs and English-language blogs with respect to recent Islamic state declarations and high-profile *murtad* (apostasy) cases. While English-language blogs comprise individuals from a variety of ethnic and religious backgrounds, it is likely that Malay-Muslims monopolize Malay-language blogs.[127] In addition, several general trends can be further discerned. Regardless of ethnicity and religion, the perspectives on English-language blogs regarding the status of Malaysia as an Islamic state are relatively in accord. However, between the English and Malay blogs there is a clear disjuncture of opinions on the issue. In the same vein, on the matter of reactions to the high-profile apostasy cases that have emerged in recent years, sentiments were divided along religious lines, regardless of the language. Nonetheless, the sharpest differences in opinions were found between the Malay and English blogs, with the former purveying more conservative and exclusionary sentiments and the latter expressing more openness to the idea of conversion out of Islam and protection of religious freedom.

These trends of social networks in virtual space appear to mirror face-to-face patterns of interaction in physical space, wherein there is a tendency to communicate and associate (by virtue of participants leaving comments and linking one's blog to another) with like-minded individuals with generally compatible perspectives on any given set of issues. For example, a large proportion of Malay bloggers who demonstrate more accommodative proclivities also tend to express their opinions on English blogs, whereas those who defend Malay-Muslim primacy are usually more active on Malay blogs. Moreover, comments in response to a blog post are usually more conciliatory than they are critical. Although virtual space accommodates and facilitates honest, open, anonymous exchange (not to mention temerity), the impermeability of ideas between the English-language and *Bahasa Melayu* (Malay language) blogs is a possible reflection of the latent desire in Malaysia to avoid dialogue, engagement, and bridging of opinions between conflicting ideas and mindsets.

Blog Discourse on the Islamic State

When Deputy Prime Minister Najib Tun Razak claimed that "we [Malaysia] have never, never been secular. . . . We are an Islamic state," his proclamation triggered passionate and effusive reactions from bloggers in Malay and English blogs, with the former generally representing views of the Muslim community.[128] Despite the expediency of the hour—Najib needed to shore up his Islamic credentials ahead of an upcoming general election and in the wake of a potentially damning murder trial involving his closest advisor—his comment touched a raw nerve in Malaysian society. Concomitantly, it is hardly surprising to find that Malaysia's grassroots harbor strong opinions on this issue, especially at a time when the country's public administration, its legislation, and the conduct of its leaders appeared to promote an increasingly Islamic form of government.

The majority of English-language bloggers vehemently disagreed with the claim that Malaysia was an Islamic state. They cited various reasons for this position, such as how the Malaysian constitution and judicial system were not based upon the tenets of the Qur'an and the *hadith*, which to their understanding was a requirement for an authentic Islamic state. Many pointed to the existence of licensed casinos (albeit mostly contained in the resort highlands of Genting in Pahang state), lotteries, and draconian laws such as the ISA as clear transgressions of Islamic fundamentals.[129] Many bloggers also mentioned in passing that for Malaysia to be an Islamic state, the ruler of the state has to be an *ulama* without affiliation with any political party.

The majority of English-language bloggers pointed out that the establishment of an Islamic state was irreconcilable with the inclusive tenets of the 1957 Malaysian constitution. In most of these blogs, authors validated their argument by invoking the now-infamous Article 11, arguing that while Article 3 stipulates that Islam is the religion of the federation and that only Islam can be preached to Muslims, Article 11 guarantees freedom of religion for all, including Muslims. According to the logic of this riposte, although the constitution states that Islam is the religion of the federation, there is an equal recognition of the right of non-Muslims to practice their religion. The reiteration of the Article 11 argument in many of the English-language blogs reflects the implicit but collective desire by like-minded individuals to transcend the exclusivism of Malay-Muslim dominance toward a racially and religiously blind Malaysia.[130] Notably, this opinion was espoused not only by non-Muslim bloggers but also a large majority of the Malay-Muslim bloggers who contributed to English blogs and chat rooms.[131]

By citing official documents like the constitution, *Rukunnegara*, and the Mahathir administration's "Strategic Challenges of *Wawasan 2020* (Vision 2020)" developmental blueprint, several bloggers also made an oblique attack on moral policing. Such criticisms claimed that, despite the primacy of Islam in Malaysia, non-Muslims should be allowed to practice their own religion and should not be admonished or treated unfairly if they failed to abide by Islamic codes of conduct and morality, which in any case may not necessarily be standards they subscribe to personally. For example, authors of the blog *Compass Direct News*, which claims to represent the interests of minorities, commented that discussion on the issue of "Malaysia as an Islamic state" has "alarmed non-Muslims, who make up forty percent of the country's population. Various religious and civil society groups have voiced their concerns over what they see as gradual Islamization and infringement of minority rights which may jeopardize the right to freedom of religion."[132] Another blogger, writing under the pseudonym Ktemoc, expressed consternation with UMNO's increased Islamization rhetoric, which, Ktemoc argued, may result in the misogynistic treatment of women, as witnessed in PAS's stronghold, Kota Bharu, Kelantan. Ktemoc recalled how religious police would "hunt down" working Muslim women who wore "sexy clothing," such as blue jeans, or those who did not wear a head scarf.[133]

While these bloggers accepted some measure of involvement on the part of the state in formulating policies and organizing religious activities, such as the building of mosques, the administration of the *haj* pilgrimage, the establishment of Islamic schools, and Islamic awareness through public broadcasting channels, they argued that non-Muslims should not be marginalized, excluded, or treated unjustly as a result, given that all three official documents cited above advocate the establishment of a just, united, democratic, liberal, progressive nation, all values that many non-Muslims understand to be congruent with the core tenets of Islam. This view was reinforced by Chandra Muzaffar, president of the International Movement for a Just World, who (as a Muslim) explained that "it is important to emphasize that most of the principles and goals articulated by the three documents do not in any way contradict the universal values of the Qur'an and the *sunnah*. Indeed in certain respects, they seek to give meaning to some of the eternal concerns of the religion about justice, accountability, and ethical conduct."[134] A prominent ethnic Chinese blogger, Ronnie Liu, argued the federal constitution had always been consistent with the values of Islam, and further added: "The people have no problems if our political leaders wish to introduce Islamic values such as clean and trustworthy governance and helping the poor and needy in the society. These values are universal and could readily [be] accept[ed] by the followers of different faiths."[135]

Additionally, there is growing concern regarding the Islamization of government policies that have led to infringement of non-Muslim rights and imposition of unwarranted restrictions on non-Muslims' lifestyles. Activists are also worried about the widening influence of the *shari'a* courts at the expense of civil laws. Ivy Josiah, executive director of the Women's Aid Organization, which runs a refuge for female victims of abuse and campaigns on human rights issues, expressed her concern that "Islam is gaining such power to affect our personal rights. We should have been outraged sooner but we let things happen. We said it was tolerable. But in fact the intrusions are cumulative. Now we can't not deal with religion. It is a human rights issue."[136]

A major reservation expressed by English-language bloggers was the possible unravelling of Malaysia's multiethnic and multireligious social fabric should it become an Islamic state where current discriminatory practices are further codified. Concern was also articulated that an Islamic state in Malaysia would both reinforce and lead to the tyranny of the majority. Nathaniel Tan, a popular blogger known for voicing vociferous criticisms of the government, blamed UMNO for the deteriorating relations between the different races, especially with the recent declaration made by Najib, and Mahathir before him, which represents one of the "underlying driving forces that may feed ethnic riots." He asserted that "ethnic conflict can only occur when there is real ethnic division. Ethnic division can only be eradicated when the inherently racist UMNO-led BN [*Barisan Nasional*] system is abolished completely."[137] Another non-Muslim blogger, David, shared Nathaniel's sentiments, claiming that UMNO's invoking of Islamic state rhetoric ignored "Malaysia's multireligious and multiracial reality, thereby causing fear and consternation among its non-Muslim population."[138] He further blamed UMNO for being "insensitive to the concerns of over 40 percent of its non-Muslim population who do not want the country to be arbitrarily declared Islamic."[139] Moreover, it was UMNO "who is preaching unity but at the same time causing schisms just when Malaysia is celebrating fifty years of *Merdeka* [independence]."[140] In other words, these popular perspectives essentially see UMNO not only as responsible for the Islamization of Malaysia but also for the intensification of the Islamic state debate.

The point to stress here is that the misgivings expressed in English-language blogs have less to do with Islam per se or the principles behind heightened Islamic consciousness than with the specific nature of the Islamization that frames the Najib and Mahathir Islamic state declarations, which to non-Muslim minds are hegemonic, exclusionary, unconstitutional, and ultimately a product of UMNO's ideological proclivities and political machinations.

Insofar as Malay-language public opinion was expressed on blogs, the most common sentiment reflected was that of repugnance toward Najib for comparing Malaysia to an Islamic state. Many felt that Malaysia under UMNO was not worthy of being called an Islamic state and regarded Najib's declaration as arbitrary, politically motivated, and a "disgrace to Islam." A majority of Malay-language bloggers reasoned that Malaysia should not be called an Islamic state because it did not meet the criteria for one. According to Muhd Razin, a Malaysian student studying Islamic law at Al-Azhar University, "In terms of government administration and the judicial system, it is clear that Islamic laws are not fully implemented in Malaysia. In fact, there are existing laws that condone acts, which are prohibited, by the *shari'a* law. Therefore, it is inaccurate, at least from the perspectives of Muslim scholars and religious leaders, if Malaysia is labeled as an Islamic state."[141] The presence of nightclubs, casinos, brothels, and other forms of vice contradicts any assertion that Malaysia is an Islamic state, Razin wrote. Another blogger made disparaging and sarcastic comments on Abdullah's conception of *Islam Hadhari* (Islamic Civilization), stating that "Malaysia is not an Islamic state but an Islamic *Hadhari* state which is infused with debauchery and oppression. Furthermore, Malaysian leaders do not possess the ability and attributes of Islamic leaders with most of them involved in corruption cases and with female politicians seen wearing clothes that do not cover their *aurat* [parts of body that should not be exposed according to Islamic belief] as well as failing to follow proper Islamic teachings."[142] A few Malay blogs even voiced support for the Chinese-led MCA's protest against the Islamic state declaration.

Some Malay bloggers were less effusive and objectively questioned whether Malaysia indeed met the qualifications of an Islamic state. Referring to the teachings of Muslim scholars, one blogger concluded that a state can only be declared an Islamic state if two conditions are met: Islamic laws and regulations have to be administered as official state legislation, and the leader of the state has to be a Muslim. Given that the first criterion was not met to its fullest potential, Malaysia was not yet an Islamic state. Bloggers of this persuasion also expressed skepticism over Malaysia's legitimacy as an Islamic state from a demographic perspective, emphasizing that there were differences between an Islamic state and a majority-Muslim state ruled by Muslim leaders.[143]

While the chairman of UMNO Youth, Hishammuddin Hussein, agreed with Najib and admonished MCA for contesting his remark, Prime Minister Abdullah, in an attempt to resolve opposing perspectives and cease all discussion on the contentious issue, declared that Malaysia is neither a theocratic nor a secular state and is instead a "parliamentary democracy." For Malay-language bloggers, this ambivalence raised doubts about the government's commitment to Islamic principles in politics and governance. The government's inconsistent position was seen as betraying the classic political strategy of using Islam to secure votes. For example, Al Husyen, a Muslim-Malay blogger, asked, "Why has PM Abdullah refused to acknowledge that Malaysia is an Islamic state unlike what is stated on his Web site? Why has he refused to acknowledge that Malaysia is an Islamic state when he was the first to introduce the concept of *Islam Hadhari*? If we are not an Islamic state and neither are we a secular state, what are we? Is Malaysia an Islamic state only in name and are we religious hypocrites?"[144] Anis Nazri echoed Al-Husyen's sentiments, stating that "all the fuss on the issue has only been about labels and not about the proper implementation of *shari'a* laws or the implementation of Islamic values within the state."[145]

Most Muslims agreed that Malaysia was not an Islamic state, but their disagreement was not based on a belief that the concept was no longer relevant for Muslim governance in the contemporary era, as some Muslim intellectuals claimed. Instead, they premised their opposition on the argument that Malaysia was "not yet" an Islamic state and that UMNO may not be the ideal vehicle for the realization of the Islamic state. If this opinion represents the majority of Malay-Muslims in Malaysia, the portents of what is to come are clearly profound.

The Apostasy Debate

The high-profile apostasy case of Lina Joy generated a vast amount of Internet traffic. In evaluating discussions and debates on the issue, several key trends can be discerned. The main concern for the majority of Malay-Muslim bloggers was not so much her personal faith or conversion but the infallible authority of the *shari'a* court over all legal matters concerning Muslim life. Many Muslim bloggers considered it a victory that the civil courts did not approve Lina Joy's conversion because it meant that there would not be a precedent for conversion from Islam without the approval of the *shari'a* courts. Rehman Razak, a Malay-Muslim blogger from Kuala Lumpur, exclaimed triumphantly:

> Alhamdullillah! [Praise be to Allah!] The federal court has made a historically significant decision yesterday. Allahuakbar! [God is

Great!] This decision has reinstated the sole authority and power of the *shari'a* court. It has altogether rejected Lina Joy's appeal to conversion from Islam. This is the ultimate victory for Islam, not because Lina remains Muslim legally . . . but because all issues pertaining to Muslims will remain under the *shari'a* court and not the civil courts.[146]

Another blogger, Faridul, was also grateful for the decision of the civil courts, stating that although Lina Joy is still not a Muslim by faith, "we have to be thankful for the superior position of the *shari'a* courts in this issue and the enshrinement of Islamic laws which are still revered and respected."[147] If opinions expressed on these blogs are any measure, then general consensus among the Muslim public was that because Lina Joy was a Muslim, the sole authority empowered to authenticate conversion from Islam was the *shari'a* courts.[148]

For many Muslims, the Lina Joy verdict was timely because it coincided with a resurgence of debate over the creation of an Inter-Faith Commission, which to their minds further threatened to interfere with the authority of the *shari'a* court as such an organization would advocate for the rights of Muslims based on international norms of human rights and not *shari'a*. The majority of Muslim bloggers expressed reservations regarding the establishment of the IFCM for fear that the intention of its proponents was to undermine the primacy of Islam. One such blogger proclaimed:

If the establishment of the Inter-Faith Commission is realized, it will threaten and erode the faiths of all Muslims in this country. This is because the main objective of the Inter-Faith Commission is to weaken the fundamental principles and teachings of Islam. Any form of external authority influencing decisions in this matter will threaten the superiority of Islam and the right of Muslims to adjudicate on all matters relating to Muslims.[149]

Another Malay-Muslim blogger said that the foremost objective of the Commission is to "deny the revelations of Allah and the actions and deeds of the prophet." He asserted further: "Islam is not a religion in which teachings and principles are open to discussion. We have to follow the teachings of Islam and it is not for us to define what the teachings of Islam are."[150] Detractors claimed that the main demands of the IFCM, such as allowing a Muslim youth to choose his faith at the age of eighteen and allowing for conversion cases to be tried at the civil instead of the *shari'a* courts, presented an underlying threat to Islam and its followers.[151] These bloggers emphasized that it is imperative that civil courts not be allowed to rule on matters under the jurisdiction of *shari'a* courts. Going by the tone of these postings, the notion of "defending the faith" against non-Muslim attempts to undermine it—a point consistently alluded to by Muslim politicians, civil society leaders, and religious authorities—has clearly gained some currency among Malay-Muslims in Malaysia.

Several bloggers also expressed concern at how the Lina Joy case had attempted to pit the constitution and Islamic *shari'a* law against each other. According to this perspective, Article 11, which legislates the rights of individuals to profess and practice their chosen religion, threatens to undermine the inviolability of Islam as well as the sanctity of the *shari'a* court when it is "incorrectly invoked," such as in this case, where there was a clear circumvention of *shari'a* court rulings.[152] So virulent were some of the recriminations that even UMNO leaders were denigrated for giving the impression that they were receptive to the Article 11 Coalition, which, akin to the IFCM, aimed to promote basic human rights that are deemed in some Muslim quarters to be incompatible with *shari'a* law. Tarmizi, a Muslim blogger, echoed these sentiments when he said, "It was during Abdullah's weak leadership that the Inter-Faith Commission was established. . . . Such groups have been gaining authority and are able to achieve their objectives because of the utter naïveté and folly of UMNO's current leadership."[153] The ACCIN added, "Because the establishment of the Inter-Faith Commission opens the doors for non-Muslims to interfere with Muslims' affairs, the organization is ultimately anti-Islam."[154] Additionally, ACCIN's Web site contended that "if Muslims are to abide by the norms and laws of basic human rights, this means that their lives will no longer be governed by Islamic values and principles. Therefore, any aspect of Islamic teachings that are antithetical to basic human rights norms will have to be abolished. This means that human right norms are superior to Allah. If we [Muslims] accept this premise then our faith in Allah will be severely shattered."[155]

In contrast to the Malay-language blogs, most non-Muslim English-language bloggers predictably expressed sympathy for Lina Joy.[156] At the heart of this outpouring of sympathy was a sense that Malaysian authorities were beginning to fundamentally restrict freedom of worship and religion, especially with regard to issues related to religious conversion involving Muslims. One such posting said, "It's a sad ruling for freedom of religion in Malaysia. . . . It's no joy for Lina . . . no joy for all Malaysians who cherish freedom of religion. My deep sympathy for Lina and all others who were affected by the sad ruling. Where can you go if you cannot get justice from the highest courts in our land."[157] A peeved Chinese blogger, Chee Yong, further intimated, "A big thumbs down for the decision. Only radical people accept this kind of decisions. Talk about freedom of religion. Those who are happy with the decision, I feel sorry for your state of mind."[158]

While some of the sympathetic bloggers were prepared to concede that Joy should not have bypassed the *shari'a* courts (which she in fact didn't), many argued otherwise, claiming that the rigorous and dogmatic procedures undertaken by the *shari'a* courts before one can be declared a convert from Islam would have invalidated her case, no matter how convincing it was.[159] The majority of these bloggers also wrote that while apostasy within Islam may be considered a major sin, the issue of faith is ultimately a personal matter between oneself and one's God and should not be given over to regulation by the state. Hence, even if Lina Joy was forced to be legally recognized as a Muslim, she was no longer a believer of the faith, much less a practicing one.[160]

In sum, the positions of Muslim and non-Muslim bloggers were clearly polarized on the issue of apostasy. While most of the non-Muslim bloggers did not feel that there was a need for the *shari'a* courts to authorize Lina Joy's conversion, many Muslim bloggers asserted that because she was born a Muslim she should be governed by the "appropriate procedures" in having her conversion out of the faith acknowledged and endorsed. Many Muslim bloggers said that conversion should not be taken lightly, and Islam should be given due respect by adhering to the thorough "rehabilitation process" designed for apostates.[161] A few also claimed that if Joy had followed the appropriate procedures, conversion from Islam would have been possible. It was noted, for example, that the *shari'a* courts in Negeri Sembilan had already authorized sixteen cases of apostasy.[162]

It is evident from this discussion that discourses on and reactions to the rising tide of Islamism have not been confined to the realm of "high politics." Malaysia has witnessed a proliferation of civil society and NGO actors that have engaged and challenged, or at times even reinforced, the political discourse of the UMNO-PAS Islamization race. It bears noting that active civil society discussion and debates have surfaced in cyberspace among increasingly politically conscious and concerned private citizens in conjunction with sociopolitical trends. This new discourse is further supplemented by a range of alternative independent media sources and news portals on the Internet such as Malaysiakini, Bangkit.net, and *Aliran Monthly* (many of which are outgrowths of the reform movement of the late 1990s) that seek to facilitate critical interrogation of mainstream news media and reportage and to provide alternative views.

Despite the panoply of outlets for political expression, two trends are worthy of note. First, given the prevalence of entrenched views on the primacy of Islam among most Malay-Muslim civil society groups, NGOs, and bloggers, it is evident that the parameters of discourse have not discernibly expanded even if the number of avenues have. One can argue that Malay-Muslim popular opinion has at times been more "fundamentalist" than either UMNO or PAS with regard to such issues as moral policing, sanctity of the *shari'a*, defense of the faith, and Malaysia's continued pursuit of the Islamic state ideal, whatever that ideal may be. Second, it is worth noting that national debates over a range of issues at the heart of the rise of Islamism in Malaysia—such as apostasy, Islamic governance and government, and the sanctity of the constitution and of *shari'a* law—have taken on dimensions beyond mainstream partisan politics. Some of the most intense debates are found not in the corridors of power or halls of Parliament but in cyberspace among ordinary citizens. This situation indicates the polarization of Malaysian society over the question of Islam's salience as an ordering principle for law and politics, and it has been most clearly demonstrated in the discourse concerning apostasy legislation, where it appears that Malaysian society is gradually being divided along ethnic and creedal lines.

5

"Securing" Islam in
a Time of Turbulence

The gradual intensification of conservative Islamist discourse discussed in this book, and the concurrent constriction of discursive and political space, have for the past several years been taking place against the broader international backdrop of yet another global resurgence of Islamic consciousness, this time driven by post–September 11 messianism on the part of the United States toward "radical Islam" in authoritarian Muslim societies. A major tenet of neoconservatism in American foreign policy, captured in the problematic phraseology of a "global war on terrorism," has been the subjection of Islam to increasing scrutiny, which clearly has further implications for understanding the contours and trajectories of Islamism in the Malaysian context, particularly in terms of its ideological and external dimensions, even as Islamist discourse is amplified.

The September 11 terrorist attacks in the United States thrust Muslim militancy to the forefront of the international security agenda. In the immediate wake of Washington's global offensive against the Al-Qaeda international terrorist network, terrorism experts quickly warned that Southeast Asia, with its porous borders and traditional receptivity to foreign Islamic ideologies and movements, might well shape up to be international terrorism's "Second Front" and "Crucible of Terror."[1] Not surprisingly, Muslim-led governments in the region took umbrage at these insinuations. The predictions of these terrorism experts were superseded by events that shifted attention to Afghanistan and Iraq. Be that as it may, Southeast Asia did witness an unnerving string of terrorism-related incidents that were cause for apprehension and concern. The uncovering of a plot to bomb the American and other Western embassies in Singapore in December 2001, the Bali bombings of 12 October 2002 and 31 August 2005, and the Jakarta Marriott attack of 5 August 2003 brought home the reality that Muslims in the region were conducting terrorism in the name of Islam.

As the war on terror rages on, the regional spotlight has increasingly fallen on the governments of Southeast Asia and their hunt for Muslim militants within their own territorial boundaries. Malaysia has stood out for particular scrutiny in this regard. While the Malaysian government under Mahathir Mohamad had undoubtedly committed itself to curbing extremism, the reality evidently appeared more ambivalent in the early years of the war on terror, leading some to be critical of Malaysia's efforts. A Singapore media report suggested in 2002 that "for years, Malaysia has played host to the network of terrorists who have emerged as key suspects in the Bali attacks and other devastating strikes against the West."[2] Likewise, a *South China Morning Post* report questioned Malaysian commitment in the fight against terrorism by noting that "the Malaysians are hauling in low-level members of *Jemaah Islamiyah*, questioning and then releasing them."[3] Malaysia's harboring of terrorists was also alluded to in the widely read International Crisis Group report on the activities of *Jemaah Islamiyah*.[4] Separately, Malaysia has also been accused by Thailand of harboring Malay-Muslims engaged in a low-level but escalating armed insurgency in its southern provinces.

On the other hand, others have accused the Malaysian government of capitalizing on the alarmist atmosphere by tenuously connecting terrorists with political dissidents and the Islamist opposition, and by mobilizing state authority to detain and incarcerate "suspected terrorists" without trial under the auspices of its vast array of instruments of coercion. These critics have further argued that the war on terror and attendant concern for "threats" to "national security" have been employed to further legitimize the surveillance state to even greater extents.

Indeed, the contradictions inherent in these two perspectives of the Malaysian government's approach to the war on terror demonstrate the complexities associated with the government's policy on Muslim extremism and militancy in the country and how it has been conflated, deliberately or otherwise, with the intensification of Islamist politics on the part of both the opposition and the government in Malaysia.

Muslim Militancy: The Malaysian Experience

The Malaysian government has a long track record of encounters with militancy and terrorism within its borders, which it often highlights to draw attention to its extensive "experience" in fighting violent antigovernment extremists.

While the Communist insurgency remains by far the most oft-cited and scrutinized, Malaysia also has had experiences with militancy and extremism that
claim religious justification.

The work of Malay historians has drawn attention to the pivotal role that
Islam played as a driver of anticolonial activity, including violence, in British
Malaya. For instance, it has been contended in certain quarters of Malaysian
historiography that Malays often "resisted the British by making references
to their religion."[5] The historical record appears to bear this out. In 1875, violence in Sungei Ujong saw British colonial authorities confronted by armed
Muslim bands waving the Turkish flag, which was indicative of the sway of
pan-Islamic aspirations in the Malay world long before *Jemaah Islamiyah*'s
regional footprint came into being. The Dato Bahaman rebellion in Pahang
between 1891 and 1895 mobilized Islamic identity among the Malay and Bu-
ginese community by rallying around Sayyid Abd al-Rahman bin Muhammad Al-Idrus, also known as Ungku Sayyid or Tunku Paloh, a Sufi scholar
from Terengganu.[6] In 1928, Terengganu, where "Islam tenaciously defied
British political control until the 1920s," when it was forced to accept a British advisor, witnessed its own uprising against central authorities when Haji
Abd al-Rahman Limbung challenged both the colonial administration and
the Terengganu Sultanate on somewhat familiar grounds—for privileging
English constitutional law over and above the *shari'a* in legal disputes concerning individual property.[7] Some have also attempted to portray the famous
Tok Janggut peasant rebellion in Pasir Puteh, Kelantan, as "inspired by the
concept of *jihad*," though this particular narrative has been challenged by
revisionist Malay historians.

Two observations come to mind in this brief sketch of Muslim extremism
across colonial Malay history. First, Islam has long resonated as a key element
of the narrative of anticolonial resistance, and it has often informed challenges
to central authority in British Malaya. Second, as a result of Islam's fusion with
Malay nationalism, Islam has proven to be immensely political in the Malaysian context, defined by the defense of Malay rights and primacy, whether it be
the colonial or postcolonial eras.

Militancy couched in religious language was, of course, not confined to
the period of British administration. Indeed, the postcolonial Malaysian government has had its fair share of confrontations with groups that justify their
attempts to challenge the authority of the state through extremism and violence with reference to religion. By the 1970s, radical and extremist groups had
already started to surface. The Penang-based Crypto cult movement, formed
in 1977, claimed that the Malaysian government was not giving Islam its due
attention and aimed to set up a theocratic order by means of violent *jihad*. It
was only in 1992 that the Malaysian government took action to clamp down
on the movement. Another group whose interpretation of Islam threatened

the incumbent regime was the *Koperasi Angkatan Revolusi Islam Malaysia* (Malaysian Islamic Revolutionary Front, or KARIM). Formed in 1974 in Kuala Lumpur, KARIM preached the overthrow of the government through violence. It was later banned and its leaders detained under the ISA. In 1980, riots in Kedah by farmers demonstrating against the government's move to introduce a forced-savings scheme were believed to be provoked by yet another militant organization called *Pertubuhan Angkatan Sabillullah*, which, according to the government, had a number of members who were also members of PAS.

In 1988, elements from within the Malaysian government moved again to incriminate PAS by linking it to Muslim militancy. This time, members of PAS Youth were accused by their UMNO nemeses of concealing weapons in the PAS seminary *Muassasah Darul Ulum* in Kedah. Though a subsequent crackdown by security forces yielded nothing, several PAS members were later rounded up under "*Ops Kenari*" in response to UMNO's further complaint that these "militants" were attempting to disrupt an UMNO rally in Semarak. During this crackdown, however, weapons were apparently discovered in the possession of PAS members. Nevertheless, attempts to censure the party failed because of insufficient evidence to implicate PAS of institutionalized involvement in militancy. It was in November 1985, however, that Malaysian security forces recorded their first armed encounter with Muslim militants when they clashed with PAS stalwart Ibrahim Mahmood and his supporters in Kedah in what has come to be known in national memory as the "Memali incident."

Ibrahim Mahmood, known also by the moniker "Ibrahim Libya," was a member of PAS and had held senior positions in the party organization at both district and state levels. Trained at the University of Tripoli and al-Azhar, Ibrahim was a popular religious teacher from Kampung Memali in Baling, Kedah, who was also a fiery critic of UMNO and the Mahathir administration. In his capacity as religious teacher and PAS leader, Ibrahim was accused by the Malaysian government of exploiting Islam by spreading radical teachings in the states of Kedah, Penang, and Perak that incited Muslims to conduct *jihad* against the state. The government labeled Ibrahim a "deviant" Muslim and moved to censure him and circumscribe his school's activities. This showdown reached its climax when government security forces stormed the compound of Ibrahim Mahmood's residence while he was conducting religious lessons. After apparent armed resistance from Ibrahim's supporters, the event reached a tragic end, with eighteen deaths and 160 arrests.[8] Several years later and in response to public outcry over their handling of the incident, the government released "video evidence" of the operation in an attempt to exonerate themselves from accusations of brutality and overzealousness in the conduct of operations in Memali. The video, however, was heavily edited and did little to quell residual popular discontent with the manner in which the Mahathir administration dealt with the issue.[9] A heated contest further ensued between the Kedah State *Fatwa* Council, representing the federal government, and the *ulama* leadership of PAS over the status of Ibrahim and his fallen supporters as *shahid* (martyrs).[10]

Recent Militant Movements

More recent manifestations of Muslim militancy surfaced in the form of the Al-Maunah (Brotherhood of Inner Power) movement, which managed to successfully carry out an arms heist from two Malaysian Armed Forces military camps in Perak in June 2000. When the Al-Maunah arms heist occurred, it proved not only a surprise for the Malaysian people but also an embarrassment for the government, given the manner in which members of the group managed to penetrate the camp's security infrastructure by dressing up in military fatigues and driving jeeps painted in camouflage green, indicating the likelihood that the heist was an inside job. According to police reports, the membership of Al-Maunah, a little-known cult led by a former army corporal, Mohammad Amin Razali, numbered several hundred (although the movement's now-defunct Web site, www.al_maunah.tripod.com, had once claimed a membership of 1000) and claimed to be an NGO involved in martial arts training and instruction. According to some reports civil servants, security services personnel, and even some UMNO members numbered among its ranks.[11]

After ascertaining Al-Maunah's responsibility for the arms heist, Malaysian security forces launched a high-profile operation against the organization's camp in Sauk, Perak, in July 2000. During the standoff nineteen members were captured, but only after four hostages were taken and two non-Muslims among them executed. Following this, members of Al-Maunah apprehended in the raid were subsequently charged with treason and plotting to overthrow the government in order to bring into being an Islamic state. While the organization was consequently disbanded and outlawed, what remains most alarming about the episode was the ease with which the militants breached security and gained access to a large cache of weapons.

In June 2001, the spectre of Muslim militancy reared its head again in Malaysia when nine members of another organization that claimed to champion the creation of a purist Muslim society in Malaysia via armed *jihad* were arrested in a failed bank robbery. Known as the *"Jihad* Gang," this group of militants was connected to a range of crimes over a period of two years, including the bombing of a church, an Indian temple, and a video arcade, an attack on a police station, the murder of a local politician, attempted murder involving the shooting of two ethnic Indians, and armed robbery. Police investigations subsequently revealed that all nine members were Malaysians who were educated in the Middle East and Pakistan, had fought with the Afghan Mujahideen during the 1980s, and more recently had participated in religious riots in Ambon (Indonesia). It was during investigations into the activities of the *Jihad* Gang that information on another, apparently more insidious, jihadist organization surfaced.

Several months after apprehending the *Jihad* Gang, Deputy Home Minister Zainal Abidin Zin informed the Malaysian Parliament that ten more Islamist militants had been detained by the government on grounds that they were members of an underground militant group called *Kumpulan Militan Malaysia* (Malaysian Militant Group, or KMM). KMM was discovered when a Malaysian was arrested for an attempted bombing of a shopping mall in Jakarta in August 2001. Investigations allegedly revealed that KMM was formed on 12 October 1995 by Zainon Ismail and had its roots in *Halaqah Pakindo*, a clandestine movement formed in 1986 as an alumni association for Malaysian graduates from religious institutions in Pakistan, India, and Indonesia.[12] The government later disclosed that eight of the ten KMM detainees were PAS members, including Nik Adli Abdul Aziz, the son of Kelantan *Mentri Besar* and PAS *Musyidul 'Am* Nik Aziz Nik Mat. Nik Adli was allegedly elected leader of KMM at a meeting of twelve senior members in Kampung Seri Aman, Puchong, in early 1999, though it was later contended by the government that real leadership came from Abu Bakar Bashir and Hambali (Riduan Isamuddin), the notorious spiritual and operational leaders of the Indonesia-based regional terrorist network *Jemaah Islamiyah*. According to government investigations and, supposedly, Nik Adli's own confession, the 34-year-old religious teacher had made frequent trips to Afghanistan.[13] This confession formed the basis of the government's case against Nik Adli that he was active in the Mujahideen resistance in Afghanistan during the era of the Afghan-Soviet war and that upon his return evidently maintained connections with "the key leaders of radical groups in the region."[14] To date, however, these allegations have not been conclusively proven in open trial, and Nik Adli remained in detention under the ISA until his release in October 2006 along with sixteen other detainees who were suspected of being members of either KMM or *Jemaah Islamiyah*.

What differentiated KMM from other militant organizations uncovered in Malaysia was the purported regional scope of its operations. Though established in Malaysia, it has been suggested in several quarters, including the Malaysian government, that the KMM enjoyed close links with the *Jemaah Islamiyah* in Indonesia, though the exact nature of this relationship remains murky.[15] Along that line of reasoning, Malaysian government sources insist that the KMM was in fact led by Abu Bakar Bashir and Hambali, while Nik Adli was merely a "nominal leader." KMM was suspected of participating in religiously inspired riots in Maluku and Ambon and of having supplied arms to the radical Muslims in the case of the latter, although no information has thus far surfaced about how these arms were obtained, how they were transported to Ambon, or even if they indeed were sent there. Upon their arrests, leaders were reportedly found to have in their possession "documents on guerrilla warfare and map reading, along with studies of militant groups in the Philippines,

Chechnya, Afghanistan and Indonesia."[16] Following this, Malaysian security forces launched a nationwide operation to weed out remaining KMM members. At the peak of arrests up to seventy individuals were detained without trial under the ISA for allegedly trying to overthrow the government through violent means in the name of *jihad*.

Operations against an array of extremist groups indicate that even before September 11 the Malaysian government was already sensitized to the threat of Muslim militancy. Political leaders, senior members of government, and the security establishment were openly discussing the problem of growing radicalization among sections of Malaysian society, particularly the younger cohort of Malay-Muslims returning from religious studies abroad and members of local Islamic organizations. By the turn of the century, the discourse in policy circles had apparently shifted from the preoccupation with economic recovery following the 1997 financial crisis to the growing threat of Islamist militancy, and "the political scene was abuzz with stories about *jihadi* and Mujahideen cells operating all over the country."[17]

Malaysia and International Terrorism

Not only did Malaysia have problems with homegrown Muslim militancy; evidence soon surfaced of the country's role as a staging point for international Muslim terrorist operations. Investigations by American intelligence agencies and their Southeast Asian counterparts after the attacks of September 11 uncovered Malaysia's pivotal role as a rendezvous point for the planning of the terrorist attacks in New York and Washington, D.C. Indeed, some have suggested that "since the early 1990s, Al-Qaeda has found Malaysia to be a convenient base of operations," where militant Islamic ideology "has been able to graft onto a small but growing community of Islamic radicals."[18] There were already indicators that Malaysia was proving to be a reliable transit point, if not an actual haven, for international Islamic militants long before the September 11 attacks. In 1995, Wali Khan Amin Shah, an international terrorist and a known accomplice of Ramzi Ahmed Youssef, the man who was responsible for the 1993 World Trade Center bombings in New York, was arrested in Malaysia. Another known terrorist linked to Ramzi Youssef, Khalid Shaikh Mohammad, who emerged as a chief plotter of the September 11 attacks, was also believed to have operated out of Malaysia on a number of occasions throughout the 1990s.

One of the suspects involved in the planning and implementation of the September 11 attacks, Zacarias Massaoui, who had been accused of conspiring with Osama bin Laden and the Al-Qaeda network to launch the attack on civilians in the United States, was known to have entered Malaysia. During his stay, he was tracked by the Malaysian Special Branch and is believed to have received assistance in the country from a former Malaysian military officer, Yazid

Sufaat. Yazid was also accused of providing shelter to two Yemeni hijackers who participated in the September 11 attacks, Khalid Al-Midhar and Nawaf Al-Azmi, as well as Tawfiq bin Atash, who would later be identified as one of the masterminds behind the October 2000 bombing of the USS *Cole* in Yemen. Through telephone intercepts, it further emerged that *Jemaah Islamiyah* operations chief Hambali used Malaysia as a platform for orchestrating the activities of the terrorist organization. Malaysia was apparently also the location for three meetings of the *Rabitatul Mujahideen,* said to be an ambitious coalition of Jihadist groups from Southeast Asia organized around the *Jemaah Islamiyah* and which attempted to cobble together a coherent agenda across these groups during 1999 and 2000. Malaysia's place in the web of international terrorism extended beyond its apparent role as a "launching pad" for terrorist activities, for it was also insinuated by American intelligence reports that the necessary raw materials required to mount terrorist bomb attacks could also be purchased in Malaysia relatively easily, though no concrete evidence was provided to prove that material was indeed purchased in Malaysia toward that end.[19]

The fact that Malaysia has been identified in the international antiterrorism dragnet as a base from which militant Muslim groups and individuals operated led Washington to label Malaysia a "Terrorist-Risk State" in 2002.[20] In certain respects, there was some substance to Washington's concern. While Malaysian leaders have publicly expressed their annoyance at being linked in any way to terrorist activity, Malaysian security officials have admitted in private that Kuala Lumpur's problems were rooted in its "visa-free" policy toward most Middle Eastern states, and it was this that might have enabled international terrorists and sympathizers to enter the country in the guise of financiers, businessmen, and tourists.[21] This process, they are quick to note, was almost impossible to monitor because of the sheer number of travelers visiting or transiting in Malaysia.

Though the Malaysian government appeared to be confronted with obstacles in monitoring the activities of foreign militant networks in Malaysia, it nevertheless moved to deal with the threat of Muslim militancy on the domestic frontier with impressive efficiency and effectiveness, at least from an operational perspective. Extremists suspected of being associated with the Al-Maunah and KMM organizations were swiftly rounded up in a series of security operations. The Malaysian Special Branch proved to be an instrumental component of the regional counterterrorism intelligence network that exposed *Jemaah Islamiyah* and its connections with Al-Qaeda, tracked down members of the organization, and foiled potential attacks. The ISA, in particular, was employed as a decisive counterterrorism policy instrument against militants "identified" via state-sanctioned surveillance.

Another successful component of Malaysia's operational strategy against terrorism has been its commitment to multilateral cooperation initiatives. The Malaysian government signed an antiterrorism pact with Indonesia and the Philippines in May 2002. Similar agreements were signed with Australia and the United States, in the case of the latter as part of the Association of Southeast Asian Nations (ASEAN). Malaysia is also part of the Five-Power Defense Agreement that pledged to reorient its security cooperation to counter international terrorism more effectively. Of particular interest was the establishment of a regional antiterrorism center in Malaysia, ostensibly in collaboration with the United States, in November 2002. Given Mahathir's vehement opposition to Washington's conduct of its war on terror and the potentially heavy political cost of being seen as a conduit for American interests, the establishment of the antiterrorism center posed a problem for the Malaysian government insofar as its domestic political legitimacy was concerned. A quandary was quickly averted, however, when Malaysian leaders swiftly declared that Washington would have neither influence over nor representation in the antiterrorism center, and that as far as the Malaysia was concerned, the initiative was undertaken independently as part of its own counterterrorism strategy.

The Counterterrorism Poser

In the aftermath of September 11 there has been a mounting sense, even among erstwhile opponents of Southeast Asian authoritarian regimes, that heightened state surveillance and control were probably the best means to address the threat of terrorism. This certainly appeared to be the case in Malaysia, where instruments of the state deployed against Muslim militancy have managed to significantly disrupt the operational capacity of the *Jemaah Islamiyah* network (at least in Malaysia). It has been surmised that a combination of intelligence gathering, the swift mobilization of the ISA, the state's effective control of the national media, and close cooperation with neighboring states have enabled the Malaysian government to detain suspected militants, dismantle militant cells, and, presumably through all this, curb future terrorist activities. Even terrorism experts and security analysts of different persuasions who had expressed reservations regarding the Malaysian government's management of the problem will surely admit that Muslim militants are today finding Malaysia less hospitable than they might have previously thought. Yet before one gives Malaysian counterterrorism operations the seal of approval, one should examine the manner and content of the ideological counteroffensive launched by the Malaysian state, which has perhaps been less categorical in its effectiveness yet more subtle in its long-term implications for the larger picture of Islamist trends in Malaysia.

It is important to note first of all that in challenging the political legitimacy of the incumbent regime, most of Malaysia's militant groups have clear domestic political agendas. For example, the Al-Maunah perpetrators of the raid on the army camps in Kedah pressed their political objectives when they demanded the resignation of Prime Minister Mahathir and his cabinet. Even in the case of the KMM, it is evident that of the three key objectives the organization allegedly espoused, namely (1) "to seek religious purity among Malay-Muslims," (2) "to ensure that PAS's political struggle was maintained and encouraged," and (3) "to implement *shari'a* within Malaysia," all pertained to domestic political concerns.[22] This consideration is important given the fixation of many terrorism analysts with the transnational nature of terrorism, which, though certainly a matter of concern, may at times detract from the real problem.

Second, results of investigations into links between these militant movements and external groups remain inconclusive. All indicators thus far point to these groups being "home-grown" and not under the control of external organizations, even if they did share some degree of ideological affinity as well as rudimentary contacts. The nature and extent of links between the KMM and the *Jemaah Islamiyah* network, drawn emphatically by a host of security analysts, have proven difficult to ascertain, to say nothing of ties with Al-Qaeda. While purportedly supported by international terrorist groups sympathetic to their agendas, it was telling that the charges leveled by the state against the members of KMM under the ISA mentioned only their attempt to overthrow the government. Despite attempts to associate KMM with external groups and regional objectives, such as the grandiose vision of a *Darul Islam Nusantara* in the region, no mention was made of links with either *Jemaah Islamiyah* or Al-Qaeda in the formal charges against the organization, nor have such charges been formally made since. On the contrary, a cursory survey of the history of Muslim militancy in Southeast Asia will reveal that more often than not, it has been Malaysians who have supported the struggles of foreign militant groups, such as the Mujahideen in Afghanistan, the Pattani United Liberation Organization in southern Thailand, the Free Aceh Movement in Aceh, and Muslim fighters in Maluku. Indeed, Malaysians are known to have made their own way to Afghanistan, southern Thailand, and Mindanao—at times without even establishing any initial contacts with local militants— to participate in what they perceived to be, and had been taught were, legitimate Muslim struggles against oppression. These observations indicate that while Muslim militants in Malaysia may draw from external sources or sympathize with the agenda of international terrorist groups (such as anti-Americanism and anti-Zionism), ultimately it has been domestic sociopolitical conditions that gave rise to them and allowed them to fester. In this respect, it is evident that not only is the ideological battle an indispensable component of counterterrorism; it can also be either constrained or enhanced by domestic considerations.

In essence, the local context of Malaysia's own struggle with terrorism post–September 11 cannot be divorced from either the Malaysian government's desire to undermine support for PAS or from its own Islamization project. In the immediate aftermath of the 2001 terrorist attacks and American operations against the Taliban in Afghanistan, Mahathir quickly leveraged on the mood on the ground toward terrorism by implying that PAS's brand of Islam lent itself to precisely the sort of extremist ideology that spawned terrorists. In characteristically opportunistic fashion, Mahathir projected himself and UMNO as the representatives of a modern, tolerant, inclusive form of Islam, while PAS was equated—very visually, through the use of television propaganda—with Taliban-style governance and terrorism. This agenda was facilitated by the arrest of the alleged members of KMM. It was the arrest of Nik Adli Nik Aziz in particular that provided crucial fuel for the government's anti-PAS propaganda.

The way the Malaysian government has attempted to gain greater currency from the war on terrorism raises some fundamental questions about the ideological component to its counterterrorism strategy. A major drawback here is the fact that the instruments for the identification and castigation of Muslim militants by the Malaysian government have become subsumed into the broader framework of exclusivist religiopolitical discourse that has descended upon Malaysia. At the heart of this discourse lies the government's codification of an interpretation of deviancy that appears, at least in part, politically inspired. Additionally, this interpretation of deviancy also paradoxically forecloses Islamist counterdiscourses that can potentially function as a structural check on the emergence of fringe, extremist interpretations of Islam of the kind that motivates groups such as Al-Maunah and *Jemaah Islamiyah*. The net effect of this discourse is that rather than exposing the "un-Islamic" character of some of these groups, the government has inadvertently fostered a religio-intellectual environment and precipitated conditions that allow such narrow, militant interpretations to surface and garner appeal.

Not surprisingly, the basis of government allegations against these groups has also been contested by a broad spectrum of critics including human rights groups, opposition parties, and many quarters in the academic community (both secular and Islamic). Chief among these criticisms is the fact that the government has yet to provide sufficient evidence of the existence of some of these organizations, their purported militant intentions, or their alleged intimate connections to international terrorist networks. This in turn has fed suspicions and conspiracy theories that the charges were manufactured toward political ends. Indeed, to its detractors, the government's case against these "deviant" movements appears to be politically motivated, given the regular reference to the relationship between these movements and PAS.

The situation with the KMM stands as a case in point. Given that several members of the KMM were apparently members of PAS, suggestions swiftly surfaced that the accusations were contrived by the Mahathir administration in order to legitimize a clamp down on the Islamic opposition. Seeking to exploit the situation, PAS quickly responded with counterallegations that the government had manipulated evidence in order to pander to Washington. Others have raised doubts as to whether the KMM in fact exists, at least in the form described in government statements.[23] While the case against Al-Maunah was handled in civil courts, where conclusive evidence was provided on their activities to back the charges leveled by the government, KMM members were charged under the ISA, meaning that its members were detained without trial. Upon its detention of alleged KMM members, the government had also declared that a white paper on the movement's activities and connections was being prepared. This white paper has yet to see the light of day. Without substantial evidence, UMNO's alacrity in making allegations that PAS and the KMM are linked may well have allowed PAS to exploit this as an instance of UMNO's pandering to Western paranoia toward Islam, as well as another example of the arbitrary application of state power to advance the interests of the ruling regime.

To be sure, the Malaysian government's operational actions against Islamic "extremists" and "radicals" are but one dimension of a complex relationship between religion, the state, and Malaysian society today. At the same time that the government is identifying and clamping down on extremists and radicals— including some rather dubious accusations based on questionable "evidence" against members of the Islamist opposition—the regime has encouraged, facilitated, and enhanced the role of the Islamic religious establishment in Malaysian society, the judiciary, and public life in general. As but one example, state-sanctioned *ulama* have come to assume prominent roles in various institutions, through which they have been empowered to govern various aspects of Malaysian intellectual, cultural, and social life, not to mention the media and education system. While deploying a vast surveillance and coercive apparatus at its disposal to demonize and demobilize Islamic political opposition, the regime has permitted—indeed, facilitated—a remarkable degree of penetration by the conservative Muslim clergy of the institutions of the state.

At first glance, these two facets to the Malaysian government's dealings with Islamic social and political forces appear to contradict each other. In reality, they are intimately related. Recognizing the utility and potency of Islamic symbols, in the interest of bolstering their own power and credentials the state has allowed the conservative Islamic clergy an active role in government and society. Rather than head off oppositionist Islamic forces with a turn to secularism, democratization, and "liberal Islam," the state has in fact mobilized Islam not only to shore up its credentials and support the base, but also to undercut the opposition. The state-sanctioned clerics who address the public in government mosques and who run the inflated religious bureaucracy through the *Jabatan Kemajuan Islam Malaysia* (the Islamic Development Department of Malaysia) are more often than not highly conservative in their outlook. In some instances, they have proven more critical (at times, vocally and animatedly) of the pluralism of values and lifestyles in Malaysia today than some segments of the Islamist opposition. In other words, many of the clerics who have state endorsement are more "radical" in their efforts to bring Malaysia into conformity with a conservative and rigid interpretation of Islamic law even as they castigate alternative expressions of Islamic religiosity and spirituality, not to mention legal opinions, as "deviant."

These, then, are the deeper conundrums behind the Malaysian government's responses to Islamic radicalism and extremism. As the preceding chapters have demonstrated, the UMNO-led Malaysian government has over the past two decades or so permitted—indeed facilitated—an enormous degree of penetration by Islamic forces into mainstream society, thereby undercutting the argument, often made by militant Muslim groups, that the government is in fact "not Islamic enough" and is in bed with *kafir* (infidel) forces. One outcome of this, however, is that the socioreligious climate in Malaysia has also seen Islam become increasingly "radical" in its fundamentalism and conservatism. Given the trajectory and pace of state-driven Islamization in Malaysia, this phenomenon will undoubtedly have significant impact on a country that has a sizeable non-Muslim minority. Far beyond the question of the presence or absence of terrorist groups in Malaysia, this phenomenon has precipitated conditions for narrow interpretations to surface and garner appeal, thereby threatening to fundamentally transform the norms and configuration of Malaysian society.

Discourses of Deviancy

For a long time, studies on Islam in Malaysia have focused on its intersection with rich and vibrant indigenous cultures that have given rise to syncretic understandings and practices of the faith. Even when Islam took on political hues in the precolonial Malay *kerajaan* (traditional court government), it seldom spawned militant activity. While the general consequence of this interaction between Islam and indigenous culture has been the production of a peaceful, status quo version of Sunni Islam in a multicultural society, there have on occasion been Islamic teachings that have evidently gone against the grain of the "approved" ideas of the religion as defined by ruling authorities, both past and present. From that vantage, it also proved convenient and expedient for these authorities to trade on their legitimacy as "authentic" commissars of the faith by framing such teachings as a challenge to mainstream traditional Islam and labeling them "deviant" for their supposed contravention of *aqidah* (faith) and *shari'a* derived from the Qur'an and *sunnah*. It follows that the prerogative of state religious authorities has been to outlaw and stamp out such "deviancy." Discourses of deviancy are then wielded as a major instrument of repression.

At an April 2002 parliamentary session, parliamentary secretary to the prime minister's department Noh Omar declared that the government had identified twenty-four "deviationist" groups, with a total membership of 7,210.[24] According to figures provided by JAKIM, there have been up to ninety-eight "deviant" strains of Islam practiced in the country, of which twenty-five are apparently still active.[25] While they may not have found their way onto the "official" list of outlawed deviant groups yet, mainstream organizations such as Forum Iqra (The Qur'anic Society of Malaysia) and Sisters in Islam, who regularly question prevailing state-sanctioned interpretations of Islam, have also been subject to demonization through accusations of deviancy by religious leaders and the religiopolitical elite.

The concept of deviancy refers to the distortion of Qur'anic teachings as defined by established religious authorities. Simply put, this definition implies a "right" or "authentic" Islam from which certain interpretations have "deviated." Needless to say, such an assertion is clearly controversial, particularly given the recognition that Islam lacks any notion of centralized religious authority. For example, conceptual lines are blurred when the idea of deviancy is juxtaposed against the notion of *ijtihad* or "informed interpretation" of the religious texts by individuals. Conceptual vagueness notwithstanding, it is a fact that accusations of deviancy remain arguably the most scathing in Islam. In Malaysia, the concept of deviancy has been the ideological cornerstone of the state's counter-offensive against Muslim extremism, not to mention other potential sources of opposition, where the ideological strategy has been premised on a policy of discrediting renditions and interpretations of Islam that are incongruent with the state-sanctioned version. At the heart of this strategy is the mobilization of state *ulama* and state-sanctioned *fatwa* against what are deemed to be deviant Islamic teachings.

While it is important to consider theological and doctrinal debates over deviancy and interpretation of the Qur'an, this is beyond the scope of this project. For current purposes, it is the political ramifications associated with such contestations within Islam that assume paramount importance with respect to the Malaysian government's conduct of its war against Muslim militancy, and, more broadly, how the Malaysian government has dealt with sources of opposition and threats—real or constructed—to its narrative on Islamism. The Malaysian state is more than equipped with the requisite instruments to identify, regulate, and discipline deviancy. As Patricia Martinez puts it, "What the Federal government does have is the power to discipline Muslims using instruments of civil law such as the Internal Security Act and the Penal Code."[26] Government control has been further expressed in the practice of sermon-policing and the close scrutiny of the political proclivities of preachers so as to attenuate support for PAS and to monitor the popularity of fringe Muslim groups. As mentioned earlier, state religious departments have taken to providing mosques with standardized sermon texts and have instituted a system of monitoring to ensure that these texts are used accordingly. Likewise, the government has an active hand in the posting of preachers, ensuring that *imam* with opposition sympathies are removed from mosques and replaced with others more amenable to the government.

"Securitizing" Islamism: Shi'a Islam and the Arabization Debate

The notion of deviancy in the history of Islam can be traced back to the struggle for legitimacy after the reign of the four rightly guided caliphs between the followers of Ali (Shiat Ali), the cousin of the Prophet Muhammad, and Abu Bakar, deemed to be the most qualified of the Prophet's followers and his immediate successor. At the heart of this tension was the debate over whether credentials for the leadership of the Muslim community rested on lineage or ability. Shi'a Islam, which grew out of the Shiat Ali movement that challenged Abu Bakar's legitimacy, has at times come to be viewed as deviationist ideology by Sunni Muslims.[27] This antagonism is considerably more palpable in Malaysia, where the propagation of Shi'a teaching is deemed an offense in the predominantly Sunni country, and Shi'a Islam is officially banned. In 1997 the Malaysian government even proposed to entrench this distinction by amending the constitution to make Sunni Islam Malaysia's official Islamic sect.[28]

Further demonstrative of the Malaysian government's propensity toward labeling and "securitizing" perceived deviancy is the fact that Shi'a Muslims have regularly been apprehended by the authorities. In the early 1990s, a concentrated onslaught of media articles warned of the threat that Shi'a Islam posed to Malay-Muslim unity in Malaysia.[29] In 1997, seven Shi'a Muslims were reportedly detained for spreading "deviationist teachings" that purportedly threatened religious harmony and "the nation's political and economic development."[30] These detainees were forced to undergo rehabilitation courses where they had to internalize the "right" Islam before they could be released. Six more Shi'a Muslims were detained under the ISA in Malaysia between October 2000 and January 2001 on similar charges.[31] Describing the security impetus for some of these arrests, a Shi'a news Web site reported: "Those who were released in early 1997 were told to renounce their Shi'a faith and to revert to the Sunni sect as a precondition of their release from ISA. The reason of arrest according to the police then was activities 'prejudicial to national security and Muslim unity.'"[32] The prejudice of established orthodoxy that dictates the nature and sources of Islamic deviancy is clearly demonstrated here in how the "challenge" posed by Shi'a Islam in Malaysia has been framed as a national security issue. Indeed, the fact that Shi'a Muslims are prosecuted under the ISA and not by the *shari'a* court, as should be the case if the matter was purely religious in nature, speaks of the overtly political nature of the government's handling of Shi'a "deviancy."

A further permutation of the security discourse on Islamism is the debate on Arabization of Southeast Asian Muslims, which has gained currency in recent times as the region comes to terms with the influx of Arabic customs and ideas, chiefly Wahhabism.[33] At the heart of the Arabization debate is the move by some religious figures to equate Arab culture with the Islamic faith, which in turn signifies the encroachment of Arab culture into traditional Malay society. This issue was taken up by Arts, Culture, and Heritage Minister Rais Yatim, who spoke out against the Arabization of Malay culture and took PAS to task for its rejection of certain aspects of Malay tradition and cultural heritage.[34] Commonly cited examples include the banning of *wayang kulit* and *dikir barat* by the PAS state government in Kelantan, and the rejection of *adat bersanding* in certain quarters among northern Malay-Muslims because of its Hindu origins. The popularity of Arabic dress as a visible marker of Islamic identity and personal piety is also regularly cited as a major indicator of Arabization in Malaysia.

Beyond attacking PAS for fostering and encouraging Arabization, UMNO has also sought to counter this influence by drawing attention to the multireligious roots of Malaysian Islam.[35] Yet PAS members and leaders are not the only channel of Arab influence in Malaysia. If Malaysian students returning from the Middle East are conduits of Arabization, as opponents of Arabization are wont to believe, then state religious officials who have been recipients of government funds and scholarships and who are now employed in the religious bureaucracy are equally culpable. At the same time that UMNO leaders are criticizing PAS for facilitating the influx of external influences that undermine local Malay culture, government-linked religious officials have been complicit in perpetuating the very fundamentalist and conservative Arabization that their political masters purport to critique. It was officials from the education ministry, for instance, and not PAS opposition backbenchers, who had "discouraged" the teaching of music in schools on the grounds that such extracurricular activities were "un-Islamic."[36]

The subtext of the concept of "deviation" implies the existence of an authentic interpretation of Islam. In the case of Malaysia, authenticity has come to translate to government-sanctioned Islam, where all other variations, including those of Islamists who argue that state policies contradict the teachings of the Qur'an, are considered "deviationist." This is clearly evident on the discursive terrain of *hudud* law, where the Mahathir government has gone on record to accuse PAS of being "deviationist" for wanting to implement *hudud* legislation that UMNO deems to be unjust.[37] Indeed, the manipulation of the concept for political ends continues to be a pressing concern for those anxious about the politicization of religion in Malaysia.

Through its *ulama*, the government has attempted to exercise hegemony over Islamic matters and has worked to ban interpretations of the religious tenets and texts that differ from the official rendition. Consequently, discursive and doctrinal debate over the Qur'an and *hadith* have been construed as the "heretical" questioning of divine will and are thus proscribed. In its religio-political jousting with PAS, the Mahathir and Abdullah administrations created a mode of representation and inquiry that portrays the Islamist opposition in Malaysia not only as fundamentalists in their desire to transform Malaysia into an Islamic polity based on the reassertion of some form of the Caliphate, but also as a deviant movement for wanting to do so. Consequently, the state mobilized accusations of deviancy as a political tool to curtail the influence of Muslim-based political opposition. Yet, paradoxically, the fact that the label of "deviationist" has become more political than scriptural has been attested to by the fact that at the end of the day, the state has not been able to take concrete action against PAS for the supposed spread of "deviationist" teaching despite UMNO's saber-rattling.

No doubt such an approach circumscribes the potential for militant interpretations of scripture to establish roots within Malaysia's Muslim society. Yet such a strategy also runs the obvious risk of being savagely double-edged. Because it is premised on casting a wide enough net, it also forecloses introspection and self-criticism within Islam and in so doing denies the possibility of the emergence of alternative, progressive interpretations of the religion from sources other than the government, which in many ways is already confronted with a credit deficit in the eyes of many in Malaysia. Seyyed Vali Nasr's notion of the "Islamic Leviathan" is perhaps apposite here to depict this process of how the state has attempted to harness Islamism to serve state interests, thereby sustaining the UMNO-PAS Islamization contest and ensuring the potential and survivability of extremist mindsets, however modest their numbers, within the Muslim community.

A major battlefront in the debate over deviancy and security was the realm of religious education. Mahathir assailed the private religious school system at the 2001 UMNO assembly as an antigovernment vehicle and mouthpiece of PAS.[38] Mahathir's remarks were soon followed by a policy of interdiction against these schools. In February 2003 some seventy-four thousand students of 268 private religious schools (Sekolah Agama Rakyat),[39] mostly run by PAS supporters and members, were forced to transfer to national schools on the pretext that the religious schools taught narrow and deviant interpretations of Islam and fostered extremism.[40] Rather than addressing the problem at root by revamping the curriculum in these religious schools, however, the government opted to cut their funding.[41] To justify this policy, the education ministry revealed that nineteen out of twenty-five alleged members of KMM apprehended in 2001 had been students of these schools. These included Nik Adli Nik Aziz, the son of PAS Mursyid'ul Am Nik Aziz Nik Mat and headmaster of Darul Anuar Islamic School in Kelantan. Another religious school alumnus, Mohammad Amin Razali, was apparently the leader of the Al-Maunah gang. This move to draw a connection between extremism, militancy, and religious education was a marked escalation from the state's initial disclosure that the "problem" with these schools was merely the "fact" that they were being used as vehicles to disseminate PAS propaganda and sow antigovernment sentiments within the traditional Malay-Muslim community.[42]

The inconsistency behind the government's rationale for the closure of these schools was not lost on the public, and the policy received an icy reception.[43] Given the Mahathir administration's declaration that Malaysia was already an Islamic state, the Malay population, for whom these schools remain a bastion of traditional Malay culture and identity, questioned the wisdom of cutting funding to Islamic schools while still giving support to Chinese and Indian schools. Civil society organizations, many of which opposed the closing down of these schools, challenged the government to provide more concrete evidence of links between terrorists and these religious institutions to justify their closure of the system.

Without denying the possibility that militants might indeed have sprung from private religious schools, PAS has countered by alleging that the security impetus was but a veil for a policy of circumscription of support for the opposition. The PAS response was understandable, given that Islamic teachers and students have traditionally been a bulwark of support for the Islamist opposition party. To be fair, PAS itself has acknowledged the political impulse behind its policy on religious education. In a document entitled *Tarbiyah* (Islamic Education) available on the party Web site, PAS made plain its ideological position that "Islam has been colonized and many Muslims have been forced to deviate from their religion as a result of their acceptance of the separation of religion from politics. To rectify this, there needs to be a realization of the intimate link between Islam and politics."[44] PAS said its support base consisted of teachers and Islamic school leaders who are "conscious that Islam *is* politics and governance."[45]

Separately, PAS leaders have on occasion also admitted that private religious schools do encounter a problem when it comes to the question of dealing with cultural pluralism in terms of the narrow nature of its curriculum.[46] The situation of the private religious schools was partly resolved when government funding was reinstated in 2005 after intense lobbying by various segments of Muslim society, on the condition that these schools register with the education ministry and endorse the *akujanji* (pledge of loyalty).[47] Another cohort of students targeted by the state were those returning from religious education institutions in Pakistan and the Middle East. This concern was informed by the fact that members of the *Jihad* Gang apprehended in 2001 were found to be graduates of Islamic education institutions in Pakistan and the Middle East.[48] From January 2002, these students were required to register with the government, apparently for purposes of assessment and monitoring.[49] Concerned about PAS influence over this cohort through numerous student organizations established by the party in the Middle East, particularly in al-Azhar and Medina but also Britain, the Malaysian government issued a directive that Malaysian students should refrain from political activities abroad, and those on government scholarships should not participate in antigovernment activities.[50]

Fraternity of Faith

An important element of Malaysia's handling of the problem of religious extremism has been the latter's connection to developments elsewhere in the Islamic world. In the immediate aftermath of the September 11 terrorist attacks,
Malaysia stepped forward as an unlikely but welcome ally in Washington's ensuing war on terrorism. Prime Minister Mahathir swiftly linked his government's
efforts at fighting Muslim militants on the domestic front to the global war on
terror. Kuala Lumpur moved to enhance bilateral security ties with Washington
by signing an antiterrorism accord and agreeing to set up the aforementioned
regional counterterrorism center. The upturn in relations, which had soured
over American criticisms of the detention of former deputy prime minister
Anwar Ibrahim several years earlier, peaked with the red-carpet reception given
to Mahathir when he visited Washington in May 2002. At the time, Mahathir
was even prepared to countenance the Bush administration's increasingly bel-
ligerent attitude toward Iraq. During his Washington visit, Mahathir reportedly
made the portentous comment: "If you can overthrow Saddam, by all means do
it. Just don't make the Iraqi people pay for it."[51]

Shared interests, however, belied fundamental differences over the road
map of the counterterrorism campaign, and U.S.-Malaysian solidarity was soon
fragmented by contrasting opinions regarding its scope, strategy, and trajectory. In the wake of the American invasion of Iraq, Islamization policies can
be further understood as a reflection of Malaysian foreign policy concerns. Despite Mahathir's reported comments, the Malaysian government soon became
a staunch opponent of Washington's attempt to extend the war on terrorism
to Iraq, which the latter justified on the basis of highly questionable evidence
linking the Iraqi regime and Al-Qaeda, evidence that was soon discredited.[52]
Mahathir tersely rejected the logic of the Bush administration, which linked
the regime of Saddam Hussein to Al-Qaeda, retorting instead that Iraq was no
more than "a side issue" in the terrorism war. Insofar as Kuala Lumpur was
concerned, the key to victory against terrorist elements was not military but
political. The Malaysian government believed that it was not the dismantling
of "tyrannical regimes" such as those in Iraq, or Afghanistan and Iran for that
matter, that would pull the rug out from under the feet of Muslim militants,
but the reformulation of American policy toward Israel and Palestine, which to
Malaysian minds was where the "root cause" of terrorism lay.

Predictably, the Malaysian government has been proactive in orchestrating
opposition to and condemnation of the American invasion of Iraq at both international and domestic levels. In his final presidential address at the UMNO
general assembly, Mahathir vehemently criticized the U.S.-led war against Iraq
and accused "Anglo-Saxon Europeans" of using the September 11 attacks as a

pretext to return to their "violent old ways" by attacking Islamic nations. He pointed out that "their strategy to fight terrorism is through attacking Muslim countries and Muslims, whether they are guilty or not. . . . By making all kinds of baseless accusations they launched attacks against Muslim countries, using their weapons of mass destruction, killing civilians and destroying the towns."[53] UMNO's position on the Iraq war, epitomized by Mahathir's sentiments, was also echoed by PAS. Party president Abdul Hadi condemned the attack on Iraq by charging "this despicable war exposes the ugliness of America and its allies." He also said that "PAS is convinced that this war is the start of America's destruction because Allah will not let any major power reign supreme forever."[54] Prior to the outbreak of hostilities in Iraq, Malaysia was already actively involved in marshaling international diplomatic opinion in opposition to American policy. Mahathir had taken advantage of Malaysia's chairmanship of the Non-Aligned Movement to formulate a resolution rejecting the case presented by the United States for its attack on Iraq, replying that ultimately the attack took place without the sanction of the United Nations. The Malaysian government has also led the OIC (Organization of Islamic Conferences) in protest against military action. At home, Malaysian leaders portrayed the war as a violation of the sovereignty of an Arab-Muslim state by Western imperialist powers.

What is striking about Malaysia's strident condemnation of American policy is the conspicuous congruence of opinions among local political actors that was also evident within Malaysian society in general. Noticeably, both ruling and opposition parties, as well as Muslim and non-Muslim NGOs, have shared the same platform and united in condemning the invasion of Iraq. The Malaysian Parliament unanimously adopted a motion reproving the unprovoked military action against Iraq by the United States and its allies, and Parliament passed seven resolutions setting out an official position on the Iraq war. In a rare display of camaraderie, the leaders of the youth movements of UMNO and PAS led a joint demonstration outside the American embassy on 25 March 2003. This followed a massive, government-organized antiwar demonstration at the Merdeka Stadium that was attended by fifty thousand people, including the entire Malaysian cabinet. UMNO Youth spearheaded a national peace movement (*Aman Malaysia*) that attempted to lobby the United Nations to investigate the "war crimes" of America and its allies and bring the "perpetrators" to court.

Clearly, a major premise of Malaysian opposition to the Iraq war stemmed from a domestic political imperative that drove the ruling party to reject American-led military action. Yet Malaysian opposition was also linked to wider concerns shared in many quarters of the Muslim world that Washington's policy was tantamount to a neoconservative American "crusade" against Islam. In the eyes of many Muslims this correlation appeared justified. Beyond these instrumental and ideological motives, there was likely also an element of pride at stake for Malaysia. Despite declaring Malaysia an ally in the war against terrorism post–September 11, Washington incensed Malaysia by subjecting Malay-Muslim students and tourists to stringent customs and immigration checks at American airports. In a visit to the United States in September 2002 as deputy prime minister, Abdullah was forced to take off his shoes and belt as part of security checks prior to a domestic flight from Los Angeles to New York City. As mentioned earlier, Malaysia also found itself listed as a "terrorist-risk" country by the American government despite its contributions to the war on terror. Given the political constellation in Malaysia, such a perception no doubt held implications for the political fortunes of Malaysia's ruling coalition government, which has traditionally enjoyed close relations with the United States.

Notwithstanding the efforts on the part of the Bush administration to emphasize that aggression against Iraq was not a war against Islam (or even against Iraqis, for that matter) but was merely targeted at the secular totalitarian regime of Saddam Hussein, an attack against a Muslim country like Iraq can very easily and quickly be perceived as an attack against Muslims, particularly if it was precipitated by questionable (and at times contradictory) policy statements. This point was repeatedly stressed by Mahathir and his successor Abdullah Badawi, although both also noted that given the number of Western states that had opposed the American action, the offensive had to be viewed as an American, not Western, war against Islam. Needless to say, this logic gained much currency among Malaysia's Muslim community, to say nothing of the larger *ummah*, for whom the contradictory American positions on Iraq and North Korea, which ironically had by then demonstrated that it possessed highly advanced nuclear and missile technology, served to further heighten suspicions by drawing attention to glaring inconsistencies in Washington's strategic logic.

While Iraq emerged as the key point of reference for more recent manifestations of Malaysia's increasingly Islamist foreign policy, Malaysian foreign policy activism for the cause of Islam has certainly not been confined to this issue, nor did it begin or end with Iraq. Of late, the Malaysian government under Abdullah has also been active in condemning Israeli retaliatory attacks on Hamas and has called on Muslim governments to provide financial aid and other forms of support to Hamas to help the party lead the Palestinian Authority. Leaders from both UMNO and PAS further criticized Western states for cutting off aid to Palestine after the Islamist victory in open elections in January 2006. Hishammuddin Hussein, head of UMNO Youth, labeled Israel's aggression in Palestine and Lebanon as *"tindakan hina biadab"* (uncivilized conduct) and blasted the United States for *"cakap tak serupa bikin"* (not walking the talk) and *"bikin tak suka cakap* (preferring action to dialogue)."[55]

In July 2006 about a thousand PAS members armed with flags, banners, and posters marched on the American embassy in Kuala Lumpur to protest what they felt was systematic Israeli aggression against Palestinian people as well as Washington's support for the Zionist state. The march was led by party (reformist) stalwarts Mohammad Sabu and Hassan Ali, whose speeches indicted that "United States should be condemned for their continuing hypocrisy in the Middle East. We will give Condoleezza Rice something to think about. We will also give her boss something to think about."[56] Reacting against Israel's policy on Palestine by alleging that the Israelis have consistently breached the Geneva conventions, Salahuddin Ayub further described them as *"bangsa bangsat"* (a race of thugs), saying that pressure should be kept up until "Jews are expelled from Arab lands."[57] Indeed, the Palestinian issue has been one that has preoccupied the Malaysian foreign policy establishment for a long time. In this regard, Malaysia rejected Washington's ill-informed conflation of the Palestinian struggle with global terrorism in the following manner: "It is Malaysia's view that the operations of Al-Qaeda and *Jemaah Islamiyah* in the nation-states of Southeast Asia lack legitimacy, whereas the struggle of the Palestinians for self-determination is grounded in international law and human rights."[58]

Notwithstanding this inclination to exhibit foreign policy dispositions in opposition to those of the United States and the larger Western world toward their Muslim coreligionists, Malaysian political leaders, and in particular Mahathir himself, have been equally caustic in their criticisms of Muslim countries, particularly in terms of their weakness and inability to stand united against the pressures of what he saw as resurgent Western imperialism. Reflecting upon this, Mahathir has lamented:

> We must admit that the Muslim *ummah* and Muslim countries
> are still under threat and are very weak. We do much damage to
> ourselves by our lack of cooperation and our frequently violent and
> debilitating struggles for power in our own countries. As a result,
> whenever our brothers are in need of help, not only are we unable to
> extend meaningful help, we are even unable to influence those agen-
> cies whose decisions and actions will affect the fate of our brothers.[59]

As mentioned earlier, the Malaysian position on the Iraq invasion was merely the latest expression of a long tradition of activism on issues relating to the Islamic world. The genesis of this activism is traceable to the early ventures of the *Hizbul Muslimin*, predecessor to the religious leaderships in both UMNO and PAS, which established a Palestine Aid Committee immediately after the end of the Second World War to support the Palestinian struggle. The *Hizbul Muslimin* also actively supported the cause of Malay-Muslim separatism in the southern provinces of Thailand.[60] This activism carried over into the 1960s when Malaysia joined the chorus of opposition from other Muslim states against the Israeli occupation of Palestine, spoke in support of Algeria's struggle for independence, and took up the Bosnian cause in the 1990s, of which Malaysia was a particularly vocal and assiduous proponent. At other times, Malaysia's Islamic foreign policy agenda was expressed in more innocuous forms such as the organization of the annual international Qur'an reading competition, the provision of humanitarian assistance and asylum for Cambodia's Muslims who had fled the killing fields of the Khmer Rouge regime, and more recently for Thai Malay-Muslims fleeing anticipated persecution by Thai security forces, which suspected elements among the kingdom's minority Malay-Muslim community in the southern provinces of engaging in separatist violence.

Shanti Nair discerned a definitive political mien to Malaysia's pro-Muslim foreign policy, which she described in the following manner: "While bilateral relations with other Muslim countries have been useful to the Administration in legitimizing its own 'Islamic' character . . . they also serve as appropriate fora for promoting the Administration's vision of what the 'right' Islam constitutes."[61] Given this domestic political imperative, it is conspicuous that notwithstanding the sharpening acrimony that defines the political jousting between UMNO and PAS, on foreign policy issues pertaining to the Muslim world both parties often find themselves aligned in the same camp. Indeed, on many of the issues identified above, the UMNO-led Malaysian government has been vociferously supported by PAS. At the height of the most recent crisis in Lebanon, for instance, PAS joined UMNO in dispatching missions to Beirut to provide medical and diplomatic support in Lebanon's struggle against Israel. Like UMNO, PAS has vehemently condemned Israeli policy in the Middle East and has supported the cause of oppressed Muslim minorities in Bosnia, Thailand, and the Philippines.

PAS's support for UMNO on this range of issues should not be mistaken for a lack of initiative on its own part, nor does the party lag behind in its own rhetoric on the plight of Muslims across the world. In fact, the opposite is true, and PAS has long had an active, if low-key, foreign policy of its own toward the Muslim world. An issue that has particularly vexed the PAS leadership (and UMNO as well) is the ongoing insurgency in the southern provinces of Thailand that border Northern Malaysia, and the attendant question of the plight of the Thai Malay-Muslims residing in the south who have been subjected to heavy-handed policies emanating from Bangkok.[62] PAS has supported the cause of Malay-Muslim separatism in southern Thailand since the party's formation.[63] In fact, not only has PAS expressed sympathy with the cause of the southern Thai Malay-Muslims; its leaders have on occasion also evidently articulated highly controversial remarks that could easily be construed as overt support for separatism.

Perhaps the most notorious of these were remarks allegedly uttered by former party president Asri Muda, who reportedly said in 1974 that "the request for autonomy with specific conditions in the administration of the four southern provinces of Thailand . . . seems credible and could be a wise move toward reconciliation and peace."[64] PAS sympathy for their Malay-Muslim co-religionists was raised again in 1992, when Abdul Hadi was reported to have expressed in his capacity as party vice-president that PAS had to consider helping Thailand's

Malay-Muslims "because our Moslem brothers are being discriminated against in all aspects of life in Southern Thailand."[65] After the October 2004 massacre of more than eighty protesters by Thai security forces in Tak Bai, a village in the southernmost province of Narathiwat, PAS representatives, supported by their UMNO counterparts, successfully submitted and pushed through a motion in the Malaysian Parliament that openly and unambiguously condemned the actions of Thai security forces. Likewise, in a telling demonstration of how Malaysia is perceived by the Malay-Muslims in southern Thailand, during a standoff between southern Thai villagers and Thai security forces in Tanyong Limo village in Narathiwat in September 2005, villagers established a "Thai media-free zone" to deny the Thai media entry into the village, but they welcomed Malaysian TV reporters.[66] Since then, Abdul Hadi has publicly called for a referendum on autonomy for the southern provinces, while Nik Aziz has petitioned for the intervention of the Thai king in the crisis.

More recently, PAS advanced its foreign policy activism to a higher plane in August 2006 when it organized the "Southeast Asia Organizations Roundtable Conference on Palestine and Lebanon in Facing Zionist and Anglo-American Imperialism" in Kuala Lumpur.[67] The conference, which featured the attendance of representatives from Hamas and Iran, shaped up to be a proverbial "who's who" of transnational Islamist political parties and civil society movements. What emerged at the meeting, apart from the customary tongue-lashing of Israel and the United States, was an effort to coordinate and institutionalize aid to Palestine and Lebanon through the formation of a transnational network of Islamist groups, beginning with the establishment of a secretariat in Kuala Lumpur. While it remains unclear if this initiative will be successful in the long run, it does demonstrate a move on the part of PAS not only to forge a larger imprint for itself and for Malaysia on the issues of Palestine and Lebanon but also to enhance its already active foreign network and policies in the Muslim world.

PAS is also attempting to extend its foreign policy activism toward non-Muslim, non-Western countries. Consider, for instance, the efforts of PAS to build relations with China. The Kelantan state government has recently enhanced cultural cooperation with various Chinese provinces, and advanced discussions are taking place between it and local and regional Chinese counterparts to enhance trade ties. PAS also invites an *imam* from China annually to Malaysia to lead prayers during Ramadan. According to PAS officials, this policy is part of the party's attempt both to demonstrate to local audiences that Chinese can be and are Muslims, and to illustrate the cosmopolitan nature of PAS's Islamist credentials as compared to the exclusivist Malay agenda of UMNO.[68]

Both PAS and UMNO have been complicit in exporting their "Islamization race" beyond Malaysian shores. By far the clearest and most intense expression of this has been the parties' respective attempts to mobilize support from

Malaysian Muslim students attending tertiary education institutions abroad. Much of the "unofficial" foreign policy activity of UMNO and PAS has been conducted by their respective youth movements, both of which have an international bureau that functions as the movement's representative in the arena of global affairs. Both parties are active among the Malaysian community in the "*kampung melayu*" in Cairo, where seminars and speaking engagements are organized regularly for some 3,500 Malaysian students attending Cairo University and al-Azhar University.[69] Both parties are also active in Saudi Arabia and Pakistan, where there are major concentrations of Malaysian students.

In addition, UMNO has long had strong student movement networks in Britain, traditionally the most popular destination for Malaysian students (including Malay-Muslims), and Australia, through which they disseminate party propaganda and solicit for new members through the various Malaysian Student Association bodies. On the other hand, PAS influence on Malaysian students overseas has largely concentrated on the Middle East (and Indonesia, where it has traditionally enjoyed close relations with Islamist groups), where it has a strong presence in terms of student networks and relations with various Middle Eastern states. The party has begun to signal its intention to establish formal student networks in Western countries as well, where politicized Malaysian Muslim student organizations have until now been mostly an exclusively UMNO sphere of influence. These networks will serve to institutionalize the existing loose links between the party and student communities, particularly in Britain, established over the years through regular visits by party members. Fully aware of the "threat" posed by the increasing activism of PAS among the Malaysian Muslim student diaspora, UMNO leaders have been quick to issue "warnings" to the latter not to be involved with student organizations linked to PAS "in order not to be associated with militant activities."[70] This was the case with Al-Hizbul Islami or HIZBI in Britain, whose student members received these warnings, despite the fact that there was no evidence that HIZBI was aligned with PAS (though student support for PAS in the organization is apparently quite strong) or that it was engaged in "militant activities."

At the same time that UMNO was extending its recruitment drive to Malaysian student networks overseas, the Malaysian state was also aware that these very networks could be prone to extremism and could be used as vehicles through which such ideas were imported back home. Thus, a number of measures were taken during the Mahathir administration to carefully monitor the activities of Malaysian Muslims studying overseas. These included the introduction of a "*dakwah* attaché" in the Malaysian diplomatic missions in London, Jakarta, and Cairo, and the creation of Malaysian student departments in international cities where large numbers of Malaysian students congregate, which would operate under the purview of the embassy. These offices served the function of policing and governing student activities abroad, and correcting "wrong" interpretations of Islam that Malaysian students brought home.[71]

The exertions of UMNO and PAS youth in the international arena represent a form of "Track Two" foreign policy making, while Islamic civil society groups have also embarked on their own "Track Three" form of activism abroad. Indeed, the activities of civil society organizations such as JIM and ABIM are illustrative of the scope of Malaysian representation on issues affecting the broader Muslim world. As an upshot of the Islamic resurgence in Malaysian politics, Islamist NGOs have issued statements and provided support to Muslims from other countries deemed to be unfairly or unjustly treated. For instance, JIM president Zaid Kamaruddin vocally supported the Malaysian government's criticisms of Thailand's handling of their Malay-Muslim issue and likened the October 2004 clampdown on protests in Tak Bai to a "massacre."[72] He further urged the Thai government to "give a thorough explanation of the true situation as it was information sought by Muslims in Patani and the international community," called for the Malaysian government to "seek an explanation from the Thai government and propose that it give top priority to peaceful approaches to resolve this issue," and noted that the "government should not stay silent in the name of diplomacy, neighborly relations or regional friendship, as Muslims in the country [Malaysia] were dismayed by the clashes."[73]

ABIM and JIM also actively protested the Iraq war and submitted a memorandum to the American embassy in Malaysia, "urging Washington to stop their soldiers from oppressing women in Iraq."[74] According to a JIM official, "this memorandum represents the views of the women in Malaysia who condemn the action by the U.S. soldiers who raped and killed Iraqi women after killing members of their families, including children."[75] JIM also called for the International Investigative Commission to "carry out a thorough investigation on such incidents by U.S. soldiers."[76] With regard to Israeli aggression in Palestine and Lebanon, JIM urged Malaysia to play a more proactive role to bring an end to Israeli military action in its capacity as chair of the Non-Aligned Movement and the OIC. JIM's vice president of international affairs, Azahari Abdul Kadir, commented that "Israel had no right on Palestine, nor over Baitulmuqadis, which had been made its capital," and thus "urged Muslim countries under the OIC to play a more proactive role at the international level in getting the recognition for Hamas."[77] He also called on Malaysians of all races and religions to "assist the people of Palestine and Lebanon by helping to raise funds for them."[78]

This chapter has sought to explore two important and intertwined facets of broader trends of Islamism in Malaysia today. The first pertains to the question of expressions of militancy and extremism as they have emerged in Malaysia. While small in numbers, increasingly enervated as an ideology, and hardly a primary axis for political activism, militant extremism is nevertheless an important expression of Islamism that has occasionally surfaced in Malaysia and has to some degree influenced thinking on trends and patterns. Here, the crucial point is that while operational counterterrorism measures have proven effective in curtailing the activities of both local and international terrorist groups in recent times, the fact that ideological aspects of counterterrorism remain ultimately premised on the narrowing of religiopolitical space, undoubtedly with one eye cast toward PAS's growing popularity, is further indicative of the intensely politicized nature of the Malaysian experience in this age of the so-called global war on terror, not to mention the increasing conservatism that has come to characterize much of Islamic discourse and praxis in the country.

This political imperative informing government policy on religiopolitical matters is further amplified when one considers the factor of Islam in Malaysian foreign policy, especially with regard to post–September 11 developments that occasioned a further reconfiguration of foreign policy outlooks and objectives. The assertion of a foreign policy oriented toward the Islamic world, one that entailed a liberal amount of anti-Western rhetoric and posturing, served a number of political purposes. First, it complemented Mahathir's hallmark vision of South-South cooperation in opposition to the Western-dominated world order. Second, an Islamic foreign policy was used to stress the religious credentials and legitimacy of his administration. These twin imperatives appear to have been carried on into the administration of Abdullah Badawi, and in fact have also been echoed by the Islamist opposition and Islamic civil society groups. In sum, both foreign and counterterrorism policy have been mobilized as integral parts of the expansion of the Islamic agenda by the Malaysian state.

Conclusion

The eminent scholar William Roff once ended one of his numerous articles on Malaysian politics with a series of probing questions concerning the increasing salience of Islam on the Malaysian political scene. He asks:

> What, for the individual rather than society, is "Islamization" and how is it to be measured? What are and have been the effects of the kinds of Islamization I have described on the 45 percent of the Malaysian population that is neither Malay nor Muslim? What more might be said of contestation within the Muslim community itself? What of the international context?[1]

More recently, in an interview with the *International Herald Tribune*, prominent Malaysian analyst Farish Noor said, "The idea of a secular state is dead in Malaysia. . . . An Islamic society is already on the cards. The question is what kind of Islamic society this will be."[2] This book has attempted to address the concerns articulated by Roff, Noor, and other observers of Malaysian politics.

There is no doubt that Islam has emerged as a highly vocal and entrenched facet of Malaysian politics today, where it is defended as religion and race. The interplay between religion and politics in Malaysia reveals the complexity of a context that defies easy characterization. Accordingly, the observations made above dovetail into a glaring paradox that typifies this complexity: even as Malaysia continues to be fêted in many scholarly and media quarters as a progressive, moderate Muslim country based on economic growth indices and the absence of major social and political strife, its political and civil society landscapes are undergoing a major transformation marked by the discernible amplification of conservative and exclusionary Islamic voices. Given that Islamic symbols and idioms feature more prominently in Malaysian social and political discourse and practice than ever before, Malaysia watchers ask: what are the nature, contours, trends, and trajectories of this rising Islamism in Malaysian politics, and what do they portend for Malaysian society?

To some extent, the gradual Islamization of Malaysian society is predictable, given the impact of major social and political upheavals in the Muslim world on the mindsets and outlooks of Malaysian Muslims over the past three decades, beginning with the global Islamic resurgence in the early 1970s. This book has been less concerned with the religiosociological phenomenon of Islamization than with how this phenomenon has translated into politics and political engagement. Of interest is how this process of Islamization in Malaysian society has spilled over into the political realm and prompted the rise of Islamism, expressed most profoundly in the intensification of the discourse on the Islamic state, the introduction of various permutations of Islamic law (by both UMNO and PAS-led state legislatures, we should add), the debates these measures have fostered, and, notwithstanding the presence of a significant non-Muslim minority, the deployment of conservative Islamic precepts as a point of reference for the organization of Malaysian society by political parties and civil society groups with visibly "Islamist" objectives.

The process of Islamization and its patently observable reframing of contemporary politics is even more striking given the relatively marginal role that Islam has traditionally played in Malaysian political affairs. While this book is not contending that Malaysia is today a bona fide Islamic state as defined by a nonnegotiable adherence to Islamic law—and certainly there is still much to say about pluralism and inclusivism in many spheres of Malaysian society today—it does suggest that over the past two and a half decades, discernible trends of conservatism and orthodoxy have emerged even as Muslim politics take on new meanings and alternative referents. The point to stress here is that these dynamics demand a reexamination of received wisdom regarding the nature and function of Islam in Malaysia today.

Conceptually, the contours of Islamism in Malaysia capture the complexities that define the field and that are expressed in longstanding debates over the compatibility of Islam with democracy, the relationship between Islamists and the state, and the nature of Islamist commitment to mainstream political processes. Islamism in Malaysia is proving to be both fragmented and variegated in substance and expression, where Islamist vocabulary and idioms have been mobilized by the state, oppositionist forces, and a wide array of civil society groups as the language of legitimacy, dissidence, and reform all at once. Several points are worth noting in this regard. First, while the prevailing conceptual concern in the literature on Islamism is with Islamists' commitment to operating within the boundaries of mainstream political processes in Malaysia, Islamists are not only operating within the boundaries; they are defining them through the vehicle of the state itself. Second, it appears that even as the Islamist opposition struggles to shed its doctrinaire image in pursuit of an agenda of reform, the erstwhile "moderate" UMNO-led government has pursued an agenda that ultimately has resulted in banning books and Bibles, demolishing temples, and constricting cultural and religious space despite a constitutionally enshrined right of freedom of worship.

Finally, the continued preoccupation with party politics and electoral participation in the study of Islamist politics belies the expansion of the scope of actors and the discursive terrain of Muslim politics in Malaysia itself. Developments in Malaysia draw attention to the fact that Islamist parties no longer have a monopoly on questions of power, legitimacy, and authenticity; or if they still do, at least this monopoly is being challenged. While conventional wisdom holds that civil society exists and operates within boundaries established and regulated by the state, in the case of Malaysia there is increasing evidence that, insofar as Islamic social and political concerns are at stake, civil society is equally capable of setting the agenda.

Contradictions and Paradoxes: UMNO and State-Orchestrated Islamism

An appreciation of the role that the Malaysian state and UMNO, the dominant party in the coalition government, have played in driving the narrative of Islamism and shaping the politicization of Islam in Malaysia is key to understanding how the current state of affairs has come about. This knowledge is all the more important because of prevailing perceptions that UMNO was in fact a secularist, moderate Muslim party that was compelled to "Islamize" in response to pressures originating from the Islamist opposition party PAS. To properly understand UMNO's role in this process, one needs to first understand how and why the party moved from being a nationalist-centrist party (albeit with some elements of its earlier leadership clearly ethnonationalist in orientation) to one that has come to frame its protection of Malay-Muslim interests along religious lines.

To suggest that UMNO was a nationalist-centrist party rather than a Malay nationalist party, as it is often understood, may raise some eyebrows. After all, UMNO is a party that regularly, and at times unabashedly, showcases its ethnonationalist credentials at party conventions with timeless clarion calls of "*hidup melayu*" (long live the Malays) and the occasional wielding of the *kris*, the traditional Malay weapon that is also a cultural symbol, by its leaders during these events. The fact that membership in the party remains the exclusive preserve of Malay-Muslims appears to point to its communal orientation. While all this is true, and there are probably more compelling reasons why scholars continue to see UMNO as ethnonationalist in nature, it is nevertheless possible to think of the party more broadly as a nationalist-centrist party on at least two counts.

First, UMNO has for the past fifty years worked closely with non-Malay parties, initially under the auspices of the Alliance and later the *Barisan Nasional*, in a manner that bestowed de facto legitimacy upon it in the eyes of most of Malaysia's non-Muslim minority.[3] Second, with specific reference to Islam, UMNO leaders before Mahathir demonstrated considerable restraint in how they framed the religious imperative for their political agenda, choosing to locate the party diametrically opposite voices that called for Islamic government and Islamic state, as well as resisting the temptation to rush headlong to deliberately engage in discernibly Islamist discourse and praxis. During the leadership of Mahathir Mohamad, however, the party all but abandoned this tradition as its leaders oversaw and orchestrated a progressive Islamization of the country and its institutions of government that precipitated the escalation of the Islamic state discourse; in this way, Islam soon became a catalyst for remaking the "modal personality" of the Malays.[4] A direct result of this process has been the imposition, both in word and deed, of an increasingly Islamic agenda on mainstream Malaysian politics in a way that has sharpened Islamist discourse and threatened the pluralistic foundations of Malaysian society.

It is important to stress here the essence of the former prime minister's vision of Islamic governance, which was governed by a modernization ethic. The Mahathir administration was intent on harnessing popular Islamic consciousness and husbanding it for the modernization drive he had envisioned for Malaysia. This was underscored by his attempt to reconcile Islam with notions of entrepreneurship, economic development, and an efficient Islamic work ethic, and by his call for Malay-Muslims to undergo a mental revolution and cultural transformation to that end.[5] This initiative was encapsulated in his concept of "Islamic modernism," through which Islam was made compatible with development and economic advancement, and has been advanced by his successor, Abdullah Ahmad Badawi, in his own concept of *Islam Hadhari*.

Yet Mahathir's Islamization drive had controversial aspects that relate directly to the rise of Islamism or "political" Islam in Malaysia. First, Mahathir was known not only as a modernizer but also as a leader who did not hesitate to employ the coercive instruments of the state in order to advance his Islamization agenda. For instance, in order to define the parameters of Islamism on his own terms, during his tenure Mahathir made occasional use of the Internal Security Act (ISA), which had a particularly devastating effect on several "deviationist" groups and individuals in Malaysia, including mainstream and legitimate political organizations and leaders, even though they posed no realistic threat to his or UMNO's position of power. The use of instruments of the state to define and police the boundaries of Islam came to the fore during Malaysia's war on extremism and terrorism. Yet while tools such as the ISA enhanced the operational capacity of the Malaysian state to deal with terrorists and extremists, the effect of this manner of mobilization of state authority was the substantial narrowing of religiopolitical space by portraying renditions of Islam as "heresy" and "deviancy" if they were not approved by the state, as the administration facilitated and enhanced the role of a conservative religious establishment in state affairs.

Second, following from the previous point, it was during Mahathir's tenure in office that the state became a vehicle for Islamization, as religion became bureaucratized. UMNO oversaw, formulated, and implemented a host of policies that gave extensive institutional expression to Islamic orthodoxy at both federal and state levels of government. This process was manifested most strikingly in the bureaucratization of Islam at the level of state governance, which, elevated *fatwa* to sources of law and empowered state religious authorities through the institution of a parallel system of legislation and governance that rested on the introduction of Islamic family laws, apostasy bills, and aspects of *hudud* legislation. Unlike Egypt, for instance, where some have suggested that the Mubarak regime "permitted a remarkable degree of Islamic penetration of the state apparatus," Malaysia's ruling party consciously facilitated this penetration, rather than sitting back and passively "permitting" it.[6] A number of these legislative initiatives have proven highly controversial for how they are forcing Malaysian society to rethink the balance between *shari'a* law, civil law, and the Malaysian constitution. In light of these developments, any suggestion that an Islamist opposition might be forced to moderate dogmatic agendas if it came to power is suspect at best, simply because the terrain in which they find themselves operating would not lend itself to such moderating influences given how government-endorsed religious clerics have many a time proven even more conservative and insular in their outlook than their counterparts in the Islamist opposition.

To be sure, UMNO is not monolithic in its Islamist disposition. Consequently, this bureaucratization of Islam caused predictable friction within the party between leaders sympathetic to the need to navigate it away from the slippery slope of exclusivist Islamist orthodoxy (though not necessarily for altruistic reasons, given the impact that Islamization might have on UMNO's extensive patronage system), and members who espouse a brand of narrow conservatism that is more commonly associated in the popular imagination with the PAS opposition and that paradoxically undermines the image of a modernist Malaysian Islam that Mahathir and Abdullah attempted to construct.[7] These more conservative UMNO members come particularly from the ranks of party *ulama* (or *ulama* affiliated to state governments) and officials from the various state religious departments. These emergent contradictions suggest that the Malaysian state is subject to contestations within the UMNO ruling and religious elite, in that it has become the arena in which they are expressed and institutionalized.[8] Thus, Mahathir himself cannot be held solely responsible for the government's complicity in orchestrating the rise of Islamism in Malaysia, although his role has been significant.

Tension among the various strands of Islamism in Malaysia is heightened by a diffusion of power among governmental bodies and institutions endowed with the authority to define the parameters of Islamic discourse and to enforce "proper" Islamic practice. A proliferation and contestation of views has been caused by the dispersal of religious and political authority rooted in this structural conundrum, wherein regulations are not mandated by Parliament but are instituted by instruments of government possessing bureaucratic powers that cannot be contested. In the Malaysian federal system of government, religious authority is officially vested in the sultan, but sultans are advised on religious issues by state *mufti* and *ulama*. States also have religious departments, *shari'a* courts, and *fatwa* councils that formulate, recommend, and implement policies relating to religion. Manifestations of religious authority also exist at the federal level. These take the form of JAKIM, a ministerial-level appointment in the cabinet and the prime minister's office, and a National Fatwa Council made up of state *mufti*. In many ways, this plurality of reference points in terms of religious authority demonstrates how Islamism in the state is clearly contested terrain, not only between political parties but within them as well.

The appointment of a Grand *Mufti* has been proposed as a way to rectify the diffusion of religious authority.[9] It remains to be seen if this centralization of authority will be the cure for this problem, and there are several reasons to be skeptical of such an outcome. Islam celebrates a number of jurisprudential schools and has never known hierarchy in its legal history. Furthermore, some in Malaysia see centralization of power as an unwelcome trend that might further entrench, rather than mitigate, authoritarian practices in Malaysia. Also, the creation of such an office would contravene constitutional principles that enshrine the sultan as the final arbiter on religious issues.

The point here is that the popular portrayal of UMNO as a "moderate," "progressive" Muslim-led party, often in contradistinction to PAS, may not be entirely accurate, and the ideological divide between the two Muslim parties may not be as sharp as it seems at first glance. UMNO under Mahathir was firmly committed to the capitalist enterprise of industrialization and development, and this remains the case with the current administration. Yet during this time, deep undercurrents of religious conservatism within UMNO and across the Malaysian state apparatus have become entrenched, permeating the judiciary, education, media, and civil society. Rather than differentiating itself from the opposition by becoming more democratic, liberal, and secular, the UMNO-led government's state religious apparatus is growing more conservative and orthodox, and Islamic credentials are becoming increasingly important. This has been most profoundly expressed in UMNO leaders' declaration that Malaysia is an Islamic state. While offered in part for popular consumption, such declarations also provide clear indications of the aspirations of some UMNO and Malaysian government officials and of the emergent terms of reference of Malaysian politics from the party's perspective.

The implications of these statements, made by senior leaders of UMNO, are likely to reverberate far beyond mere rhetorical acrobatics. Numerous policies enacted by UMNO-run state governments have given substance to the conception of Islam as a political ideology and a comprehensive system of law. Thus, statements by Mahathir, Najib, and others that Malaysia was already an "Islamic state" (including Abdullah's conception of *Islam Hadhari*) have not only reopened fundamental questions about whether the Malaysian state is at heart secular or Islamic; they further mark an intensification of the narrative of Islamism and a major departure from UMNO's traditional reluctance to engage directly in the discourse of the Islamic state.[10]

Of course, one should remember that there was a fair amount of brinkmanship and politicking driving these statements. But the point is that pronouncements of this nature, which are made with increasing regularity, resonate with segments of the Muslim population. This indicates that the shift is not merely discursive but has followed broader trends in society as a whole. Combined with the gradual introduction of Islamic laws and strictures by several state governments, the introduction of the "Islamic state" axiom into UMNO's political lexicon emphasizes that the levers of Islamic government have already begun to be put in place. Moreover, as far as Malaysia's non-Muslim communities are concerned, the UMNO-led government's position (whether explicit or implicit) on the matter of constitutional rights and freedom of religion laid to rest any lingering doubts that the "secularist" government in fact harbors clearly Islamic predispositions. UMNO's position is discernible most clearly in the wake of major court decisions that have frightened or angered non-Muslims, when the UMNO rank and file celebrates with joy, and from the UMNO leadership there comes a deafening silence. In other words, the distinction between UMNO as a political party and UMNO as a religious organization of sorts has become increasingly blurred.[11]

A careful examination of UMNO's discourse and policies over the past few decades will reveal that elements of a discernibly Islamist agenda have been nurtured since the early 1980s, immediately after Mahathir assumed office. This process has gradually intensified independent of the challenge from the Islamist opposition. Rather than being a knee-jerk instrumentalist response motivated by pressure from PAS, UMNO's transformation into a party and a government with Islamist leanings was both an outgrowth of Islamic consciousness within the ranks of UMNO and a reaction to developments outside the realm of mainstream party politics, primarily in the civil society sphere (known in religiosociological parlance as the "Islamic resurgence"). This accords with Milne and Mauzy's assessment concerning the impact that developments in civil society had on mainstream politics in Malaysia: "In the late 1960s . . . government policies had inhibited doctrinal diversification within Islam, and had tended to check some dynamic and modernist trends. The Islamic resurgence, a few years later, burst through the barriers of government policies."[12] UMNO's co-optation of and competition with PAS have not arisen from a situation where an Islamist political opposition forced the UMNO-led Malaysian government to react. Rather, the ruling party and the state have shaped and orchestrated an Islamization process of their own, one that encompassed decidedly "Islamist" points of reference.

Oppositional Politics: Between Creed and Compromise

In much the same way that UMNO is uncritically depicted as the progenitor of progressive and moderate Islam, PAS is often portrayed in the mainstream media as a conservative and fundamentalist Islamic opposition uncompromisingly committed to the formation of an Islamic state in Malaysia. Careful scrutiny of its political triumphs and tragedies, however, will reveal a complicated narrative that speaks of a dynamic and fluid Islamist organization that has regularly reinvented itself in order to remain a relevant player in Malaysian politics.[13]

In its early incarnations, PAS had to balance between Islam and the imperative of Malay nationalism. The intimate relationship between race and religion in the Malay imagination permitted relatively congruent and convenient reconciliation of these two agendas. Even then, there were many instances where one overshadowed the other, and it was often the racial and ethnic imperative that dominated. The picture, however, began to change after 1982, when PAS came under the leadership of *ulama*. This change was expressed most profoundly in the introduction of the practice of *kafir-mengafir* and the issuance of the *Amanat Haji Hadi*, culminating in a 1986 election campaign platform that was built on narrow fundamentalist and conservative Islamist precepts, as PAS sought to "out-Islam" UMNO.

According to the results of the 1986 general elections, however, this agenda was unattractive to the Malaysian electorate, including the sizable Muslim constituency, and the party was compelled to reassess its tactical agenda, reconsider its message, and recalibrate its political strategy. This mood of introspection led to a conscious adoption of a more explicit reformist agenda consonant with popular grievances. As an Islamist opposition, PAS had to recalibrate its political agenda even before being subjected to the realities of governing. Furthermore, this process took place at the same time that UMNO, paradoxically, became more "Islamist."

The apex of this "mainstreaming" of PAS came about in the late 1990s, when the party appropriated the lexicon of good governance and political reform as it exploited the mood of popular discontent borne of the Asian financial crisis and the government's unceremonious dismissal of Anwar Ibrahim. The results of this shift were telling: PAS went on to win its largest number of parliamentary and state seats in its history in the 1999 general elections, and in the process became the leader of the Malaysian opposition.[14] Soon afterward, however, a combination of fate and circumstance worked to transform the fortunes of the party. The passing of the popular *ulama* president and architect of PAS' reformist turn, Fadzil Noor, was the harbinger of an immediate shift in the party's ideological and strategic direction. Latent tension between reformists, who desired to craft a more widely acceptable image for PAS while playing down the rhetoric of the Islamic state, and conservatives, who held closely to the narrow Islamist agenda that privileged above all else the immediate establishment of an Islamic state, soon surfaced and manifested itself in internal debates over the crafting of a policy document articulating the PAS vision of Islamic government. It should be noted that the mounting pressure for the articulation of this vision came from UMNO's escalation of the Islamization debate, when its then-president appropriated the "Islamic state" label for UMNO's version of an Islamized Malaysia and challenged PAS to respond.

Against the backdrop set by UMNO's raising of the political stakes, the loss of Fadzil Noor opened the way for conservatives to regain the upper hand in the party. Conservatives soon occupied the party presidency and deputy presidency, which allowed them to shape internal discussions on the Islamic state that were eventually articulated as the PAS Islamic State Document, released in December 2003, against the counsel of party reformists who had anticipated a backlash. The party's fortunes then came full circle, when its dismal showing at the 2004 general election brought back memories of 1986 and triggered yet another introspective phase among its leadership, the result of which was the surprisingly penitent admission on the part of the conservative *ulama* leadership of their shortcomings and the concomitant amplification of the reformist voice among the party ranks. This shift, in turn, deepened tension within PAS between conservatives and reformists over the direction of the party, notwithstanding the *ulama* leadership's acknowledgement that its dogmatic and scripturalist politics had hurt the party's electoral prospects. Such duality is neither alien to the sphere of Muslim politics nor unique to PAS. For instance, the Islamic Salvation Front opposition party in Algeria championed pluralism and participatory democracy as *al-shura* in the late 1980s and early 1990s under Abbasi Madani, but the party's deputy leader, Ali Belhaj, was at the same time a fiery opponent of democracy.[15]

Despite its label as a fundamentalist party, PAS's ideology has in fact varied more than UMNO's in the course of its history. Indeed, PAS has proven to be a surprisingly resilient and dynamic political party fully attuned to the "political" nature of Islamism, cognizant of political realities and its own shortcomings, and prepared to negotiate its political and ideological boundaries in order to "stay in the game" where necessary. Through its cyclical history of political success, failure, and reinvention, there is one clear constant: the success of PAS has almost always hinged on its ability to relate Islam to the pressing issues of the day. The record of the party's political fortunes mapped here indicates that the Islamist opposition has never been able to succeed in mainstream Malaysian politics on purely doctrinaire and ideological terms. PAS's attempt to engage UMNO in political contest on the back of a staunchly doctrinaire campaign in both 1986 (*kafir-mengafir*) and 2004 (the Islamic State Document) proved to be massive strategic failures that spurred the party to reconsider the viability of fundamentalist religious campaign templates.

On the other hand, the party's major political successes in 1959, 1990, and 1999 (and later in 2008) resulted from the party's ability to reconcile its Islamist agenda with the pressing social, economic, and political issues of the day. In 1959, the party reaped dividends from its ability to capitalize on Malay discontent by justifying their struggle in terms of the defense of Malay identity and primacy, of which Islam was a component. Likewise, more recent successes have stemmed from the effective deployment of Islam as a voice of dissidence, when PAS portrayed itself as a champion of civil justice, human rights, and democracy in opposition to the authoritarianism and money politics associated with the later stages of the Mahathir administration.

At first glance, there is an apparent anomaly in this assessment of the electoral fortunes of PAS. On the one hand, the case has been made that Muslim society in Malaysia has been caught up in increasingly conservative trends of Islamization; Islamic vocabulary and idioms clearly resonate with the Muslim population and have become increasingly important in governance and everyday life. On the other hand, however, decidedly Islamist agendas, such as those pursued by PAS in 1986 and 2004, have proved to be political liabilities for PAS, even though UMNO was evincing Islamist predilections at the same time. Upon closer scrutiny, however, this discrepancy is easily explained. This is because fundamental issues at stake are not a question of whether Malaysia should be more Islamic—it should be clear by now that this is a moot point—but rather what shape of Islamism is acceptable at a given point in time. Islamic idioms were as critical to UMNO's political strategy as they were to PAS's, so UMNO-PAS contests since the early 1980s have never been about "more Islam or less Islam" in the ordering of Malaysian society, as might have been the case in Egypt under Mubarak and Turkey under military rule. Rather, differences have centered on which model of Islamic order was more attractive. In 1986 it was clearly Mahathir's Islamization strategy, and in 2004 Abdullah's *Islam Hadhari*, that garnered more support.

The key point to stress here is that, contrary to popular belief, PAS's commitment to fundamentalism, epitomized by its agenda for the implementation of *shari'a* law and the formation of an Islamic state, has hardly been unflinching, monolithic, or non-negotiable. This was demonstrated most profoundly in the tension over the party's articulation of its position on the Islamic state, a discussion pursued at length in chapter 3. This tension is indicative of a party that appears prepared to accommodate, negotiate, and compromise on several aspects of its agenda in order to command a broader following, but it also speaks to resistance to change on the part of conservatives. It is still unclear if the reformists in PAS have mobilized enough to achieve their goals of reinvigorating and transforming the party, if indeed the party is as committed to pluralism and democracy as the reformists in its ranks maintain; nor is it any clearer if there would be a new generation that might eventually rise to take up the banner of *ulama*-based conservatism currently personified in the likes of Nik Aziz Nik Mat, Abdul Hadi Awang, Harun Din, and Harun Taib, all of whom are popular conservative *ulama* leaders getting on in years. In sum, PAS's Islamism, not unlike UMNO's, can best be described as context- and issue-specific, and PAS is just as likely to contain a coterie of *ulama* staunchly opposed to an unabated pursuit of the Islamic state objective as it is to have party leaders from the ranks of the professionals who endorse moral policing by state religious authorities and the primacy of the *shari'a* over civil law in the ordering of private lives of Muslims.

PAS will likely never find itself to be democratic in a manner understood as such in the Western lexicon of political science. The party remains deeply patriarchal, and its leaders see themselves as the guardians of faith, tradition, and authenticity, and are likely to vehemently oppose expansion of social liberties. Nonetheless, PAS has also realized the need to rethink some of their obscurantist positions; as a result, the party has managed to internalize a culture of *realpolitik* by learning to make compromises and cooperate with various groups, including religious civil society groups, NGOs, and secular political parties.

The crucial point of this discussion is that despite the efforts of UMNO and PAS to win votes by differentiating themselves from each other, in truth they are two sides of the same coin, and the Islamic discourse and debates in which they engage belie the fact that their brands of Islamism are at least imbricated, if not altogether mirrored in each other. The bifurcation that is commonly assumed to exist between UMNO and PAS is false, a fact that has grave implications for the trajectory of Islamism in Malaysia for the foreseeable future.

Popular Islam and "Defending the Faith"

In addition to a careful and critical deconstruction of Islamic discourse and praxis of the main protagonists of "political" Islam, this book has also attempted to provide a fuller sense of the cultural context, meanings, and practices of contemporary Islam in Malaysia, particularly of how these factors interplay with mainstream elite politics encapsulated in the UMNO-PAS "Islamization race" that is the *sine qua non* of Islamist politics in the country. By looking at the contributions of those who have emerged outside the elites and parallel to the intensification of the "Islamization race" to respond to UMNO's and PAS's mutually reinforcing Islamisms, this book has assessed how elements of society (as opposed to the state and political parties) have acted as vehicles for or buffers against Islamization.

In that regard, it is important to note the recent proliferation of civil society groups and NGOs that can be defined as Islamist by virtue of their articulation of relatively clear and deliberate Islamic agendas, contribution to ongoing debates, and the potential influence they wield over the trajectory of Islamism in the country. While activism on the part of Islamic NGOs and civil society groups is hardly distinct to Malaysia, this book has shown that these alternative voices emerging from outside the mainstream Islamist parties have come to assume great importance in the shaping of Islamic discourse and practice in Malaysian politics.

Several observations can be made of this alternative Islamist discursive terrain. First, these movements are diverse and fragmented. There are groups that are virulently exclusivist in character and orientation (PUM and PEMBELA); those that are less provocative but which nevertheless propound discernibly Islamist agendas (ABIM and JIM); "moderate" and "liberal" Islamic movements (Sisters in Islam); and groups located outside the parameters of mainstream Malaysian Islamism (*Hizbut Tahrir* and *Al Arqam*). Despite the variations in their doctrine and politics, all these groups share the desire to bring about change in the terms of public engagement with Islam, to expand the space for public discussion of laws and policies made in the name of religion, and to extend their influence in the public sphere by interpreting and reinterpreting categories of Islam to legitimize and motivate their activism and intervention. This phenomenon is not unlike what Dietrich Reetz has observed in India, where, according to his research, the heightened activism of Islamic groups was driven "as much by the desire to revive religious faith as by the intention to carve out for themselves and their groups a place in a rapidly changing political and social environment, to find their place in the new society."[16]

The upshot of this activism is the beginning of a gradual but observable shift in the center of gravity of political Islam away from mainstream party politics. Of course, this by no means implies that UMNO and PAS will be rendered redundant by this process any time soon. Islamist parties will continue to play a major role in framing the Islamist agenda in Malaysia for some time to come. Having said that, it must be noted that, at least on certain issues, these movements, as representatives of "popular" Islam, are facilitating the gradual bypassing of mainstream parties by Muslims who choose instead to focus their activities and energies on the civil society sector. This phenomenon has been most intensely demonstrated in the politics behind apostasy controversies in recent years, where the terrain of debate in Malaysia has been characterized as much by the cacophony in the civil sphere (including cyberspace) as it has by the silence on the part of UMNO and PAS in response to legal rulings on high-profile cases such as Lina Joy and Moorthy Maniam. Put differently, this has resulted in the emergence of an alternative Islamist discourse, articulated in an increasingly vocal civil society sphere, which both reinforces and undermines the dominant narrative emanating from UMNO and PAS. Any discussion of civil society and Islamist alternatives should not preclude non-Muslim responses to rising Islamism in Malaysia, most of which have rallied and mobilized over the issue of apostasy and the Islamic state, and which have contributed to the attempted drawing and dismantling of the boundaries of Islamist discourse described above.

This activism points to a number of trends. In accordance to conventional understandings of the autonomy of civil society from the state, the vibrancy of this parallel civil society appears to indicate a healthy democratic practice of debate focused on fundamental issues such as democracy, secularism, human and constitutional rights, and freedom of belief and religion, even as public space for such exchanges has gradually opened up, despite the Malaysian government's attempts to constrain the burgeoning counterdiscourse.[17] Indeed, the Malaysian state has noted the increasingly important role that these NGOs and civil society organizations play in Malaysian politics and society and has thus to some extent been compelled to provide room for their activities. As Saliha Hassan noted:

> This more recent Islamic reawakening has prompted activism extending beyond the conventional circle of rural-based religious *ulama* and teachers or graduates of Islamic religious studies. Instead the current activists and leaders are from the new crop of urban-based, Malay, middle-class professionals. Their advocacy extends also beyond the traditional aims of encouraging a more upright Islamic community from a moral and social perspective. Instead these activists have promoted political Islam. They may not have all joined partisan politics but their *dakwah* has now emphasised the Islamic obligation to enjoin good and deny evil within the political life of the nation.[18]

At the same time, however, this relative autonomy from the state does not necessarily imply opposition to it, even if it does entail some measure of critical interrogation of state narratives and policies. Similarly, a vibrant civil society need not always be consonant with the interests of the minority, particularly when it reinforces and entrenches the "tyranny of the majority"—the bane, as it were, of democracy. Notwithstanding the resistance of fringe Islamic groups like SIS or non-Muslim movements like MCCBCHS and the Article 11 Coalition, in the Malaysian case it is striking that, paradoxically, the proliferation of voices has not brought about any discernible expansion of the parameters of debate. Obvious examples of this paradox can be found in the debates over apostasy, freedom of religion, and the primacy of *shari'a* in Muslim life as well as the question of moral policing. Indeed, on these issues one finds a sizable number of vocal Muslim civil society groups and NGOs that have at times championed positions even more conservative and hardline than those taken by either UMNO or PAS.

Particularly instructive in this regard is the all-too-frequent discourse of "defending the faith," which has become a characteristic clarion call for the vast majority of Islamic NGOs and civil society groups. Unlike the situation in Indonesia, where a "cultural Islam" emerged in the 1980s that offered a trenchant critique of the prevailing political agenda of the country's Islamist political forces and sought to redefine Islam's relations with the state, a close perusal of the dominant civil society agenda in Malaysia reveals discourses that in fact mostly impose limits on debates about Islam.[19] Moreover, given that engaging in a discourse of "defense of the faith" implies a belief that the faith is coming under some sort of attack, it is not surprising to find that these limits are imposed less for altruistic purposes than to deny non-Muslims and those perceived to be "lesser" Muslims a voice on matters relating to Islam, which, to these Islamists is equivalent to an attack on Islam. Thus, this discourse clearly does not arise from a perspective that is self-critical.

In many respects, the trends in popular perspectives about the direction of Islam are echoed in a much wider arena of popular discourse. Set against the context of mainstream politics, a broader range of responses from Malaysia's Muslim and non-Muslim population to Islamist trends, as illustrated in debates and discourses in blogs, listserves, and alternative media outlets, have demonstrated that these perspectives are playing an increasingly important role in helping define the scope of Islam in Malaysia. Again, this in no way implies an erosion of mainstream elite politics as represented by UMNO and PAS. As a matter of fact, as in the case of NGO language and activism, this parallel discourse often intersects with mainstream debates, such as when popular opinion on apostasy and the sanctity of *shari'a* reflects the sentiments of conservative religious leaders from both UMNO and PAS. Still, such voices also sometimes criticize the dominant discourse.

Islamism in Malaysia must ultimately contend with the fact that the Malaysian context is essentially one of religious and ethnic diversity. Given the current shape of Islamization, this structural "fact" does not appear to be significantly constraining the increasingly conservative and exclusionary discourses that are emanating from the political and public realms. Over the past two and a half decades, the regulatory and administrative functions of the state have been gradually framed in Islamist terms, even as the public articulation of Islamism becomes more pronounced. The culmination of this process has not inspired hope or optimism among Malaysia's significant ethnoreligious minorities. In recent times, Hindu temples and Christian churches have been torn down under the supervision of state religious authorities empowered by the Malaysian system of federalism. While the official reason given for these acts was the lack of a recognized permit for the building, the move itself has been disconcerting from the perspective of non-Muslims, for it demonstrates disregard for their rights and further constriction of their already limited social and political space.[20]

Over the last few years, a strong undercurrent of dissatisfaction has been building up against increasing encroachment of Islam into everyday non-Muslim life. This encroachment has been manifested in numerous forms, ranging from inconspicuous everyday examples such as municipal legislation against alcohol sales and dog licenses to highly publicized debates over religious conversion, freedom of religion, and the nature of the Malaysian constitution. As a result, "two parallel societies—Muslim and non-Muslim—have gradually replaced what was a pluralistic, secular Malaysian society based on common law that was the legacy British colonials handed over upon independence in 1957."[21]

The ongoing legal controversy over Article 121 1(A) of the Malaysian constitution, amended in 1988 to circumscribe civil court jurisdiction over *shari'a* courts, captures the essence of this perplexing problem. There is serious disagreement in Malaysian society over whether individual Muslims enjoy the right and freedom to make their own decisions on issues of personal piety or to interpret religious injunctions, not to mention the sanctity of constitutionally guaranteed rights of religious freedom. In addition, in the wake of the creeping influence of Islamic law, non-Muslims have also pressed their rights as citizens to define the shape of a politicized Islam that they perceive to be increasingly infringing upon these rights. As with the case of the Islamist agenda, non-Muslims have increasingly looked to alternative avenues, beyond political parties (including the non-Muslim component parties of the *Barisan Nasional*), for ways and means to advance their agendas. They have mobilized and coalesced into their own organizations, such as MCCBCHS and Hindu Rights Action Force (HINDRAF), and they have worked with more moderate Muslim groups that share similar reservations regarding the tenor and shape of Islamic discourse today. They have also used alternative media outlets in order to amplify their concern for the steady, if at times inadvertent, encroachment upon their rights.

Be that as it may, their activism has done little to alter the trajectory of an increasingly exclusivist Islamism. Nor has the non-Muslim cause received much assistance from the state or the ruling elite. The UMNO-led government has reacted cautiously to the petitions and candlelight vigils, calling for restraint but otherwise doing little.[22] Government coalition parties have been equally reticent in their response, careful not to strain relations with UMNO, for which they would likely pay a high political price. Not surprisingly, opposition parties and civil society groups have been more vocal and unequivocal in

their response, though they too have achieved little success is stalling the jug-
gernaut of the Islamic exclusivism taking hold in Malaysia.

The Road Ahead

There should be little doubt that Islamization is gaining momentum in Malaysia and will continue to do so. In addition, the overall tenor of Muslim
attitudes—at least in terms of Islamic religious authorities, political entities,
and certain segments of the Muslim population—is becoming discernibly
more conservative as the state religious apparatus grows in profile and influence. As for the Malaysian government, it is clear that, despite the occasional
deployment of the ISA during the Mahathir administration against the Islamist
opposition and fringe Islamic groups, any large-scale clamping down on Muslim political assertiveness such as that seen in Nasserite Egypt or Ataturk's
Turkey is unlikely. As this book has argued, this is simply because the rules of
engagement in Malaysia are significantly different, where the state itself is at
the forefront of this Islamization process as its chief architect, orchestrating,
shaping, and harnessing Islamization as it rejects the logic of secularism and
engages in pathological "piety-trumping" with its political opposition. Consequently, Islam is becoming more politically salient, and Islamic credentials
are assuming greater importance in the contest for popular support and votes.
Such is the extent of the penetration of Islamic consciousness into conceptions
of order and governance that the main debate is no longer the question of
whether Malaysia is an Islamic or secular state, but what type of Islamic state
Malaysia is today and will be in the future.

There is a common perception that one of the problems associated with the
rise of political Islam in Malaysia has been the inordinate amount of influence
that a small coterie of *ulama* has been able to bring to bear on the Islamism
debate. Zainah Anwar, the tireless activist from SIS, laments the implications
for democracy when "only a small group of people, the *ulama*, as traditionally
believed, have the right to interpret the Qur'an, and codify the text in a manner
that very often isolates the text from the sociohistorical context of its revelation,
isolates classical juristic opinion, especially on women's issues, from the sociohistorical context of the lives and society of the founding jurists of Islam, and
further isolates our textual heritage from the context of contemporary society,
the world that we live in today."[23]

While this is a fair observation, it merely touches the tip of the iceberg.
No doubt the *ulama* play a central role in defining the terms of any debate on
Islamic issues anywhere in the Muslim world, yet they are hardly the center
of gravity, given how political and moral authority has fragmented in Malaysia. As a microcosm of the challenges confronting traditional religious authority across the Muslim world today, in Malaysia the rise of Islamism and its

ongoing debate has been influenced by a far more disparate assemblage of actors and voices than merely the *ulama*. These have included politicians, activists (including Zainah herself), academics, government officials and bureaucrats, non-Muslim organizations, and an increasingly vocal public sphere. In Malaysia, one is confronted with a curious paradox, for while discursive and political space has expanded, allowing for more debate and discussion and the creation of a far more cacophonous concoction of alternative Islamic narratives and actors than elsewhere in the Islamic world (save perhaps for democratized Indonesia), it has at the same time contracted, such that the dominant narrative emerging from this kaleidoscope of actors appears to point, on balance, to a gradually narrowing exclusivist conservatism.

Eminent scholars have argued that Islamist political contestations have in the past given rise to two diametrically opposing trends. On the one hand, Islamism has led to radicalization and extremism as camps seek to outbid their opponents in order to cement their authority over Islam. On the other hand, Islamist groups have encountered what Piscatori terms a "de facto structural pluralism" wherein they realize the impossibility of outright domination over their competition and are forced to compromise and engage in the give-and-take of normal politics. Neither trend conclusively describes Islamism in Malaysia, where paradoxes and contradictions abound. It remains to be seen how these paradoxes and contradictions will be, or can be, reconciled. One thing is clear, though: while the political competition taking place between UMNO and PAS, with each trying to "out-Islam" the other in the realm of mainstream politics, remains as pertinent as ever to efforts to understand political Islam in Malaysia, parallel tracks of Islamist activism are intensifying in terms of their vibrancy and activity. Thus, the future trajectory of Islamism will be shaped as much by what happens outside the boundaries of mainstream partisan politics as it will by what happens in the UMNO-PAS "Islamization race." Meanwhile, the passionate debates rage on, and Malaysia remains as divided as ever, this time over how Islamic teachings are to be interpreted, propagated, and institutionalized within the context of a modern, pluralistic society.

Epilogue

Malaysia held its twelfth general election on 8 March 2008. In its best performance ever, Malaysia's political opposition—consisting of *Parti Keadilan Rakyat* (People's Justice Party), PAS, and DAP—combined to deny the ruling *Barisan Nasional* coalition a two-thirds parliamentary majority. Even more astonishing was their victory in an unprecedented five state legislatures—Kelantan (which PAS successfully defended), Kedah, Perak, Penang, and Selangor.

The abysmal performance of the *Barisan*, which led immediately to calls for the resignation of *Barisan* chairman, UMNO president, and Malaysian prime minister Abdullah Badawi, was a consequence of a number of factors: increasing inflation and rising prices of food staples and fuel; pervasive corruption; emaciation of the judiciary; and discriminatory policies toward non-Malays and non-Muslims on the part of federal and state administrations. All these culminated in an overall perception that the Abdullah-led government had failed to fulfill the electoral promises it made in 2004 of a more consultative, *rakyat*-oriented government that would weed out corruption. The elections were notable on three further counts. First, PAS put up a strong electoral showing, comparable to its 1999 performance. While the party's twenty-three parliamentary seats and eighty-two state seats fell somewhat short of their achievement eleven years ago, they did secure the *Menteri Besar* (chief minister) post in three states—Kelantan, Kedah, and Perak. In addition, a striking similarity between the PAS campaigns in 1999 and 2008 was the deliberate attempt of party leaders to stress issues such as reform, justice, and democracy, and to deemphasize the Islamic state. Also similar was how PAS benefited more from popular rejection of Abdullah and *Islam Hadhari* than from endorsement of their ideological positions. Second, civil society movements, as anticipated, played a major role in the campaign hustings. Islamic civil society groups were particularly forceful in their presence, and many among their ranks in fact stepped forward to contest the elections on either PAS or *Keadilan* tickets. Third, Islam played a predictably instrumental role in the elections, particularly in the Malay-Muslim heartland, where Islamic credentials were brandished by the candidates of both UMNO and PAS. In order to keep with the major themes of the book, this epilogue confines itself to a discussion of the role played by the factor of Islam in electoral politics, and a reflection on developments immediately following the elections.

The Context

Many analysts have opined (with, it should be noted, the benefit of hindsight) that the writing was already on the wall for UMNO and its allies long before 8 March. Since 2004, the ruling coalition had been confronted with a litany of grievances that it failed to address convincingly and that eventually created the "political tsunami," as many have termed it, that hit the *Barisan*. Chief among these grievances were issues of judicial integrity, electoral reform, and minority rights, all of which led to massive street protests in Malaysia in the last four years. Furthermore, Abdullah, chief architect of *Islam Hadhari*, was unwilling or unable during his tenure to rein in the tide of Islamization—overseen by Malaysia's inflated religious bureaucracy—that was polarizing Malaysian society in the wake of controversial cases of apostasy (such as those discussed at length in earlier chapters). In choosing to skirt dialogue and discussion with concerned minority groups rather than confront these issues head on—or worse, endorsing some of the actions of Islamic religious authorities—the Abdullah administration showed itself to be elusive and unwilling to lend an ear to the grievances of those whose rights were gradually impinged upon by government-sanctioned Islamization policies. Matters came to a head on 25 November 2007 when HINDRAF, a religious NGO championing the interests of the Hindu minority in Malaysia, orchestrated a public protest at the Batu Caves, a site of religious significance for Hindus, involving an estimated ten thousand ethnic Indians to draw attention to the plight of the Indian community. While the issue of marginalization of Malaysia's ethnic Indian minority was hardly a new one, this protest was a direct consequence of the increasing pace and scope of Islamization in Malaysia and the constriction of religious and cultural space for the non-Muslim minority. Two issues, in particular, weighed heavily on the minds of Hindu protesters who took to the streets: the mounting number of "body-snatching" cases, instances where deceased ethnic Indians were deemed by state religious authorities to have converted to Islam and hence were denied Hindu burial rites despite protestations from family members, and the egregious demolition of Hindu temples by religious authorities affiliated with UMNO-led state governments. The plight of the Hindu minority was further compounded by the fact that earlier appeals by community leaders to the prime minister and the leaders of the MIC—the political party that purportedly represented the interests of the ethnic Indian minority—had fallen on deaf ears.

This acute sense of non-Malay and non-Muslim marginalization was not confined to the Indian minority. Ethnic Chinese, too, faced increasing encroachment of religion and state religious authorities into their private cultural and religious space. This concern was tellingly captured in the following cryptic comments made by an MCA leader about his UMNO colleagues: "If MCA continues to focus on the threats of opposition PAS as perceived to be against the Chinese community, it is fighting a shadow game. Basically UMNO has done more sociopolitical damage to other minority communities compared to PAS."[1]

Echoing Hindu concerns, in the buildup to the elections Malaysian Christians had taken umbrage at a number of incidents, such as the confiscation of Bibles by Malaysian customs authorities and efforts by local authorities to ban Christian usage of the pre-Islamic term for God, Allah. Prior to these events, government officials had also confiscated Christian children's books from several bookstores on the pretext that they included illustrations of prophets, which, they claimed, Muslims found offensive. These moves elicited a defiant response from the chairman of the Christian Federation of Malaysia, Bishop Paul Tan, who in an official statement retorted that on the matter of "their faith and practice," Christians in Malaysia were "answerable only to God." His concluding remark was even more pointed: "In the run-up to the national elections, it is important for the churches to be convinced that the policy of the *Barisan Nasional* guarantees religious freedom and would not tolerate any actions that undermine the religious rights of all citizens of Malaysia."[2] These sentiments were reinforced by Hermen Shastri, secretary of the Council of Churches of Malaysia, who made it clear that the CCM would use the pulpit to exhort Malaysian Christians to "vote wisely" at the elections.[3] From this buildup to the election, it was clear that issues of religion would be a major bone of contention for both Muslims and non-Muslims. Islam was poised to be the point of reference, and departure, for Malaysian politics yet again.

The (Islamist) Contest

While minority communities were preoccupied with the erosion of cultural and religious freedoms by a Muslim-dominated hegemonic government, UMNO and PAS busied themselves with the all-too-familiar ritual of mobilizing and employing the vocabulary and metaphors of Islam in their contests for Malay-Muslim hearts, minds, and ballots in the northern states. Predictably, UMNO campaigned in the northern states on a decidedly Islamic platform. As suggested in chapter 3, UMNO's sights had been trained on Kelantan since 2004, which on the eve of elections was controlled by PAS via a paper-thin majority of a single seat in the state assembly. UMNO's strategy to take Kelantan rested on the use of UMNO-run Terengganu in incumbent propaganda as the staging post and "model" of *Islam Hadhari* for the anticipated capture of the PAS stronghold. Thus, UMNO's campaign in the northern Malay-Muslim-majority states centered on profiling *Islam Hadhari's* "achievements" in the state—the impressive number of mosques built by the UMNO-led state government, the number of Islamic students who had learned to recite the Qur'an in government religious schools, and the government's *Taman Tamadun Islam* (Islamic Civilization Theme Park) project, which was engineered to be a manifestation of *Islam Hadhari* and which was profiled extensively in the government-controlled media as a feather in Abdullah's cap.

PAS, as expected, fell back on its proven organic network of *ceramah*, which it mobilized with characteristic efficiency. Through these small-scale traveling campaign rallies, PAS leaders worked to discredit the religious credentials of their UMNO opponents. At times, these tactics took somewhat extreme forms, most strikingly in the personal attacks on Abdullah Badawi. PAS campaigners displayed countless pictures of the prime minister in the company of Michelle Yeoh, a prominent Malaysian actress. Meanwhile, Abdullah's *Islam Hadhari* agenda also came under heavy fire when it was attacked as a new school of Islam that stressed materialism over spiritual well-being. The elections also witnessed the full-scale mobilization of PAS political leaders as religious functionaries, drawing on the dual roles that the party's leadership has always occupied. This came across most prominently during the *Sembahyang Hajat*, a mass prayer session conducted a day before the elections in the Sultan Muhammad ke-IV Stadium, Kota Bharu, where senior PAS political figures conducted prayers for their political campaign and for the "glory of Islam" in Kelantan and Malaysia.

Islamic credentials aside, PAS was at the same time also cognizant of the need to carefully calibrate its Islamic agenda to achieve maximum leverage from the widespread disenchantment with the Abdullah administration. This realization translated into a conscious move to avoid making references to the Islamic state outside of the party's strongholds in the rural north, to the extent that even leaders such as Nik Aziz, Abdul Hadi Awang, and Harun Din were uncharacteristically muted on the matter of *shari'a* and the Islamic state (again though, not unlike 1999). Instead, the party promulgated slogans such as *Negara Kebajikan* ("Welfare State"), *Kembalikan Demokrasi* ("The Return of Democracy"), *Pembangunan Seimbang* ("Balanced Development"), and *Pembangunan bersama Islam* ("Development with Islam"), slogans that captured the mood of the day and resonated with the masses. At a tactical level, candidates seen as technocrats and "moderate professionals" were sent to contest in largely urban and ethnically mixed seats across the country, while the party's base of religious teachers contested mostly in the north in order to maximize the potential of the party's slate of candidates. So confident was PAS that several of the party's moderates, notably deputy president Nasharuddin Mat Isa and Central Executive Committee member Hatta Ramli, found themselves contesting, and winning, in UMNO strongholds.[4]

Apart from the UMNO-PAS contest, this election was notable for the anticipated mobilization of Islamic NGOs behind the banner of Islamization. NGOs and civil society movements had already begun to play an increasingly salient and visible role in the buildup to the election. In late February 2008, eighty-eight Islamic NGOs rallied together and called for political parties, election candidates, and prospective state and federal governments to acknowledge and address issues concerning the interests of Islam and Muslim society, and to endorse the primacy of Islam in the country. Among the NGOs represented were ABIM, JIM, the Malaysian Chinese Muslim Association, the Shari'a Lawyers Association of Malaysia, the Allied Coordinating Council of Islamic NGOs, the Muslim Lawyers Association, PUM, and TERAS. Their demands were articulated in a document titled "Malaysia's Twelfth General Election: Islamic NGOs Election Demands." The document sought to address: (1) the special constitutional position of Islam, (2) Islamic education and *dakwah*, (3) good governance, (4) civil society and democracy, (5) interethnic and interreligious relations, and (6) Islamic faith and morals. Notably, these demands were made immediately after Christian groups began circulating their own document, titled "Vote Wisely," and secularist civil society movements circulated a "Malaysian Peoples' Declaration" that sought the reaffirmation of the centrality of the Constitution.

In a clear riposte to secularist and non-Muslim concerns, the Islamist document made a list of demands: the defense of Islam as the religion of the Federation, an assertion of the significant role of Islam in the state, the rejection of the notion that Malaysia was a secular state, the defense and strengthening of the position and jurisdiction of the *shari'a* courts, the strengthening of legislation against the propagation of non-Muslim religions, the prosecution of those who make offensive remarks against Islam, an increase in the time allocated to the learning of Islam in national schools, sensitivity toward the Muslim majority in devising media and broadcasting policies, the rejection of political parties and politicians who disregard the special position of Islam in Malaysia and who advocate secularism, the careful regulation by Muslim authorities of the building of non-Muslim houses of worship, the rejection of religious pluralism, the rejection of the use of specific terms from the lexicon of the Islamic creed ("Allah," "Ka'abah," "Solat") to refer to similar concepts in non-Muslim religions, an increase in the number of religious enforcement officers, and the enforcement of existing laws on religious crimes. This comprehensive list of demands draws attention once again not only to the acutely Islamist nature of a large majority of Islamic NGOs in Malaysia today but also to their heightened political consciousness and activism.

The Implications

While campaigning in northern Malaysia, Awang Adek, who had been unveiled as UMNO's choice for *Menteri Besar* of Kelantan in the event of a victory, proudly proclaimed, "When we win, we will usher in a new era in Kelantan, by building a grand mosque."[5] After the elections, PAS *Musyidul 'Am* Nik Aziz Nik Mat explained that the results were an "endorsement of the Islamic government" ("*Kerajaan Islam*") that Kelantan had instituted eighteen years ago and a rejection of the UMNO model of Islam.[6] Meanwhile, civil society groups mobilized along religious lines: HINDRAF articulated the general concerns of the ethnic Indian minorities in religious language, Christian churches mobilized through the pulpit, and Muslim groups responded by making demands for all political parties to reaffirm the primacy of Islam. Clearly, the increasing salience of religion continues to define the political terrain in the country in ways consistent with trends already identified in the preceding chapters.

Cognizant of the miscalculations following the 1999 elections, there are initial indications that PAS is exercising care not to misread the massive swing of support in its favor by pressing aggressively its Islamic agenda. For instance, PAS leaders moved immediately to quell rumors that they were already planning the formulation of *hudud* laws in Kedah, along the way providing repeated assurances of their commitment to the broader oppositionist cause. On the other hand though, provocative remarks were made by the vice-chief of PAS Youth, Azman Shapawi, indicating that the party will press for the implementation of *Siasat Shari'a* (Shari'a regulations) in opposition-ruled states. Beneath this contradiction lies the matter of internal tensions within the party leadership over whether to interpret the result of the election as a resounding mandate for greater Islamic strictures and governance on the one hand, or, on the other hand, merely the outcome of an avalanche of protest votes. Given the simmering tensions between professionals and the conservative *ulama* ranks, internal party stability will hinge on the management of these different perspectives. At the same time, PAS would do well to learn from its missteps during the period 1999–2004, when conservative forces implemented short-sighted policies and made ill-informed statements that alienated it from the Malaysian public and made cooperation with other opposition parties difficult.

In addition, the sustainability of the nascent opposition alliance is another matter that has commanded attention. Whether the Pakatan Rakyat will remain a viable force will depend on the ability of PAS and DAP to reconcile what appear to be fundamental differences in their longstanding party ideologies. It should be noted that neither leadership dealt head-on with this issue during the campaign, choosing instead to shelve differences, as they did in 1999. Nevertheless, the opposition's surprise victories in several state legislatures, particularly Selangor and Perak, may well prove a litmus test of the pliability of the working relationship between two opposition parties who possess fundamentally divergent ideological inclinations.

Turning to UMNO, Abdullah's immediate response after the election was to extend an olive branch to PAS. In a move that rekindled memories of events in 1974, UMNO leaders—not least the party president himself—floated the prospect of Malay and Islamic "unity" talks with PAS leaders, even as the latter were instructed by opposition leader Anwar Ibrahim to encourage UMNO members to break ranks and join the opposition coalition in order for him to secure enough defections for a simple majority in Parliament. The issue of cooperation with UMNO was subject to heated discussion and debate in PAS between elements in the party who were amenable to cooperation with UMNO on the principle of Malay-Muslim primacy (though not necessarily amounting to PAS membership in the *Barisan* as was the case in 1974) and who were quietly concerned that the electoral gains of DAP and *Keadilan* might obstruct its Islamic agenda, and those who shunned UMNO and its political culture. This tension was resolved when PAS rejected overtures from UMNO and reiterated its commitment to the opposition *Pakatan Rakyat* coalition at the Muktamar of August 2008, but not before vociferous debate between party leaders and the rank and file. Indeed, the debates at the Muktamar included a caustic rebuke from deputy *Musyidul 'Am* Harun Din, who took the party rank and file to task for questioning a decision by the *Majlis Shura* to explore the possibilities of dialogue with UMNO. Harun Din's harsh response was all the more telling given that none other than *Musyidul 'Am* Nik Aziz himself declared that he did not support talks with UMNO.

Given that cooperation with PAS is no longer a viable prospect, it is possible that UMNO will return to its Islamization script, as it did after the 1999 elections, in order to regain lost ground. The concern here would be that this could translate to a more unwavering approach, not only in its brand of Islamic politics but also in its endorsement of the conduct of the religious bureaucracy, in order to strengthen its Islamic credentials (particularly if the party leadership remains weak). Such a move would have significant impact on a number of levels. First, it would ensure that the UMNO-PAS Islamization race continues to be the definitive feature of the Malaysian political landscape and that the discourse of Islamism escalates while Islamic referents remain in place. Second, it would likely also set the tone for further activism on the part of nonpartisan actors. Given the size of the voting bloc controlled by Islamic NGOs such as ABIM and JIM, both of which have clearly articulated their demands for "more Islam" in Malaysia, these actors would be even more instrumental in

shaping and determining the contours and course of Islamism in contemporary Malaysia. Third, the presence of "more Islam" in Malaysian politics after
the 2008 elections would undoubtedly be met with further consternation on
the part of non-Muslims in Malaysia. This would in turn have negative repercussions not only for the respective political alliances (*Barisan Nasional* and the
Pakatan Rakyat) but also for Malaysian society at large. Finally, the elections
will likely have an impact on Malaysia's stature in the international community.
The categorical rejection of Abdullah's *Islam Hadhari* model of Islamic governance, previously promoted as the epitome of "moderate" and "progressive"
Islam, will undoubtedly reverberate across the Muslim world, considering how
the Organization of the Islamic Conference had wanted *Islam Hadhari* to be
"a central pillar in its new look."[7]

Concluding Observations

Given the magnitude of the opposition's success at the elections, it should not
be surprising to hear talk of a new dawn in Malaysian politics. At first glance,
there are persuasive reasons for such a view. While tensions have surfaced
within the opposition coalition, as seen in the contradictory statements of
its leaders on several issues, at the time of this writing the coalition remains
united. In addition, PAS has continued to keep its Islamic state agenda away
from the spotlight, as its reformist leaders continue to try to improve its image
in the eyes of the non-Muslim electorate. Amplifying these positive developments, voting patterns are further indicative of possible shifts in the demo-
graphics of PAS support. For instance, in the states of Perak and Selangor,
both of which fell into opposition hands, PAS had lost many rural seats where
Malay-Muslims formed the majority electorate, but the party won some urban,
mixed-constituency seats. This phenomenon speaks to a wider trend of Malaysians breaking ranks with traditional ethnoreligious partisan alignments.
Indeed, anecdotal evidence abounds of non-Malays voting for PAS and Malay-
Muslims for DAP.

Yet there are equally compelling reasons to avoid premature conclusions
regarding the implications of the 2008 elections. While a fair number of voters
jettisoned traditional race- and religion-based party allegiances, many have also
subsequently voiced regret for doing so, for various reasons. In most instances,
the reason expressed for this regret was that the voter had grossly under-
estimated the prospects for DAP or PAS success in several seats, or that they
were "caught up in the moment." Second, while the tide of reform was clearly
evident at this election, an opportunity to break out of the traditional political
configurations was lost, as the rhetoric that pointed to a shift away from ethnic
alignments and agendas was not matched by the creation of a truly "postcom-
munal" political movement. It is instructive to note that the opposition coalition

has configured itself along a similar constellation as the *Barisan Nasional*: PAS and DAP remain primarily Malay-Muslim and non-Malay secularist parties, respectively, while the *Parti Keadilan Rakyat* has morphed into a Malay-Muslim majority party, despite its assertions of multiculturalism and the presence of a handful of non-Malays in positions of leadership. Third, the persistence of ethnically based coalitions further accentuates the ideological gulf that remains. Notwithstanding laudable efforts to bridge their differences, the foundational ideological premises of PAS and DAP remain fundamentally at odds: the former will never abandon its Islamic state objective, just as the latter will never accept it. The implications of these differences can at best be postponed, as they have been thus far, but it is unlikely that they can be skirted indefinitely.

Fourth, it remains to be seen how executive authorities in opposition state governments can deal with Islamic councils and local religious bureaucracies, given the relative autonomy of state religious authorities on matters of faith and how their actions have in recent times exacerbated tensions and polarized communities. For instance, tensions between executive authority and royalty in the states of Penang and Perak have already surfaced over matters of appointment and dismissal of officers from the state religious bureaucracy, while temple demolitions have persisted in Selangor despite a change to a *Pakatan Rakyat* administration. Even within UMNO, while there is clearly a realization that the party is paying the price for allowing the process of Islamization to advance unabated, any move on the part of Abdullah or his successor to retrench Islamic political forces will have to contend with increasing pressure by various elements within the party to defend the Malay—and by extension the Islamic—agenda. Likewise, while it is clear that a main reason for the non-Muslim electorate's rejection of Abdullah and the *Barisan* was its endorsement and facilitation of a narrow and exclusivist Islamization process, this logic may be less explanatory of voting trends among the Malay-Muslim electorate, especially considering the vocal Malay-Muslim NGO activism that lobbied both incumbent and opposition for "more Islam."

All said, it should be quite clear that the dynamics behind the 2008 general election have reinforced many of the contentions made in the preceding chapters about the nature, state, contours, and impact of Islamism in Malaysia. It is not likely that Islam's influence on Malaysian affairs will diminish anytime in the near future. If anything, Islam is likely to take on a greater role as an organizing principle and point of reference for politics and society in the country.

Notes

PREFACE

1. There has, however, been active debate over the question of who is Malay and how to define the concept of "Malay," particularly with reference to religion, given that a significant minority of Muslims in Malaysia are not ethnically Malay. See, for example, Judith Nagata, "What is a Malay? Situational Selection of Ethnic Identity in a Plural Society," *American Ethnologist* 1, no. 2 (1974): 331–50; Timothy P. Barnard, ed., *Contesting Malayness: Malay Identity across Boundaries* (Singapore: Singapore University Press, 2004).

2. "Increasing Religiosity in Malaysia Causes a Stir," *Straits Times,* 5 September 2006.

3. While Malay sultans and rulers retained their offices, power lay in the hands of the British Resident. It was the British who regulated Islam and contained it in the private sphere, with legislative councils forming a supporting cast.

4. Mahathir Mohamad, keynote address delivered at the conferment of the King Faisal International Prize, Riyadh, Saudi Arabia, 22 March 1997.

INTRODUCTION

1. For example, a recent survey of 1,000 respondents revealed that 77 percent wanted stricter Islamic laws in place, and 44 percent supported a more active role for state religious authorities to police morality. See Patricia Martinez, "Islam, Pluralism, and Conflict Resolution in Malaysia: The Case of Interfaith Dialogue," paper presented at the Association of Asian Studies Annual Conference, San Francisco, Calif., 6–9 April 2006.

2. Consider, for example, how current UMNO president and Malaysian prime minister Abdullah Badawi regularly makes references to Islam

in his public speeches, or how *Mingguan Malaysia* [*Malaysia Weekly*], a best-selling government-linked daily, has weekend columns offering advice on various matters pertaining to religion in everyday life. Malaysia has also regularly hit the country-level limit set by the Saudi government for Haj pilgrims, and there is now a three-year waiting list for Malaysians wanting to make the pilgrimage.

3. As A. G. Noorani writes, "The Latin suffix attached to the Arab original more accurately expresses the relationship between the pre-existing reality (in this case a religion) and its translation into a political ideology." See A. G. Noorani, *Islam and Jihad: Prejudice versus Reality* (London: Zed Books, 2002), 68.

4. Judith Nagata, "Open Societies and Closed Minds: The Limits of Fundamentalism in Islam," *ICIP Journal* 2, no. 2 (2005): 2.

5. See International Crisis Group, *Indonesia Backgrounder: Why Salafism and Terrorism Mostly Don't Mix*, Asia Report No. 83 (Brussels, Belgium: 2004). Salafism refers to a movement that seeks to replicate the purest form of Islam in daily life, which to Salafis is the period of the Prophet and the three generations that came after him.

6. Indeed, this is the argument put forth by the *Jamaat Tabligh*, the transnational Islamic proselytization movement that originated in South Asia.

7. Azza Karam, "Transnational Political Islam and the USA: An Introduction," in *Transnational Political Islam: Religion, Ideology and Power*, ed. Azza Karam (London: Pluto Press, 2004), 6.

8. Michael Laffan, "The Tangled Roots of Islamist Activism in Southeast Asia," *Cambridge Review of International Affairs* 16, no. 3 (2003): 411.

9. See, for example, R. Hrair Dekmejian, *Islam in Revolution: Fundamentalism in the Arab World* (Syracuse, N.Y.: Syracuse University Press, 1995); Mahmud A. Faksh, *The Future of Islam in the Middle East: Fundamentalism in Egypt, Algeria, and Saudi Arabia* (Westport, Conn.: Praeger, 1997).

10. In any case, the argument that wealth gives rise to democracy has been challenged by the work of scholars such as Larbi Sadiki, who counterproposes that Arab democratization "seems to benefit from austerity, not bounty." See Larbi Sadiki, "Popular Uprisings and Arab Democratization," *International Journal of Middle East Studies* 32, no. 1 (2000): 90.

11. See James Piscatori, "Islam, Islamists, and the Electoral Principle in the Middle East," *ISIM Papers* 1 (2000): 10. See also Dale Eickelman and James Piscatori, *Muslim Politics* (Princeton, N.J.: Princeton University Press, 1996).

12. John L. Esposito and John O. Voll, *Islam and Democracy* (New York: Oxford University Press, 1996), 16.

13. In that regard, the exertions of the *Ikhwanul Muslimin* have already been well-documented in the literature. Less studied but no less salient are groups, such as the Gulen movement in Turkey, that advocate greater Islamic consciousness across Muslim society but toward inclusiveness and democracy. See Etga Ugur, "Intellectual Roots of 'Turkish Islam' and Approaches to the 'Turkish Model,'" *Journal of Muslim Minority Affairs* 24, no. 2 (2004): 327–46; Kuru T. Ahmet, "Globalization and Diversification of Islamic Movements: Three Turkish Cases," *Political Science Quarterly* 120, no. 2 (2005): 253–74.

14. See the remarks of Mohammed Ayoob in Hudson Institute, transcript of conference, *Beyond Radical Islam?* 2nd session, "Political Islam: Image and Reality,"

Washington, D.C., 16 April 2004, http://www.hudson.org/files/publications/Beyond_Radical_Islam-Transcript_2.pdf; see also Ghadbian Najib, "Democratization and the Islamist Challenge in the Arab World" (Ph.D. diss., City University of New York, 1995).

15. See Khaleed Sayeed, *Politics in Pakistan* (New York: Praeger Publishers, 1980), 86; John Walsh, "Egypt's Muslim Brotherhood: Understanding Centrist Islam," *Harvard International Review* 24, no. 4 (2003): 32–36.

16. Ayoob suggests that "competition" almost always results in admission of incapacity, as it leads to what Ayoob intimates will be "a failure to live up to its own words." See Ayoob, *Beyond Radical Islam.*

17. Jan Stark, "Constructing an Islamic Model in Two Malaysian States: PAS Rule in Kelantan and Terengganu," *Sojourn* 19, no. 1 (2004): 59.

18. See Salbiah Ahmad, "Islam in Malaysia: Constitutional and Human Rights Perspectives," *Muslim World Journal of Human Rights* 2, no. 1 (2005): 18; Stark, "Constructing an Islamic Model in Two Malaysian States," 54.

19. Some might argue, for instance, that PAS's electoral gains in 1999, in which the party wrested two states from UMNO's grasp, increased its standing in Parliament from seven to twenty-seven seats, and won 15 percent of the popular vote, indicated the emergence of a viable political alternative that posed a threat to UMNO's dominance of the Malay-Muslim electorate. The decrease in UMNO votes seemed to indicate the same, as did the reduction of UMNO seats from eighty-nine to seventy-two. However, in the larger scheme of things, UMNO still commanded slightly more than half of the Malay-Muslim electorate, a level of support just below their average. In any case, the process of Islamization in UMNO predated the 1999 elections, so it cannot be used to falsify this hypothesis. On the shift in support from UMNO to PAS, see John Funston, "Malaysia's Tenth Elections: Status Quo, Reformasi or Islamization?" *Contemporary Southeast Asia* 22, no. 1 (2000): 23–59; Maznah Mohamad, "The Contest for Malay Votes in 1999: UMNO's Most Historic Challenge?" in *New Politics in Malaysia,* ed. Francis Loh Kok Wah and Johan Saravanamuttu (Singapore: ISEAS, 2003), 66–86. Chandra Muzaffar, former deputy president of Keadilan and a losing candidate in the 1999 elections, mentioned at a public seminar in Singapore in 2003 that after the opposition coalition assessed voting trends, it discovered that the common perception that UMNO had lost the majority of Malay-Muslim votes was false; they still managed to retain more than 50 percent of that group's votes.

20. Importantly, however, the circumscription of Islamic opposition in Malaysia never reached the stage where the Islamist opposition was banned altogether, as had happened in many other Muslim countries.

21. "King of Morocco Outlaws Islamic Parties on Fourth Anniversary of His Reign," *Independent,* 1 August 2003.

22. Seyyed Vali Reza Nasr, *Islamic Leviathan: Islam and the Making of State Power* (New York: Oxford University Press, 2001), 4.

23. Ibid., 14.

24. Thereby speaking to the salience of the pragmatic and conciliatory trends, albeit still very rudimentary at this stage in Malaysia, exemplified by the arguments of Piscatori, Esposito, and Voll, discussed earlier.

25. John Funston, *Malay Politics in Malaysia: A Study of UMNO and PAS* (Singapore: Heinemann Educational Books, 1983); Hussin Mutalib, *Islam in*

Malaysia: From Revivalism to Islamic State (Singapore: Singapore University Press, 1993); Kamarulnizam Abdullah, *The Politics of Islam in Contemporary Malaysia* (Bangi, Malaysia: Penerbit Universiti Kebangsaan Malaysia, 2002). To be fair, Funston's analysis took place before major shifts within both UMNO and PAS toward a more Islamic register. Even so, as the first major book-length study of the UMNO-PAS relationship, Funston's study has proven critical as a resource and point of entry for subsequent attempts to understand the dynamics of this relationship.

CHAPTER I

1. William R. Roff, *The Origins of Malay Nationalism* (Kuala Lumpur, Malaysia: Oxford University Press, 1967) remains the classic study on the early Islamic reformists and their impact throughout the Malay world.

2. George McTurnan Kahin, *Nationalism and Revolution in Indonesia* (Ithaca, N.Y.: Cornell University Press, 1952), 38.

3. See Azyumardi Azra, "The Transmission of al-Manar's Reformism to the Malay-Indonesian World: The Cases of al-Imam and al-Munir," *Studia Islamika* 6, no. 3 (1999): 75–100.

4. See John Funston, *Malay Politics in Malaysia: A Study of UMNO and PAS* (Singapore: Heinemann Educational Books, 1980), 87.

5. Hussin Mutalib, *Islam and Ethnicity in Malay Politics* (Singapore: Oxford University Press, 1990), 107.

6. Nabir Haji Abdullah, *Maahad Il-Ihya Assyariff Gunung Semanggol, 1934–1935* (Kuala Lumpur, Malaysia: Jabatan Sejarah, Universiti Malaya, 1976), 149; Firdaus Abdullah, *Radical Malay Politics: Its Origins and Early Developments* (Petaling Jaya, Malaysia: Pelanduk Publications, 1985), 38–46.

7. Funston, *Malay Politics in Malaysia*, 88.

8. The religious character of MATA was emphasized in the composition of its advisory board, which included a number of prominent *ulama* such as Haji Fadhlullah Suhaimi, Haji Abdullah Pahim, Haji Abdul Jalil Hassan, and Ustaz Abu Bakar al-Bakir. See Abdullah, *Maahad Il-Ihya Assyariff Gunung Semanggol*, 149.

9. Funston, *Malay Politics in Malaysia*, 87–88.

10. Alias Mohamed, *PAS' Platform: Development and Change 1951–1986* (Petaling Jaya, Malaysia: Gateway Publishing House, 1994), 9.

11. N. J. Funston, "The Origins of Parti Islam Se Malaysia," *Journal of Southeast Asian Studies* 7, no. 1 (1976): 66.

12. Funston, *Malay Politics in Malaysia*, 91.

13. The relevant portion of the memorandum reads as follows: "The religion of Malaya shall be Islam. The observance of this principle shall not impose any disability on non-Muslim natives professing and practicing their religions and shall not imply that the State is not a secular State." See M. Sufian Hashim, "The Relationship between Islam and the State in Malaya," *Intisari* 1, no. 1 (1957): 8. Alliance (*Perikatan*) here refers to the coalition agreement between UMNO, the Malayan Chinese Association, and the Malayan Indian Congress to contest the 1955 elections. The Alliance itself was formed in 1952 by UMNO and the Malayan Chinese Association to contest the 1952 Kuala Lumpur municipal elections.

14. Describing the competition between the two, Alias argued that "while Dato Onn fought for the defusion [*sic*] of communal tension among the different communities through the creation of a single political organization for all, the Tunku strove for the maintenance and preservation of a separate political party for the Malays, but at the same time, recognizing the inherent rights of the non-Malays." See Mohamed, *PAS' Platform*, 26.

15. Gordon P. Means, "Public Policy towards Religion in Malaysia," *Pacific Affairs* 51, no. 3 (1978): 399.

16. Ibid., 24.

17. Farish A. Noor, *Islam Embedded: The Historical Development of the Pan-Malaysian Islamic Party PAS, 1951–2003* (Kuala Lumpur, Malaysia: Malaysian Sociological Research Institute, 2004), 1:72–73.

18. See Clive Kessler, *Islam and Politics in a Malay State: Kelantan 1839–1969* (Ithaca, N.Y.: Cornell University Press, 1978), 166.

19. Salim bin Osman, "UMNO-PAS Rivalry in Malaysia" (B.A. diss., National University of Singapore, 1979), 18.

20. Ibid., 23.

21. See Shafie Ibrahim, *The Islamic Party of Malaysia: Its Formative Stages and Ideology* (Kuala Lumpur, Malaysia: Nuawi bin Ismail, 1981), 26–27.

22. Parti Islam Se-Malaysia, *Perlembagaan Parti Islam SeMalaysia* [Constitution of the Islamic Party of Malaysia] (Kuala Lumpur, Malaysia: Pejabat Agung PAS, 1977), 2–4. Along with the *Dewan Ulama*, youth and women's councils were also established in the form of the *Dewan Pemuda* and *Dewan Muslimat*.

23. Ibid., 3.

24. Ibid.

25. Alias Mohamed, *Malaysia's Islamic Opposition: Past, Present and Future* (Kuala Lumpur, Malaysia: Gateway Publishing House, 1991), 11.

26. See Funston, *Malay Politics in Malaysia*, 94.

27. Farish Noor, *Islam Embedded*, 1:77–78.

28. Gordon P. Means, *Malaysian Politics: The Second Generation* (London: Oxford University Press, 1990), 17.

29. *Utusan Zaman*, 13 January 1952, quoted in Alias Mohamed, *PAS' Platform*, 32.

30. Kessler noted, for instance, how PAS grassroots organizations helped Malay peasants navigate the bureaucratic waters of taxation. See Kessler, *Islam and Politics in a Malay State*, 167–68. Indeed, as we have witnessed in the track record of Islamist political parties worldwide, most popular and successful Islamist parties began their activism as welfare organizations, providing services that the state was unable or unwilling to provide.

31. See Gordon P. Means, *Malaysian Politics*, 2nd ed. (London: Hodder and Stoughton, 1976), 155.

32. Funston, *Malay Politics in Malaysia*, 94.

33. Karl von Vorys, *Democracy without Consensus: Communalism and Political Stability in Malaysia* (Kuala Lumpur, Malaysia: Oxford University Press, 1976), 147.

34. Burhanuddin played a key role in the formation of *Hizbul Muslimin, Partai Kebangsaan Melayu Malaya* (Malay Nationalist Party of Malaya), *Parti Rakyat Malaya* (People's Party of Malaya), and *Parti Buruh Malaya* (Labor Party of Malaya).

35. See Farish Noor, *Islam Embedded*, 1:114–15. Noor suggests, for instance, that Burhanuddin's call for Malay-Muslims to transcend the narrow ethnocentrism and parochialism of the day was driven by the Islamic argument against all forms of *assabiyyah* (chauvinistic communalism).

36. Hussin Mutalib, *Islam in Malaysia: From Revivalism to Islamic State?* (Singapore: Singapore University Press, 1993), 24.

37. See Alias Mohamed, *PAS' Platform*, 70. It should be noted, though, that Burhanuddin's defeat of Zulkiflee Muhammad by a substantial margin (84 to 12) perhaps indicated that the PAS delegates who voted in the elections were generally satisfied with his credentials. In any case, Alias Mohamed noted John Funston's argument that the difference between Burhanuddin and Zulkilfee may have been less an issue of Islamist credentials than one concerning schools of thought: "It seems more accurate to describe their differences as those between an adherent to Islamic reformism on the one side, and on the other to a more quietistic Sufism." See Funston, *Malay Politics in Malaysia*, 122.

38. It is a well-known fact that Burhanuddin was personally close to Sukarno, the charismatic Indonesian nationalist leader whom Burhanuddin admired. Their relationship can be traced to the prewar nationalist struggles in British Malaya and the Dutch East Indies, where Sukarno's anticolonial agitation became somewhat of a model for Malayan anticolonialists like Burhanuddin, Ahmad Boestamam, and Ibrahim Yaacob. See Joseph Chinyong Liow, *The Politics of Indonesia-Malaysia Relations: One Kin, Two Nations* (London: RoutledgeCurzon, 2005), 54–72. For Burhanuddin's reference to the mantra of nationalism, religion, and socialism in the ideology of PAS, see Burhanuddin's 1956 policy speech titled "Ucapan Dasar Parti PAS" [Speech on PAS's Fundamentals], reproduced in K. S. Jomo, ed., *Islam dan Sosialisme* [Islam and Socialism] (Kuala Lumpur, Malaysia: Ikraq Press, 1988).

39. This claim was made in Kamarulnizam Abdullah, *The Politics of Islam in Contemporary Malaysia* (Bangi, Malaysia: Penerbit Universiti Kebangsaan Malaysia, 2002), 46. See also T. G. McGee, "The Malayan Elections of 1959: A Study in Electoral Geography," *Malayan Journal of Tropical Geography* 16 (1962): 68–69.

40. See Shafie Ibrahim, *The Islamic Party of Malaysia*, 86. The five principles were: (1) the Malay nation was to be the rightful owner of Malaya, (2) the Malays should be granted special rights, (3) there should be stricter conditions for Malayan citizenship, (4) Islam should be the official religion, and (5) Malay should be the official national language.

41. That said, it appears that during his tenure as PAS president Burhanuddin did draft an Islamic state document that sought to outline his vision of an Islamic government in Malaya. This document however, is not available to the public. Interview with officials from the PAS archives, Kota Bharu, Malaysia, 2 June 2007.

42. A concise summary of the intra-Alliance problems in the run-up to the 1959 elections can be found in Leonard Andaya and Barbara Watson Andaya, *A History of Malaysia*, 2nd ed. (Basingstoke, UK: Palgrave, 2001), 277–82.

43. See T. E. Smith, "The Malayan Elections of 1959," *Pacific Affairs* 33, no. 1 (1960): 41–42.

44. The importance of the language issue to the stability of the Alliance coalition, especially in the early years of independence, was emphasized in Leon Comber, "Chinese Education: Perennial Malayan Problem," *Asian Survey* 1, no. 8 (1961): 30–35.

45. For example, with these new laws the Chinese electorate expanded from 11.2 percent in 1955 to 35.6 percent at the 1959 general elections.

46. See von Vorys, *Democracy without Consensus*, 147. Under these new laws, citizenship was granted on the principle of *jus soli*. This was a marked change from the earlier laws under the Federation Agreement, wherein citizenship required residence for at least 15 out of 25 years, a declaration of permanent settlement, and competence in Malay and English.

47. *Siaran PAS Kelantan* 3 (1968): 11.

48. Kessler, *Islam and Politics in a Malay State*, 120–21.

49. Alias Mohamed, *PAS' Platform*, 79.

50. Kessler, *Islam and Politics in a Malay State*, 35.

51. Sukarno's *Konfrontasi* or Confrontation denoted a policy of harsh diplomacy coupled with limited military action. His government first employed the term against the Dutch in the West Irian campaign, and Sukarno used it again in his attempt to disrupt the formation of Malaysia, which sought to bring Malaya, Singapore, Sarawak, and Sabah together as one singular terrestrial political entity.

52. Liow, *The Politics of Indonesia-Malaysia Relations*, 105.

53. This event has been the subject of several major studies, including John Slimming, *Malaysia: Death of a Democracy* (London: J. Murray, 1969); Felix Gagliano, *Communal Violence in Malaysia 1969: The Political Aftermath* (Athens, Ohio: Ohio University Center for International Studies, 1970); Goh Cheng Teik, *The May Thirteenth Incident and Democracy in Malaysia* (Kuala Lumpur, Malaysia: Oxford University Press, 1971); W. Donald McTaggart, *The May 1969 Disturbances in Malaysia: Impact of a Conflict on Developmental Pattern* (San Diego, Calif.: Association for Asian Studies, 1971); and Leon Comber, *13 May 1969: A Historical Survey of Sino-Malay Relations* (Kuala Lumpur, Malaysia: Heinemann Asia, 1983).

54. K. J. Ratnam and R. S. Milne, "The 1969 Parliamentary Elections in West Malaysia," *Pacific Affairs* 43, no. 2 (1970): 203–26.

55. Von Vorys, *Democracy without Consensus*, 261.

56. Ibid., 249–50.

57. Alias Mohamed, *PAS' Platform*, 96–97.

58. It is interesting to note that, in contrast, von Vorys felt that PAS had expanded its popularity *in spite* of its rather incoherent organizational approach to the elections. See von Vorys, *Democracy without Consensus*, 261–62.

59. Ibid., 271–72.

60. See Alias Mohamed, *PAS' Platform*, 91.

61. Quoted in Ibid., 271.

62. Hussin Mutalib, *Islam and Ethnicity in Malay Politics*, 51.

63. Ibid., 53.

64. Harold Crouch, *Government and Society in Malaysia* (Ithaca, N.Y.: Cornell University Press, 1996), 24–25.

65. Funston, *Malay Politics in Malaysia*, 294.

66. Ibid., 245.

67. Kamarulnizam Abdullah, *The Politics of Islam in Contemporary Malaysia*, 191.

68. Interview with Ustaz Hassan Shukri, 16 August 2006.

69. Details of the UMNO-PAS alliance can be found in Means, *Malaysian Politics*.

70. Details on this struggle can be found in L. Ismail, *Berakhirnya Zaman Keagungan PAS* [The End of a Prolific Era for PAS] (Kuala Lumpur, Malaysia: Penerbitan Pena, 1978).

71. For instance, Ahmad Fauzi Abdul Hamid, "Islamic Resurgence: An Overview of Causal Factors, A Review of 'Ummatic' Linkages," *Jurnal IKIM* 10, no. 2 (2001): 87–123; Khoo Boo Teik, *Searching for Islam in Malaysian Politics: Confluences, Divisions, and Governance*, Working Paper Series No. 72 (Hong Kong: City University of Hong Kong, Southeast Asia Research Centre, 2004).

72. See Clive Kessler, "Malaysia: Islamic Revivalism and Political Disaffection in a Divided Society," *Southeast Asia Chronicle* 75 (1980): 3–11.

73. Salim bin Osman, "UMNO-PAS Rivalry," 36.

74. The *Yayasan Dakwah Islamiah Malaysia* (YDIM) was in fact led predominantly by PAS members. See YDIM, *Dakwah* [Proselytization] (Kuala Lumpur, Malaysia: Yayasan Dakwah Islamiah Malaysia, 1977).

75. Asri Muda's attempt to forge an alliance with the Chinese-dominated DAP was also seen as contributing substantially to PAS's defeats. It should be recognized, however, that PAS did generally maintain much of its support in the Northern Malay states, and its best performances were in Malay-majority constituencies. See Diane Mauzy, "A Vote for Continuity: The 1978 General Elections in Malaysia," *Asian Survey* 19, no. 3 (1979): 281–96.

76. Cited in Zainon Ahmad, "Of PAS, Present, and Future," *Sun*, 11 June 2005.

77. Yusof Rawa, "Ke Arah Pembebasan Ummah" [Toward the Liberation of the Ummah], in *Memperingati Yusof Rawa* [Commemorating Yusof Rawa], ed. Kamarudin Jaffar (Kuala Lumpur, Malaysia: IKDAS, 2000), 43–44.

78. Hussin Mutalib, *Islam and Ethnicity in Malay Politics*, 113–14.

79. "Laporan Tahunan Dewan Pemuda PAS Untuk Dikemukakan Dimuktamar Tahunan Ke-23" [Yearly Report from PAS Youth Wing to be Discussed at the 23rd Annual Conference], Bukit Mertajam, Seberang Perai, 31 July 1982, 6.

80. Mohamed Nawab bin Mohamed Osman, "Religio-Political Activism of Ulama in Malaysia" (M.A. diss., National University of Singapore, 2006), 57.

81. Farish A. Noor, *Islam Embedded*, 2:337. This account contradicts Alias Mohamed's reading that Yusof Rawa, known to have harbored a personal grudge against Asri Muda, was exploited by the Young Turks and "was no more than a figure head." See Alias Mohamed, *PAS' Platform*, 182.

82. See Kamarulnizam Abdullah, *The Politics of Islam in Contemporary Malaysia*, 141.

83. One of the clearest indicators of this change came in the form of the establishment of the *Majlis Shura Ulama* (Consultative Council of Religious Scholars) to coordinate decision-making in the party leadership. The formation of this institution within the party epitomized the reemphasis on *ulama* leadership in the rejuvenated PAS.

84. See "Laporan Tahunan Dewan Pemuda PAS" [Yearly Report from PAS Youth Wing], 5.

85. PAS, *Perlembagaan Parti Islam Se Malaysia* [Constitution of the Islamic Party of Malaysia], 5–6.

86. Jabatan Penerangan PAS, *Memahami dan Mengenali Perjuangan Parti Islam Se Malaysia* [To Understand and Identify PAS's Struggles] (Kuala Lumpur, Malaysia: Jabatan

Penerangan PAS Pusat, undated), 6–7, cited in Kamarulnizam Abdullah, *The Politics of Islam in Malaysia*, 141.

87. Kamarudin Jaffar, ed., *Memperingati Yusof Rawa* [Commemorating Yusof Rawa] (Kuala Lumpur, Malaysia: IKDAS, 2000), 30.

88. This group of student organizations has been called the Islamic Republic Group. See Zainah Anwar, *Islamic Revivalism in Malaysia: Dakwah among the Students* (Petaling Jaya, Malaysia: Pelanduk Publications, 1987), 34–36.

89. Ahmad Fauzi Abdul Hamid, "Islamic Doctrine and Violence: The Malaysian Case," paper presented at the Institute of Defence and Strategic Studies Conference on "Anatomies of Religious Conflict in South and Southeast Asia," Singapore, 3–4 May 2005, 7.

90. In fact, this polarization of Malaysia's Muslim community was not new. It echoed developments at the turn of the century when the challenge posed by younger, reformist Muslim intellectuals to the old order anchored by the orthodox, traditional *ulama*—known in popular parlance as the *Kuam Tua* (Old Generation)–*Kaum Muda* (Young Generation) debate—generated similar communal cleavages across rural Malaya. See Roff, *The Origins of Malay Nationalism*, 75–87.

91. Ahmad Fauzi Abdul Hamid, "Islamic Doctrine and Violence: The Malaysian Case," 7.

92. "Fundamentalism on Trial," *Far Eastern Economic Review*, 8 May 1986; "Amanat Haji Hadi Bawa Padah" [Haji Hadi's Edict Bears Disastrous Results], *Mingguan Malaysia* [*Malaysia Weekly*], 13 June 1999; "Prayers Held in Two Mosques," *New Straits Times*, 8 December 2004.

93. "Countering a Crusade," *Far Eastern Economic Review*, 23 August 1984.

94. "Malaysia: Islam on the Screen," *Economist*, 27 October 1984; "They Shall Not Pass," *Far Eastern Economic Review*, 18 October 1984.

95. "Reminder to Gazette Fatwa Council Ruling on Amanat Hadi," *Bernama*, 21 April 2001.

96. Farish A. Noor, "Blood, Sweat, and Jihad: The Radicalization of the Political Discourse of the Pan-Malaysian Islamic Party (PAS) from 1982 Onwards," *Contemporary Southeast Asia* 25, no. 2 (2003): 200–232.

97. Alias Mohamed, *PAS' Platform*, 184.

98. "Fadzil: Prove Decree Goes against Islamic Teaching," *New Straits Times*, 29 March 2001.

99. K. S. Jomo and Ahmad Shabery Cheek, "Malaysia's Islamic Movements," in *Fragmented Vision: Culture and Politics in Contemporary Malaysia*, ed. Joel S. Kahn and Francis Loh Kok Wah (Honolulu: University of Hawaii Press, 1992), 98.

100. See Hussin Mutalib, *Islam and Ethnicity in Malay Politics*, 118.

101. See PAS, *Manifesto: PAS Negeri Kelantan 1986* (Kota Bharu, Malaysia: Perhubungan PAS Negeri Kelantan, 1986).

102. For insightful elaboration of the Islamic state concept of governance as it may apply in Malaysia's case, see Hussin Mutalib, *Islam in Malaysia: From Revivalism to Islamic State* (Singapore: Singapore University Press, 1993).

103. This is enshrined in the party's manifesto, available at http://www.parti-pas. org or http://www.pas.org.my/index.php?option=com_content&task=view&id=1370& Itemid=86. See also Nasharuddin Mat Isa, *The Islamic Party of Malaysia (PAS): Ideology,*

Policy, Struggle and Vision towards the New Millennium (Kuala Lumpur, Malaysia: Islamic Party of Malaysia, 2001).

104. Abdul Hadi, it will be remembered, was arguably the most vehement and scathing critic of UMNO among the new PAS leadership. It was he who upped the ante in the so-called Islamic race by labelling UMNO leaders infidels and calling the PAS struggle against UMNO a *jihad*.

105. Jan Stark, "Constructing an Islamic Model: PAS Rule in Kelantan and Terengganu," *Sojourn* 19, no. 1 (2004): 63.

106. See S. Ramanathan and M. H. Adnan, *Malaysia's 1986 General Election: The Urban-Rural Dichotomy*, Occasional Paper No. 83 (Singapore: Institute of Southeast Asian Studies, 1988), 32–33. Needless to say, these accusations subsequently proved groundless.

107. Ibid., 59.

108. Ibid., 60.

109. See Syed Ahmed Hussein, "Muslim Politics and the Discourse on Democracy," in *Democracy in Malaysia: Discourses and Practices*, ed. Francis Loh Kok Wah and Khoo Boo Teik (Richmond, UK: Curzon, 2002), 93.

110. Hussin Mutalib, *Islam in Malaysia*, 115.

CHAPTER 2

1. Chandra Muzaffar, "Islamisation of State and Society: Some Further Critical Remarks," in *Shari'a Law and the Modern Nation-State*, ed. Norani Othman (Kuala Lumpur, Malaysia: Sisters in Islam, 1994), 113.

2. See Judith Nagata, "Religious Ideology and Social Change: The Islamic Revival in Malaysia," *Pacific Affairs* 53, no. 3 (1980): 405–39.

3. Zainon Ahmad, "Of PAS, Present, and Future," *Sun*, 11 June 2005.

4. Mohamad Abu Bakar, "Islamic Revivalism and the Political Process in Malaysia," *Asian Survey* 21, no. 10 (1981): 1044.

5. Nagata, "Religious Ideology and Social Change," 49.

6. Anne Katherine Larsen, "The Impact of the Islamic Resurgence on the Belief System of Rural Malays," *Temenos* 32 (1996): 137–54.

7. Judith Nagata, *The Reflowering of Malaysian Islam: Modern Religious Radicals and Their Roots* (Vancouver: University of British Columbia Press, 1984), 81.

8. Mohamad Abu Bakar, "Islamic Revivalism and the Political Process in Malaysia," 1050.

9. Syed Ahmad Hussein, *Muslim Politics in Malaysia: Origins and Evolution of Competing Traditions in Malaysian Islam*, Occasional Paper No. 15 (Braamfontein, South Africa: Foundation for Global Dialogue, 1998), 24.

10. See Khoo Boo Teik, *Paradoxes of Mahathirism: An Intellectual Biography of Mahathir Mohamad* (Kuala Lumpur, Malaysia: Oxford University Press, 1995), 163–74.

11. See Mahathir's speech at the 33rd Annual UMNO General Assembly, Kuala Lumpur, Malaysia, 10 September 1982.

12. Mahathir's drive to create a Muslim work ethic was part of his broader Look East Policy, which aimed for Malaysia to emulate the developmental and modernization strategies of Japan, a nation that attained a high rate of industrialization without compromising indigenous culture and tradition.

13. Hussin Mutalib, "Islamisation in Malaysia: Between Ideals and Realities," in *Islam, Muslims and the Modern State: Case Studies of Muslims in Thirteen Countries*, ed. Hussin Mutalib and Taj ul-Islam Hashmi (New York: St. Martin's Press, 1994), 155.

14. Norhashimah Mohd. Yasin, *Islamisation/Malaynisation: A Study on the Role of Islamic Law in the Economic Development of Malaysia: 1969–1993* (Kuala Lumpur, Malaysia: A. S. Noordeen, 1996), 232.

15. See Kikue Hamayotsu, "Islamisation, Patronage and Political Ascendancy: The Politics and Business of Islam," in *The State of Malaysia: Ethnicity Equity and Reform*, ed. Edmund Terence Gomez (London: RoutledgeCurzon, 2004), 247.

16. See Seyyed Vali Reza Nasr, *Islamic Leviathan: Islam and the Making of State Power* (Oxford, UK: Oxford University Press, 2001), 105–29.

17. See Nagata, *The Reflowering of Malaysian Islam*, 159; Nasr, *Islamic Leviathan*, 120.

18. Georg Stauth, *Politics and Cultures in Islamisation in Southeast Asia: Indonesia and Malaysia in the Nineteen-nineties* (Bielefield, Germany: Transcript Verlag, 2002), 205.

19. R. S. Milne and Diane K. Mauzy, *Malaysian Politics under Mahathir* (London: Routledge, 1999), 85.

20. See Hussin Mutalib, *Islam in Malaysia: From Revivalism to Islamic State?* (Singapore: Singapore University Press, 1993), 31.

21. Shanti Nair, *Islam in Malaysian Foreign Policy* (London: Routledge, 1997), 33.

22. Department of Islamic Development Malaysia, http://www.islam.gov.my/english/function.php (accessed 31 July 2006).

23. Stauth, *Politics and Cultures in Islamisation in Southeast Asia*, 206. The crimes that come under *hudud* include *sariqah* (theft), *hirabah* (robbery), *zina* (adultery), *qazaf* (false accusations of *zina*), *syurb* (alcoholism), *irtidad* or *riddah* (apostasy), and *bughah* (rebellion against Islam). *Qisas* covers offenses involving bodily injury or death. *Ta'azirat* refers to types and quantities of punishments that have not been determined by *shari'a* and hence have to be determined by a *hakim* (judge).

24. Ibid.

25. "Govt. Explains Hesitancy in Arresting Ayah Pin," *Bernama*, 22 September 2005.

26. "Book on Ashaari's Views on Islam Hadhari Deviating: Dr Abdullah," *Bernama*, 30 June 2005.

27. "JAKIM Views Spread of Wahhabi Practices Seriously," *Bernama*, 27 November 2005.

28. "Empowering JAKIM with Authority to Arrest, Prosecute," *Bernama*, 5 November 2005.

29. "Shahrizat Says Holding Back Law Will Give Time for Views," *Bernama*, 13 January 2006.

30. "Stiffer Fines for SMS Divorce," *New Straits Times*, 12 February 2006.

31. "Johore Made Tests Compulsory for Couples in 2001," *New Straits Times*, 10 July 2006.

32. "JAKIM Won't Wait for Decency Guidelines," *New Straits Times*, 19 April 2006.

33. Ibid.

34. "Group to Handle Apostasy Issue," *New Straits Times*, 18 July 2006.

35. "PAS: Go Directly to the Government," *New Straits Times*, 20 May 2006.

36. Ibid.

37. "Another Tussle over Religious Status," *New Straits Times*, 21 January 2006.

38. "Probe into Perak Mufti's Apostate Claims," *New Straits Times*, 13 July 2006.

39. Ibid.

40. "Abdullah: JAKIM Can Enhance Branding Malaysia as *halal* Hub," *Bernama*, 14 April 2006.

41. "Techpark@enstek Attracts Health Ministry, JAKIM," *Business Times*, 3 March 2006.

42. "M'sia to Pursue '*halal*' Food Hub Status to Lure ASEAN Tourists," *Bernama*, 22 July 2006.

43. "JAKIM Drafting Cosmetic Standard," *Bernama*, 11 May 2006.

44. "Religious Guidelines on Entertainment: Consult Others," *New Straits Times*, 23 May 2005.

45. See Kikue Hamayotsu, "Islam and Nation Building in Southeast Asia: Malaysia and Indonesia in Comparative Perspective," *Pacific Affairs* 75, no. 3 (2002): 353–98.

46. IKIM.FM, http://www.ikim.gov.my/ikim.fm/ikimfm.htm (accessed 6 August 2006).

47. *Yayasan FELDA* (FELDA Foundation), http://www.felda.net.my/yayasan felda/start.htm (accessed 6 August 2006).

48. Milne and Mauzy, *Malaysian Politics under Mahathir*, 86.

49. "Ahmad Sarji Reappointed IKIM Chairman," *Bernama*, 27 March 2006.

50. Patricia Martinez, "Mahathir, Islam and the New Malay Dilemma," in *Mahathir's Administration: Performance and Crisis in Governance*, ed. Ho Khai Leong and James Chin (Singapore: Times Book International, 2002), 235.

51. Ibid.

52. Anthony S. K. Shome, *Malay Political Leadership* (London: RoutledgeCurzon, 2003), 161.

53. Milne and Mauzy, *Malaysian Politics under Mahathir*, 86.

54. Hajrudin Somun, *Mahathir: The Secret of the Malaysian Success* (Kuala Lumpur, Malaysia: Pelanduk Publications, 2004), 163.

55. Ibid., 262. This should not be surprising given Anwar's popularity among tertiary students. The second rector of the university, Iraqi scholar Abdul Hamid Abu Sulayman, was known to have been a mentor of Anwar's during his time as a student leader in ABIM, and his term as rector at IIUM (1988–1998) coincided with Anwar's ascent and subsequent downfall.

56. See Norhashimah Mohd. Yasin, *Islamisation/Malaynisation*, 261–64. The bank did not offer any interest on deposits it received. Instead, it would share the profits earned from investing the deposits with the bank's customers. The bank was also not charging interest on credit that it extended.

57. Hajrudin Somun, *Mahathir*, 164.

58. Martinez, "Mahathir, Islam and the New Malay Dilemma," 233.

59. Interview with PAS officials, Petaling Jaya, Malaysia, 18 August 2006.

60. Harold Crouch describes the Mahathir administration as a case of "soft authoritarianism." See Harold Crouch, *Government and Politics in Malaysia* (Ithaca, N.Y.: Cornell University Press, 1990).

61. Norani Othman, "Islamisation and Democratization in Malaysia in Regional and Global Contexts," in *Challenging Authoritarianism in Southeast Asia: Comparing Indonesia and Malaysia*, ed. Ariel Heryanto and Sumit K. Mandal (London: Routledge-Curzon, 2003), 127.

62. Printers and publishers now have to apply for new licenses annually, whereas previously they were only required to renew the licenses they already had.

63. Norani Othman, "Islamisation and Democratization in Malaysia in Regional and Global Contexts," 128.

64. Milne and Mauzy, *Malaysian Politics under Mahathir*, 87.

65. "Malaysian Opposition Chief Slams Detention Proposal," *New Straits Times*, 29 July 1995.

66. For details on how the ISA was mobilized against PAS, see Nicole Fritz and Martin Flaherty, *Unjust Order: Malaysia's Internal Security Act* (New York: The Joseph R. Crowley Program in International Human Rights, 2003), 25–29.

67. Milne and Mauzy, *Malaysian Politics under Mahathir*, 88.

68. Ibid.

69. Martinez, "Mahathir, Islam and the New Malay Dilemma," 239. Naturally, the inclusion of wives and children would inflate the overall membership figure.

70. Ibid.

71. Milne and Mauzy, *Malaysian Politics under Mahathir*, 88.

72. "10 Anti-Hadith Lecturers, Politicians, under Probe," *New Straits Times*, 22 June 1995.

73. "Muslims First, Malaysians Second," *Straits Times*, 21 August 2006.

74. Norhashimah Mohd. Yasin, *Islamisation/Malaynisation*, 224.

75. Ibid., 223.

76. See Judith Nagata, "How to Be Islamic without Being an Islamic State," in *Islam, Globalisation, and Postmodernity*, ed. Akbar Ahmed and Hastings Donnan (London: Routledge, 1994), 71.

77. "Blunt Message," *Far Eastern Economic Review*, 8 August 1996.

78. "How Far Should Islamic Law Go?" *Straits Times*, 22 August 1997.

79. "Stuck in an Islamic Time Capsule," *muslimedia.com*, 1–15 August 1997, http://www.muslimedia.com/archives /sea98/capsule.htm (accessed 12 June 2007). The report also noted that the women "had admitted that it [their arrest] was a blessing in disguise and they now realized the meaning of dignity in Islam."

80. Norhashimah Mohd. Yasin, *Islamisation/Malaynisation*, 223.

81. Mahlon Meyer, "Stopped in Its Track," *Newsweek*, 30 October 2000.

82. Sean Yoong, "Malaysian State Legislature Passes Bill on Strict Islamic Criminal Code," *Associated Press*, 8 July 2002, http://www.highbeam.com/doc/1P1-54163924.html (accessed 8 July 2002). The other four seats were held by UMNO politicians.

83. "Terengganu Hudud Laws Expected to Be Gazetted by Dec 31," *New Straits Times*, 18 September 2002.

84. Yoong, "Malaysian State Legislature Passes Bill on Strict Islamic Criminal Code."

85. Ibid.

86. Rose Ismail, *Hudud in Malaysia: The Issues at Stake* (Kuala Lumpur, Malaysia: SIS Forum Berhad, 1995), 175.

87. Kikue Hamayotsu, "Politics of Syariah Reform," in *Malaysia: Islam, Society and Politics*, ed. Virginia Hooker and Norani Othman (Singapore: ISEAS, 2003), 72.

88. "Don't Like *Hudud*? Blame UMNO, Not PAS," *Free Anwar Campaign News*, 9 September 2002, http://www.freeanwar.net/june2002/facnews090902b.htm (accessed 30 July 2006).

89. Ibid.

90. "Amendments Made to Bill," *Straits Times*, 9 July 2002.

91. Ibid.

92. Zainah Anwar, *Islamisation and Its Impact on Laws and the Law-Making Process in Malaysia*, http://www.whrnet.org/fundamentalisms/docs/doc-wsf-zainah-malaysia-0311.rtf (accessed 30 July 2006). Shafi'i and Maliki are two of the four mainstream schools of jurisprudence in Sunni Islam, the other two being Hanbali and Hanafi. Shafi'i is the dominant school practiced in Malaysia.

93. Ibid.

94. See "Lawyer Attempts to Block Sharia Bills," *South China Morning Post*, 23 October 2003.

95. "Police Deal Blow to PAS Hudud Laws," *Straits Times*, 11 July 2002.

96. Ibid.

97. Ibid.

98. "Mahathir Blasts Blind Support for PAS," *Straits Times*, 20 July 2002.

99. Jan Stark, "Constructing an Islamic Model in Two Malaysian States: PAS Rule in Kelantan and Terengganu," *Sojourn* 19, no. 1 (2004): 51–75.

100. Ibid. See also John Hilley, *Malaysia: Mahathirism, Hegemony and the New Opposition* (London: Zed Books, 2001), 187–88.

101. See, for example, "Racial Politics versus PAS," *Harakah*, 30 November 1998.

102. "PAS Will Not Force Islam on Malaysia If It Runs Government," *Straits Times*, 1 January 2003.

103. "PAS Quietly Shifts Election Tactics," *Straits Times*, 14 January 2003.

104. "Hadi: Role for All Communities in Islamic State," *malaysiakini.com*, 27 August 2002, http://www.malaysiakini.com/news/12724 (accessed 14 January 2006).

105. See Patricia Martinez, "A Response to Dr. Tom Michel," *CTC Bulletin* 18 (2002), http://www.cca.org.hk/resources/ctc/ctc02-01/ctc0201e.htm.

106. Ibid. To the author's knowledge, many non-Muslims as well as Muslims laud PAS's curbing of such activities, as they are associated with the "social ills" that even the federal government has acknowledged have become a problem in Malaysia.

107. Reme Ahmad, "UMNO Wants to Shut Out PAS in Terengganu," *New Straits Times*, 9 February 2005.

108. Statement cited in Zainah Anwar, *Islamisation and Its Impact on Laws*, http://www.whrnet.org/fundamentalisms/docs/doc-wsf-zainah-malaysia-0311.rtf (accessed 20 July 2006).

109. Norani Othman, "Islamisation and Democratization in Malaysia in Regional and Global Contexts," 129.

110. Zainah Anwar, *Beyond the Veil: Rethinking Gender, Modernity and Islam*, http://asialink.unimelb.edu.au/cpp/pdf/0912FinalAnwarTranscript.pdf (accessed 21 June 2007).

III. Since October 1999, all Muslim Malaysian citizens have been required to have their religion indicated on their identity cards. Non-Muslims, however, are not required to do so.

112. Interview with PAS *ulama* and officials, Petaling Jaya, Malaysia, 15 August 2006.

113. Ibid.

114. Martinez, "Mahathir, Islam and the New Malay Dilemma," 240.

115. Norani Othman, "Islamisation and Democratization in Malaysia in Regional and Global Contexts," 128.

116. Article 11(4) stipulates: "State law . . . may control or restrict the propagation of any religious doctrine or belief among persons professing the religion of Islam."

117. Norani Othman, "Islamisation and Democratization in Malaysia in Regional and Global Contexts," 129.

118. Ibid.

119. Ibid.

120. This was demonstrated in the *Shari'a* Criminal Offenses Enactments of Penang, Perak, Terengganu, Kelantan, and Federal Territories, among others.

121. Stark, "Constructing an Islamic Model in Two Malaysian States," 69.

122. The bill was only withdrawn after protests by non-Muslim communities.

123. This observation was made by DAP stalwart Lim Kit Siang in "UMNO-PAS Islamic Competition More Far-reaching Consequences Than 2003 Budget," *dapmalaysia. org*, http://www.dapmalaysia.org/english/lks/sep02/lks1866.htm (accessed 15 July 2005).

124. "When State-Sponsored Firebrands Are Just as Confusing to Muslims," *New Straits Times*, 19 September 2002.

125. Again, this is an outcome of the role that the British accorded to the sultans as heads and guardians of Islam and Malay culture.

126. Patricia A. Martinez, "The Islamic State or the State of Islam in Malaysia," *Contemporary Southeast Asia* 23, no. 3 (2001): 479.

127. "Malaysia's Muslim Authorities Oppose Public Kissing, Hugging," *Agence France Presse*, 20 April 2006, http://www.malaysia-today.net/Blog-e/2006/04/no-kissing-please-we-are-malaysians.htm.

128. "Malaysians Protest against Laws That Make Public Kissing a Crime," *Agence France Presse*, 13 April 2006, http://www.malaysia-today.net/Blog-e/2006/04/no-kissing-please-we-are-malaysians.htm.

129. Carolyn Hong, "KL Kissing Case Sparks Debate on Indecency," *Straits Times*, 7 April 2006.

130. "Malaysia's Muslim Authorities Oppose Public Kissing, Hugging," *Agence France Presse*, 20 April 2006, http://www.malaysia-today.net/Blog-e/2006/04/no-kissing-please-we-are-malaysians.htm.

131. Salbiah Ahmad, "Islam in Malaysia: Constitutional and Human Rights Perspectives," *Muslim World Journal of Human Rights* 2, no. 1 (2005): 8.

132. The evidence of which was apparently a letter written by Moorthy himself stating that he had converted to Islam. This letter, alluded to during the hearing of the case in the *shari'a* court, was never made public.

133. "Malaysia's Thin Line between State and Faith," *Straits Times*, 25 January 2006.

134. Salbiah Ahmad, "Islam in Malaysia," 12.

135. Shad Faruqi, "Thoughts for the Future," *Sunday Star*, 14 July 2002.

136. Salbiah Ahmad, "Islam in Malaysia," 14.

CHAPTER 3

1. Dale F. Eickelman and James Piscatori, *Muslim Politics* (Princeton, N.J.: Princeton University Press, 1996).

2. See Farish A. Noor, "Blood, Sweat, and Jihad: The Radicalization of the Political Discourse of the Pan-Malaysian Islamic Party (PAS) from 1982 Onwards," *Contemporary Southeast Asia* 25, no. 2 (2003): 226.

3. John Hilley, *Malaysia: Mahathirism, Hegemony, and the New Opposition* (London and New York: Zed Books, 2001), 193–99.

4. On its Web site, PAS maintains a column devoted to reports on the party in the Chinese media.

5. In a groundbreaking study, the noted Malaysian ethnographer Tan Chee Beng concluded that the Chinese communities in Terengganu have not felt their identities to be threatened by the presence of a PAS state government. See Tan Chee Beng, *Chinese Minority in a Malay State: The Case of Terengganu in Malaysia* (Singapore: Eastern Universities Press, 2002).

6. Interviews in Kelantan, Malaysia, 6 March 2008.

7. See "Najib, You Are Wrong," 7 January 2008, http://www.dq6633.blogspot.com (accessed 8 March 2008).

8. Farish A. Noor, *Islam Embedded: The Historical Development of the Pan-Malaysian Islamic Party PAS, 1951–2003* (Kuala Lumpur, Malaysia: Malaysian Sociological Research Institute, 2004), 2:445.

9. See Syed Ahmad Hussein, "Muslim Politics and the Discourse of Democracy," in *Democracy in Malaysia: Discourses and Practices*, ed. Francis Loh Kok Wah and Khoo Boo Teik (Richmond, UK: Curzon Press, 2002), 93–95.

10. Fadzil Noor, "Penghayatah Pemerintahan Islam dalam Demokrasi Abad ke-21 Masehi" [Understanding Islamic Rule within a Democracy in the 21st Century], address delivered at *Muzakarah Penghayatan Pemerintahan Islam Dalam Demokrasi Abad ke-21 Masehi*, Kuala Terengganu, Terengganu, 12–13 October 2001.

11. Ibid.

12. Cited in Zainon Ahmad, "Of PAS, Present, and Future," *Sun*, 11 June 2005.

13. Formed on 24 October 1999, the *Barisan Alternatif* comprised PAS, DAP, *Parti Keadilan Rakyat* (People's Justice Party), and *Parti Rakyat Malaysia* (Malaysian Peoples' Party). This was the first formal multiethnic coalition of opposition parties in Malaysia.

14. PAS was at the time allied with *Semangat '46* (Spirit of 46), a Malay-Muslim party formed by ex-UMNO members who had attempted to challenge Mahathir's presidency of the party in 1987. In accordance with their respective campaign strategies, *Semangat '46* entered into a separate pact with DAP in 1989. It was through the *Semangat '46* pact that PAS was seen to have worked with DAP, albeit unofficially.

15. "The Issue is Change: Fadzil Noor on the PAS Agenda," *Asiaweek*, 26 November 1999, http://www.asiaweek.com/asiaweek/magazine/99/1126/nat.malaysia3.pas.html (accessed 11 July 2005).

16. See Mustapha Ali, "The Islamic Movement and the Malaysian Experience," in *Power-Sharing Islam?* ed. Azzam Tamimi (London: Liberty Publications, 1993), 120.

17. Even on this matter, the leadership of the party has yet to arrive at a definite decision at the time of writing.

18. "PAS: Parti Ajaran Sesat?" [PAS: Party Espousing Deviant Doctrines?], *Harakah*, 9 March 2006.

19. Led by Nik Aziz, PAS won twenty-four seats in the state legislature, while *Semangat 46* won fourteen. This worked out to a clean sweep for the opposition, as UMNO failed to win any of the thirty-eight contested seats. In addition, PAS also won six federal parliamentary seats out of fourteen in Kelantan.

20. Hilley, *Malaysia*, 189; Jan Stark, "Beyond 'Terrorism' and 'State Hegemony': Assessing the Islamist Mainstream in Egypt and Malaysia," *Third World Quarterly* 26, no. 2 (2005): 312.

21. A. L. Othman, *Wajah Baru Politik Malaysia* [The New Face of Malaysian Politics] (Kuala Lumpur, Malaysia: Penerbitan Pemuda, 1995); T. M. Jam., *Ketahanan PAS Ancam Masa Depan UMNO* [PAS's Resolve Threatens UMNO's Future] (Kuala Lumpur, Malaysia: Pangkaian Minda Publishing, 1995); "Racial Politics versus PAS," *Harakah*, 30 November 1998.

22. See Hilley, *Malaysia*, 206–209.

23. See John Funston, "Malaysia's Tenth Elections: Status Quo, Reformasi or Islamization?" *Contemporary Southeast Asia* 22, no. 1 (2000): 38. This claim was later reiterated by PAS deputy president Nasharuddin Mat Isa, who stated that PAS will not establish a theocratic state because "responsibility of leadership must be derived from a mandate through consent of citizens." See "No Plan for PAS to Set Up 'Theocratic' State: Nasharuddin," *malaysiakini.com*, 16 July 2003, http://www.malaysiakini.com/news/16364 (accessed 21 July 2003).

24. The same cannot be said for the DAP, which lost substantial support because of its decision to work with PAS.

25. Greg Barton, "The Ties That Do Not Bind," *Asiaweek*, 16 June 2000; Patricia Martinez, "The Islamic State or the State of Islam in Malaysia," *Contemporary Southeast Asia* 23, no. 3 (2001): 474–529.

26. Yusof Rawa, "Ke Arah Pembebasan Ummah" [Toward the Liberation of the Ummah], in *Memperingati Yusof Rawa* [Commemorating Yusof Rawa], ed. Kamarudin Jaffar (Kuala Lumpur, Malaysia: IKDAS, 2000), 55–56.

27. There had been attempts to explain the relationship between Islam and politics, though no explicit effort was made to explain the Islamic state in great detail. See Dewan Ulama PAS Pusat, *Islam dan Politik* [Islam and Politics] (Kuala Lumpur, Malaysia: Dewan Ulama PAS Pusat, 1980); Abdul Hadi Awang, *Konsep Negara Islam dan Matlamatnya* [The Concept of an Islamic State and Its Aims] (Kuala Lumpur, Malaysia: G. G. Edat, 1986).

28. Cited in Hussin Mutalib, *Islam in Malaysia: From Revivalism to Islamic State* (Singapore: Singapore University Press, 1993), 99–100.

29. See, for instance, Abdul Razak Baginda and Peter Schier, eds., *Is Malaysia an Islamic State? Secularism and Theocracy: A Study of the Malaysian Constitution* (Kuala Lumpur, Malaysia: Malaysian Strategic Research Centre and Konrad Adenauer Foundation, 2003).

30. Wan Zahidi Wan Teh, *Malaysia Is an Islamic State* (Kuala Lumpur, Malaysia: Ministry of Information, 2001).

31. It was a shift in the sense that it marked the first instance where a Malaysian political leader declared publicly that Malaysia was already an "Islamic state."

32. "Islamic State Debate Should Be on Whether Malaysia Is an Islamic State," *The Free Media*, 19 November 2003, http://thefreemedia.com/index.php/articles/3619 (accessed 19 October 2007).

33. PAS Youth chief Salahuddin Ayub said that PAS's Islamic state document was a direct response to Mahathir's challenge for the party to articulate its vision of Islamic governance in Malaysia. Interview with Salahuddin Ayub, Kota Bharu, Kelantan, 7 March 2008.

34. Minutes of PAS Executive Committee Meeting, 11 May 2003, 5.

35. According to PAS sources, the United Kingdom was chosen over existing Islamic states because it was perceived as providing a viable model of the marrying of modernization and Islamization. Telephone interview with PAS official, Kuala Lumpur, Malaysia, 18 August 2006.

36. Interview with PAS official, Kota Bharu, Malaysia, 7 March 2008.

37. Since then, the first three drafts have been taken out of circulation by the party, and only the fourth and final draft, formally published by the party as the Islamic State Document, is in circulation. Copies of all four drafts are in the author's private collection.

38. Parti Islam SeMalaysia, *Memorandum PAS kepada Rakyat Malaysia: Penghayatan Pemerintahan Islam Dalam Demokrasi Abad ke-15H/21M* [PAS Memorandum to the Malaysian People: The Understanding of Islamic Rule in the Context of 15th Hijrah/21st Century Democracy], author's personal copy, undated, 1.

39. Ibid., 2.

40. Ibid., 4.

41. Fadzil Noor, "*Penghayatah Pemerintahan Islam dalam Demokrasi Abad ke-21 Masehi*" [Understanding Islamic Rule within a Democracy in the 21st Century], address delivered at *Muzakarah Penghayatan Pemerintahan Islam Dalam Demokrasi Abad ke-21 Masehi*, Kuala Terengganu, Terengganu, 12–13 October 2001, 2–3.

42. Ibid., 5–6.

43. Parti Islam SeMalaysia, *Memorandum PAS kepada Rakyat Malaysia*, 2.

44. This commitment to democracy was also affirmed in the other two preliminary documents. See Parti Islam SeMalaysia, *Draf Memorandum Negara Islam* [A Draft of the Memorandum for an Islamic State], undated, and Parti Islam SeMalaysia, *Kertas Kerja Dasar Negara Islam* [Working Paper on the Foundations of an Islamic State], undated.

45. Parti Islam SeMalaysia, *Memorandum PAS kepada Rakyat Malaysia*, 10.

46. See Ibid., 8.

47. Fadzil Noor, "*Penghayatan Pemerintahan Islam Dalam Demokrasi Abad Ke-21 Masehi*," 19.

48. "PAS' New Deputy President on Malaysian Politics and the Islamic Movement," *muslimedia.com*, http://www.muslimedia.com/archives/movement05/my-intvw.htm (accessed 3 August 2006).

49. Telephone interview with PAS officials, 16 August 2006.

50. For an important discussion of the anticipated impact of Fadzil's death on PAS, see Farish Noor, *PAS post-Fadzil Noor: Future Directions and Prospects* (Singapore: ISEAS, 2002).

51. Interestingly, Zulkefly Ahmad had expressed in private in March 2004 that the party leadership would be satisfied if they successfully defended Kelantan and Terengganu, thereby maintaining the status quo of 1999. Interview with Zulkefly Ahmad, Petaling Jaya, Malaysia, 15 March 2004.

52. Some skeptics might be quick to discount Mustapha's candidacy because he was a firm believer in the PAS policy of *ulama* rule as expressed in the authority of the *Majlis Shura Ulama*, and he had openly declared his reluctance to contest. As PAS Youth chief in the early 1980s, Mustapha had stoutly championed the need for *ulama* leadership of the party.

53. According to sources, there was only one holdout against the *shura* committee's general feeling that Harun Din should assume the deputy presidency by consensus, and that was Hasan Shukri himself. It is possible that Harun Din's last-minute withdrawal was to avoid a contest for the deputy presidency, which nevertheless still materialised.

54. Badruzaman Yusoff, *Penjelasan Dokumen Negara Islam* [Clarification on the Islamic State Document] (Petaling Jaya, Malaysia: Pusat PAS, 2003).

55. PAS, *The Islamic State Document*, http://www.wluml.org/english/news/pas-islamic-state-2003.pdf.

56. Ibid., 13.

57. Ibid., 19. The Document further quotes Surah Al-Maaidah: 38, "As to the thief, male or female, cut off his or her hands: punishment by way of example, from Allah, for their crime; And Allah is exalted in power, full of wisdom" and emphasizes that "the above stated injunction is mandatory and must be implemented."

58. Ibid., 20.

59. Ibid., 21.

60. Ibid., 25.

61. Ibid., 27.

62. Ibid., 32.

63. Ibid., 34.

64. Ibid., 30.

65. Ibid., 21.

66. Abdullah Badawi, "Islam Hadhari and the Malay Agenda," speech delivered at the 55th UMNO General Assembly, Kuala Lumpur, Malaysia, 23–25 September 2004, reproduced in Abdullah Ahmad Badawi, *Islam Hadhari: A Model Approach for Development and Progress* (Selangor, Malaysia: MPH Group Publishing, 2006), 3.

67. Anwar Ibrahim, address at the Sixth Malaysia-Singapore Forum, Petaling Jaya, Malaysia, 6 December 1996.

68. See Yukiko Ohashi, "Malaysia: The Elusive Islamic State," *Asia Times*, 9 June 2004, http://www.atimes.com/atimes/Southeast_Asia/FF09Ae02.html (accessed 10 June 2004).

69. Abdullah Badawi, *Islam Hadhari*, 5.

70. Farish Noor, "Race, Racism, and Islam Hadhari," *malaysiakini.com*, 2 October 2004, http://www.malaysiakini.com/columns/30474 (accessed 13 October 2006).

71. See Khoo Boo Teik, "The House of the Rising Sons: What They Didn't Debate at the UMNO General Assembly," *Aliran* 24, no. 9 (2004), http://www.aliran.com/oldsite/monthly/2004b/9c.html (accessed 3 September 2006).

72. Nazish Ansari, "Malaysia: Limitations of the Human Rights Discourse and the Deployment of Rights in a Religious Identity Debate," *Muslim World Journal of Human Rights* 1, no. 1 (2004): 14.

73. See Abdul Hadi Awang, *Hadharah Islamiyah bukan Islam Hadhari* [Hadharah Islamiyah Is Not Islam Hadhari] (Kuala Lumpur, Malaysia: Nufair Street, 2005).

74. For a detailed analysis of the implications of the elections, see Joseph Chinyong Liow, "The Politics behind Malaysia's 11th General Elections," *Asian Survey* 45, no. 6 (2005): 907–930.

75. "Malaysia's Ruling Party Routs Islamists," *Channelnewsasia.com*, 22 March 2004, http://www.channelnewsasia.com/stories/afp_asiapacific/view/76543/1/.html (accessed 12 December 2006).

76. "Interview: Facing High Expectations," *Newsweek*, 5 April 2004.

77. "Election Numbers to Watch," *Straits Times*, 15 March 2004.

78. This statistic should be considered in the context of a general increase in the number of candidates that PAS fielded in 2004 compared to 1999.

79. "PAS Legacy Becomes Problem for UMNO," *Straits Times*, 27 November 2004.

80. Ibid.

81. "Tackling Education, Poverty, Islamic Mindset," *New Straits Times*, 20 March 2006.

82. Ibid.

83. Abdul Halim Muhammady, "Undang-Undang Jenayah Syariah dan Perlaksanaannya di Malaysia" [Syariah Criminal Law and its Implementation in Malaysia], *Seminar Perlaksanaan Hukum Syarak di Malaysia* [A Seminar on the Implementation of Islamic Law in Malaysia], Pulau Pinang, Malaysia, 9–10 February 2001.

84. Wan Zahidi Wan Teh, "Ciri-Ciri Sebuah Negara Islam" [Characteristics of an Islamic State], *Seminar Perlaksanaan Hukun Syarak di Malaysia* [A Seminar on the Implementation of Islamic Law in Malaysia], Pulau Pinang, Malaysia, 9–10 February 2001.

85. Nakhaie Ahmad, "Hudud dalam Konteks Perlaksanaan Syariat Islam yang Menyeluruh" [Hudud in the Context of a Holistic Implementation of Islamic Laws], *Seminar Kebangsuun Cabaran Perlaksanaan Islam dalam Konteks Masyarakat Malaysia* [A Seminar on the National Challenge of the Implementation of Islam in the Context of Malaysian Society], Kuala Lumpur, Malaysia, 28 June 1992.

86. Faisal Haji Othman, *"Perlaksanaan Hudud di Zaman Nabi dan Khulafa Rashidun"* [Implementation of Hudud Laws in the Era of the Prophet and Khulafa Rashidun], *Seminar Kebangsaan Cabaran Perlaksanaan Islam dalam Konteks Masyarakat Malaysia* [A Seminar on the National Challenge of the Implementation of Islam in the Context of Malaysian Society], Kuala Lumpur, Malaysia, 28 June 1992.

87. Ibid.

88. "Terengganu Getting the Economy Going Again," *New Straits Times*, 20 March 2006.

89. It should be stated here that neither did PAS table any official legislation on women's dress.

90. Interview with Abdul Rahman Dahlan, Kuala Lumpur, Malaysia, 18 August 2006.

91. K. J. Ratnam, "Religion and Politics in Malaysia," in *Readings on Islam in Southeast Asia*, ed. Ahmad Ibrahim, Sharon Siddique, and Yasmin Hussain (Singapore: Institute of Southeast Asian Studies, 1985), 145.

92. "Wajar Larang Orang Islam Masuk Premis Jual Arak" [It Is Right to Prohibit Muslims from Entering Premises Where Alcohol Is Sold], *Harakah*, 20 December 2003.

93. "Youth Chief: PAS Ulama Council 'Neither Dead Nor Alive,'" *malaysiakini. com*, 2 June 2005, http://www.malaysiakini.com/news/36622 (accessed 19 October 2006).

94. "Q&A: Agenda for Change Depends on New Line-up," *malaysiakini.com*, 19 May 2005, http://www.malaysiakini.com/opinionsfeatures/36274 (accessed 22 May 2005).

95. To date there has not been any move to formalize this proposal.

96. For instance, while conservative leaders arriving from other states had made the journey to Kota Bharu by car, some among the reformist camp, otherwise known as the "professionals," flew in from Kuala Lumpur in business class.

97. Interview with Anwar Ibrahim, Singapore, 21 August 2007.

98. Comments by outgoing PAS vice-president Hassan Ali at the 53rd PAS Muktamar, Kota Bharu, Malaysia, 3 June 2007.

99. M. Shamsul Haque, "The Role of the State in Managing Ethnic Tensions in Malaysia," *American Behavioral Scientist* 47, no. 3 (2003): 245.

100. Mohammad Hashim Kamali, *Islamic Law in Malaysia: Issues and Developments* (Kuala Lumpur, Malaysia: Ilmiah Publishers, 2000), 30, cited in Peter G. Riddell, "Islamization, Civil Society, and Religious Minorities in Malaysia," in *Islam in Southeast Asia: Political, Social and Strategic Challenges for the 21st Century*, ed. K. S. Nathan and Mohammad Hashim Kamali (Singapore: Institute of Southeast Asian Studies, 2005), 163.

101. Harold Couch, *Government and Society in Malaysia* (Ithaca, N.Y.: Cornell University Press, 1996), 169.

102. For information on the riots, see Leon Comber, *13 May 1969: A Historical Survey of Sino-Malay Relations* (Singapore: Graham Brash, 1983).

103. Cited in Greg Fealy and Virginia Hooker, eds., *Voices of Islam in Southeast Asia: A Contemporary Sourcebook* (Singapore: ISEAS, 2006), 254.

104. Judith Nagata, "How to Be Islamic without Being an Islamic State: Contested Models of Development in Malaysia," in *Islam, Globalization, and Postmodernity*, ed. Akbar S. Ahmed and Hastings Donnan (London: Routledge, 1994), 72.

105. See "No Plan for PAS to Set Up 'Theocratic' State: Nasharuddin," *malaysia kini.com*, 16 July 2003, http://www.malaysiakini.com/news/16364 (accessed 21 July 2003).

106. Claudia Derichs, *Looking for Clues: Malaysian Suggestions for Political Change* (Duisburg, Germany: Institut für Ostasienwissenschaften, 2001), 12.

107. Interview with PAS leaders, Kuala Lumpur, Malaysia, 15 August 2006.

108. Comments by Hu Pang Chua at the 53rd PAS Muktamar, Kota Bharu, Malaysia, 3 June 2007.

109. Sang Harimau, "This is a Muslim country, leave Malaysia if you don't like it, says Jerai MP," *Cicak*, 29 April 2006, http://thecicak.com/?p=102 (accessed 18 October 2007). The video of this parliamentary debate, where a heated exchange of words occurred among the MPs, has been posted on YouTube: http://www.youtube.com/watch?v=pkqyhBDU5HM (accessed 18 October 2007).

110. Martinez, "The Islamic State or the State of Islam in Malaysia," 490.

111. "929" refers to the date on which Mahathir made the controversial declaration (September 29).

112. See "We Were Not Forced to Withdraw Memo: Ong," *Sun*, 22 January 2006. Abdullah was quoted as saying that it was "not normal or proper" for ministers to publish a memorandum instead of raising the issue at the weekly cabinet meeting.

113. "Uproar over Claim of Islamic State Is Silenced," *Christians in Crisis Online*, 10 August 2007, http://www.christiansincrisis.net/index.php?option=com_content&task=view&id=660&Itemid=2 (accessed 19 August 2007).

114. "Historical Documents Show Malaysia Is Secular, Says MCA," *Straits Times*, 21 July 2007.

115. Ling Rong Xiang, "Apart From UMNO Leaders, No One Is Allowed to Talk about the Islamic State Issue," *merdekareview.com*, 23 July 2007, http://www.merdekareview.com/news.php?n=4559 (accessed 21 October 2007).

116. "Furor over Najib's Islamic State Remark," *Straits Times*, 21 July 2007.

117. Ibid.

118. "Three Responses to Najib's '717 Declaration': Malaysia is an Islamic State and has never been a Secular State," http://blog.limkitsiang.com/?p=410 (accessed 19 August 2007).

119. "Press Release: Malaysia Is Not an Islamic State," http://www.hindusangam.org.my/newsmgr/index.php?id=92, http://www.hindusangam.org.my/news/?id=37 (accessed 20 August 2007).

120. "Malaysia's Christians Protest 'Islamic State' Comments ahead of Elections," *Christian Today*, http://www.christiantoday.com/article/malaysia.christians.protest.islamic.state.comments.ahead.of.elections/11854–2.htm (accessed 19 August 2007).

121. Ng Ling Fong and Soon Li Tsin, "Ministry Bans Islamic State Debate in Media," http://www.jeffooi.com/2007/07/umnos_islamic_state_damage_con.php (accessed 20 August 2007).

122. "No Debate on Islamic State," http://tonypua.blogspot.com/2007/07/no-debate-on-islamic-state.html (accessed 20 August 2007).

123. Zari Bukhari, "Temple Demolitions Stoke Malaysian Tensions," *Asia Times*, 11 July 2006, http://www.atimes.com/atimes/Southeast_Asia/HG11Ae01.html (accessed 5 August 2007).

124. "Hindu Temple Demolished by Malaysian Authorities," *ACV/Kerala*, 22 April 2006, http://www.freerepublic.com/focus/f-news/1619629/posts (accessed 8 August 2007); K. Kabilan, "Temple Row: A Dab of Sensibility Please," *malaysiakini.com*, 16 June 2006:, http://www.malaysiakini.com/opinionsfeatures/52600 (accessed 8 August 2007).

125. M. V. Kamath, "Our Secular Cowards," *NewsToday Online*, 21 April 2007, http://newstodaynet.com/guest/2104gu1.htm (accessed 8 August 2007).

126. "Anger over Malaysia Temple Razzings," *Aljazeera Online*, 24 June 2006, http://english.aljazeera.net/English/archive/archive?ArchiveId=23828 (accessed 8 August 2007).

127. "Hindu Group Protests 'Temple Cleansing' in Malaysia," *Associated Press Online*, 23 May 2006, http://www.financialexpress.com/old/latest_full_story.php?content_id=128069 (accessed 8 August 2007).

128. "Religion-Malaysia: Rediscovering Secularism," *Asian Media Forum*, 3 April 2006, http://www.asiamediaforum.org/node/409 (accessed 19 December 2006).

129. The Sky Kingdom Cult was led by Ayah Pin, who caused shockwaves across Malaysia's generally traditional Muslim community by proclaiming that he was God and that his followers were free to practice whatever religion they pleased.

130. "Nazri Ticked Off for Backing Article 11," *Suaram*, 6 September 2006, http://www.suaram.net/display_article.asp?ID=516 (accessed 15 September 2006).

131. See "Memorandum kepada Raja-Raja Melayu dan Perdana Menteri Malaysia" [Memorandum to the Malay Kings and the Prime Minister of Malaysia], *myislam network.net*, 29 September 2006, http://myislamnetwork.net/portal/modules/news/article.php?storyid=105 (accessed 15 October 2006).

132. "Police Reports Filed over 'Enemy of Allah' Statement," *malaysiakini.com*, 1 June 2006, http://www.malaysiakini.com/news/51929 (accessed 2 June 2006).

133. "PM: Stop Debate on Religious Issues," *Star*, 28 July 2006.

CHAPTER 4

1. Meredith L. Weiss, "Malaysian NGOs: History, Legal Framework and Characteristics," in *Social Movements in Malaysia: From Moral Communities to NGOs*, ed. Meredith L. Weiss and Saliha Hassan (London: Routledge, 2003), 7.

2. Consider, for example, the arguments made in Michael Mann, "The Autonomous Power of the State: Its Origins, Mechanisms and Results," *European Journal of Sociology* 25 (1984): 185–203; and in Gabriel Almond and Sidney Verba, *The Civic Culture: Political Attitudes and Democracy in Five Nations* (London: Sage, 1989). In the case of Asia, see Muthiah Alagappa, ed., *Civil Society and Political Change in Asia* (Stanford, Calif.: Stanford University Press, 2004).

3. Clive Kessler, "Malaysia: The Long March towards Desecularisation," *Asian Analysis*, October 2006, http://www.aseanfocus.com/asiananalysis/article.cfm?articleID=989 (accessed 15 November 2006).

4. Saliha Hassan, "Islamic Non-governmental Organizations," in *Social Movements in Malaysia*, ed. Weiss and Saliha Hassan, 105.

5. See K. S. Jomo and Ahmad Shabery Cheek, "Malaysia's Islamic Movements," in *Fragmented Vision: Culture and Politics in Contemporary Malaysia*, ed. Joel S. Kahn and Francis Loh Kok Wah (Honolulu: University of Hawaii Press, 1992), 85. ABIM claimed the Ikhwani pedigree by virtue of its association with the Egyptian-based *Ikhwanul Muslimin* (Muslim Brotherhood), the archetypal Islamist social-political movement that has provided inspiration for generations of Islamic activists worldwide since its formation in 1928.

6. It has been estimated that the membership of ABIM had grown exponentially from nine hundred at its inception to more than thirty-five thousand in 1980. The current membership is around sixty thousand.

7. Unofficial statistics indicate that 1,169 ABIM members were arrested for the Baling demonstrations.

8. Describing his impression of differences between Kelantan chief minister Nik Aziz's vision of an Islamic state as compared to that of ABIM, Malaysian scholar Ahmad Fauzi Abdul Hamid writes: "In contrast with *dakwah* movements' gradualist approach, Haji Nik Aziz plainly rejected the notion that an Islamic state could come about step-by-step, starting from the individual, then progressing to the family, the society and finally the state. He surmised that such a theory was concocted by the enemies of Islam to obstruct the Islamic struggle. Ruling out the conception of the diversity of movements and methods, he insisted if there had to be diversity after all, one movement needed to be installed as the parent movement, by which he meant none other than PAS." See Ahmad Fauzi Abdul Hamid, "Reforming PAS?" *Aliran* 6 (2003): 11–13.

9. Interview with Anwar Ibrahim, Washington, D.C., 15 November 2005.

10. See "Abim Has to Look into Conscience to Decide Its Future," *New Straits Times*, 11 December 2000.

11. Cited in Farish Noor, "Reality after the Dream," *Impact International* 28, no. 1 (1998), http://www.galway.iol.ie/~afifi/BICNews/Impact/impact2.htm (accessed 16 December 2006).

12. ABIM's role as the heartbeat of *Reformasi* should not be surprising, given that it was essentially students who embraced the nationwide reform movement when it erupted in 1998. That said, ABIM's attempt to take over the top posts in *Keadilan* was rebuffed by the party rank and file. See "Keadilan lupa jasa pemimpin ABIM" [Keadilan Fails to Acknowledge ABIM Leaders' Help], *Utusan Malaysia*, 26 November 2001.

13. "Interview with Hatta Ramli and Farid Shahran," *Dialogue with the Islamic World*, 9 December 2006, http://www.qantara.de/webcom/show_article.php/_c-478/_nr-541/i.html?PHPSESSID=5869 (accessed 12 December 2006).

14. "Religious Right Vows to Uphold Status of Islam," *Straits Times*, 24 July 2006.

15. Ibid.

16. "Group to Handle Apostasy Issue," *New Straits Times*, 18 July 2006.

17. Mohamed Nawab Mohamed Osman, "Religio-Political Activism of Ulama in Malaysia" (M.A. diss., National University of Singapore, 2006).

18. Cited in Ibid., 90.

19. See Persatuan Ulama Malaysia and Persatuan Ulama Kedah, *Islam Dicabar, Rasulullah Dan Ulama Dihina* [Islam Is Challenged, the Prophet and Religious Scholars Are Disparaged] (Penang, Malaysia: Jutaprint, 2002).

20. Ibid.

21. In response to this pressure, Abdul Hamid Othman, religious advisor to the Prime Minister, announced that "the media will no longer be allowed to publish articles penned by freelance writers concerning the principles of Islam or Prophet Muhammad." See "No More Articles on Islamic Tenets or the Prophet, Media Told," *malaysiakini.com*, 12 April 2002, http://www.hakam.org/news120402_4.htm (accessed 5 October 2007).

22. "PUM Told to Question 'Dubious Decrees from Religious Scholars,'" *New Straits Times*, 2 June 2002.

23. "Only Fatwa Council Has Right to Degree Religious Edicts," *malaysiakini. com*, 3 December 2001, http://www.freeanwar.com/facnewsoct2001/facnews0312016.htm (accessed 5 October 2007).

24. Jamaah Islah Malaysia, http://www.jim.org.my/kenal/sejarah02.php (accessed 16 August 2006).

25. Jamaah Islah Malaysia, http://www.jim.org.my/kenal/visi.php (accessed 16 August 2006).

26. Ibid.

27. See William Case, "Testing Malaysia's Pseudo-democracy," in *The State of Malaysia: Ethnicity, Equity and Reform,* ed. Edmund Terence Gomez (London: Routledge-Curzon, 2004), 33.

28. See Norani Othman, Zainah Anwar, and Zaitun Mohamad Kasim, "Malaysia: Islamisation, Muslim Politics and State Authoritarianism," in *Muslim Women and the Challenge of Islamic Extremism,* ed. Norani Othman (Kuala Lumpur, Malaysia: Sisters in Islam, 2005), 83.

29. "Make It a Tall, Cold Glass . . . ," *Weekend Mail,* 15 July 2006.

30. "PAS Chief Slammed over Remarks (HL)," *New Sunday Times,* 7 March 2004.

31. Ibid.

32. Ibid.

33. "Marriage of Equals," *Asian Wall Street Journal,* 24 September 2004.

34. "Fathers, Your Family Needs You," *New Straits Times,* 21 June 2004.

35. Ibid.

36. Ibid.

37. "Poor Knowledge Leads to Misinterpretation of Islamic Family Law," *Bernama,* 13 February 2006.

38. "Muslim Sisters Fight for Their Rights," *Straits Times,* 4 April 2002.

39. "Consider Wife's View First before Deciding on Second Spouse," *New Straits Times,* 13 January 2003. This remark was made in response to a statement by Perlis Mufti Datuk Mat Jahaya Husin, who said that Perlis would allow men to practice polygamy without getting the consent of the first wife.

40. "Women's Groups Oppose MBSA Action," *New Straits Times,* 14 May 2004.

41. Ibid.

42. "PAS Policies a Failure, Says NCWO," *New Straits Times,* 25 June 2005.

43. Maznah Mohamad, "Women in the UMNO and PAS Labyrinth," in *Risking Malaysia: Culture, Politics and Identity,* ed. Maznah Mohamad and Wong Soak Koon (Kuala Lumpur, Malaysia: Universiti Kebangsaan Malaysia Press, 2001), 117.

44. "Muslim Women Raise Funds for Shelter Home," *New Straits Times,* 26 February 2004. "Bohsia" (which means "silent" in the Hokkien vernacular dialect) was a colloquial term for prostitutes.

45. "LEPAK Way to Promote Positive, Constructive Objectives," *Bernama,* 4 June 2005.

46. See Maznah Mohamad, "Women in the UMNO and PAS Labyrinth," 118.

47. See Norani Othman, Zainah Anwar, and Zaitun Mohamed Kasim, "Malaysia: Islamization, Muslim Politics and State Authoritarianism," 100.

48. Hence, one could argue that with the advent of Mahathir's Islamization project, the once-progressive Islamic family law in Malaysia in effect regressed.

49. Norani Othman, Zainah Anwar, and Zaitun Mohamed Kasim, "Malaysia: Islamization, Muslim Politics and State Authoritarianism," 91.

50. "Sisters for Justice," *New Straits Times,* 11 August 2003.

51. See "Malaysian Islamic Group Accused of Disrespect, Sowing Disharmony," *BBC Monitoring Asia-Pacific*, 31 March 2005.

52. "Sisters for Justice," *New Straits Times*, 11 August 2003.

53. "No Faith in Politics: Women decry the erosion of their rights in Malaysia, which once had the most progressive family law in the Muslim world," *Montreal Gazette*, 23 June 2006.

54. Zainah Anwar, "The Struggle for Women's Rights within the Religious Framework: The Experience of Sisters in Islam," in *Modern Malaysia in the Global Economy: Political and Social Change into the 21st Century*, ed. Colin Barlow (London: Edward Elgar, 2001), 180.

55. In Muslim divorces, the word *talaq* had to be publicly uttered three times for a divorce to take place.

56. Zainah Anwar, "The Struggle for Women's Rights," 181.

57. "No Faith in Politics: Women decry the erosion of their rights in Malaysia, which once had the most progressive family law in the Muslim world," *Montreal Gazette*, 23 June 2006.

58. "*Shari'a* Court Biased against Women," *Straits Times*, 12 November 2002.

59. "Selangor Family Law Enactment Discriminates against Women," *New Sunday Times*, 18 May 2003.

60. "KL Rewording Family Law after Raft of Complaints," *Straits Times*, 10 February 2006. The Johore state government clarified that "inherited property, personal property, and gifts are not part of matrimonial assets" and that the case of Zaidah Rahman was an isolated incident. See "SIS Wants Govt. to Review Language Use in Laws," *Bernama*, 29 March 2006.

61. Ibid.

62. *Baraza!* is available on the SIS Web site: www.sistersinislam.org.

63. Norani Othman, Zainah Anwar, and Zaitun Mohamed Kasim, "Malaysia: Islamization, Muslim Politics and State Authoritarianism," 91.

64. Zainah Anwar, "The Struggle for Women's Rights," 181.

65. "Sisters-in-Islam Wants Enactment Reviewed," *Malay Mail*, 3 February 2005.

66. Ibid.

67. See John Hilley, *Malaysia: Mahathirism, Hegemony, and the New Opposition* (London: Zed Books, 2001), 192.

68. See "Stop All Forms of Vigilante Action," *New Straits Times*, 15 March 2003.

69. Zainah Anwar, "The Struggle for Women's Rights," 181.

70. "Sisters Take On Scholars in Battle for Islam," *Guardian*, 1 June 2005.

71. Zainah Anwar, "Facing the Fundamentalist Challenge in Malaysia," *Straits Times*, 9 January 2003.

72. See Zainah Anwar, "The Struggle for Women's Rights," 179.

73. "Sisters in Islam—Take Terengganu Government to Court," *New Straits Times*, 29 October 2003.

74. Ibid.

75. Ibid.

76. "It Victimizes Women, No Equal Justice for Offenders, Says SIS," *New Straits Times*, 25 October 2003.

77. Zainah Anwar, "Facing the Fundamentalist Challenge in Malaysia."

78. "Advocates for Women in Islam," *Malay Mail*, 3 August 2003.

79. "18,000 Sign Article 11 Petition," *Sun*, 8 May 2006.

80. The MCCBCHS has repeatedly said that its role is in congruence with the Malaysian constitution, which provides for religious freedom, and with the national ideology of *Rukunnegara*, which has as its first principle *Kepercayaan kepada Tunan* (Belief in God).

81. "Religious Tolerance a Duty of All Malaysians," *Business Times*, 22 March 1994.

82. Ibid.

83. Ibid.

84. U.S. Department of State, "Report Says Civil Liberties Scarce in Malaysia: State Department Project on Human Rights Practices in Malaysia," press release, 3 April 2003.

85. "Guidelines on Places of Worship Not Issued Yet," *New Straits Times*, 19 February 2000.

86. Under the guidelines, while applications for land for non-Muslim places of worship required proof that the particular area had at least a population of two to three thousand followers of the particular religion, no such requirements existed for Muslim places of worship. See U.S. Department of State, "Report Says Civil Liberties Scarce in Malaysia: State Department Project on Human Rights Practices in Malaysia," press release, 3 April 2003.

87. "Council Raps Terengganu over Enactment," *New Sunday Times*, 21 July 2002.

88. "Religious Consultative Council Pledges Support for BN," *Bernama*, 24 November 1999.

89. "Kit Siang: Inter-religious Group's Support for BN a Major Blow," *New Straits Times*, 26 November 1999.

90. "Groups Object to Plan to State Religion on ICs," *Straits Times*, 11 October 1999.

91. Ibid.

92. "Reconsider Including Religion on ICs, Says Consultative Council," *Sun*, 10 October 1999.

93. Ibid.

94. "Suhakam to Consider Proposal to Set Up Interreligious Council," *New Straits Times*, 27 August 2002.

95. Ibid.

96. "Interfaith Commission: Why Fear It?" *malaysiakini.com*, 2 March 2005, http://www.malaysiakini.com/columns/34017 (accessed 1 September 2006).

97. Interview with Hermen Shastri, Singapore, 26 February 2008.

98. "No Need for Inter-Faith Commission, Says ACCIN," *Sun*, 22 February 2005.

99. Ibid.

100. "Help Safeguard Our Religious Harmony," *New Straits Times*, 21 March 2005.

101. "Over His Dead Body," *Guardian*, 30 December 2005.

102. Ibid.

103. "Finding Solutions to a Touchy Matter," *New Sunday Times*, 1 January 2006.

104. "Over His Dead Body," *Guardian*, 30 December 2005.

105. "Finding Solutions to a Touchy Matter," *New Sunday Times*, 1 January 2006.

106. Ibid.

107. "Malaysian Interfaith Group Backs Constitutional Reform after Conversion Ruling," *BBC Monitoring Asia-Pacific*, 9 December 2005.

108. "Memo to PM," *New Straits Times*, 20 January 2006.

109. The movement's activities in Central Asia have been discussed in Ahmed Rashid, *Jihad: The Rise of Militant Islam in Central Asia* (New Haven, Conn.: Yale University Press, 2002), 115–37; Zeyno Baran, *Hizb ut-Tahrir: Islam's Political Insurgency* (Washington, D.C.: Nixon Center, 2004).

110. See http://www.mykhilafah.com/index.php?option=com_content&view=cate gory&layout=blog&id=51&Itemid=18. The *Hizbut Tahrir Indonesia* is now a prominent Islamic group in the country, with its membership estimated at a few hundred thousand. They have established chapters in various parts of the country, including Java, Sumatra, Sulawesi, and Aceh.

111. For more on *Hizbut Tahrir Indonesia*, see A. Maftuh Abegebriel and A. Yani Abeveiro, *Negara Tuhan: The Thematic Encyclopedia* (Jakarta, Indonesia: SR-Ins Pub., 2004), chapter 8.

112. See http://www.mykhilafah.com/index. php?option=com_content&view=category&layout=blog&id=51&Itemid=18.

113. This rejection of democracy is clearly stated in most of its seminars and publications.

114. See http://www.mykhilafah.com/index.php?option=com_content&view= category&layout=blog&id=51&Itemid=18.

115. These comments were made at a seminar titled *Hijrah: Titik Mula Islam Sebagai Tamadun Baru Dunia* [Hijrah: The Beginning of Islam as a New Civilization for the World], Petaling Jaya, Malaysia, 20 January 2007.

116. Conversation with members of HTM, Kuala Lumpur, Malaysia, 20 January 2007.

117. The first edition of *Sautun Nahdhah* was published in 2000.

118. Examples of such seminars are *Khilafah Dan Alam Melayu* (*Sejarah Yang Disembunyikan*) [Khilafah and the Malay World (The Concealed History)], held on 3 September 2006 at Pusat Perindustrian Pontian, Johore, and *Sempena Hari Kemerdekaan* (*Merdeka Menjadi Sekular Atau Merdeka Menjadi Islam*) [In Conjuction with Independence Day (Moving from Independence into Secularism or Islam)], held on 11 June 2006 in Kuala Lumpur. However, HTM also capitalizes on international issues, such as the Israeli-Lebanese conflict in 2006, to galvanize support for the group. For instance, they held a seminar titled *Selamatkan Pelestin Dan Lubnan* (*Isu-Isu Sejagat Kaum Muslimin*) [Save Palestine and Lebanon (International Muslim Issues)] on 10 September 2006 at Wisma Darul Manar, Al-Islamiyyah, Parit Sakai, Jalan Temenggung Ahmad, Muar, Johore.

119. According to HTM members, membership has increased greatly over the past eight years.

120. Interview with PAS Youth, Kota Bharu, Malaysia, 2 June 2007.

121. Researcher interview with an HTM member who was formerly a member of PAS, Petaling Jaya, Malaysia, 20 January 2007.

122. Researcher interview with PAS officials, Kuala Lumpur, Malaysia, 21 January 2007.

123. Researcher interview with PAS officials, Petaling Jaya, Malaysia, 22 January 2007.

124. *Hizbut Tahrir* seminar titled *Hijrah: Titik Mula Islam Sebagai Tamadun Baru Dunia* [Hijrah: The Beginning of Islam as a New Civilization for the World], Petaling

Jaya, Malaysia, 20 January 2007. In his address, HTM member Esa Abdullah openly gave his salaam to members of the Malaysian Security Branch.

125. See, for example, Marc Lynch, *Voices of a New Arab Republic: Iraq, Al Jazeera, and Middle East Politics Today* (New York: Columbia University Press, 2006).

126. A weblog is a regularly updated Web page that provides unedited commentary and hyperlinks to other Web sites and weblogs. Weblogs focus on a variety of topics, ranging from hobbies and celebrity gossip to personal diaries and politics.

127. Needless to say, this general remark is made based on bloggers who actually sign their names to their posts.

128. "Malaysia Is an Islamic State," *Bernama*, 17 July 2007.

129. See Ronnie Liu, "Najib, Malaysia Is Not an Islamic State," http://zfikri.word press.com/2007/07/19/malaysia-an-islamic-state/ (accessed 30 August 2007); Lim Kit Siang, "Malaysia an 'Islamic State': Now Pak Lak Says It in a Threatening Manner," http://blog.limkitsiang.com/2007/08/28/malaysia-an-islamic-state-now-pak-lah-says-it-in-a-threatening-manner/ (accessed 30 August 2007); M. Bakri Musa, "Rooting for an Islamic State," http://www.bakrimusa.com/archives/rooting-for-an-islamic-state (accessed 3 September 2007); Jules, "Malaysia Islamic State?" *Garam Masala*, http://chappatiandcurry.blogspot.com/2007/07/malaysia-islamic-state.html (accessed 30 August 2007).

130. Maznah Mohamed, "Is Malaysia an Islamic State?" http://commentisfree. guardian.co.uk/maznah_mohamad/2006/09/post_406.html (accessed 30 August 2007); "Malaysia Morphing into Islamic Law State," *Rojak and Cocktail*, http://linken lim.blogspot.com/2007/09/malaysia-morphing-into-islamic-law.html (accessed 6 September 2007).

131. The biographies of these Malay-Muslim bloggers indicate that most are young undergraduates and graduates; others are academics or older Malays who have settled abroad.

132. "Malaysia: Prime Minister Calls Country 'Islamic State,'" *Compass Direct News*, http://www.compassdirect.org/en/display.php?page=news&lang=en&length=long& idelement=5019 (accessed 6 September 2007).

133. Ktemoc, "Is Malaysia an Islamic State?" *Ktemoc Konsiders,* http://ktemoc. blogspot.com/2007/07/is-malaysia-islamic-state.html (accessed 30 August 2007).

134. Chandra Muzaffar, "A Secular State or an Islamic State?" *The Other Malaysia*, http://www.othermalaysia.org/content/view/102/1/ (accessed 1 September 2007).

135. Ronnie Liu, "Opposition Must Unite to Fight the Common Enemy," *Colour-blind because there's a strong resemblance between different colours*, http://ronnieliutiankh iew.wordpress.com/2006/12/26/opposition-must-unite-to-fight-the-common-enemy/ (accessed 1 September 2007).

136. Vaudine England, "Malaysia Struggles with Islamic Path," *International Herald Tribune*, 30 August 2007.

137. Nathaniel Tan, "Ong Ka Ting Condemns Chinese to Eternity of 2nd Class Citizenship," http://jelas.info/2007/08/21/ong-ka-ting-condemns-chinese-to-eternity-of-2nd-class-citizenship/ (accessed 28 August 2007).

138. David, "The Selling-Out of Malaysia," *On the Shoulders of Giants*, http://dbc tan.blogspot.com/2007/08/selling-out-of-malaysia.html (accessed 15 September 2007).

139. Ibid.

140. Ibid.

141. Muhammad Razin, "Malaysia Negara Islam?" [Is Malaysia an Islamic State?] *NurCahayaMu*, http://zinzam.blogspot.com/2007/08/malaysia-negara-islam.html (accessed 6 September 2007).

142. DPPBK, "Najib Muka Tidak Malu Mengaku Malaysia Negara Islam" [Najib Is Unashamed to Declare That Malaysia Is an Islamic State], *Ke Arah Kepimpinan Berakhlak*, http://pemudabukitkatil.blogspot.com/2007/07/najib-muka-tidak-malu-mengaku-malaysia.html (accessed 30 August 2007).

143. Muhammad Razin, "Malaysia Negara Islam?" [Is Malaysia an Islamic State?], *NurCahayaMu*, http://zinzam.blogspot.com/2007/08/malaysia-negara-islam.html (accessed 6 September 2007); Diya, "Apakah Malaysia Sebuah Negara Islam?" [Is Malaysia an Islamic State?], *Diary of My Life*, http://diya1902.blogspot.com/2007/06/apakah-malaysia-sebuah-negara-islam.html (accessed 6 September 2007).

144. Al Husseyn, "Adakah Malaysia Negara Munafiq?" [Is Malaysia a State That Endorses Hypocrisy?], *Guna Akal Untuk Berfikir*, http://taraknamav2.wordpress.com/2007/08/05/adakah-malaysia-negara-munafiq/ (accessed 30 August 2007).

145. Anis Nazri, "Negara Islam Hanya Propoganda Politik UMNO" [The Islamic State Rhetoric Is Just UMNO's Propaganda Tool], *Bukankerananama*, http://bukankerananama-aburazzi.blogspot.com/2007_08_01_archive.html (accessed 30 August 2007).

146. Rehman Razak, "Kes Lina Joy: Apa Yang Perlu Anda Tahu" [The Lina Joy Case: What You Need to Know], *Urban Influence*, http://urbaninfluence.blogspot.com/2007/05/kes-lina-joy-apa-yang-perlu-anda-tahu.html (accessed 7 September 2007).

147. Faridul, "Kenapa Orang Murtad Dihukum" [Why Apostates Are Punished], *Tadabbur al-Engineer*, http://faridul.wordpress.com/2007/08/09/kenapa-orang-murtad-dihukum/ (accessed 5 September 2007).

148. Mohamed Azam Mohamed Adil, "Jangan Pinggirkan Kuasa Sebenar Makamah Syariah" [Do Not Disregard the Definite Authority of the Syariah Courts], *Utusan Malaysia*, 6 September 2007.

149. Meor Saiful Nazli, "Ancaman Terhadap Islam di Malaysia" [The Threat toward Islam in Malaysia], *PeduliRakyat Infogo*, http://infogo07.blogspot.com/2007/08/ancaman-terhadap-islam-di-malaysia_02.html (accessed 6 September 2007).

150. Anak Bapak, "Kes Lina Joy . . . Bukan Disini Nokta Perjuangan" [The Lina Joy Case . . . The Victory Does Not End Here], *Minda Kritis Anak Bapak*, http://anakbapak8385.blogspot.com/2007/06/kes-lina-joy-bukan-di-sini-noktah.html (accessed 7 September 2007).

151. Meor Saiful Nazli, "Ancaman Terhadap Islam di Malaysia" [The Threat toward Islam in Malaysia], *PeduliRakyat Infogo*, http://infogo07.blogspot.com/2007/08/ancaman-terhadap-islam-di-malaysia_02.html (accessed 7 September 2007).

152. Tarmizi Mohd Jam, "Rancangan Apa Sebalik Lina Joy?" [What Are the Steps That Need to Be Taken after the Lina Joy Case?], *sanggahtoksago.com*, http://sanggahtoksago.blogspot.com/2007/08/pikio-tarmizi-mohd-jam-kes-lina-joy.html (accessed 6 September 2007).

153. Ibid.

154. ACCIN, "Penubuhan Interfaith Commission," *The Abused Hunggermugger*, http://fayestillcrapping.wordpress.com/2006/08/09/ifc-ifc/ (accessed 7 September 2007).

155. Ibid.

156. Many also commented that the decision to have her religion unchanged on the Malaysian identity card, also known as Mykad, entails greater repercussions for her personal life, because she will not be able to marry her Christian partner.

157. Ronnie Liu, "A Sad Ruling for Freedom of Religion in Malaysia," *Colour-blind because there's a strong resemblance between different colours*, http://ronnieliutiankhiew. wordpress.com/2007/05/30/a-sad-ruling-for-freedom-of-religion-in-malaysia/ (accessed 8 September 2007).

158. "Chee Yong" in Liu, ibid.

159. "Aniamus" in Farouk A. Peru, "Save One: Lose a Million," *Malaysia Today*, http://www.malaysia-today.net/blog2006/guests.php?itemid=5051 (accessed 8 September 2007).

160. Peru, "Save One: Lose a Million."

161. This blog entry captures a female Chinese blogger's response to a female Malay-Muslim blogger's opinions on the issue of apostasy in Islam. While the Malay-Muslim blogger asserts that Lina Joy failed to follow the proper procedures to convert from Islam, the Chinese blogger argues otherwise. Refer to "Something to Be Pondered Upon," *Mystical Thoughts: Secrets of Flying Time*, http://winterspringchange. blogspot.com/2007/08/something-to-be-pondered-upon.html (accessed 9 September 2007).

162. "Biggum Dogmannsteinburg" in "Lina Joy: The Aftermath," *O.B.E.*, http:// shar101.wordpress.com/2007/05/31/lina-joy-the-aftermath/ (accessed 6 September 2007).

CHAPTER 5

1. See John Gershman, "Is Southeast Asia the Second Front?" *Foreign Affairs* (July/August 2002): 60–74; Zachary Abuza, *Militant Islam in Southeast Asia: Crucible of Terror* (Boulder, Colo.: Lynne Reiner, 2003).

2. "School for Bombers: Malaysia Haven for Terror Trainees," *Sunday Times*, 15 December 2002.

3. "Anti-terror Drive in Southeast Asia Is 'Half-hearted,'" *South China Morning Post*, 5 September 2003.

4. See International Crisis Group, *Jemaah Islamiyah in Southeast Asia: Damaged But Still Dangerous*, Asia Report No. 63 (Brussels, Belgium, 2003).

5. Mohamad Abu Bakar, "Islam and Nationalism in Contemporary Malay Society," in *Islam and Society in Southeast Asia*, ed. Taufik Abdullah and Sharon Siddique (Singapore: ISEAS, 1986), 156.

6. Leonard Andaya and Barbara Watson-Andaya, *A History of Malaysia* (London: Macmillan, 1982), 170.

7. A. C. Milner, "Rethinking Islamic Fundamentalism in Malaysia," *Review of Indonesian and Malaysian Affairs* 20, no. 2 (1986): 55.

8. "The Battle for Memali," *Far Eastern Economic Review*, 5 December 1985.

9. It should be noted that Mahathir was away in China during this time, and it was his deputy and home minister Musa Hitam who issued the orders for the assault in Memali.

10. Briefly, the Kedah State *Fatwa* Council issued a decree declaring that those who died at Memali were not *shahid*. PAS leaders maintained that they were and contested the *fatwa*.

11. "Two Policemen and Nine More Soldiers Identified as Belonging to the Movement," *New Straits Times*, 13 July 2000.

12. It is not clear how many members *Halaqah Pakindo* had or how regular its meetings were.

13. "Nik Adli Identified as Militant Group Leader," *Star*, 9 August 2001.

14. Zachary Abuza, "Tentacles of Terror: Al Qaeda's Southeast Asia Network," *Contemporary Southeast Asia* 24, no. 3 (2002): 430.

15. Greg Fealy, "Is Indonesia a Terrorist Base?" *Inside Indonesia* 71 (2001), www.insideindonesia.org/edit71/fealy1.htm (accessed 24 June 2004).

16. "Asian Militants with Alleged Al Qaeda Ties Are Accused of Plotting against Embassies," *Asian Wall Street Journal*, 2 January 2002.

17. Farish Noor, "Reaping the Bitter Harvest after Twenty Years of State Islamization: The Malaysian Experience Post–September 11," in *Terrorism in the Asia-Pacific: Threat and Response*, ed. Rohan Gunaratna (Singapore: Eastern Universities Press, 2003), 182.

18. Abuza, "Tentacles of Terror," 444.

19. "Nik Adli Identified as Militant Group Leader," *Star*, 9 August 2001.

20. "Eye of the Storm," *Time*, 10 February 2002.

21. Interview with a retired Malaysian security agency official, Kuala Lumpur, Malaysia, 8 September 2003.

22. Kamarulnizam Abdullah, "Islamic Militancy Problems in Malaysia," *SEACSN Bulletin* (January–March 2003): 7.

23. See Fealy, "Is Indonesia a Terrorist Base?"

24. Habbard, Anne-Christine, *Malaysia—"The Boa Constrictor": Silencing Human Rights Defenders* (Geneva, Switzerland, and Paris: World Organisation Against Torture and International Federation of Human Rights, 2003), 28.

25. "Govt. Explains Hesitancy in Arresting Ayah Pin," *Bernama*, 22 September 2005.

26. Patricia Martinez, "The Islamic State or the State of Islam in Malaysia," *Contemporary Southeast Asia* 23, no. 3 (2001): 480.

27. That said, it should be noted that an Al-Azhar *fatwa* has since declared Shi'ism to be a religiously correct school of thought with the same status as Sunni schools of thought.

28. See "Religious Freedom World Report," *International Coalition for Religious Freedom*, 8 June 2001, http://www.religiousfreedom.com/wrpt/asiapac/malaysia.htm (accessed 12 June 2005).

29. For example, "Pensyarah Sebar Faham Syiah" [A Lecturer Spreads Shia Teachings], *Berita Minggu*, 25 February 1990; "Ajaran Syiah Boleh Jejas Perpaduan" [Shi'a Teachings May Jeopardize Unity], *Berita Harian*, 3 March 1990.

30. Human Rights Watch, "Malaysia: World Report 2002," http://hrw.org/wr2k2/asia8.html (accessed 13 June 2005).

31. Ibid.

32. "Shias under Attack in Malaysia," *shianews.com*, 19 July 2002, http://www.shianews.com/hi/asia/news_id/0001668.php (accessed 13 June 2005).

33. See Cris Prystay, "Bits of Malay Culture Now Vanishing under Muslim Rules," *Wall Street Journal*, 19 April 2006.

34. See "Beware of Arabisation," *Straits Times*, 23 April 2004.

35. "Malaysia's Lessons for Indonesia," *South China Morning Post*, 1 April 2004.

36. "Flawed Foundations of Arabisation," *New Straits Times*, 2 May 2004.

37. "PM Who Turned Dissident," *Australian*, 30 December 2006. The report cites Mahathir as having said, "Many deviant ideas which do not properly reflect true Islam are popular. Many Muslims like to link Islam with the so-called *hudud* laws, where the punishment is invariably cutting off hands and legs and things like that. But the religion, the Koran, stresses not forms of punishment, not even the methods of juridical procedures, but that justice must be done."

38. See Mahathir's presidential address to the 2001 UMNO General Assembly, 21 June 2001, http://www.utusan.com.my/utusan/SpecialCoverage/UMNO2001/index.asp?pg=speech_mahathir.htm (accessed 23 June 2001). See similar remarks in "Islam Tidak Pernah Halal Keganasan: Dr. Mahathir" [Islam Does Not Permit Violence: Dr. Mahathir], *Berita Harian*, 16 October 2001. For studies on Islamic education in Malaysia, see Awang Had Salleh, "Institusi Pondok di Malaysia" [Institution of Religious Boarding Schools in Malaysia], in *Masyarakat Melayu: Antara Tradisi dan Perubahan* [The Malay Community: Between Tradition and Change], ed. Zainal Kling (Kuala Lumpur, Malaysia: Utusan Publications, 1977); Rosnani Hashim, *Educational Dualism in Malaysia: Implications for Theory and Practice* (New York: Oxford University Press, 1996).

39. These private Islamic schools were previously known as *pondok* (hut), referring to the huts in which students at these boarding schools lived. *Pondok* schools focus solely on the teaching of Islam. Despite the fact that they have been eclipsed in terms of prominence by the *madrasah* (modern Islamic schools that teach academic subjects along with religious studies) and public schools, *pondok* schools are still romanticized in traditional Malay communities as a bastion of religious knowledge and culture.

40. See "KL Shows Proof of Danger from Religious Schools," *Straits Times*, 18 March 2003.

41. Previously, the government provided grants of between RM60 and RM150 per student for these schools.

42. "BN and PAS Poised for Battle over Islamic Schools," *Straits Times*, 25 January 2003.

43. "Islamic School Issue: PAS' New Election Weapon against UMNO," *Straits Times*, 20 March 2003.

44. Parti Islam Se-Malaysia, *Tarbiyah*, http://www.parti-pas.org/tarbiyah.php (accessed 7 November 2006).

45. Ibid.

46. See, for example, "What PAS Promises . . . If It Comes to Power," *malaysia kini.com*, 19 March 2003, http://www.malaysiakini.com/news/14810 (accessed 12 October 2006).

47. See "*Banyak Sekolah Tolak Bantuan Semula Kewangan Kerajaan*" [Numerous Schools Have Rejected Government's Financial Aid], *malaysiakini.com*, 25 October 2005, http://www.malaysiakini.com/news/42248 (accessed 12 October 2006).

48. "Bungling Robbers Were All Graduates in Islamic Studies," *Straits Times*, 25 May 2001.

49. C. van Dijk, "The Hearts and Minds of the People: Southeast Asia after 11 September 2001," in *Islamic Movements in Southeast Asia* (Jakarta: UIN, 2003), 17.

50. Ibid.

51. "Malaysia Backs Saddam Ouster," *Washington Times*, 16 May 2002.

52. It was only in the wake of its inability to conclusively prove Iraqi links with Al-Qaeda or to locate weapons of mass destruction in Iraq that the discourse to legitimize the invasion of Iraq shifted to the "spread of democracy."

53. Quoted from "Mahathir Accuses West of 'Attacking Muslim Countries,'" *Financial Times*, 20 June 2003.

54. "Asian Muslims Denounce Attack on Iraq," *People's Daily*, 20 March 2003.

55. Quoted from Hishammuddin Hussein in "BN, PAS, DAP Youth Ink Joint Memorandum," *malaysiakini.com*, 23 August 2006, http://www.malaysiakini.com/news/55776 (accessed 25 August 2006).

56. "Anti-Israel March to U.S. Embassy Draws 1,000," *malaysiakini.com*, 7 July 2006, http://www.malaysiakini.com/news/53589 (accessed 5 February 2007).

57. "BN, PAS, DAP Youth Ink Joint Memorandum," *malaysiakini.com*.

58. K. S. Nathan, "Malaysia and the Palestinian Issue: The Need for a Balanced Approach to the Two-State Formula," in *Malaysia and the Islamic World*, ed. Abdul Razak Baginda (London: ASEAN Academic Press, 2004), 201.

59. Mahathir Mohamad, speech delivered at the Seventh Islamic Summit Conference, Casablanca, Morocco, 13 December 1994.

60. Alias Mohamed, *PAS' Platform: Development and Change 1951–1986* (Petaling Jaya, Malaysia: Gateway Publishing House, 1994), 10.

61. Shanti Nair, *Islam in Malaysian Foreign Policy* (London: Routledge, 1997), 97.

62. The situation has been complicated by southern Thai militants who have, since the beginnings of political resistance in the 1940s, used northern Malaysia as a base from which to operate (including armed resistance) against the Thai state.

63. See Joseph Chinyong Liow, "The Security Situation in Southern Thailand: Towards an Understanding of Domestic and International Dimensions," *Studies in Conflict and Terrorism* 27, no. 6 (2004): 531–48.

64. "Residue of Mistrust," *Far Eastern Economic Review*, 30 August 1974. The same source would later report that Asri's comments were quoted out of context by the Thai media. See "Looking South with Increasing Suspicion," *Far Eastern Economic Review*, 9 September 1974.

65. "Malaysia's Opposition Party Offers Sanctuary for Thai Moslem Separatists," *Agence France-Presse*, 16 August 1992.

66. "Village Bans Entry of Thai News Media," *Bangkok Post*, 22 September 2005.

67. See Mohamed Nawab Mohamed Osman, "Israel, Lebanon, and the Rise of the Islamists," *IDSS Commentaries*, 24 August 2006.

68. Interview with PAS officials, Kuala Lumpur, Malaysia, 21 January 2007.

69. "Informal Relations between Egypt and Malaysia Have Come a Long Way," *arabicnews.com*, 8 February 1997, http://www.arabicnews.com/ansub/Daily/Day/970802/1997080219.html (accessed 24 September 2006).

70. "'PAS Linked' Organization Spells Trouble, Students Warned," *malaysiakini.com*, 5 March 2003, http://www.malaysiakini.com/news/14642 (accessed 9 November 2007).

71. Nair, *Islam in Malaysian Foreign Policy*, 157.

72. "Islamic Groups Shocked over Bloody Clashes," *New Straits Times*, 30 April 2004.

73. Ibid.

74. "JIM Submits Memorandum Asking US to Stop Suppression of Women," *Bernama*, 5 July 2006.

75. Ibid.

76. Ibid.

77. "JIM Wants Malaysia to Play Role to Stop Israeli Assault," *Bernama*, 20 July 2006.

78. Ibid.

CONCLUSION

1. William R. Roff, "Patterns of Islamization in Malaysia, 1890s–1990s: Exemplars, Institutions, and Vectors," *Journal of Islamic Studies* 9, no. 2 (1998): 210–28.

2. See "Malaysia's Secular Vision vs. 'Writing on the Wall,'" *International Herald Tribune*, 28 August 2006.

3. Arguably, non-Muslim support for oppositionist forces, which can at times be substantial, is often more of a rejection of non-Malay component parties because of their perceived inability to extract concessions from UMNO than a rejection of UMNO itself.

4. See Virginia Matheson Hooker, "Reconfiguring Malay and Islam in Contemporary Malaysia," *Review of Indonesian and Malaysian Affairs* 34, no. 2 (2000): 1–27.

5. At the heart of his argument lay a somewhat similar logic to that of orientalist scholars who believed that there was "something wrong" with Islam that prevented it from embracing modernity.

6. See Carrie Rosefsky Wickham, *Mobilizing Islam: Religion, Activism, and Political Change in Egypt* (New York: Columbia University Press, 2002), 211.

7. For instance, on the matter of moral policing, state *mufti* such as Zainol Abidin from Perlis (a state that is known to be more Hanbali than Shafi'i in jurisprudential orientation) and Ismail Yahya from Terengganu have criticized the practices of moral policing and polygamy, even as others, such as Perak's Harussani Idris, have enthusiastically supported these actions.

8. For theorists of the state, this would not be altogether surprising, given their contention that the state is an arena for condensation, crystallization, and summation of social relations within its defined territories. See Nikos Poulantzas, *Pouvoir Politique et Classes Sociales* [Political Power and Social Classes] (Paris: Maspero, 1972).

9. See "Confusing Voices of Malaysia's Islamic Leaders," *Straits Times*, 15 January 2007.

10. Indeed, before this UMNO had already declared itself to be the third-largest Islamic party in the world. See R. S. Milne and Diane K. Mauzy, *Malaysian Politics under Mahathir* (London: Routledge, 1999), 88.

11. Hermen Shastri, secretary of the Council of Churches in Malaysia, raised this paradox when he asked in rhetorical fashion: "When dealing with UMNO, are we dealing with a government or a religious organization?" Conversation with Hermen Shastri, Singapore, 26 February 2008.

12. Milne and Mauzy, *Malaysian Politics under Mahathir*, 80–81.

13. For a more detailed mapping of the various permutations of PAS over time, see Joseph Chinyong Liow, "Exigency or Expediency? Contextualising Political Islam and the PAS Challenge in Malaysian Politics," *Third World Quarterly* 25, no. 2 (2004): 359–72.

14. This performance was surpassed in 2008. The 2008 general elections are discussed in the Epilogue.

15. Whether this dualism translated into factionalism within the FIS was pretty much a moot point, because Abassi and Belhaj were charged with conspiracy against the state before any tension could be resolved. They were arrested and the FIS was outlawed in a government crackdown.

16. Dietrich Reetz, *Islam in the Public Sphere: Religious Groups in India, 1900–1947* (New Delhi, India: Oxford University Press, 2006), 299.

17. See, for instance, Timothy Mitchell, "The Limits of the State," *American Political Science Review* 85, no. 1 (1991): 77–96.

18. Saliha Hassan, "Islamic Non-governmental Organizations," in *Social Movements in Malaysia: From Moral Communities to NGOs*, ed. Meredith L. Weiss and Saliha Hassan (London: RoutledgeCurzon, 2003), 113–14.

19. Robert W. Hefner, *Civil Islam: Muslims and Democratization in Indonesia* (Princeton, N.J.: Princeton University Press, 2000).

20. "Pressure on Multifaith Malaysia," *BBC News*, 16 May, 2006, http://news.bbc.co.uk/2/hi/asia-pacific/4965580.stm (accessed 17 May 2006).

21. Baradan Kuppusamy, "Malaysia's Non-Muslims Unite against Shari'a," *Inter-Press Service*, 14 January 2006.

22. In extreme cases UMNO politicians had in fact threatened to incriminate non-Muslims for criticizing or insulting Islam by speaking out on issues related to Islamic legislation. See "Malaysia: Minister Threatens Jail over Islam Slurs," *South China Morning Post*, 22 March 2006.

23. Zainah Anwar, "Islamisation and Its Impact on Democratic Governance and Women's Rights in Islam: A Feminist Perspective," keynote address delivered at the Center for the Study of Islam and Democracy, Washington, D.C., 17 May 2003.

EPILOGUE

1. "Can MCA Pull Off Another Big Victory?" *malaysiakini.com*, 13 February 2008, http://www.malaysiakini.com/news/78005 (accessed 14 February 2008).

2. "Our Religious and Civil Liberties," *malaysiakini.com*, 12 February 2008, http://www.malaysiakini.com/columns/77941 (accessed 14 February 2008).

3. Conversation with Hermen Shastri, Singapore, 26 February 2008. See also "Polls Role for Churches, Hindu Temples," *Straits Times*, 18 February 2008.

4. Nasharuddin contested in Bachok against Awang Adek, who was publicly announced as the "new" *Menteri Besar* of Kelantan if UMNO won the state. Hatta Ramli contested in the Kuala Kerai seat in Terengganu. Both won their contests.

5. "Promise of Mosques in Malaysia Polls," 25 February 2008, http://tvnz. co.nz/view/tvnz_portable_story_skin/1600333 (accessed 26 February 2008).

6. "Abdullah tolak Islam punca Allah beri kekalahan kepada UMNO/BN" [Abdullah Denies That Islam is the Reason behind God-Ordained UMNO/BN Loss], *Harakahdaily.net*, 9 March 2008, http://mindacergas.wordpress.com/2008/03/09/ malaysian-elections-islam-vs-islam-hadhari/ (accessed 23 March 2008).

7. Marwaan Macan-Markar, "Islamic Push for Malaysian Moderation," *Asia Times*, 7 June 2005, http://www.atimes.com/atimes/Southeast_Asia/GF07Ae02.html (accessed 23 March 2008).

Glossary

adat bersanding.   Customary practice of newlyweds sitting side by side on a dais

ad-din.   A way of life

akal.   Reason

akujanji.   Pledge of loyalty

al halal wal haram fil Islam.   The lawful and prohibited acts in Islam

Alhamdullillah.   Praise be to Allah

alim.   Religious leader

Allahuakbar.   God is great

al-li'an.   Termination of marriage by a husband's accusation

Al-Maunah.   Brotherhood of Inner Power

Aman.   Malaysia national peace movement

amanat.   Edict

Angkatan Belia Islam Malaysia.   Malaysian Islamic Youth Movement

aqidah.   Faith

assabiyyah.   Chauvinistic communalism or tribalism

aurat.   Parts of the body that should not be exposed, according to Islamic belief

bangsa bangsat.   A race of thugs

Barisan Alternatif.   Alternative Front

Barisan Nasional.   National Front

bumiputra.   Sons of the soil

ceramah.   Dialogue session/political meeting

dakwah.   Proselytization

Dewan Muslimat.   Women's Wing

Dewan Rakyat.   House of Parliament

Dewan Ulama.   *Ulama* Council

dikir barat.   Traditional Malay performing art, characterized by call-and-response singing

din wa dawla.   Faith along with polity

diyat.   Compensation for death or injury to a woman

fatwa.   Religious decree/legal opinion

fiqh.   Islamic jurisprudence

Gerakan Aceh Merdeka.   Free Aceh Movement

Gerakan Pemuda Melayu Raya.   Greater Malaysia Youth Movement

haj.   Pilgrimage

halal.   That which is permissible in Islam

halaqah.   Study/discussion circles in Mecca

Harakah.   Magazine of the *Parti Islam Se-Malaysia* (Islamic Party of Malaysia, or PAS)

Hidup melayu.   Long live the Malays

Hizbul Muslimin.   A reformist party, and the first overtly Islamist political organization in Malaya

hudud.   Islamic penal code

ibadah.   Worship

ijtihad.   Reinterpretation and informed reasoning

Ikhwanul Muslimin.   Muslim Brotherhood

imam.   Leader during prayers/leader of the mosque

Institut Kajian Dasar.   Institute of Policy Studies

Institut Kefahaman Islam Malaysia.   Malaysian Institute of Islamic Understanding

Islam Hadhari.   Civilizational Islam

jabatan agama.   Religious departments

Jabatan Kemajuan Islam Malaysia.   Malaysian Islamic Development Department

jangan ikut tuhan.   Don't conform to God

Jemaah Islah Malaysia.   Malaysia Islamic Reform Society

jihad.   Qur'anic injunction for believers to strive and struggle with their entire being to carry out the commandments of God as part of their submission to God's will.

jus soli.   Birthright

kafir.   Unbelievers or infidels

kafir-mengafir.   Muslims labeling fellow Muslims as infidels

kampung melayu.   Malay communities

Kaum Muda.   Young Generation

Kaum Tua.   Old Generation

keadilan sosial.   Social justice

Kelab Penyokong PAS.   PAS Supporters' Club (club for non-Muslim supporters of *Parti Islam Se-Malaysia* [PAS], the Islamic Party of Malaysia)

kerajaan.   Traditional court government

keris.   Traditional Malay weapon, which is also a cultural symbol

Kesatuan Melayu Muda.   Young Malays Union

ketuanan melayu.   Malay primacy

khalwat.   To indulge in illicit association

khutbah.   Sermon

Konfrontasi.   Confrontation, a foreign policy of harsh diplomacy coupled with limited military action, popularized by the Sukarno regime in Indonesia

Koperasi Angkatan Revolusi Islam Malaysia. Malaysian Islamic Revolutionary Front
Kumpulan Militan Malaysia. Malaysian Militant Group
Lembaga Islam Se Malaya. All-Malaya Islamic Council
lepak. Loitering
Majlis Agama Tertinggi Malaya. Malayan Supreme Religious Council
Majlis Kebangsaan Halehwal Islam Malaysia. National Council of Islamic Affairs
Majlis Shura Ulama. Consultative Council of Religious Scholars
Majlis Ugama. Religious Council
masjid. Mosque
Masjid Kristal. Crystal Mosque
Masyarakat Madani. Civil Society
mazhab. School of Islamic jurisprudential thought
Menteri Besar. Chief executive of the state governments
menumpang. Temporarily reside
Merdeka Day. Independence Day
mufti. Muslim jurist
muktamar. General assembly
munaqashah. Special convention
murtad. Apostate
Musyidul 'Am. Spiritual leader
Nasionalisme, Agama, Komunisme. Nationalism, Religion, Communism
negara Islam. Islamic state
nilai-nilai Islam. Islamic values
nusrah. Political support
Pakatan Rakyat. Peoples' Pact
Parti Buruh Malaya. Labor Party of Malaya
Parti Keadilan Rakyat. People's Justice Party
Parti Kebangsaan Melayu Malaya. Malay Nationalist Party of Malaya
Parti Rakyat Malaya. People's Party of Malaya
Pembela Tanah Ayer. Defenders of the Fatherland; a leftist Malay organization
Persatuan Bahasa Melayu Universiti Malaya. University of Malaya Malay Language Society
Persatuan Islam. Islamic student associations and societies
Persatuan Islam Se-tanah Malaya. Pan-Malayan Islamic Association
Persatuan Kebangsaan Pelajar-Pelajar Islam Malaysia. National Union of Malaysian Muslim Students
Persatuan Ulama Se-Malaya. Ulama Association of Malaya
Persidangan Ekonomi Agama Se-Malaysia. Malay Nationalist and Religious Leaders' Conference
Pertubuhan Angkatan Sabillullah. Sabillullah Armed Forces
Pertubuhan-Pertubuhan Pembela Islam. Defenders of Islam
perundangan Islam. Islamic law
pondok. Traditional Malay religious boarding school
Pusat Islam. Islamic Center
qazaf. Accusation of *zina* (adultery/illicit sex) without witnesses
qisas. Laws of retaliation covering homicide and injury

rakyat.   Common folk

riba.   Profit maximization through usury

Rukunnegara.   Values of the Nation

Sekolah Agama Rakyat.   Private Religious Schools

shahid.   Martyr

shari'a.   Islamic way of life, including Islamic law

shura.   Consultation

Siaran PAS.   PAS Broadcast (broadcast of *Parti Islam Se-Malaysia* [PAS], the Islamic Party of Malaysia)

Siasat Shari'a.   Policies and regulations in accordance with Islamic law

Suara Felda.   Voice of the Federal Land Development Authority

sunnah.   Religious actions of the Prophet

surau.   Prayer house

tadaruj.   Evolutionary stages

tafsir.   Interpretation of the Qur'an

takfir.   The act of claiming that a person or group is an unbeliever or infidel

talaq.   Repudiation

Taman Tamadun Islam.   Islamic Civilization Theme Park

tarbiyah.   Islamic education

tauliah.   Formal letter of authority

tawhid.   Oneness and unity in the name of Allah

ta'zirat.   Penal stipulations

tindakan hina biadab.   Uncivilized conduct

tok guru.   Religious teacher from a pondok (traditional Malay religious boarding school)

tudung.   Head scarf

ulama.   Religious scholar or community of religious scholars

ummah.   Community of Muslim believers

usrah.   Discussion groups

ustaz.   Religious teachers in Islamic schools

waqf.   Foundations

wawasan sihat.   Healthy Vision

Wawasan 2020.   Vision 2020

wayang kulit.   Shadow puppet theatre

Yang di-Pertuan Agong.   King of Malaysia

Yayasan Dakwah Islamiah Malaysia.   Islamic Missionary Foundation

Yayasan Islam Hadhari.   Islam Hadhari Foundation

zakat.   Tithes

zina.   Adultery/illicit sex

Selected Bibliography

Abdul Hamid, Ahmad Fauzi. "Islamic Resurgence: An Overview of Causal Factors, A Review of 'Ummatic' Linkages." *Jurnal IKIM* 10, no. 2 (2001): 87–123.

———. "Reforming PAS?" *Aliran* 6 (2003): 11–3.

———. "Islamic Doctrine and Violence: The Malaysian Case." Paper presented at IDSS Conference on "Anatomies of Religious Conflict in South and Southeast Asia." Singapore, May 2005.

Abdullah, Firdaus. *Radical Malay Politics: Its Origins and Early Development.* Petaling Jaya, Malaysia: Pelanduk Publications, 1985.

Abdullah, Kamarulnizam. *The Politics of Islam in Contemporary Malaysia.* Bangi, Malaysia: Penerbit Universiti Kebangsaan Malaysia, 2002.

———. "Islamic Militancy Problems in Malaysia." *SEACSN Bulletin* (January–March 2003): 4–7.

Abdullah, Nabir Haji. *Maahad Il-Ihya Assyariff Gunung Semanggol, 1934–1935.* Kuala Lumpur, Malaysia: Jabatan Sejarah, Universiti Malaya, 1976.

Abegebriel, A. Maftuh, and Abeveiro, A. Yani. *Negara Tuhan: The Thematic Encyclopedia.* Jakarta, Indonesia: SR-Ins, 2004.

Abu Bakar, Mohamad. "Islamic Revivalism and the Political Process in Malaysia." *Asian Survey* 21, no. 10 (1981): 1040–59.

———. "Islam and Nationalism in Contemporary Malay Society." In *Islam and Society in Southeast Asia,* ed. Taufik Abdullah and Sharon Siddique, 155–74. Singapore: ISEAS, 1986.

Abuza, Zachary. "Tentacles of Terror: Al Qaeda's Southeast Asia Network." *Contemporary Southeast Asia* 24, no. 3 (2002): 427–65.

Ahmad, Salbiah. "Islam in Malaysia: Constitutional and Human Rights Perspectives." *Muslim World Journal of Human Rights* 2, no. 1 (2005): 24–29.

Alagappa, Muthiah, ed. *Civil Society and Political Change in Asia.* Stanford, Calif.: Stanford University Press, 2004.

Ali, Mustapha. "The Islamic Movement and the Malaysian Experience." In *Power-Sharing Islam?* ed. Azzam Tamimi, 109–24. London: Liberty Publications, 1993.

Almond, Gabriel, and Verba, Sidney. *The Civic Culture: Political Attitudes and Democracy in Five Nations.* London: Sage, 1989.

Andaya, Leonard, and Andaya, Barbara Watson. *A History of Malaysia.* 2nd ed. Basingstoke, UK: Palgrave, 2001.

Ansari, Nazish. "Malaysia: Limitations of the Human Rights Discourse and the Deployment of Rights in a Religious Identity Debate." *Muslim World Journal of Human Rights* 1, no. 1 (2004): 1–34.

Anwar, Zainah. *Islamic Revivalism in Malaysia: Dakwah among the Students.* Petaling Jaya, Malaysia: Pelanduk Publications, 1987.

———. "The Struggle for Women's Rights within the Religious Framework: The Experience of Sisters in Islam." In *Modern Malaysia in the Global Economy: Political and Social Change into the 21st Century,* ed. Colin Barlow, 178–88. London: Edward Elgar, 2001.

Awang, Abdul Hadi. *Konsep Negara Islam dan Matlamatnya* [The Concept of an Islamic State and Its Aims]. Kuala Lumpur, Malaysia: G. G. Edat, 1986.

———. *Hadharah Islamiyah bukan Islam Hadhari* [Hadharah Islamiyah Is Not Islam Hadhari]. Kuala Lumpur, Malaysia: Nufair Street, 2005.

Ayoob, Mohammed. *Beyond Radical Islam?* Hudson Institute, 16 April 2004. Available at: http://www.hudson.org/files/publications/Beyond_Radical_Islam-Transcript_2.pdf. Accessed 12 February 2007.

Azra, Azyumardi. "The Transmission of al-Manar's Reformism to the Malay-Indonesian World: The Cases of al-Imam and al-Munir." *Studia Islamika* 6, no. 3 (1999): 75–100.

Badawi, Abdullah Ahmad. *Islam Hadhari: A Model Approach for Development and Progress.* Kuala Lumpur, Malaysia: MPH Group Publishing, 2006.

Baginda, Abdul Razak, and Schier, Peter, eds. *Is Malaysia an Islamic State? Secularism and Theocracy: A Study of the Malaysian Constitution.* Kuala Lumpur, Malaysia: Malaysian Strategic Research Centre and Konrad Adenauer Foundation, 2003.

Baran, Zeyno. *Hizb ut-Tahrir: Islam's Political Insurgency.* Washington, D.C.: Nixon Center, 2004.

Case, William. "Testing Malaysia's Pseudo-Democracy." In *The State of Malaysia: Ethnicity, Equity and Reform,* ed. Edmund Terence Gomez, 29–48. London: RoutledgeCurzon, 2004.

Crouch, Harold. *Government and Politics in Malaysia.* Ithaca, N.Y.: Cornell University Press, 1990.

———. *Government and Society in Malaysia.* Ithaca, N.Y.: Cornell University Press, 1996.

Dekmejian, R. Hrair. *Islam in Revolution: Fundamentalism in the Arab World.* Syracuse, N.Y.: Syracuse University Press, 1995.

Derichs, Claudia. *Looking for Clues: Malaysian Suggestions for Political Change.* Duisburg, Germany: Institut für Ostasienwissenschaften, 2001. Project Discussion Paper No. 10/2001.

Dewan Ulama PAS Pusat. *Islam dan Politik* [Islam and Politics]. Kuala Lumpur, Malaysia: Dewan Ulama PAS Pusat, 1980.

Eickelman, Dale, and Piscatori, James, eds. *Muslim Politics.* Princeton, N.J.: Princeton University Press, 1996.

Esposito, John L., and Voll, John O. *Islam and Democracy.* New York: Oxford University Press, 1996.

Faksh, Mahmud A. *The Future of Islam in the Middle East: Fundamentalism in Egypt, Algeria, and Saudi Arabia.* Westport, Conn.: Praeger, 1997.

Fealy, Greg, and Hooker, Virginia, eds. *Voices of Islam in Southeast Asia: A Contemporary Sourcebook.* Singapore: ISEAS, 2006.

Fritz, Nicole, and Flaherty, Martin. *Unjust Order: Malaysia's Internal Security Act.* New York: Joseph R. Crowley Program in International Human Rights, 2003.

Funston, John, N. "The Origins of Parti Islam Se Malaysia." *Journal of Southeast Asian Studies* 7, no. 1 (1976): 58–71.

———. *Malay Politics in Malaysia: A Study of UMNO and PAS.* Singapore: Heinemann Educational Books, 1983.

———. "Malaysia's Tenth Elections: Status Quo, Reformasi or Islamization?" *Contemporary Southeast Asia* 22, no. 1 (2000): 23–59.

Gagliano, Felix. *Communal Violence in Malaysia 1969: The Political Aftermath.* Athens, Ohio: Ohio University Center for International Studies, 1970.

Goh, Cheng Teik. *The May Thirteenth Incident and Democracy in Malaysia.* Kuala Lumpur, Malaysia: Oxford University Press, 1971.

Habbard, Anne-Christine. *Malaysia—"The Boa Constrictor": Silencing Human Rights Defenders.* Geneva, Switzerland, and Paris: World Organisation against Torture and International Federation of Human Rights, 2003.

Hamayotsu, Kikue. "Islam and Nation Building in Southeast Asia: Malaysia and Indonesia in Comparative Perspective," *Pacific Affairs* 75, no. 3 (2002): 353–75.

———. "Politics of Syariah Reform." In *Malaysia: Islam, Society and Politics,* ed. Virginia Hooker and Norani Othman, 55–79. Singapore: ISEAS, 2003.

———. "Islamisation, Patronage and Political Ascendancy: The Politics and Business of Islam." In *The State of Malaysia: Ethnicity Equity and Reform,* ed. Edmund Terence Gomez, 229–52. London: RoutledgeCurzon, 2004.

Haque, M. Shamsul. "The Role of the State in Managing Ethnic Tensions in Malaysia." *American Behavioral Scientist* 47, no. 3 (2003): 240–66.

Hashim, M. Sufian. "The Relationship between Islam and the State in Malaya." *Intisari* 1, no. 1 (1957): 7–21.

Hashim, Rosnani. *Educational Dualism in Malaysia: Implications for Theory and Practice.* New York: Oxford University Press, 1996.

Hassan, Saliha. "Islamic Non-governmental Organizations." In *Social Movements in Malaysia: From Moral Communities to NGOs,* ed. Meredith L. Weiss and Saliha Hassan, 97–114. London: Routledge, 2003.

Hefner, Robert W. *Civil Islam: Muslims and Democratization in Indonesia.* Princeton, N.J.: Princeton University Press, 2000.

Hilley, John. *Malaysia: Mahathirism, Hegemony and the New Opposition.* London: Zed Books, 2001.

Hooker, Virginia Matheson. "Reconfiguring Malay and Islam in Contemporary Malaysia." *Review of Indonesian and Malaysian Affairs* 34, no. 2 (2000): 1–27.

Hudson Institute. Transcript of conference, *Beyond Radical Islam?* 2nd session, "Political Islam: Image and Reality," Washington, D.C., 16 April 2004. Available at: http://www.hudson.org/files/publications/Beyond_Radical_Islam-Transcript_2.pdf. Accessed 12 February 2007.

Hussein, Syed Ahmed. *Muslim Politics in Malaysia: Origins and Evolution of Competing Traditions in Malaysian Islam.* FGD Occasional Paper No. 15. Braamfontein, South Africa: Foundation for Global Dialogue, 1998.

———. "Muslim Politics and the Discourse on Democracy." In *Democracy in Malaysia: Discourses and Practices*, ed. Francis Loh Kok Wah and Khoo Boo Teik, 74–107. Richmond, UK: Curzon, 2002.

Ibrahim, Shafie. *The Islamic Party of Malaysia: Its Formative Stages and Ideology.* Kota Bharu, Malaysia: Nuawi bin Ismail, 1981.

International Crisis Group. *Jemaah Islamiyah in Southeast Asia: Damaged but Still Dangerous.* Asia Report No. 63. Brussels, Belgium: 2003.

———. *Indonesia Backgrounder: Why Salafism and Terrorism Mostly Don't Mix.* Asia Report No. 83. Brussels, Belgium: 2004.

Ismail, L. *Berakhirnya Zaman Keagungan PAS* [The End of a Prolific Era for PAS]. Kuala Lumpur, Malaysia: Penerbitan Pena, 1978.

Ismail, Rose. *Hudud in Malaysia: The Issues at Stake.* Kuala Lumpur, Malaysia: SIS Forum Berhad, 1995.

Jaffar, Kamarudin, ed. *Memperingati Yusof Rawa* [Commemorating Yusof Rawa]. Kuala Lumpur, Malaysia: IKDAS, 2000.

Jam, T. M. *Ketahanan PAS Ancam Masa Depan UMNO* [PAS's Resolve Threatens UMNO's Future]. Kuala Lumpur, Malaysia: Pangkaian Minda Publishing, 1995.

Jomo K. S., ed. *Islam dan Sosialisme* [Islam and Socialism]. Kuala Lumpur, Malaysia: Ikraq Press, 1988.

Jomo K. S., and Cheek, Ahmad Shabery. "Malaysia's Islamic Movements." In *Fragmented Vision: Culture and Politics in Contemporary Malaysia*, ed. Joel S. Kahn and Francis Loh Kok Wah, 79–106. Honolulu: University of Hawaii Press, 1992.

Kahin, George McTuman. *Nationalism and Revolution in Indonesia.* Ithaca, N.Y.: Cornell University Press, 1952.

Karam, Azza. "Transnational Political Islam and the USA: An Introduction." In *Transnational Political Islam: Religion, Ideology and Power*, ed. Azza Karam, 1–27. London: Pluto Press, 2004.

Kessler, Clive. *Islam and Politics in a Malay State: Kelantan 1839–1969.* Ithaca, N.Y.: Cornell University Press, 1978.

———. "Malaysia: Islamic Revivalism and Political Disaffection in a Divided Society." *Southeast Asia Chronicle* 75 (1980): 3–11.

Khoo Boo Teik. *Paradoxes of Mahathirism: An Intellectual Biography of Mahathir Mohamad.* Kuala Lumpur, Malaysia: Oxford University Press, 1995.

———. *Searching for Islam in Malaysian Politics: Confluences, Divisions, and Governance.* Working Paper Series No. 72. Hong Kong: City University of Hong Kong, Southeast Asia Research Centre, 2004.

Laffan, Michael. "The Tangled Roots of Islamist Activism in Southeast Asia." *Cambridge Review of International Affairs* 16, no. 3 (2003): 397–414.

Larsen, Anne Katherine. "The Impact of the Islamic Resurgence on the Belief System of Rural Malays." *Temenos* 32 (1996): 137–54.

Liow, Joseph Chinyong. "Exigency or Expediency? Contextualising Political Islam and the PAS Challenge in Malaysian Politics." *Third World Quarterly* 25, no. 2 (2004): 359–72.

———."The Security Situation in Southern Thailand: Towards an Understanding of Domestic and International Dimensions." *Studies in Conflict and Terrorism* 27, no. 6 (2004): 531–48.

———.*The Politics of Indonesia-Malaysia Relations: One Kin, Two Nations.* London: RoutledgeCurzon, 2005.

———. "The Politics behind Malaysia's 11th General Elections." *Asian Survey* 45, no. 6 (2005): 907–30.

Lynch, Marc. *Voices of a New Arab Republic: Iraq, Al Jazeera, and Middle East Politics Today.* New York: Columbia University Press, 2006.

Mann, Michael. "The Autonomous Power of the State: Its Origins, Mechanisms and Results." *European Journal of Sociology* 25 (1984): 185–212.

Martinez, Patricia. "The Islamic State or the State of Islam in Malaysia." *Contemporary Southeast Asia* 23, no. 3 (2001): 474–529.

———. "Mahathir, Islam and the New Malay Dilemma." In *Mahathir's Administration: Performance and Crisis in Governance,* ed. Ho Khai Leong and James Chin, 120–60. Singapore: Times Book International, 2002.

———. "A Response to Dr. Tom Michel." *CTC Bulletin* 18 (2002). Available at: http://www.cca.org.hk/resources/ctc/ctc02-01/ctc0201e.htm.

———. "Islam, Pluralism, and Conflict Resolution in Malaysia: The Case of Interfaith Dialogue." Paper presented at the Association of Asian Studies Annual Conference, San Francisco, Calif., April 2006.

Mat Isa, Nasharuddin. *The Islamic Party of Malaysia (PAS): Ideology, Policy, Struggle and Vision Towards the New Millennium.* Kuala Lumpur, Malaysia: Islamic Party of Malaysia, 2001.

Mauzy, Diane. "A Vote for Continuity: The 1978 General Elections in Malaysia." *Asian Survey* 19, no. 3 (1979): 281–96.

McGee, T. G. "The Malayan Elections of 1959: A Study in Electoral Geography." *Malayan Journal of Tropical Geography* 16 (1962): 57–69.

McTaggart, W. Donald. *The May 1969 Disturbances in Malaysia: Impact of a Conflict on Developmental Pattern.* San Diego, Calif.: Association for Asian Studies, 1971.

Means, Gordon P. *Malaysian Politics.* 2nd ed. London: Hodder and Stoughton, 1976.

———. "Public Policy towards Religion in Malaysia." *Pacific Affairs* 51, no. 3 (1978): 384–405.

———. *Malaysian Politics: The Second Generation.* London: Oxford University Press, 1990.

Milne, R. S., and Mauzy, Diane K. *Malaysian Politics under Mahathir.* London: Routledge, 1999.

Milner, A. C. "Rethinking Islamic Fundamentalism in Malaysia." *Review of Indonesian and Malaysian Affairs* 20, no. 2 (1986): 48–75.

Mitchell, Timothy. "The Limits of the State." *American Political Science Review* 85, no. 1 (1991): 77–96.

Mohamad, Mahathir. Speech given to UMNO General Assembly, Kuala Lumpur, Malaysia, June 21, 2001. Available at: http://www.utusan.com.my/utusan/Special Coverage/UMNO2001/index.asp?pg=speech_mahathir.htm.

Mohamad, Maznah. "Women in the UMNO and PAS Labyrinth." In *Risking Malaysia: Culture, Politics and Identity*, ed. Maznah Mohamad and Wong Soak Koon, 216–40. Kuala Lumpur, Malaysia: Universiti Kebangsaan Malaysia Press, 2001.

Mohamed, Alias. *Malaysia's Islamic Opposition: Past, Present and Future*. Kuala Lumpur, Malaysia: Gateway Publishing House, 1991.

———. *PAS' Platform: Development and Change 1951–1986*. Petaling Jaya, Malaysia: Gateway Publishing House, 1994.

Mohamed Osman, Mohamed Nawab. "Religio-Political Activism of Ulama in Malaysia." M.A. diss., National University of Singapore, 2006.

Mutalib, Hussin. *Islam and Ethnicity in Malay Politics*. Singapore: Oxford University Press, 1990.

———. *Islam in Malaysia: From Revivalism to Islamic State?* Singapore: Singapore University Press, 1993.

———. "Islamisation in Malaysia: Between Ideals and Realities." In *Islam, Muslims and the Modern State: Case Studies of Muslims in Thirteen Countries*, ed. Hussin Mutalib and Taj ul-Islam Hashmi, 152–73. New York: St. Martin's Press, 1994.

Muzaffar, Chandra. "Islamisation of State and Society: Some Further Critical Remarks." In *Shari'a Law and the Modern Nation-State*, ed. Norani Othman, 113–22. Kuala Lumpur, Malaysia: Sisters in Islam, 1994.

Nagata, Judith. "Religious Ideology and Social Change: The Islamic Revival in Malaysia." *Pacific Affairs* 20, no. 3 (1980): 405–39.

———. *The Reflowering of Malaysian Islam: Modern Religious Radicals and Their Roots*. Vancouver, Canada: University of British Columbia Press, 1984.

———. "How to Be Islamic without Being an Islamic State," In *Islam, Globalisation, and Postmodernity*, ed. Akbar Ahmed and Hastings Donnan, 63–90. London: Routledge, 1994.

Nair, Shanti. *Islam in Malaysian Foreign Policy*. London: Routledge, 1997.

Najib, Ghadbian. "Democratization and the Islamist Challenge in the Arab World." Ph.D. diss., City University of New York, 1995.

Nasr, Seyyed Vali Reza. *Islamic Leviathan: Islam and the Making of State Power*. New York: Oxford University Press, 2001.

Nathan, K. S. "Malaysia and the Palestinian Issue: The Need for a Balanced Approach to the Two-State Formula." In *Malaysia and the Islamic World*, ed. Abdul Razak Baginda, 185–216. London: ASEAN Academic Press, 2004.

Noorani, A. G. *Islam and Jihad: Prejudice versus Reality*. London: Zed Books, 2002.

Noor, Farish A. *PAS post–Fadzil Noor: Future Directions and Prospects*. Singapore: ISEAS, 2002.

———. "Blood, Sweat, and Jihad: The Radicalization of the Political Discourse of the Pan-Malaysian Islamic Party (PAS) from 1982 Onwards." *Contemporary Southeast Asia* 25, no. 2 (2003): 200–232.

———. "Reaping the Bitter Harvest after Twenty Years of State Islamization: The Malaysian Experience post–September 11." In *Terrorism in the Asia-Pacific: Threat and Response,* ed. Rohan Gunaratna, 178–201. Singapore: Eastern Universities Press, 2003.

———. *Islam Embedded: The Historical Development of the Pan-Malaysian Islamic Party PAS, 1951–2003.* 2 vols. Kuala Lumpur, Malaysia: Malaysian Sociological Research Institute, 2004.

Norhashimah, Mohd Yasin. *Islamisation/Malaynisation: A Study on the Role of Islamic Law in the Economic Development of Malaysia: 1969–1993.* Kuala Lumpur, Malaysia: A. S. Noordeen, 1996.

Osman, Salim bin. "UMNO-PAS Rivalry in Malaysia." B.A. diss., National University of Singapore, 1979.

Othman, A. L. *Wajah Baru Politik Malaysia* [The New Face of Malaysian Politics]. Kuala Lumpur, Malaysia: Penerbitan Pemuda, 1995.

Othman, Norani. "Islamisation and Democratization in Malaysia in Regional and Global Contexts." In *Challenging Authoritarianism in Southeast Asia: Comparing Indonesia and Malaysia,* ed. Ariel Heryanto and Sumit K. Mandal, 117–44. London: RoutledgeCurzon: 2003.

Othman, Norani, Anwar, Zainah, and Mohamad Kasim, Zaitun. "Malaysia: Islamisation, Muslim Politics and State Authoritarianism." In *Muslim Women and the Challenge of Islamic Extremism,* ed. Norani Othman, 78–108. Kuala Lumpur, Malaysia: Sisters in Islam, 2005.

Parti Islam Se-Malaysia. *Perlembangan Parti Islam SeMalaysia* [Constitution of the Islamic Party of Malaysia]. Kuala Lumpur, Malaysia: Pejabat Agung PAS, 1977.

———. *Tarbiyah.* Available at: http://www.parti-pas.org/tarbiyah.php.

———. *Manifesto: PAS Negeri Kelantan 1986.* Kota Bharu, Malaysia: Perhubungan PAS Negeri Kelantan, 1986.

———. *The Islamic State Document.* Available at: http://www.wluml.org/english/news/pas-islamic-state-2003.pdf.

Persatuaan Ulama Malaysia, Persatuan Ulama Kedah. *Islam Dicabar Rasulullah Dan Ulama Dihina* [Islam Is Challenged, the Prophet and Religious Scholars Are Disparaged]. Penang, Malaysia: Jutaprint, 2002.

Piscatori, James. "Islam, Islamists, and the Electoral Principle in the Middle East." *ISIM Papers* 1 (2000): 1–64.

Ramanathan, S., and Adnan, M. H. *Malaysia's 1986 General Election: The Urban-Rural Dichotomy.* Occasional Paper No. 83. Singapore: Institute of Southeast Asian Studies, 1988.

Rashid, Ahmed. *Jihad: The Rise of Militant Islam in Central Asia.* New Haven, Conn.: Yale University Press, 2002.

Ratnam, K. J. "Religion and Politics in Malaysia." In *Readings on Islam in Southeast Asia,* ed. Ahmad Ibrahim, Sharon Siddique, and Yasmin Hussain, 143–50. Singapore: Institute of Southeast Asian Studies, 1985.

Ratnam, K. J., and Milne, R. S. "The 1969 Parliamentary Elections in West Malaysia." *Pacific Affairs* 43, no. 2 (1970): 203–26.

Rawa, Yusof. *"Ke Arah Pembebasan Ummah"* [Towards the Liberation of the Ummah]. In *Memperingati Yusof Rawa* [Commemorating Yusof Rawa], ed. Kamarudin Jaffar, 27–68. Kuala Lumpur, Malaysia: IKDAS, 2000.

Reetz, Dietrich. *Islam in the Public Sphere: Religious Groups in India, 1900–1947.* New Delhi, India: Oxford University Press, 2006.

Roff, William R. *The Origins of Malay Nationalism.* Kuala Lumpur, Malaysia: Oxford University Press, 1967.

———. "Patterns of Islamization in Malaysia, 1890s–1990s: Exemplars, Institutions, and Vectors." *Journal of Islamic Studies* 9, no. 2 (1998): 210–28.

Sadiki, Larbi. "Popular Uprisings and Arab Democratization." *International Journal of Middle East Studies* 32, no. 1 (2000): 71–95.

Salleh, Awang Had. *"Institusi Pondok di Malaysia"* [Institution of Religious Boarding Schools in Malaysia]. In *Masyarakat Melayu: Antara Tradisi dan Perubahan* [The Malay Community: Between Tradition and Change], ed. Zainal Kling, 31–49. Kuala Lumpur, Malaysia: Utusan Publications, 1977.

Sayeed, Khaleed. *Politics in Pakistan.* New York: Praeger Publishers, 1980.

Shome, Anthony S. K. *Malay Political Leadership.* London: RoutledgeCurzon, 2003.

Slimming, John. *Malaysia: Death of a Democracy.* London: J. Murray, 1969.

Smith, T. E. "The Malayan Elections of 1959." *Pacific Affairs* 33, no. 1 (1960): 38–47.

Somun, Hajrudin. *Mahathir: The Secret of the Malaysian Success.* Petaling Jaya, Malaysia: Pelanduk Publications, 2004.

Stark, Jan. "Constructing an Islamic Model in Two Malaysian States: PAS Rule in Kelantan and Terengganu." *Sojourn* 19, no. 1 (2004): 51–75.

———. "Beyond 'Terrorism' and 'State Hegemony': Assessing the Islamist Mainstream in Egypt and Malaysia." *Third World Quarterly* 26, no. 2 (2005): 307–27.

Stauth, Georg. *Politics and Cultures of Islamisation in Southeast Asia: Indonesia and Malaysia in the Nineteen-nineties.* Bielefeld, Germany: Transcript Verlag, 2002.

Tan Chee Beng, *Chinese Minority in a Malay State: The Case of Terengganu in Malaysia.* Singapore: Eastern Universities Press, 2002.

Ugur, Etga. "Intellectual Roots of 'Turkish Islam' and Approaches to the 'Turkish Model.'" *Journal of Muslim Minority Affairs* 24, no. 2 (2004): 327–45.

Van Dijk, C. "The Hearts and Minds of the People: Southeast Asia after 11 September 2001." In *Islamic Movements in Southeast Asia,* 29–62. Jakarta, Indonesia: UIN, 2003.

Von Vorys, Karl. *Democracy without Consensus: Communalism and Political Stability in Malaysia.* Kuala Lumpur, Malaysia: Oxford University Press, 1976.

Walsh, John. "Egypt's Muslim Brotherhood: Understanding Centrist Islam." *Harvard International Review* 24, no. 4 (2003): 32–36.

Wan Teh, Wan Zahidi. *Malaysia Is an Islamic State.* Kuala Lumpur, Malaysia: Ministry of Information, 2001.

Weiss, Meredith L. "Malaysian NGOs: History, Legal Framework and Characteristics." In *Social Movements in Malaysia: From Moral Communities to NGOs,* ed. Meredith L. Weiss and Saliha Hassan, 17–44. London: Routledge, 2003.

Wickham, Carrie Rosefsky. *Mobilizing Islam: Religion, Activism, and Political Change in Egypt.* New York: Columbia University Press, 2002.

Yusoff, Badruzaman. *Penjelasan Dokumen Negara Islam* [Clarification on the Islamic State Document]. Kuala Lumpur, Malaysia: Pusat PAS, 2003.

Index